LIBRARY OF NEW TESTAMENT STUDIES

399

formerly the Journal for the Study of the New Testament Supplement series

Editor

Mark Goodacre

Editorial Board

John M. G. Barclay, Craig Blomberg, R. Alan Culpepper, James D. G. Dunn,
Craig A. Evans, Stephen Fowl, Robert Fowler, Simon J. Gathercole, John S.
Kloppenborg, Michael Labahn, Robert Wall, Steve Walton, Robert L. Webb,
Catrin H. Williams

'THE SUFFERINGS OF CHRIST ARE ABUNDANT IN US' (2 CORINTHIANS 1.5)

A NARRATIVE DYNAMICS INVESTIGATION OF PAUL'S SUFFERINGS IN 2 CORINTHIANS

KAR YONG LIM

t & t clark

Published by T&T Clark International
A Continuum imprint
The Tower Building, 11 York Road, London SE1 7NX
80 Maiden Lane, Suite 704, New York, NY 10038

www.continuumbooks.com

British Library Cataloguing-in-Publication Data
A catalogue record for this book is available from the British Library

ISBN: HB: 978-0-567-10728-2

Typeset by CA Typesetting Ltd, www.sheffieldtypesetting.com
Printed in Great Britain by the MPG Books Group, Bodmin and King's Lynn

CONTENTS

TABLES

ACKNOWLEDGMENTS

The topic of Paul's sufferings has been a focus of my interest for almost a decade. This project could not have come to completion without the support, help and encouragement of a network of people. First of all, I would like to thank Dr William Campbell, from the University of Wales, Lampeter, who has been a constant source of inspiration and encouragement in guiding me in my research journey. I must also mention Dr Rollin Grams, from the Oxford Centre for Mission Studies, who provided much assistance in helping me shape the methodology for my research, and Dr David Horrell and Dr Paul Middleton, who sharpened loose arguments and provided further insights to improve my work.

A very generous scholarship jointly awarded by the Department of Theology & Religious Studies and the Oxford Centre for Mission Studies for faculty development from the Two-Thirds world made this research possible. Further grants from the Department of Theology & Religious Studies provided the opportunity to present aspects of my research at the Society of Biblical Literature International Meetings in Singapore (2005) and Edinburgh (2006).

My research has also taken me to libraries in Britain, Europe and Asia. I spent many stimulating moments working in Tyndale House, Cambridge; Bodleian Library, Oxford, and Katholieke Universiteit Leuven. The libraries of Trinity Theological College, Singapore, Seminari Theoloji Malaysia, and Malaysia Bible Seminari provided me with many works written by Asian scholars which, unfortunately, are not available in the United Kingdom.

Many friends and churches in Malaysia provided much encouragement and support, and there are too many to name – you know who you are! A special word of thanks is due to Vic Cern Wong for painstakingly compiling the indexes and Ruth Ng and Sarah Yap for checking the references.

Over the course of my research, I have seen my mother suffer much pain as a result of health complications and the countless times she was admitted to the hospital. Being so far away from my family in the UK, countless sleepless nights and anxious moments were my companion throughout these years. In the midst of these adverse circumstances, I have found comfort in the words of the Lord to Paul, "My grace is sufficient for you, for my power is made perfect in weakness" (2 Cor. 12.9). In some ways, I have also experienced that "For when I am weak, then I am strong," (2 Cor. 12.10) and completing this project is a testimony to this paradoxical reality. And I would like to thank my family who encouraged, supported, and sacrificed much for me during my absence from home. As such, this book is lovingly dedicated to them.

Kar Yong Lim
Seremban, March 2009

ABBREVIATIONS

AB	Anchor Bible
ABD	*Anchor Bible Dictionary*
ABR	*Australian Biblical Review*
AcBib	Academia Biblica
ACNT	The Augsburg Commentary on the New Testament
AJT	*Asia Journal of Theology*
AnBib	Analecta Biblica
ASV	American Standard Version
BDAG	W. Bauer, F. W. Danker, W. F. Arndt and F. W. Gingrich. *Greek-English Lexicon of the New Testament and Other Early Christian Literature*, 3rd edn
BBE	The Bible in Basic English
BBR	*Bulletin for Biblical Research*
BDB	F. Brown, S. R. Driver and C. A. Briggs, *Hebrew and English Lexicon of the Old Testament*
BETL	Bibliotheca ephemeridum theologicarum lovaniensium
BHT	Beiträge zur historischen Theologie
Bib	*Biblica*
BiBh	*Bible Bhashyam*
BibSac	*Bibliotheca Sacra*
BJS	Brown Judaic Studies
BNTC	Black's New Testament Commentaries
BR	*Biblical Research*
BTB	*Biblical Theology Bulletin*
BTS	Biblical Tools and Studies
BZ	*Biblische Zeitschrift*
BZAW	Beihefte zur Zeitschrift für die alttestamentliche Wissenschaft
BZNW	Beihefte zur Zeitschrift für die neutestamentliche Wissenschaft
CB	Coniectanea Biblica
CBET	Contributions to Biblical Exegesis and Theology
CBNTS	Coniectanea Biblica New Testament Series
CBQ	*Catholic Biblical Quarterly*
CBR	*Currents in Biblical Research*
CE	Common Era
CMSJ	*Chinese Missionary Society Journal*
COQG	Christian Origins and the Question of God
CR:BS	*Currents in Research: Biblical Studies*
CTM	*Concordia Theological Monthly*
CTR	*Criswell Theological Review*
DPL	*Dictionary of Paul and His Letters*, ed. Gerald F. Hawthorne, Ralph Martin and Daniel G. Reid
EB	Études bibliques

EC	Epworth Commentaries
EDNT	*Exegetical Dictionary of the New Testament*, ed. H. Balz and G. Schneider
ETL	*Ephemerides theologicae lovanienses*
ERT	*Evangelical Review of Theology*
ESV	English Standard Version
EvQ	*Evangelical Quarterly*
EvT	*Evangelische Theologie*
ExpT	*Expository Times*
FB	Forschung zur Bibel
FRLANT	Forschungen zur Religion und Literatur des Alten und Neuen Testaments
HBT	*Horizons in Biblical Theology*
HTR	*Harvard Theological Review*
HTS	Harvard Theological Studies
IBC	Interpretation: A Bible Commentary for Teaching and Preaching
ICC	International Critical Commentary
Int	*Interpretation*
IVPNTC	InterVarsity Press New Testament Commentary
JAC	*Jahrbuch für Antike und Christentum*
JB	Jerusalem Bible
JBL	*Journal of Biblical Literature*
JBV	*Journal of Beliefs and Values*
JCE	*Journal of Christian Education*
JDDS	Jian Dao Dissertation Series
JETS	*Journal of the Evangelical Theological Society*
JPT	*Journal of Pentecostal Theology*
JSJSup	Supplement to the Journal for the Study of Judaism
JSNT	*Journal for the Study of the New Testament*
JSNTSup	Journal for the Study of the New Testament Supplement Series
JSOT	*Journal for the Study of the Old Testament*
JSOTSup	Journal for the Study of the Old Testament Supplement Series
JSS	*Journal of Semitic Studies*
JTS	*Journal of Theological Studies*
KEK	Kritisch-exegetischer Kommentar über das Neue Testament (Meyer-Kommentar)
KJV	King James Version
LEC	Library of Early Christianity
LNTS	Library of New Testament Studies
LS	*Louvain Studies*
LTQ	*Lexington Theological Quarterly*
LXX	Septuagint
MBPS	Mellen Biblical Press Series
MNTC	Moffatt New Testament Commentary
MNTS	McMaster New Testament Studies
MT	Massoretic Text
NA^{27}	Nestle-Aland, *Novum Testamentum Graece* 27th edn
NAB	The New American Bible
NAC	The New American Commentary
NASB	New American Standard Bible
NCB	New Century Bible
NCBC	New Cambridge Bible Commentary

Neot	*Neotestamentica*
NGTT	*Nederduitse gereformeerde teologiese tydskrif*
NIB	The New Interpreter's Bible
NIBC	New International Bible Commentary
NICNT	The New International Commentary on the New Testament
NICOT	The New International Commentary on the Old Testament
NIDNTT	*New International Dictionary of New Testament Theology*, ed. Colin Brown
NIGTC	New International Greek Testament Commentary
NIV	New International Version
NIVAC	The NIV Application Commentary
NJB	New Jerusalem Bible
NKJV	New King James Version
NLT	New Living Translation
NovT	*Novum Testamentum*
NovTSup	Supplements to Novum Testamentum
NRSV	New Revised Standard Version
NSBT	New Studies in Biblical Theology
NT	New Testament
NTC	New Testament in Context
NTL	New Testament Library
NTS	*New Testament Studies*
OBO	Orbis biblicus et orientalis
OT	Old Testament
OTL	Old Testament Library
OTWSA	*Die ou-Testamentiese werkgemeenskap in Suid-Afrika*
PBM	Paternoster Biblical Monographs
PRS	*Perspectives in Religious Studies*
PTMS	Pittsburgh Theological Monograph Series
RB	*Revue biblique*
ResQ	*Restoration Quarterly*
RevExp	*Review and Expositor*
RHPR	*Revue d'Histoire et de Philosophie Religieuses*
RSV	Revised Standard Version
RTR	*Reformed Thelogical Review*
SANT	Studien zum Alten und Neuen Testaments
SBEC	Studies in the Bible and Early Christianity
SBL	Studies in Biblical Literature
SBLDS	Society of Biblical Literature Dissertation Series
SBLMS	Society of Biblical Literature Monograph Series
SBLSP	*Society of Biblical Literature Seminar Papers*
SBLSymS	Society of Biblical Literature Symposium Series
SBT	Studies in Biblical Theology
SDSSRL	Studies in the Dead Sea Scrolls and Related Literature
SE	*Studia evangelica*
SEAJT	*South East Asia Journal of Theology*
SJ	Studies in Judaism
SJLA	Studies in Judaism in Late Antiquity
SJT	*Scottish Journal of Theology*
SNTSMS	Society for New Testament Studies Monograph Series
SNTW	Studies of the New Testament and Its World

SO	*Symbolae osloenses*
SP	Sacra Pagina
ST	*Studia theologica*
TAPS	*Transactions of the American Philosophy Society*
TD	*Theology Digest*
TDNT	*Theological Dictionary of the New Testament*, ed. G. Kittel and G. Friedrich
TGST	Tesi Gregoriana Seri Teologia
TJT	*Taiwan Journal of Theology*
TNTC	Tyndale New Testament Commentary
TTJ	*Torch Trinity Journal*
TynBul	*Tyndale Bulletin*
UBS	United Bible Societies
VC	*Vigiliae Christianae*
VT	*Vetus Testamentum*
WBC	Word Biblical Commentary
WC	Westminster Commentaries
WestBC	Westminster Bible Companion
WMANT	Wissenschaftliche Monographien zum Alten und Neuen Testament
WTJ	*Westminster Theological Journal*
WUNT	Wissenschaftliche Untersuchungen zum Neuen Testament
WWSup	Word and World Supplement Series
YLT	Young's Literal Translation
ZNW	*Zeitschrift für die neutestamentliche Wissenschaft und die Kunde der älteren Kirche*

Chapter 1

INTRODUCTION

Of the letters in the Pauline canon, 2 Corinthians stands out as Paul's most intense and personal letter where he intimately displays his pastoral heart and theological mind as he deals with a very difficult Christ-believing community. Throughout this letter, one theme that frequently emerges with greater intensity and detailed description compared to his other letters is the description of his apostolic suffering. This is noticeably obvious in his epistolary introduction, where he thanks God for the comfort he received in his afflictions (1.3-11). Moving on to the body of the letter, Paul highlights specific references to his apostolic suffering. On one occasion, he employs Roman triumphal imagery to convey his self-presentation as an apostle (2.14-17). At other times, he lists his suffering in catalogue fashion (4.7-12; 6.4-10; 11.23–12.10). Paul tells his readers that the sufferings he endures are intimately related to Christ; indeed his weaknesses and marks of suffering are the matter of his boasting in Christ (1.5; 4.10-11; 12.9-10; 13.4). So key to his understanding is the role of affliction in his faith that, throughout this letter, Paul frequently interjects the theme of suffering in the midst of his argument on various issues confronting the Corinthians.

The frequent repetitions about Paul's suffering strongly suggest that this theme not only plays a crucial role in Paul's thought but also is fundamental to his argument in 2 Corinthians. But why does Paul so strongly emphasize his apostolic suffering in his correspondence to a Christ-believing community that does not seem to have much evidence of suffering as a result of their faith in Christ?[1] Why is Paul's description of his suffering much more illustrative and detailed in 2 Corinthians than in his epistles elsewhere (cf. Rom. 8.18, 35-9; Phil. 3.7-11)? Before we proceed with our investigation, a review of previous studies on Paul's suffering is carried out.

I. *Critical Review of Scholarship*

The review of scholarship on Paul's suffering covers a survey of significant research done since the 1960s. Despite numerous studies carried out on the topic,

---

1. Cf. John M. G. Barclay, 'Thessalonica and Corinth: Social Contrasts in Pauline Christianity', *JSNT* 47 (1992): 49–74.

the literature survey demonstrates that previous studies have resulted in opposing interpretations of Pauline suffering. There remain a number of central issues
unresolved and several others unexplored. To assess these studies critically, a
detailed literature review will be carried out according to the following methodological approaches: (1) exegetical studies; (2) historical and background studies;
and (3) topical and thematic studies. While these categories are not always mutually exclusive, nonetheless, they offer one effective way of evaluating previous work that not only exposes some of the weaknesses of the approaches but
also furnishes a backdrop for the methodological commitments that will subsequently govern this study. At the same time, my major concern in this review is
to unearth whether previous scholarship has provided an adequate answer to the
question why Paul's suffering is a dominant theme in 2 Corinthians.

A. *Exegetical Studies*

The question of the nature of Paul's participation in the suffering of Christ has
been a central issue of debate since the 1960 article by Barnabas M. Ahern.[2]
Ahern's starting point is to determine the meaning of the phrase 'the fellowship
of his sufferings' in Phil. 3.10 by investigating it in the light of other Pauline
texts of the same subject. This leads him to conclude that suffering is seen as
solidarity with Christ at the point of a believer's baptism.

The major weakness of Ahern's approach is the neglect of the context of
the individual passages investigated. This is evident in the example of Ahern's
exegesis of 2 Corinthians where he sees it as a 'conjoined application of the
themes of Rom and 1 Cor.'.[3] In his exegesis of 2 Cor. 4.7-12, Ahern establishes
the force of 4.11-12 by reading Rom. 6.12-14 and Col. 3.5 into it. As a result of
heavy cross-references to other passages, Paul's exposition on suffering within
the context of 2 Corinthians receives inadequate attention. Hence, the force
of how Paul's argument about his suffering functions in 2 Corinthians is not
adequately explored.

In a 1963 article that summarizes the major thrust of his 1956 doctoral dissertation, C. Merrill Proudfoot seeks to establish the concept of suffering with
Christ in Paul.[4] The basis of Proudfoot's argument is that the notion of the body
of Christ as reflected in 1 Cor. 5.3-4; 6.17; 12.26; and 2 Cor. 11.29 throws considerable light on Paul's understanding of his suffering with Christ.[5] This leads
to his hypothesis that the idea of 'suffering with Christ' is to be understood in
terms not only of *imitatio Christi* but also of *participatio Christi*, which he

---

2.   Barnabas Mary Ahern, 'The Fellowship of His Sufferings (Phil. 3,10): A Study of St.
Paul's Doctrine on Christian Suffering', *CBQ* 22 (1960): 1–32.

3.   Ahern, 'Fellowship of His Sufferings', 18.

4.   C. Merrill Proudfoot, 'Imitation or Realistic Participation? A Study of Paul's Concept of
"Suffering with Christ"', *Int* 17 (1963): 140–60.

5.   Proudfoot, 'Imitation or Realistic Participation', 147.

identifies as the concept of mystical union, a real spiritual bond with the body of Christ.[6] Proudfoot then demonstrates how his hypothesis finds support in his exegesis of 2 Cor. 1.3-7; 4.10-12; Rom. 8.17; and Phil. 3.10-11.

In his approach, Proudfoot uses certain common ideas or words to formulate his hypothesis without paying sufficient attention to the context. For example, in his exegesis of 2 Cor. 1.3-7, Proudfoot uses the notion of σῶμα Χριστοῦ both to designate the body of Christ and the Church and by referring to other Pauline texts that speak of σῶμα Χριστοῦ to reach his conclusion that '(t)he sufferings of Christ are the Christians' sharing in the historical sufferings (or death) of Jesus, as these are mediated to them through their spiritual connection with the risen Christ – just as "comfort" is their sharing in the resurrection of Christ through the somatic union with him'.[7] Second, by using certain catchwords and cross-references, Proudfoot's exegesis of the selected texts also suffers from the same lack of attention to the context as seen in Ahern's work. It seems that both Ahern's and Proudfoot's interpretations of Paul's suffering as mystical union with Christ are heavily influenced by Schweitzer's *The Mysticism of Paul the Apostle*.[8]

Moving away from a mystical interpretation of Paul's suffering with Christ, Che-Bin Tan argues that Paul interprets his suffering in light of salvation history.[9] Tan's basic tenet is that the idea of suffering with Christ in Paul's thought is found in the OT and in the teaching of Jesus himself. Tan adopts a systematic approach in analysing Paul's suffering by going through the entire Pauline canon with the exception of Philemon, 1 Timothy and Titus.

Tan's study has much to commend it in relation to my approach. He argues that the suffering of Paul is related to the Christ-event, and to both the message and the proclamation of the gospel.[10] As a result, Tan rejects the interpretation of messianic woes and mystical union in relation to Paul's suffering.[11] He also recognizes that the idea of Paul's suffering is rooted in the OT.[12] However, it is unfortunate that Tan does not pay sufficient attention to the OT citations found in the context of suffering in 2 Corinthians.[13] In addition, Tan's systematic approach to the topic and his rather large scope of investigation covering

---

6. Proudfoot, 'Imitation or Realistic Participation', 147, especially 159–60.

7. Proudfoot, 'Imitation or Realistic Participation', 147.

8. Albert Schweitzer, *The Mysticism of Paul the Apostle*, trans. William Montgomery (New York: H. Holt & Co, 1931).

9. Che-Bin Tan, 'The Idea of "Suffering with Christ" in the Pauline Epistles: An Exegetical and Historical Study' (PhD dissertation, University of Manchester, Manchester, 1978).

10. Tan, 'Idea of Suffering', 279–89.

11. Tan, 'Idea of Suffering', 280, 283, 288. Cf. my discussion of these ideas in Chapter 3.

12. Tan, 'Idea of Suffering', 288.

13. See Tan, 'Idea of Suffering', 155–91, for his treatment of Paul's suffering in 2 Corinthians. Paul's citation of LXX Isa. 49.8 in 2 Cor. 6.2 is surprisingly missing in Tan's treatment. Also missing is the notion of boasting in the Lord which is a crucial key in unpacking Paul's understanding of his weaknesses in 11.23–12.10. See Chapters 6 and 7 below.

the entire Pauline corpus lead him to sacrifice paying attention to the context of the individual passages under investigation and the function of Paul's suffering within the respective epistles. Despite these shortcomings, Tan's observation that the idea of suffering is to be interpreted Christologically remains the springboard for our investigation.

The first major exegetical work that seriously takes into account Paul's suffering within the context of the Corinthian correspondence is the commendable effort by Scott Hafemann.[14] Hafemann attempts to establish the thesis that 2 Cor. 2.14 holds the key to understanding what he describes as the 'theological heart' of 2 Corinthians. By focusing on 2.14–3.3, Hafemann argues that Paul regards himself as the eschatological and mediatory agent who stands in between God and the Church, and who as the minister of the new covenant is entrusted with the gospel of Christ in his preaching and suffering. In his exegesis, Hafemann argues that this passage reveals the threefold defence of Paul's apostolic ministry characterized by suffering. First, Paul uses the triumphal procession imagery to describe himself as the captive being led to death. Second, Paul reminds the Corinthians that God has made him sufficient for ministry, and he is not dependent on them for monetary support. Hafemann argues that an essential part of Paul's suffering as an apostle is his voluntary decision to support himself and the tribulations that accompany his practice of tentmaking. Third, Paul sees himself as the Spirit-giver to the Corinthians by invoking the tradition of Moses' call in relation to himself.[15]

Hafemann's excellent historical and exegetical task is a very commendable attempt in examining the text in relation to the relevant background materials. Many of his arguments are convincing and insightful. His careful attention to both the Greco-Roman and OT background is exemplary. It is unfortunate that Hafemann's work is limited to 2.14–3.3; how the other passages of Paul's suffering in 2 Corinthians contribute to his overall argument remains unexplored.

In his study on 2 Corinthians, A. E. Harvey argues that any significant changes in Paul's theology and attitude to suffering are affected by what he personally experienced. In line with this, Harvey believes that the tribulations Paul experienced in Asia (2 Cor. 1.8) between the composition of 1 and 2 Corinthians must be taken literally because they fundamentally affected his understanding of suffering, his relationship with Christ, and the help he is thus able to give others who suffer.[16]

---

14. Scott J. Hafemann, *Suffering and the Spirit: An Exegetical Study of II Cor. 2:14–3:3 within the Context of the Corinthian Correspondence*, WUNT 2/19 (Tübingen: J. C. B. Mohr, 1986). The slightly abridged version is reprinted as *Suffering and Ministry in the Spirit: Paul's Defense of His Ministry in II Corinthians 2:14–3:3* (Grand Rapids: Eerdmans, 1990).

15. Hafemann, *Suffering and the Spirit*, 219–21.

16. A. E. Harvey, *Renewal through Suffering: A Study of 2 Corinthians*, SNTW (Edinburgh: T&T Clark, 1996).

In his investigation, Harvey adopts a chronological approach in examining the development of Paul's understanding of suffering by comparing texts in Galatians and Corinthians.[17] This leads him to propose a two-stage understanding of Paul's suffering. First, Harvey acknowledges that by the time Paul writes Galatians,[18] he is merely talking about the outward visible marks on his body as expressed in Gal. 6.17. It is not until the severe tribulations experienced in Asia that Paul begins to comprehend the second stage of his understanding of suffering – the renewal of the inner man.

The strength of Harvey's work is his emphasis on the influence of Scripture on Paul's thought and careful attention paid to the context of 2 Corinthians. While Harvey's insight of suffering as a positive spiritual renewal exercise for the sufferer is attractive, his argument of the two-stage development of Paul's understanding of his suffering appears to be less convincing. Harvey pays much attention to Paul's suffering as a personal experience, and as a result, the function of Paul's suffering in 2 Corinthians and how this is subsequently worked out in the lives of the Corinthians is neglected.

Timothy Savage's work in 1996 seeks to explore the circumstances leading to Paul's use of paradoxical language to explain his ministry in 2 Corinthians.[19] By evaluating Paul according to the prevailing cultural values, Savage argues that the Corinthians fault Paul for his: (1) lack of boasting; (2) unimpressive physical demeanour; (3) lack of rhetorical skills in public speech; and (4) refusal to accept financial support.[20] Savage contends that Paul responds to each of these criticisms by positioning himself in a paradoxical fashion in order to oppose the Corinthians' conception of what their leader should be. By focusing on 2 Cor. 3–4, Savage further examines the paradoxes where the antitheses of power through weakness, glory through shame, and life through death appear in their full force. Savage concludes that 'it was evident that the Corinthian church was embroiled in a conflict between two opposing viewpoints: the worldly outlook of the Corinthians and Paul's own Christ-centred perspective'.[21] As a minister of the gospel, Paul is bound by the pattern of cruciform weakness of his Lord as demonstrated on the cross.

Savage's work is significant in at least two aspects. First, he locates Paul within the cultural values and social prejudices of the first-century world. He sees the problems Paul has with the Corinthians are closely related to the prevailing social ethos, particularly in the ways in which people evaluated their

---

17. Harvey finds a theological approach to Paul's understanding of suffering wanting. See his critique in *Renewal through Suffering*, 123–4.

18. Harvey believes in an early dating of Galatians.

19. Timothy B. Savage, *Power through Weakness: Paul's Understanding of the Christian Ministry in 2 Corinthians*, SNTSMS 86 (Cambridge: Cambridge University Press, 1996).

20. Savage, *Power through Weakness*, 12. For further analysis of these issues, see pages 54–99.

21. Savage, *Power through Weakness*, 188.

peers and religions in the Greco-Roman world. This is particularly helpful in unpacking Paul's response to the issues surrounding his weaknesses and sufferings. While Savage sees suffering as a demonstration of Paul's weakness, he is more concerned with the paradoxical idea of power through weakness. It is unfortunate that further investigation into Paul's suffering in 2 Corinthians remains inadequate where 1.3-11 and 6.3-10 are not given attention.

Alexander Mak's work is probably the first major attempt in the last decade to construct a contextual understanding of Paul's suffering based on 2 Corinthians.[22] To establish a holistic view of Pauline suffering, Mak carries out a detailed exegesis of eight passages that speak directly of suffering. His commendable treatment of the passages extends beyond the boundaries of the four oft-quoted catalogues of hardships (4.7-12; 6.4-10; 11.23b-29; and 12.7-10) in studies on Paul's suffering to include other neglected passages (1.3-11; 2.1-7; 4.16–5.4; and 7.7-11). Although Mak clearly describes his work as a contextual study of Paul's suffering, he largely ignores the socio-historical background of the Corinthians and also Paul's use of Scripture within the passages identified. Mak focuses almost exclusively on the rhetorical effects of Paul's hardship lists within the Greco-Roman conventions. It is unfortunate that in unpacking the theological and positive meaning behind Paul's suffering, Mak seems less interested in demonstrating how Paul's suffering relates to his mission and the Corinthians.

B. *Historical and Background Studies*

In reacting against Rudolf Bultmann[23] and Wolfgang Schrage,[24] who identified the provenance of Paul's catalogues of hardships as Stoic and Jewish apocalyptic thought respectively, Robert Hodgson cautions against any background investigation into these catalogues that limits itself exclusively to either Greco-Roman or Jewish conventions.[25] Hodgson argues that Paul's catalogues stem from both conventions and any investigation of these catalogues must take into account the full range of background materials[26] and not mere superficial parallels.[27] More importantly for Hodgson is the question of how Paul subsumes such diverse tribulation traditions into his own vision of apostleship and the

---

22. Alexander Mak, 'Towards a Holistic View of Pauline Suffering: A Contextual Study of 2 Corinthians' (ThD dissertation, Bible College of Victoria, Melbourne, 1996).

23. Rudolf Bultmann, *Der Stil der paulinischen Predigt und die kynisch-stoische Diatribe*, FRLANT 13 (Göttingen: Vandenhoeck & Ruprecht, 1910), 71–2.

24. Wolfgang Schrage, 'Leid, Kreuz und Eschaton: Die Peristasenkatologe als Merkmale paulinischer theologia crucis und Eschatologie', *EvT* 34 (1974): 141–75.

25. Robert Hodgson, 'Paul the Apostle and First Century Tribulation Lists', *ZNW* 74 (1983): 59–80.

26. Hodgson, 'Paul the Apostle', 59, 80.

27. Hodgson, 'Paul the Apostle', 62–80.

gospel, a question that Hodgson never answered but hoped would stimulate further investigation into Paul's catalogues of suffering.[28]

Several studies have taken up Hodgson's appeal to investigate the provenance of Paul's catalogues of suffering. But the direction of these studies appears to have fallen into the very trap that Hodgson is advocating against in limiting the study of these catalogues exclusively to either Greco-Roman or Jewish conventions.

One such person who views Paul's catalogues of suffering in light of Greco-Roman conventions is John T. Fitzgerald.[29] Fitzgerald argues that the Hellenistic moralists and philosophers use *peristasis* catalogues as literary devices to demonstrate the various virtues and to defend the integrity of the suffering sage. Taking this cue, Fitzgerald further argues that Paul uses these catalogues in similar fashion to defend his integrity and to prove himself virtuous in his sufferings. To defend his thesis, Fitzgerald carries out a thorough investigation on the hardships of the sage. He then applies this Hellenistic background study in his exegesis of 1 Cor. 4.10-13; 2 Cor. 4.7-12; and 6.3-10 to depict Paul as an ideal Christian sage that the Corinthians should seek to emulate.

For some unsatisfactory reason, Fitzgerald omits 2 Cor. 11.23-9 from his treatment.[30] When examined closely, this passage demonstrates anything but an ideal sage. It reveals the weaknesses of Paul through his intense physical and emotional pains. His constant anxiety and concern for the welfare of the communities are clearly depicted. Such a description hardly reveals the sage who demonstrates great serenity and composure that Fitzgerald portrays Paul to be.[31]

Fitzgerald's major contribution in this study is his extensive and informative treatment of Greco-Roman background to Paul's catalogues of hardships. His study will certainly be a major reference for any future Greco-Roman background study of Paul's *peristasis* catalogues. However, Fitzgerald's argument that 'Hellenistic discussions of the sage appear to offer a better means for sharpening our understanding of Paul's catalogues'[32] results in the regrettable omission of the Jewish and OT traditions in Paul's thought, as rightfully warned against by Hodgson.[33] While recognizing that the catalogues reflect divine power in Paul's life, Fitzgerald does not see Paul's suffering as having any missiological significance. Nevertheless, Fitzgerald's work has been immensely influential in subsequent studies on Pauline suffering and major commentaries on 2 Corinthians where he has been cited approvingly in many instances.

28. Hodgson, 'Paul the Apostle', 61, 80.

29. John T. Fitzgerald, *Cracks in an Earthen Vessel: An Examination of the Catalogues of Hardships in the Corinthian Correspondence*, SBLDS 99 (Atlanta: Scholars Press, 1988).

30. Fitzgerald, *Cracks in an Earthen Vessel*, 3, cites lack of space for omitting this passage.

31. For further discussion, see Chapter 7.

32. Fitzgerald, *Cracks in an Earthen Vessel*, 30.

33. Hodgson, 'Paul the Apostle', 59–80.

Apart from a Hellenistic perspective, a number of studies also seek to trace and interpret Paul's idea of suffering solely from a Jewish perspective. In his study on *Persecution and Martyrdom in the Theology of Paul*, John Pobee attempts to locate the martyrology model in the death of Jesus, and further argues that this is the best place to begin the background investigation into Paul's suffering.[34] Pobee's thesis is that central to Paul's understanding of the death of Jesus, and of himself as a persecuted apostle, is the Jewish martyr theology set forth in the intertestamental literature, particularly in 1–4 Maccabees.

Based on this premise, Pobee argues that since Paul sees Jesus as a martyr he therefore interprets his own suffering in the same light. This is perhaps the most problematic part of Pobee's thesis that has been rigorously challenged.[35] Some statements may have been pushed too far; for example, Pobee argues that 'the whole direction of the debate about the Law in Pauline theology stems from the martyrological interpretation of the crucifixion of Christ'.[36] It remains to be convincingly demonstrated how Jewish martyr theology operates in Paul's theology, particularly Paul's Christology, soteriology, eschatology and ecclesiology, not to mention Paul's understanding of his own suffering.[37] In dealing with the scandal of the cross, Pobee argues that 'Paul took the sting out of the scandal of the cross by reinterpreting through established martyrological themes: (a) that the death was in obedience to the will of God and out of zeal for the Lord; (b) that it was a vicarious sacrifice; and (c) that it was not an accident of history but in the fore-ordained plan of God for the redemption of the world'.[38] As such, 'a martyrological understanding of the cross transforms its shame into a thing of glory'.[39] This interpretation ignores the social context of Corinth, and it is doubtful whether the Corinthians would have viewed the cross as 'a thing of glory'.[40] If it can be convincingly argued that the earliest Jewish traditions do not see Jesus' death as martyrdom, then Pobee's entire thesis collapses as well.

In relation to 2 Corinthians, Pobee briefly refers to 6.4-10 and 11.23-7 without giving much attention to the text.[41] Paul's other catalogues and crucial passages

---

34. John S. Pobee, *Persecution and Martyrdom in the Theology of Paul*, JSNTSup 6 (Sheffield: JSOT Press, 1985).

35. Michael D. Greene, Review of *Persecution and Martyrdom in the Theology of Paul*, by John S. Pobee, *PRS* 16 (1989): 169–72 (170), describes Pobee's book as one that is 'far more a work buttressed by seemingly unending proof-texts, than a work supported by the necessary exegetical interpretive depth'. See also the critique by C. Marvin Pate, *The Glory of Adam and the Afflictions of the Righteous: Pauline Sufferings in Context* (Lewiston: Edwin Mellen, 1993), 48.

36. Pobee, *Persecution and Martyrdom*, 78.

37. See Pobee's discussion in *Persecution and Martyrdom*, 74–92.

38. Pobee, *Persecution and Martyrdom*, 69.

39. Pobee, *Persecution and Martyrdom*, 72.

40. On the social shame and stigma attached to crucifixion, see Martin Hengel, *Crucifixion in the Ancient World and the Folly of the Message of the Cross* (London: SCM Press, 1977).

41. Pobee, *Persecution and Martyrdom*, 93–4, 96.

related to his suffering are either ignored without any satisfactory justification or not given adequate attention.[42] While Pobee pays attention to materials in the intertestamental period, reference to the OT is much neglected. As a result, Paul's suffering in relation to the Corinthians is not satisfactorily worked out.

In 1991, C. Marvin Pate attempted to bring together the motifs of the glory of Adam and the suffering of the righteous in his interpretation of 2 Cor. 4.7–5.21.[43] In his investigation, Pate locates terminologies such as glory (δόξα), image (εἰκών), outer and inner man (ἔξω/ἔσω ἄνθρωπος), naked (γυμνός) and groaning (στενάζομεν) and connects them to LXX Gen. 1–3. This forms the basic argument that Adam theology provides a key insight for the interpretation of the text, thus leading, in turn, to the thesis that Paul believes that the primeval glory lost by the first Adam has been restored through the righteous suffering of Christ, the last Adam. Building on this premise, Pate further expands his investigation in a subsequent publication to include other key Pauline texts on suffering.[44] Pate believes that significant light can also be shed on Paul's understanding of suffering if Jewish speculation about Adam from the writings in the period of 200 BCE to 200 CE is brought into the discussion.[45]

The major problem with Pate's thesis is that he seems more concerned to locate the interpretation of Paul's suffering within a particular model rooted in the restoration of Adam's glory through righteous suffering rather than by paying close attention to the text. For example, he interprets the heavenly ascent account in 2 Cor. 12.1-10 as a proleptic experience of the restoration of Adam's glory through righteous suffering. Reading this account in the light of Adam's loss of paradise and glory in LXX Gen. 2–3, Pate sees Paul's use of the phrases 'man in Christ', 'paradise', and 'messenger of Satan' as referring to Paul's Adam-Christ typology, the paradise lost in Adam's account and similar types of temptation that Adam and Eve faced in the Garden of Eden, respectively.[46] Pate's approach appears to be speculative and problematic.

More recently, Barry Smith revealed that Paul's language of suffering is closely related to that of the suffering righteous in Jewish thought.[47] Smith argues that there are seven explanations of the suffering righteous in Paul's thought. Suffering is seen as: (1) a result of persecution; (2) remedial; (3) salvation-historically necessary; (4) probationary; (5) effect of the sins of Adam;

---

42. For example, 2 Cor. 4.7-12 is missing in Pobee's treatment while 1.3-11 and 12.10 are only briefly mentioned.

43. C. Marvin Pate, *Adam Christology as the Exegetical and Theological Substructure of 2 Corinthians 4:7–5:21* (Lanham: University Press of America, 1991).

44. See Pate, *Glory of Adam* for the list of texts investigated.

45. Pate, *Glory of Adam*, 67.

46. See Pate, *Glory of Adam*, 107–42, for further discussion. Cf. Pate, *Adam Christology*, 77–157, for a similar approach in his reading of 2 Cor. 4.7–5.10.

47. Barry D. Smith, *Paul's Seven Explanations of the Suffering of the Righteous*, SBL 47 (New York: Peter Lang, 2002).

(6) pedagogical; and (7) participation in the suffering of Christ. In carrying out his investigation, Smith identifies the theme in the OT texts, then traces its development through Second Temple Judaism and finally brings these insights into Pauline texts to unpack Paul's thinking.

There are several flaws in Smith's argument. Smith's assumption is that the ideas found in the intertestamental literature must not only be present in Paul's thought but also heavily influence his understanding of suffering. He also includes religious-historical background materials that post-date Paul's writing with the assumption that these probably preserved pre-Pauline religious ideas.[48] This approach has attracted severe criticism from Tom Holland:

> The method of collecting texts from a range of independent Second Temple docu-
> ments and from them constructing a theological argument that supposedly represents
> the Jewish understanding of that era is theologically irresponsible. To do so denies
> these texts the voices of their own authors and their theological view points.[49]

Regrettably, Smith's topical arrangement can sometimes obscure the texts because this approach tends to ignore the context of Paul's argument. At the same time, Smith is highly critical of those who approach Pauline suffering from a Hellenistic perspective, and describes this approach as 'fundamentally misguided and [one that] will produce distortion'.[50] While Smith is correct to argue for Paul's background in Judaism, he fails to see that Paul is also at the same time writing to predominantly gentile Christ-believers. For this reason, Hellenistic influence on Paul cannot be completely discounted.

C. *Topical and Thematic Studies*

In his attempt to understand the concept of weakness in Paul, David A. Black has carried out an examination of every occurrence of ἀσθένεια and its cog-nates in the Pauline corpus.[51] Black argues that there are three sub-themes in which the theological motif of weakness is developed in Paul: the anthropo-logical, Christological and ethical.[52] Highlighted in Black's study is the concept of weakness in terms of suffering that is developed within the Christological sub-theme and that functions as the platform where the power of God is dem-onstrated through weakness. However, the major weakness of Black's study is that merely focusing on the study of a particular word will not completely reveal Paul's understanding of weakness in suffering. As a result, passages such

---

48. Smith, *Paul's Seven Explanations*, 2–3.

49. Tom Holland, Review of *Paul's Seven Explanations of the Suffering of the Righteous*, by Barry D. Smith, *Themelios* 29 (2003): 89–91 (90).

50. Smith, *Paul's Seven Explanations*, 3. Smith further argues that 'a familiarity with interpre-tations of suffering in Greek philosophical texts is unnecessary'.

51. David A. Black, *Paul, Apostle of Weakness: Astheneia and Its Cognates in the Pauline Literature* (New York: Lang, 1984).

52. Black, *Paul, Apostle of Weakness*, 222–46.

as 2 Cor. 1.5-11; 2.14-17; 4.7-12; and 6.3-10 that clearly express the idea of weakness but without using ἀσθένεια are not analysed.

In his monograph, *The Paradox of the Cross in the Thought of St Paul*, A. T. Hanson seeks to answer why Paul describes his activity in a series of remarkable contrasts and paradoxes.[53] In carrying out this task, Hanson adopts a thematic approach by focusing on the exegesis of several passages in the Pauline epistles which stress the significance of the cross for Paul's ministry. Hanson also pays careful attention to Paul's use of the OT and his locating the teaching and ministry of Jesus in these passages. Typical conclusions of Hanson's exegesis can be summarized as follows:

> We must conclude ... that Paul, in describing the life of the apostolic community, has in mind the tradition he knew of Jesus' teaching about the life and characteristics of the citizens of the kingdom, that he consciously modelled this description on the pattern of the sufferings and death of Jesus Christ, and that in doing so he was frequently inspired by his interpretation of scripture. We cannot avoid the conclusion also that Paul regarded the sufferings and possible death of the apostles as possessing an atoning, reconciling, salvific value.[54]

One of the greatest strengths of Hanson's work is his appeal to the OT as operative in Paul's thought. Another strong point is that he not only looks for parallels in Jesus' teaching in the Gospel tradition but also emphasizes how this may have been echoed in Paul's teachings. Hanson's argument that Paul not only knows elements of Jesus' teaching but applies it to the life-pattern of the apostolic community opens up new insights since the teaching of Jesus is often minimized in Pauline scholarship.[55] Hanson is certainly on track when he locates Paul's suffering in his missionary activities: 'We must not carry away the impression that the apostles suffer simply for the sake of suffering. Their suffering is incurred in the course of their great activity of declaring the good news of what God has done in Christ.'[56] However, Hanson's argument that Paul's apostolic suffering has atoning value has attracted criticism.[57] But if

53. Anthony Tyrell Hanson, *The Paradox of the Cross in the Thought of St Paul*, JSNTSup 17 (Sheffield: JSOT Press, 1987).

54. Hanson, *Paradox of the Cross*, 36.

55. Hanson, *Paradox of the Cross*, 31–2. However, Hanson's greatest strength appears to be his weakness, as he may have stretched beyond the evidence in looking for links in the OT or teachings of Jesus. For example, he believes that Paul's use of the term 'dogs' in Phil. 3.2-16 is a reflection of Jesus' conversation with the Syro-Phoenician woman in Mark 7 (89–97). He also argues that Paul has in mind Lam. 3.45 when he uses the words 'the scum of the earth, the refuse of the world' in 1 Cor. 4.13 (33–7). These connections may not be too persuasive, as reviewed by David L. Bartlett, Review of *The Paradox of the Cross in the Thought of St Paul*, by A. T. Hanson, *Int* 42 (1988): 434–6; and Eugene Hensell, Review of *The Paradox of the Cross in the Thought of St Paul*, by A. T. Hanson, *CBQ* 51 (1989): 559–60.

56. Hanson, *Paradox of the Cross*, 147–8.

57. Hanson, *Paradox of the Cross*, 139–43. See the review by Bartlett; and also Charles B.

Hanson's position is taken from a missiological perspective where Paul's apostolic suffering results in bringing the gentiles life in Christ and in the creation of Christ-believing communities (cf. 2 Cor. 2.14-17; 4.10-11), then it can be said to possess atoning value: Paul is manifesting the redemptive work of Christ through his apostolic suffering.[58]

While Hanson's contribution to understanding the subject of Pauline suffering is valuable, his study adopts a thematic approach and neglects to locate the suffering passages within the larger context of Paul's correspondence, particularly in 2 Corinthians. The significance of suffering in Paul's mission is somehow acknowledged but this subject needs to be further developed.

Charles Cousar's monograph on *The Theology of the Cross* attempts to examine the importance and role of the death of Jesus in the letters of Paul.[59] Based on the seven undisputed letters of Paul, Cousar pursues his argument thematically. Particularly related to the theme of Pauline suffering is his Chapter 5 on 'Jesus' Death and the Christian Life'. In this chapter, Cousar seeks to answer the question of how Paul's apostolic vocation is expressed in terms of Jesus' death and how this subsequently projects the identity of the community of faith.[60] To do so, Cousar examines four autobiographical passages where Paul describes his own life or ministry in connection with Jesus' death, namely, Gal. 6.11-18; 2 Cor. 4.7-15; Phil. 3.2-11; and 2 Cor. 13.1-4.

In his exegesis of 2 Cor. 4.7-15, Cousar not only sees hardships as the occasion for discerning the divine power of the gospel, but also attempts to give suffering a theological interpretation.[61] Cousar argues that sufferings are Christological in nature, and the sufferings of Paul are for the sake of Christ.[62] As such, Cousar strongly believes that the missiological context in 4.12-15 naturally becomes clear where 'sufferings are not valued simply because of what Paul experiences and perceives about himself (i.e., that the life of Jesus is manifested only in him), but for what they mean for the outreach of the church'.[63] Turning to 2 Cor. 13.1-4, Cousar argues that Paul's apostolic weakness serves as a basis for authenticating his apostleship and maintains that the entire argument of 2 Cor. 10–13 is grounded in 13.4 where Paul's weakness is seen as Christological. Cousar believes that 'through the language of hardships, insults, rejections, weakness, afflictions, [Paul] tells the story of faith, confessing the

Cousar, *A Theology of the Cross: The Death of Jesus in the Pauline Letters* (Minneapolis: Fortress Press, 1990), 155 n. 44.

58. See Chapter 4 for further discussion.

59. Cousar, *Theology of the Cross*.

60. Cousar, *Theology of the Cross*, 135–89.

61. Cousar, *Theology of the Cross*, 150–1.

62. Cousar, *Theology of the Cross*, 152: 'As it is, Jesus' way is the way of the cross, and identifying with him means that afflictions are simply part and parcel of the apostolic existence.'

63. Cousar, *Theology of the Cross*, 153.

crucified, risen and returning Christ'.[64] This insight will be further expanded in my investigation.

In his overall argument, Cousar sees sufferings in a positive light as they become opportunities to experience the risen life and power of Christ. But he is also quick to add that sufferings are not to be sought, neither are they unexpected.[65] Furthermore, Cousar argues that the theology of the cross is the lens through which the apostolic ministry is viewed.[66] He also stresses that the importance of Paul's suffering is not for himself but for the sake of the community and the creation of its identity. However, it is unfortunate that while the narrative significance of Paul's suffering is acknowledged, it is not further developed.

D. *Evaluation and Research Problems*

This review of previous studies on Paul's suffering reveals several significant implications for my study. Without doubt, all of the above studies provide helpful insights into various aspects of Paul's understanding of his suffering and the present study is obviously indebted to them. However, my survey also reveals several key shortcomings that need to be addressed.

Based on my evaluation, the final result yields a divergence of opinions with different interpretations of Paul's suffering, as highlighted below. The fundamental problem underlying this divergence of opinions appears to be tied to the categories of approaches adopted.

1. From the category of exegetical studies, I notice that despite the abundance of materials on the investigation of Pauline suffering, it is highly surprising that there remains a specific lack of any serious study on the place and function of Paul's suffering within the context of 2 Corinthians. What makes this observation even more acute is that scholars generally agree that suffering is an important theme in 2 Corinthians, but any adequate development of this theme in this letter has not been published. In attempting to locate Paul's understanding of his suffering in relation to his theology, numerous previous studies have also detached the text on Paul's suffering from the context. The fact that the significance and function Paul ascribes to his suffering in any given context is always shaped by the perception of the issues and concerns in the community at the time of writing the epistle has been largely ignored.

2. My evaluation of the category of background and historical studies reveals that scholars often allow their understanding of Paul's suffering to be shaped exclusively by either the Jewish or the Hellenistic tradi-

---

64. Cousar, *Theology of the Cross*, 169.
65. Cousar, *Theology of the Cross*, 171.
66. Cousar, *Theology of the Cross*, 153.

tion; rather than recognizing that Paul's context straddles both worlds and that it is extremely difficult to draw a strict boundary between the two. The primary concern for studies taking this approach is to identify parallels and similarities in the textual comparison. In other words, the major focus here is to be occupied with the form rather than the content of Paul's suffering. Hodgson's caution against taking an either–or standpoint has recently received strong support from both Niels Willert[67] and Alexander Mak.[68] As a native Chinese from Hong Kong, Mak suggests that parallels to the teaching of suffering in the writings of Confucius can easily be detected, but he is quick to qualify that no serious Pauline scholar would venture so far as to argue that the provenance of Paul's idea of suffering can be traced back to Confucianism.[69] Since human suffering is a common experience, it is not surprising that one is able to find parallels to Paul's idea of suffering in ancient religious and philosophical materials. What is needed is the impartial evaluation of these background materials that goes beyond mere superficial similarities between them.

3. The weakness of studies devoted to Pauline suffering often arises from generalizations drawn from a limited selection of passages rather than a comprehensive study of the texts that relate Pauline suffering to a particular context. The exegesis of a particular passage is often based upon cross-references from the Pauline corpus instead of close examination of the thrust of the argument of the passage under consideration. Such a thematic approach often ignores the context of the passages in order to fit the texts into a particular form or line of argument and, as a result, the force or the function of the passages are easily obscured.

4. Paul's use of Scripture within the context of his suffering (particularly his citation of LXX Isa. 49.8 in 2 Cor. 6.2 and LXX Jer. 9.22-3/1 Kgdms 2.10 in 2 Cor. 10.17 as background to the boasting of his weaknesses) has not received sufficient attention. This is strange as the importance of the OT background in Paul's thought has been repeatedly highlighted by Tan, Hafemann, Harvey, Hanson, and Barry Smith.

5. The treatment of Paul's understanding of the cross and how this made an impact on his understanding of suffering is surprisingly obscure. In addition, previous studies have not fully appreciated that Paul's

67. Niels Willert, 'The Catalogues of Hardships in the Pauline Correspondence: Background and Function', in *The New Testament and Hellenistic Judaism*, ed. Peder Borgen and Soren Givenson (Aarhus: Aarhus University Press, 1995), 217–43: 'I find it necessary to emphasize that it is impossible to discern between Graeco-Roman or Jewish background' (225).

68. Mak, 'Holistic View of Pauline Suffering', 37.

69. Mak, 'Holistic View of Pauline Suffering', 37.

suffering is directly related to his missionary activities and, as such, the function of suffering in the Pauline mission remains to be fully explored.

As a result, many questions regarding Paul's suffering in the context of 2 Corinthians remain unanswered and, thus, call for further investigation. Why does Paul frequently highlight his suffering in 2 Corinthians particularly in an antithetical or paradoxical fashion to a community of believers who apparently have not suffered?[70] How would the OT quotations function in Paul's understanding of his suffering? Why is it that, in Paul's description of his suffering, there is a strong allusion to the story of Jesus and how does this story function in Paul's argument to the Corinthians? What then is the function of Paul's suffering in 2 Corinthians and what does this reveal about Paul and the Corinthian community? Is Paul defending his *call* to apostleship characterized by suffering, as affirmed by an overwhelming majority of scholars, or is Paul defending the *nature* of his apostleship? Is Paul ultimately more concerned with his personal defence or is he more concerned with the status of the Corinthians? In sum, my study attempts to answer the question why the theme of suffering is central to the argument of 2 Corinthians, and I now move on to consider how I propose to proceed.

II. *Methodological Considerations*

One exciting approach in recent developments in Pauline studies is the adoption of the narrative approach in unpacking Paul's thought.[71] These studies have advanced the 'story of Jesus' as an integral ingredient in Paul's thought, and I now briefly survey some of these significant developments.

A. *Brief Overview of the Narrative Approach in Pauline Studies*

Much of the catalyst for the heightened interest in the study of narrative ingredients in Paul's thought can be traced to the groundbreaking work of Richard Hays in 1983.[72] In his monograph, Hays argues that Paul's theological thinking is grounded in a narrative structure based on the story of Jesus. In carrying out his investigation, Hays concerns himself with establishing a methodological

70. Cf. Barclay, 'Thessalonica and Corinth'.

71. For recent developments in the narrative approach to Pauline studies, see Bruce W. Longenecker, 'The Narrative Approach to Paul: An Early Retrospective', *CBR* 1 (2002): 88–111; and idem, 'Narrative Interest in the Study of Paul: Retrospective and Prospective', in *Narrative Dynamics in Paul: A Critical Assessment*, ed. Bruce W. Longenecker (Louisville: Westminster/ John Knox, 2002), 3–16.

72. Richard B. Hays, *The Faith of Jesus Christ: The Narrative Substructure of Galatians 3:1–4:11*, 2nd edn (Grand Rapids: Eerdmans, 2001). See also his article, 'Is Paul's Gospel Narratable?', *JSNT* 27 (2004): 217–39.

basis for locating the narrative substructure in Paul. By taking into account
the relationship between narrative and reflective discourse, Hays concludes as
follows:

1. There can be an organic relationship between stories and reflective
    discourse because stories have an inherent configurational dimension
    (*dianoia*) which not only permits but also demands restatement and
    interpretation in non-narrative language.
2. The reflective restatement does not simply repeat the plot (*mythos*) of
    the story; nonetheless, the story shapes and constrains the reflective
    process because the *dianoia* can never be entirely abstracted from the
    story in which it is manifested and apprehended.
3. Hence, when we encounter this type of reflective discourse, it is legiti-
    mate and possible to inquire about the story in which it is rooted.[73]

Hays suggests two phases in discerning the narrative substructures within a
particular discourse. The first phase involves the identification within the discourse of allusions to the story and the search for its general outlines. In the
second phase, an inquiry of how this story shapes the logic of argumentation in
the discourse is considered.[74]

By using Gal. 3.1–4.11 as a test case, Hays advances the argument that 'the
framework of Paul's thought is constituted neither by a system of doctrines nor
by his personal religious experience but by a "sacred story", a narrative structure'[75] that is identified as the story of Jesus Christ. It is a substructure because
in writing to the Galatians, Paul writes in a 'mode of recapitulation'.[76] This is so
because Paul has already proclaimed the gospel to the community and he could
then assume the story of Jesus as their common ground. As such, Paul's concern
is 'to draw out the implications of this story for shaping the belief and practice
of his infant churches'.[77]

In his concluding chapter, Hays suggests that his detection of a narrative substructure in Galatians can also be applied to other Pauline letters
specifically identified as 1 Cor. 15; Phil. 2.6-11; Rom. 3.21-6; and 5.12-
21.[78] What is conspicuously missing from Hays's suggestion is 2 Corinthians. As Young and Ford remark, Hays's treatment can also be extended to
2 Corinthians,[79] and the present study attempts to fill precisely this lacuna.
We have already detected that Paul alludes to the story of Jesus in his suf-

73. Hays, *Faith of Jesus Christ*, 28.
74. Hays, *Faith of Jesus Christ*, 29.
75. Hays, *Faith of Jesus Christ*, 6.
76. Hays, *Faith of Jesus Christ*, 28–9.
77. Hays, *Faith of Jesus Christ*, 6.
78. Hays, *Faith of Jesus Christ*, 209–10.
79. Frances M. Young and David F. Ford, *Meaning and Truth in 2 Corinthians* (Grand Rapids:
Eerdmans, 1988), 261 n. 3.

fering and, as such, this allows us to draw a richer portrait of Christ and to investigate how Paul draws out the implication of this story for the Corinthian community.

Hays must be credited with laying a solid foundation for further investigation into the narrative dynamics of Pauline studies. Following Hays, a similar interest has been expressed by N. T. Wright. In his extensive study on mapping out the process of human cognition, Wright argues that worldviews which express themselves through symbols and praxis provide 'the *stories* through which human beings view reality'.[80] Based on this, Wright has developed a template of a reconstructed first-century Jewish worldview centred around Christ. Applied to Paul, Wright argues that the larger narrative of the story of God, Israel and the whole world in Paul's thought can be discovered through his letters.[81] For Wright, Paul's most emphatically theological statements and arguments are 'expressions of the *essentially Jewish story now redrawn around Jesus*'.[82] While this insight is essentially true and Wright does appreciate the role the story of Jesus plays in Paul's writings, his subsequent pursuit of the story of Jesus in Paul's thought becomes problematic. To Wright, the story of Jesus is one that not only represents the story of Israel but one that embodies her story and history,[83] and in doing so, in effect, replaces her. To tell the story of Jesus' resurrection is '*to tell Israel's story in the form of Jesus' story*'.[84] As such, Wright sees the story of Jesus as one that contains a 'subversive twist at almost every point'; this is especially so in Paul's view of the Torah which '*should convict Israel of sin*, so that Israel should be cast away in order that the world might be redeemed'.[85] Wright observes Paul 'telling, again and again, the whole story of God, Israel and the world as now compressed into the story of Jesus'.[86] It is here that I take a somewhat different approach from Wright for several reasons. Christ is nowhere identified as Israel in Paul's thought. In addition, there is too much at stake if we were to compress the story of the world including the fallen nature of humanity into Christ. Finally, Wright seems to emphasize the connection of the story of Jesus with what precedes it (i.e. the story of Israel now compressed in the story of Jesus). However, the present study will take this further to highlight the story of Jesus not only in what precedes it but also in connection with what follows – how Paul and the Corinthian community are to participate in and continue the story.

80. N. T. Wright, *The New Testament and the People of God*, COQG 1 (Minneapolis: Fortress Press, 1992), 123, emphasis his.

81. Wright, *New Testament and the People of God*, 405.

82. Wright, *New Testament and the People of God*, 79, emphasis his.

83. Wright, *New Testament and the People of God*, 402.

84. Wright, *New Testament and the People of God*, 400–1, emphasis his.

85. Wright, *New Testament and the People of God*, 405–6.

86. Wright, *New Testament and the People of God*, 79.

The narrative approach has gained further recognition in Rollin Grams's dissertation, 'Gospel and Mission in Paul's Ethics'.[87] In his study, Grams attempts to define Paul's missionary ethics in relation to his community of believers, setting aside the notion of a central theme of Paul's theology in favour of a narrative framework in terms of the 'Gospel Story'.[88] Grams claims that the 'Gospel Story is a missionary Story'; which is a revelation of God's redemptive activity in the world through the historical appearing and work of Jesus Christ, and that this story is the fulfilment of God's past promises. It is this story into which Paul and his community of believers are incorporated, and it is this story that forms the character of the community of believers.[89]

Grams's study extends the conversation of the narrative approach to a new dimension by incorporating Pauline ethics. For Grams, ethics should not be seen as merely a set of ethical systems or one key ethical principle, but the entire Gospel Story.[90] Grams's argument that the gospel is a character-informing story is provocative.[91] To Grams, the community of believers that has been incorporated into this Story not only adopts 'the character, attitudes, and actions which the Gospel Story describes but also … enter(s) into the missionary purpose of the Story'.[92] This notion will be further investigated in the present study.

In 1990, Stephen Fowl carried out a detailed analysis of the function of the hymnic texts focused on the story of Jesus in Phil. 2.6-11; Col. 1.15-20; and 1 Tim. 3.16a.[93] In his exegesis, Fowl pays close attention not only to the content but also to how each of these passages functions within the argument of the respective epistles. Fowl rightly recognizes that all the communities Paul writes to were already founded on the tradition and stories of Jesus. Paul simply needed to employ the tradition to draw out ethical implications for these communities in the light of their concrete situations.[94] Fowl argues that each of these passages narrates 'a story in which Christ is the main character … the foundation of the communities to which each epistle is written', and that therefore the communities draw their identity from these traditions about Christ.[95] As such, Fowl sees these passages providing concrete examples of the relationship

---

87. Rollin G. Grams, 'Gospel and Mission in Paul's Ethics' (PhD dissertation, Duke University, Durham, 1989). The capitalizations follow Grams's usage in his dissertation.

88. Grams, 'Gospel and Mission', 5. See his further discussion in 113–212.

89. Grams, 'Gospel and Mission', 414–17. For further discussion on the 'Gospel Story', see 172–96.

90. Grams, 'Gospel and Mission', 414.

91. Grams, 'Gospel and Mission', 416–34.

92. Grams, 'Gospel and Mission', 430–1.

93. Stephen E. Fowl, *The Story of Christ in the Ethics of Paul: An Analysis of the Function of the Hymnic Material in the Pauline Corpus*, JSNTSup 36 (Sheffield: JSOT Press, 1990).

94. Fowl, *Story of Christ*, 197, 202.

95. Fowl, *Story of Christ*, 199.

between narrative and ethics, and argues that the story of Jesus in these hymnic passages functions as exemplars for the communities.[96]

Fowl's argument that Paul alludes to the story of Jesus in order to draw out implications for his readers is to be applauded. That the Christ-believing communities founded by Paul, built on the story of Jesus, are to continue the story by shaping their lives in conformity to the life of Jesus is a key idea that will be expounded in this study.

While Hays, Wright, Grams and Fowl recognize the narrative elements in Paul, Ben Witherington is to be credited with the first major attempt to establish the narrative element as an interpretive tool in a full-fledged study of Paul's theology. Witherington shows that Paul's thought is grounded in a grand narrative and in a story that has continued to develop out of the narrative.[97] This story not only involved elements from the Scriptures, but also elements from Jewish, Greco-Roman and Christian traditions, elements of logic, and elements drawn from Paul's own and other Christian experiences of God in Christ.[98] To develop his argument, Witherington proposes four interrelated stories that constitute the larger story in Paul's narrative thought world:

> (1) the story of a world gone wrong; (2) the story of Israel in that world; (3) the story of Christ, which arises out of the story of Israel and humankind on the human side of things, but in a larger sense arises out of the very story of God as creator and redeemer; and (4) the story of Christians, including Paul himself, which arises out of all three of these previous stories and is the first full instalment of the story of a world set right again.[99]

Witherington argues that, for Paul, the story of Christ is 'the hinge, crucial turning point, and climax of the entire larger drama'.[100] However, unlike Wright who focuses on what seems to precede the story of Christ, Witherington pays particular attention to reading the ongoing story of Christians in Paul and particularly in the light of how Paul believes the drama will ultimately be concluded by Christ in the Parousia.[101] This recognition, aptly described as 'the Christening of the Believer',[102] will be reinforced in this present study.

While Witherington's approach is an improvement over Wright's template of a reconstructed first-century Jewish worldview, it often ignores the context of the individual letters. This is evident in Witherington's treatment of Paul as the

---

96. Fowl, *Story of Christ*, 92–8, 203–7. For a discussion on the notion of 'exemplar', see 92–101, 152–4 and 192–4.

97. Ben Witherington III, *Paul's Narrative Thought World: The Tapestry and Tragedy of Triumph* (Louisville: Westminster/John Knox, 1994).

98. Witherington, *Paul's Narrative Thought World*, 3.

99. Witherington, *Paul's Narrative Thought World*, 5.

100. Witherington, *Paul's Narrative Thought World*, 5.

101. Witherington, *Paul's Narrative Thought World*, 5.

102. Witherington, *Paul's Narrative Thought World*, 245–337.

suffering sage and Servant.[103] While he makes reference to Paul's catalogues of suffering in 2 Corinthians, Witherington does not advance to highlight how these catalogues function within the context of 2 Corinthians.

In his magnum opus on the study of Paul's theology, James Dunn also articulates that a profitable approach for conceptualizing Paul's theology is the narrative approach. He identifies five distinct narrative ingredients that inform and influence each other:

> We could readily speak of the substructure of Paul's theology as the story of God and creation, with the story of Israel superimposed upon it. On top of that again we have the story of Jesus, and then Paul's own story, with the initial intertwining of these last two stories as the decisive turning point in Paul's life and theology. Finally, there are the complex interactions of Paul's own story with the stories of those who had believed before him and those who came to form the churches founded by them.[104]

Dunn insists that none of these stories stands on its own, and that 'by clarifying each story, each level, as it comes to expression, explicitly or implicitly, in Paul's theology, we should be able to enter more fully into Paul's theology'.[105] Like Witherington, Dunn also argues that the story of Jesus is the pivotal point in Paul's thought, and sees the continuation of the story in all the five narrative elements in Paul.[106] Departing from Wright, Dunn does not see the story of God and creation and the story of Israel end with the climax of the story of Jesus, but these stories merge with the story of Paul and the story of his churches.[107] Dunn further argues that for Paul it is crucial that his churches should read their story with and within that of Jesus, 'for the key to a realistic theological ethic was a life molded on the template of Christ'.[108] It is the story of Jesus that gives them 'a central model of living: the cruciform life, the cross as determining the character of self-sacrificing love, the story of discipleship as the story of Christ's self-giving being still lived out till that day when those who had shared in his dying would also share fully in his rising again'.[109] This portrayal of Paul's

---

103. Witherington, *Paul's Narrative Thought World*, 236–44.

104. James D. G. Dunn, *The Theology of Paul the Apostle* (Grand Rapids: Eerdmans, 1998), 18. Dunn provides further reflection on how these five levels of stories interact with each other in 'Paul's Theology', in *The Face of New Testament Studies: A Survey of Recent Research*, ed. Scot McKnight and Grant R. Osborne (Grand Rapids: Baker, 2004), 326–48.

105. Dunn, 'Paul's Theology', 328.

106. Dunn, 'Paul's Theology', 343.

107. Dunn, 'Paul's Theology', 347: 'Paul's gospel sought to reshape the stories of his churches, as it had done and was doing in Paul's own life story, by tying them into the other earlier stories. For Paul, it evidently was crucial for his converts' self-understanding that they should see themselves as those who were part of each of these stories, that these stories were incomplete without them.'

108. Dunn, 'Paul's Theology', 348.

109. Dunn, 'Paul's Theology', 348.

churches as a continuation of the story of Jesus, in its theological and ethical dimensions, will be the focus of the present study.

Based on the five narrative ingredients proposed by Dunn as a template, the edited volume of *Narrative Dynamics in Paul* is a commendable attempt by a group of British Pauline scholars to assess the feasibility of the narrative approach focused on Romans and Galatians.[110] Five contributors (Edward Adams, Bruce W. Longenecker, Douglas A. Campbell, John M. G. Barclay and Andrew T. Lincoln) each wrote an article on one of the five main stories, with five others (R. Barry Matlock, Morna D. Hooker, Graham N. Stanton, David G. Horrell and I. Howard Marshall) each providing a critical response to these articles respectively. Two others (James D. G. Dunn and Francis Watson) provide final assessment essays to wrap up the project. As a result, this book contains a collection of essays highlighting the merits and demerits of the narrative approach, with some expressing reservation about the approach and others demonstrating a more positive endorsement. There are some pertinent issues raised in this book that are relevant to the present study.[111] First, Longenecker in his analysis of the story of Israel in Romans and Galatians argues that he is 'not aware of any significant way in which a heightened attentiveness to narrative dynamics has resulted in new exegetical insights or the profiling of certain textual features in unprecedented ways'.[112] While Longenecker maintains that the narrative approach does not *advance* textual exegesis, he suggests that it offers a necessary *exegetical control* as the narrative dimension in Paul's thought is not to be ignored.[113] I hope to demonstrate in this study that the narrative approach not only offers *exegetical control* but can also be profitably used to *advance* new exegetical insights. Second, Edward Adams demonstrates that careful attention needs to be paid to the different occasional nature of the letters.[114] By doing so, Adams argues that the story of God in creation, while featured in Romans, is missing from Galatians. Taking heed of Adams's observation in our present study, I pay particular attention to the context of 2 Corinthians. Finally and surprisingly, Paul's use of Scripture and how the Scriptures inform Paul's argument are not given much attention in this

---

110. Bruce W. Longenecker, ed., *Narrative Dynamics in Paul: A Critical Assessment* (Louisville: Westminster/John Knox, 2002).

111. See also the response and further clarifications of the issues raised in this project in Hays, 'Is Paul's Gospel Narratable?'; and Kathy Ehrensperger, Review of *Narrative Dynamics in Paul: A Critical Assessment*, ed. Bruce W. Longenecker, *JBV* 24 (2003): 377–80.

112. Bruce W. Longenecker, 'Sharing in Their Spiritual Blessings? The Stories of Israel in Galatians and Romans', in *Narrative Dynamics in Paul: A Critical Assessment*, ed. Bruce W. Longenecker (Louisville: Westminster/John Knox, 2002), 58–84 (83).

113. Longenecker, 'Sharing in Their Spiritual Blessings?', 83, emphasis his.

114. Edward Adams, 'Paul's Story of God and Creation: The Story of How God Fulfils His Purposes in Creation', in *Narrative Dynamics in Paul: A Critical Assessment*, ed. Bruce W. Longenecker (Louisville: Westminster/John Knox, 2002), 19–43 (41).

project. In his article, R. Barry Matlock suggests that a narrative reading of a text should take more notice of intertextuality.[115] I hope to demonstrate this by paying careful attention to Paul's use of the Scriptures and how this can further illuminate Paul's argument.

While not every contributor to this volume expresses unqualified and enthusiastic endorsement of the narrative approach, this book demonstrates that the narrative elements in Paul are not to be ignored. In the opinion of Graham N. Stanton, it is the 'right use' of the approach, rather than 'abandonment', that is crucial.[116] Similarly, James Dunn also acknowledges the value of a narrative approach, but cautions that when it is 'pressed into service beyond its obvious competency, it raises more problems than it solves and becomes more of a hindrance than a help'.[117] With such caveats in place, I believe that this approach can provide fruitful insights and further contributions to the interpretation of 2 Corinthians.

Yet more recently, Michael Gorman has taken the narrative approach further by attempting to 'uncover what Paul means by conformity to the crucified Christ, showing that this conformity is a dynamic correspondence in daily life to the strange story of Christ crucified as the primary way of experiencing the love and grace of God'.[118] Gorman, like Grams, departs from his predecessors who sought to identify a 'centre' of Paul's theology. Instead, by adopting an 'integrative narrative experience' where a narrative is seen as 'action and movement not merely around an immovable central feature but *within* the central phenomena of the story',[119] Gorman argues that Paul's life tells a story, and that the crucified Messiah is the focal point of this story. By using this approach, Gorman provides fresh insights into understanding the centrality of the cross in Paul's thought. Particularly insightful for the present study is Gorman's treatment of Paul's suffering for the sake of the gospel.[120] However, Gorman's approach is not beyond criticism. Any claim to identify

---

115. R. Barry Matlock, 'The Arrow and the Web: Critical Reflections on a Narrative Approach to Paul', in *Narrative Dynamics in Paul: A Critical Assessment*, ed. Bruce W. Longenecker (Louisville: Westminster/John Knox, 2002), 44–57 (53–4).

116. Graham N. Stanton, '"I Think, When I Read That Sweet Story of Old": A Response to Douglas Campbell', in *Narrative Dynamics in Paul: A Critical Assessment*, ed. Bruce W. Longenecker (Louisville: Westminster/John Knox, 2002), 125–32 (130).

117. James D. G. Dunn, 'The Narrative Approach to Paul: Whose Story?', in *Narrative Dynamics in Paul: A Critical Assessment*, ed. Bruce W. Longenecker (Louisville: Westminster/John Knox, 2002), 217–30 (230).

118. Michael J. Gorman, *Cruciformity: Paul's Narrative Spirituality of the Cross* (Grand Rapids: Eerdmans, 2001), 5. For a review of Gorman's work, see Kar Yong Lim, Review of *Cruciformity: Paul's Narrative Spirituality of the Cross*, by Michael J. Gorman, *JBV* 25 (2004): 114–16.

119. Gorman, *Cruciformity*, 370–1, emphasis his.

120. Gorman's treatment of Paul's suffering is found in his chapters 9 and 11.

a single integrative framework in Paul's experience of the cross is certainly open to suspicion and debate. Identifying Phil. 2.6-11 as Paul's 'master story of the cross',[121] where at least 17 parallel patterns of cruciformity of faith, love, power and hope can be found across Paul's letters, is likely to raise questions. While I agree with Gorman that the story of Jesus Christ is central in Paul's thought, I am reluctant to impose the template where such precise parallels are to be found in all Paul's letters.

Thomas Dennis Stegman's work marks the latest contribution to the ongoing discussion of the narrative approach to Pauline studies.[122] Applying this approach to 2 Corinthians, Stegman argues that 'the character of Jesus... underlies the self-commendation of Paul's apostleship... as well as his exhortations and challenge to the Corinthians to embody a particular manner of discipleship'.[123] Stegman sustains his thesis by examining a series of passages that speak of the character of Jesus. It is by embodying the faithfulness of Jesus through suffering that Paul is able to commend himself as one who is faithful to Christ. After setting himself as an example to be emulated, Stegman argues, Paul then challenges the Corinthians to embrace the character of Jesus and thus to continue the story of Jesus.

Stegman's attempt to extend the boundary of the narrative approach to 2 Corinthians is commendable. But placing heavy emphasis on the debate of the faith/faithfulness of Jesus in Pauline studies and applying them throughout the allusions to the character of Jesus in 2 Corinthians appears to be forced at numerous places.[124] While he places some emphasis on some of the passages that speak of Paul's suffering, Stegman's primary emphasis is to locate the allusion to the theme of the character of Jesus in these passages, rather than focusing on how Paul draws on the story of Jesus and how this functions within Paul's argument in 2 Corinthians.

B. *Evaluation of the Narrative Approach*

An emerging appreciation of the narrative elements, particularly the centrality of the story of Jesus in Paul's thought, is clearly evident from the brief survey above. The terminology of 'narrative' is now widely acknowledged to have gained 'a foothold among a significant number of prominent Pauline scholars'.[125] This can be seen in the significant contributions of Hays, Wright,

---

121. Gorman, *Cruciformity*, 88–94.

122. Thomas Dennis Stegman, 'The Character of Jesus: The Linchpin to Paul's Argument in 2 Corinthians' (PhD dissertation, Emory University, Atlanta, 2003), now published as *The Character of Jesus: The Linchpin to Paul's Argument in 2 Corinthians*, AnBib 158 (Rome: Editrice Pontifico Istituto Biblico, 2005).

123. Stegman, *Character of Jesus*, 2.

124. It is interesting to note that the debate on the faith/faithfulness of Christ in Stegman's dissertation 'Character of Jesus' (140–82) is omitted in his subsequent publication.

125. Longenecker, 'Narrative Interest in the Study of Paul', 10.

Grams, Fowl, Witherington, Gorman and Stegman to this emerging trend. These works identify various narrative components (e.g., story of God, story of Israel and story of Jesus) within the narrative dynamics of Paul. These individual narratives enlighten and influence each other as Paul responds to different issues at different times and circumstances. What has been enthusiastically emphasized however, is not only that Paul continuously draws on the story of Jesus in his proclamation of the gospel but also that this story functions as a key component in Paul's subsequent communication with his communities. And within this correspondence a key strategy of Paul is to underscore the ongoing implications of the story of Jesus not only in his own life but also in the lives of the communities. This present study locates itself within this approach of reading Paul.[126]

The role of Scripture in Paul's thought also gains significance in the narrative approach in the works of Hays, Wright, Grams and Stegman. Grams argues that the study of Paul's use of Scripture 'provides additional insight into his Gospel, showing among other things the narrative character of the Gospel: it is the fulfilment of the promises which God has made to His people'.[127] In this study, Paul's quotation of Scripture will be given special attention in Chapters 6 and 7.

While the narrative elements in Paul are acknowledged, previous studies have largely been concentrated on Romans and Galatians,[128] despite the bold claim that narrative 'is rapidly becoming commonplace in analyses of Paul's letters and theology'.[129] There remains tremendous potential for extending the use of a narrative approach to other areas of Pauline studies, especially the theme of Paul's suffering in 2 Corinthians since Paul describes his suffering as being grounded in the story of Jesus. To the best of my knowledge, a full-scale narrative approach on Paul's suffering remains to be attempted.[130] This is where the significant contribution of the present study is positioned.

126. Cf. Douglas A. Campbell, *The Quest for Paul's Gospel*, JSNTSup 274 (New York: T&T Clark, 2005), 70, who suggests that 'the story of Jesus, properly understood – and this also means detecting its connections with *other* important stories – is an *irreducible* element in Paul's soteriology as it unfolds in Romans and Galatians' (emphasis his). In our study, we hope to see 2 Corinthians included in Campbell's position.

127. Grams, 'Gospel and Mission', 190. See also Grams's 15 points of scriptural references in relation to Paul's gospel in 191–3.

128. This is best illustrated in Longenecker, ed., *Narrative Dynamics in Paul*. See also A. Katherine Grieb, *The Story of Romans: A Narrative Defense of God's Righteousness* (Louisville: Westminster/John Knox, 2002).

129. Longenecker, 'Narrative Interest in the Study of Paul', 10. Cf. Campbell, *Quest for Paul's Gospel*, 5, where he describes the narrative approach as 'a currently fashionable methodological approach to Paul'.

130. The only exceptions are the brief treatment by Gorman and Cousar. While Stegman's work is an initial attempt to extend the boundary of employing the narrative approach to 2 Corinthians, its focus is on the idea of the faithfulness of Christ rather than Paul's suffering.

C. *Definitions*

Before proceeding further, a simple clarification on the use of terminology is necessary. In this study, the words 'story' and 'narrative' will be used interchangeably when both are used as nouns. As Hays has already pointed out, the English language unfortunately lacks an adjective derived from the word 'story' and the only adjective that carries the meaning 'having the form of story' is the adjective 'narrative'.[131] Hence, there is this slight distinction when the word 'narrative' is used as a noun and adjective.

'Story' refers to an account, narration or recital of an event or series of events. For the purpose of this study, whenever the word 'story' is used, my emphasis is not merely on the recital of an event or series of events that are sequentially or consequentially connected but also on the message that this story conveys concerning the event or course of events. Hence, the 'story of Jesus' for Paul is not merely the story of the earthly Jesus, narrating his birth, life, death and resurrection. It is a story that is given an interpretive function that begins and ends beyond the scope of human history. It is a story that focuses on God's redemptive act in fulfilling the purposes of creation, a story about Israel and her Messiah, a story about the community of faith created as a result of this story, and a story about divine and human actions. As such, Paul's gospel does not purely comprise the story of the birth, death, resurrection and the future appearing of Christ but it is also the story that encompasses the ongoing implications of the saving work of Christ acted out in Paul and his communities. My working definition of the story of Jesus is excellently summed up by Wedderburn:

> The story of Jesus which Paul knows is clearly a narrative of events, a 'story', but it differs from being a story of the earthly Jesus in that it tells of a 'prehistory' in Jesus' existence before his human life on earth, and it also tells of what happened to him subsequently, after Jesus' this-worldly life came to an end. It is also highly interpretive in character: not only does it repeatedly speak of God's involvement in the experiences of Jesus, either explicitly ('God sent', 'God greatly exalted') or implicitly in divine passives ('he was given up', 'he was raised'), but it also gives Christ a role in creation comparable to that of the divine wisdom (1 Cor 8.6), and speaks of his experiences being redemptive (1 Cor 15.3; 2 Cor 8.9; Gal 4.5) and according to the scriptures (1 Cor 15.3-4). The 'prehistory' and the sequel to Jesus' earthly life set the latter within the perspective of a grander, divine design.[132]

---

131. Hays, *Faith of Jesus Christ*, 18–19.

132. A. J. M. Wedderburn, 'Paul and the Story of Jesus', in *Paul and Jesus: Collected Essays*, JSNTSup 37, ed. A. J. M. Wedderburn (Sheffield: JSOT Press, 1989), 161–89 (163). For further discussion, see 161–89. Cf. Cousar, *Theology of the Cross*, 27: 'The story of the cross relates not only the story of the Son of God "who loved me and gave himself for me" (Gal. 2:20), but at the same time the story of one "who did not spare his only Son but gave him up for us all" (Rom. 8:32).' Others would describe this story as a 'myth' since it refers to a means by which truth is believed and conveyed. See David G. Horrell, *Solidarity and Difference: A Contemporary Read-*

D. *Procedures*

Taking the cue from Hays, the procedure for identifying the narrative elements in Paul's discourse on his suffering in 2 Corinthians will be carried out in two phases.[133] The first phase involves the identification within the discourse allusions to the story and seeking to discern its general outlines, and I have identified passages that speak of Paul's suffering, either by vocabulary or imagery, as 1.3-11; 2.14-16; 4.7-12; 6.1-10; 11.23–12.10; and 13.4.

In the second phase, an inquiry into how this story shapes the logic of argumentation in the discourse may then be asked. In carrying out the second phase, I shall start by close reading of the text itself[134] and by carrying out detailed exegetical study that gives careful attention to the immediate contexts of these passages and how these passages relate to the wider argument of 2 Corinthians. In doing so, I attend to the fact that Paul's contexts straddle not only the Jewish and Hellenistic world but also how his call/conversion plays an important role in shaping his thinking and his response to circumstances. This exercise not only takes into account intratextual and semantic connections but also intertextual quotations and allusions to the Scriptures.[135] The purpose of this entire task is to follow Paul's train of thought, rediscover what Paul is actually saying, ascertain his response to the circumstances confronting the Corinthians, and unearth Paul's theology embedded in his response by drawing on the story of Jesus.

In view of the methodological considerations highlighted above, the presentation of this research will be carried out as follows. In Chapter 2, I shall consider the epistolary function of the thanksgiving period in 2 Corinthians. From Chapters 3 to 7, I shall focus my exegesis on the story of Jesus in Paul's narra-

---

ing of Paul's Ethics (London: T&T Clark, 2005), 85–90. Horrell argues that while Paul's letters are not narrative in form, it can be shown that 'a narrative underpins Paul's "theologizing": the story of God's saving act in Jesus Christ' (85). It is this narrative described as a 'myth' that Paul believes finds its central focus in the Christ-event, that is 'the descending, dying, and rising of Jesus Christ, which represents the saving action of God in which believers participate' (87). For Horrell, this central focus not only has a vertical dimension (the descending and ascending of Christ) but also a horizontal dimension, where in the fulness of time God sent forth his son who died, rose and will return again (87). This Christ-story is also chronologically ordered, beginning with God's creation, the 'fall' of Adam, the promise of God to Abraham to bless all the nations, the fulfilment of this promise in Christ, and the creation of a new family in Christ that looks forward to the final consummation (87–8). This myth is also used in community-formation (90). Therefore, Horrell argues that it is entirely appropriate to conceive of Paul's letters as texts that 'depend on, echo, reproduce, reshape, the early Christian myth(s)' (86).

133. Hays, *Faith of Jesus Christ*, 29. See also the discussion on Hays's methodology above.

134. This approach is emphasized in Hafemann, *Suffering and the Spirit*, 2–3; Hays, *Faith of Jesus Christ*, xxvii; and Stegman, *Character of Jesus*, 114.

135. See Richard B. Hays, *Echoes of Scripture in the Letters of Paul* (New Haven: Yale, 1989), 1–33, for further discussion and methodology on the exercise of intertextuality.

tive of his suffering based on these passages: 1.3-11; 2.14-16; 4.7-12; 6.1-10; 11.23–12.10; and 13.4 respectively. Finally, in Chapter 8, I shall bring together the implications of the study.

III. *Summary and Advantages of the Narrative Approach*

Second Corinthians provides the springboard for understanding Paul's suffering as it contains the most numerous, explicit and detailed accounts of his suffering compared to the accounts in his other epistles. In addition, the tone of 2 Corinthians is very personal and emotional, hence making it a good candidate for testing out new ideas by employing the narrative approach, which may result in stimulating and fresh insights on Paul's theology and mission.

Building on previous works, the present research not only becomes an avenue to explore the possibilities and the potential of the narrative approach in Pauline studies but also pushes the current developments of the narrative approach further by extending the debate beyond the boundaries of Romans and Galatians to Paul's suffering in 2 Corinthians.

This research positions Paul's suffering within the context of 2 Corinthians by locating the story of Jesus in Paul's references to his own suffering. The narrative approach will be used as a tool for analysing how Paul's mind works in order to appreciate what he says and how he says it. This approach not only takes us to the heart of Paul's understanding of his gospel as well as his own apostleship but also anchors him in the culture and social conventions of his day. It also sees the continuity of the story of Israel and the story of Jesus as the climax of God's faithfulness to the covenant with Israel and pursues the continuation of these stories in Paul and his community. Therefore, it is anticipated that a new and heightened attentiveness to the narrative dynamics in Paul will also yield new exegetical insights and offer stimulating results with significant implications for reconstructing Paul's theology and mission. In brief, the study of narrative approach in Paul, while still in its infancy, offers the prospect of a fresh evaluation of Paul's theological argument.

Chapter 2

THE EPISTOLARY FUNCTION OF THE
THANKSGIVING PERIOD IN 2 CORINTHIANS 1.3-11

I. *Introduction*

In Chapter 1, I reviewed previous scholarship on Paul's suffering and set the direction for my investigation. In this chapter, I shall examine the epistolary function of the thanksgiving period in 1.3-11 by arguing that the theme of Paul's suffering is dominant throughout 2 Corinthians and appears at critical junctures in his argument.

Before proceeding, a word about my hypothesis concerning issues surrounding the integrity of the letter and the identity of Paul's opponents is in order. The history of scholarship on these two issues is long and complex, and comprehensive reviews exist elsewhere.[1] Any further review here would necessarily

---

1. For the debate on the integrity of 2 Corinthians since J. S. Semler to the early 1990s, see Reimund Bieringer, 'Teilungshypothesen zum 2 Korintherbrief: Ein Forschungsüberblick', in *Studies on 2 Corinthians*, BETL 112, ed. Reimund Bieringer and Jan Lambrecht (Leuven: Leuven University Press, 1994), 67–105, particularly the table summarizing various positions on 96–7. For a survey of the debate from 1980 to 2000, see Steven S. H. Chang, 'The Integrity of 2 Corinthians: 1980–2000', *TTJ* 5 (2002): 167–202, particularly the table on 169. In addition, see Hans Dieter Betz, *2 Corinthians 8 and 9*, Hermeneia (Philadelphia: Fortress Press, 1985), 3–35; David R. Hall, *The Unity of the Corinthian Correspondence*, JSNTSup 251 (New York: T&T Clark, 2003), 86–128; Murray J. Harris, *The Second Epistle to the Corinthians*, NIGTC (Grand Rapids: Eerdmans, 2005), 8–51; Victor S. Nicdao, 'Power in Times of Weakness according to 2 Corinthians 12,1-10: An Exegetical Investigation of the Relationship between Dynamism and Asthéneia' (PhD dissertation, Catholic University of Leuven, Leuven, 1997), 4–135; Stegman, *Character of Jesus*, 1–25; and Margaret E. Thrall, *A Critical and Exegetical Commentary on the Second Epistle to the Corinthians*, Vol. 1, ICC (Edinburgh: T&T Clark, 1994), 3–49, particularly the listing of various positions on 48–9.

For the study of Paul's opponents, from the Reformation until the 1970s, see E. Earle Ellis, 'Paul and His Opponents: Trends in Research', in *Christianity, Judaism and Other Greco-Roman Cults: Studies for Morton Smith at Sixty, Part One: New Testament*, SJLA 12, ed. Jacob Neusner (Leiden: Brill, 1975), 264–98. See also John J. Gunther, *St. Paul's Opponents and Their Background: A Study of Apocalyptic and Jewish Sectarian Teachings*, NovTSup 35 (Leiden: Brill, 1973); Dieter Georgi, *The Opponents of Paul in Second Corinthians* (Philadelphia: Fortress Press, 1986); Hall, *Unity of the Corinthian Correspondence*, 129–73; Ralph P. Martin, 'The Opponents of Paul in 2 Corinthians: An Old Issue Revisited', in *Tradition and Interpretation in the New*

be a duplication of these efforts. For the purpose of our investigation, I believe the issue of the integrity of the letter does not carry significant bearing on my investigation, and I have followed the canonical form in the present study. I shall suggest that the theme of Paul's suffering not only binds the entire 2 Corinthians together but may further support the integrity of the letter. Similarly, I believe the identity of the opponents should not drive my interpretation of 2 Corinthians.[2] Instead, I shall focus on Paul's conversation with the Corinthians and allow this to drive my exegesis. By directing my attention to Paul's relationship with the Corinthians rather than the opponents, I am able to pay close attention to Paul's voice – his intense suffering as an apostle for their sake, his deep pastoral concern as a founding father to them, his urgent appeal grounded in the Scriptures, and his earnest invitation to the Corinthians to be participants in the story of Jesus. It is this voice that must be heard in interpreting 2 Corinthians, and it must not be drowned by the voice of the opponents, reconstructed.

II. *Epistolary Function of the Thanksgiving Period in 2 Corinthians 1.3-11*

Harris has noted that Paul's theology of Christian suffering is most apparent in the thanksgiving period in 1.3-11.[3] Yet with the wealth of information this passage offers, it is surprising that 1.3-11 is rarely discussed in studies on Paul's suffering and has not received the attention it deserves.[4]

Testament: Essays in Honor of E. Earle Ellis for His 60th Birthday, ed. Gerald F. Hawthorne and Otto Betz (Grand Rapids: Eerdmans, 1987), 279–89; Nicdao, 'Power in Times of Weakness', 136–205; Stegman, *Character of Jesus*, 25–42; Jerry L. Sumney, *Identifying Paul's Opponents: The Question of Method in 2 Corinthians*, JSNTSup 40 (Sheffield: JSOT Press, 1990); Margaret E. Thrall, *A Critical and Exegetical Commentary on the Second Epistle to the Corinthians*, Vol. 2, ICC (Edinburgh: T&T Clark: 2000), 926–45; and Stanley E. Porter, ed., *Paul and His Opponents*, Pauline Studies 2 (Leiden: Brill, 2005), especially the articles by Jerry L. Sumney, 'Studying Paul's Opponents: Advances and Challenges', 7–58, and Nicholas H. Taylor, 'Apostolic Identity and the Conflicts in Corinth and Galatia', 99–127. See also the critique of the use of 'mirror reading' in identifying Paul's opponents by George Lyons, *Pauline Autobiography: Toward a New Understanding*, SBLDS 73 (Atlanta: Scholars Press, 1985), 76–121; C. J. A. Hickling, 'Is the Second Epistle to the Corinthians a Source for Early Church History?', *ZNW* 66 (1975): 284–7; and John M. G. Barclay, 'Mirror-Reading a Polemical Letter: Galatians as a Test Case', *JSNT* 31 (1987): 73–93.

2.   Contra Sumney, *Identifying Paul's Opponents*, 189–90; and Martin, 'Opponents of Paul', 280. See also C. K. Barrett, 'Paul's Opponents in 2 Corinthians', *NTS* 17 (1971): 1–54 (233).

3.   Harris, *Second Corinthians*, 123.

4.   For example, see Ahern, 'Fellowship of His Sufferings'; Pate, *Glory of Adam*; and Smith, *Paul's Seven Explanations*. Harvey's *Renewal through Suffering* is primarily concerned with the effects of Paul's devastating Asian experience (2 Cor. 1.8) on his understanding of suffering and of his relationship with Christ. While Fitzgerald, *Cracks in an Earthen Vessel* includes 1.3-11 in

A. *The Epistolary Function of 2 Corinthians 1.3-11*

The introductory thanksgiving section of Paul's letter contains an outline of the major themes that will be addressed subsequently. This significance has been established by Paul Schubert, based on his analysis of both biblical and extra-biblical Greek epistolary papyri and inscriptions.[5] Subsequent studies have confirmed and modified Schubert's work. Gordon Wiles demonstrates that Paul's thanksgiving and intercessions are not merely liturgical expressions but also, by appearing in strategic locations at the beginning of the letter, they anticipate their main thrust.[6] As for the benediction found in 2 Cor. 1.3, Wiles argues that Paul has 'clearly set the tone of the whole succeeding letter' where 'the theme of suffering and comfort, shared inseparably by apostle and people, will never be far away from his thoughts, especially in his profound meditation on the inner nature of his apostolic ministry'.[7]

In presenting a detailed investigation of the introductory periods in Paul's letters, O'Brien concludes that Paul's introductory thanksgivings were 'integral parts of their letters, setting the tone and themes of what was to follow'.[8] O'Brien's work is important as it takes the investigation of the epistolary function further in providing a detailed examination of the relationship of the various theological themes developed within the thanksgiving periods and the letter itself. Commenting on the thanksgiving periods in 2 Corinthians, O'Brien highlights the use of the εὐλογητός formulation instead of the more common εὐχαριστέω formula in the opening sentence. While the opening formula is different, O'Brien argues that both these introductory formulations have the same function of introducing the theme found in the rest of the letter.[9]

his discussion, it is brief (only four pages, 153–7) compared to his treatment of other passages. The only notable exceptions are the works of Arulsamy Innasimuthu, 'Comfort in Affliction: An Exegetical Study of 2 Corinthians 1:3-11' (PhD dissertation, Catholic University of Leuven, Leuven, 1995); and Laura Dawn Alary, 'Good Grief: Paul as Sufferer and Consoler in 2 Corinthians 1:3-7: A Comparative Investigation' (PhD dissertation, University of St. Michael's College, Toronto, 2003). Innasimuthu is primarily concerned with the exegetical-historical examination of the text while Alary concentrates on how Paul's suffering can benefit the Corinthians. Both works have not given sufficient attention to the overall discussion of Paul's suffering in 2 Corinthians. This limitation has been corrected by Mak, 'Holistic View of Pauline Suffering', 49–70. Although Mak includes this passage in his consideration, he is less concerned with demonstrating how the introductory thanksgiving section holds clues to unpacking Paul's suffering in 2 Corinthians.

    5.   Paul Schubert, *Form and Function of the Pauline Thanksgivings*, BZNW 20 (Berlin: Töpelmann, 1939).

    6.   Gordon P. Wiles, *Paul's Intercessory Prayers: The Significance of the Intercessory Prayer Passages in the Letters of St Paul*, SNTSMS 24 (Cambridge: Cambridge University Press, 1974), 229, 294.

    7.   Wiles, *Paul's Intercessory Prayers*, 227.

    8.   Peter Thomas O'Brien, *Introductory Thanksgiving in the Letters of Paul*, NovTSup 49 (Leiden: Brill, 1977), 263.

    9.   O'Brien, *Introductory Thanksgiving*, 254–5.

Together with others, O'Brien has correctly pointed out that there was more interaction between the Hellenistic and Judaistic worlds than allowed for by Schubert. While the structure of the Pauline thanksgiving periods was Hellenistic, the form did not control the content of these thanksgiving periods which showed deep Jewish influence.[10] In particular, David Pao's recent study pays close attention to the Hebrew traditions of thanksgiving in Paul's thought.[11] He argues that any investigation of Pauline thanksgiving should not be limited to the introductory thanksgiving periods but should also include its significance within the body of the letters. By locating Paul's thanksgiving within the Hebraic covenantal traditions, Pao demonstrates that thanksgiving is not merely an act of remembrance of the past; it is also a call to conduct one's life in the present in the light of the past and provides hope for the future in anticipation of the fulfilment of God's promises. Hence, Pao locates Paul's thanksgiving within an eschatological framework.[12] Pao's work is significant in my study as, apart from the thanksgiving period, the theme of thanksgiving appears twice within the context of Paul's suffering, in 2 Cor. 2.14; and 4.15. This will be elaborated on in Chapters 4 and 5 below.

The epistolary function of the thanksgiving period is now well established and acknowledged.[13] Applied to 2 Corinthians, the force of Paul's argument based on the theme of suffering cannot be more emphatically stated than when its prominent presence is undeniably displayed in 1.3-11. Its strategic location

10. O'Brien, *Introductory Thanksgiving*, 10–13. Cf. W. Bingham Hunter, 'Prayer', *DPL*, 725–34.

11. David W. Pao, *Thanksgiving: An Investigation of a Pauline Theme*, NSBT 13 (Downers Grove: InterVarsity, 2002).

12. Pao, *Thanksgiving*, 143–4.

13. See, among others, David E. Garland, *2 Corinthians*, NAC (Nashville: Broadman & Holman, 1999), 56–7; Scott J. Hafemann, *2 Corinthians*, NIVAC (Grand Rapids: Zondervan, 2000), 58–9; Frank J. Matera, *II Corinthians: A Commentary*, NTL (Louisville: Westminster/ John Knox, 2003), 41; David R. Nichols, 'The Strength of Weakness, the Wisdom of Foolishness: A Theological Study of Paul's Theologia Crucis' (PhD dissertation, Marquette University, Milwaukee, 1992), 4–10; James M. Scott, *2 Corinthians*, NIBC (Peabody: Hendrickson, 1998), 31; Thrall, *II Corinthians*, I:98; Sze-Kar Wan, *Power in Weakness: The Second Letter of Paul to the Corinthians*, NTC (Harrisburg: Trinity, 2000), 34. For a recent discussion on the epistolary structure of Paul's letters, see Runar M. Thorsteinsson, *Paul's Interlocutor in Romans 2: Function and Identity in the Context of Ancient Epistolography*, CBNTS 40 (Stockholm: Almqvist & Wiksell, 2003), 13–30. See also Jack T. Sanders, 'The Transition from Opening Epistolary Thanksgiving to Body in the Letters of the Pauline Corpus', *JBL* 81 (1962): 348–62; Stanley K. Stowers, *Letter Writing in Greco-Roman Antiquity*, LEC 5 (Philadelphia: Westminster, 1986), 22–3; M. C. Dippenaar, 'Reading Paul's Letters: Epistolarity and the Epistolary Situation', *TJT* 15 (1993): 141–57; idem, 'Prayer and Epistolarity: The Function of Prayer in the Pauline Letter Structure', *TJT* 16 (1994): 147–88; Peter Artz, 'The "Epistolary Introductory Thanksgiving" in the Papyri and in Paul', *NovT* 36 (1994): 29–46; Jeffrey T. Reed, 'Are Paul's Thanksgivings "Epistolary"?', *JSNT* 61 (1996): 87–99; M. Luther Stirewalt Jr., *Paul, the Letter Writer* (Grand Rapids: Eerdmans, 2003), 26 n. 3.

at the beginning of 2 Corinthians not only strongly suggests the importance and dominance of this theme but also sets the tone for Paul's argument throughout the letter.[14]

B. *The Function of 2 Corinthians 1.3-11 in Relation to the Argument of 2 Corinthians*

1. *Key Motifs*
After establishing the epistolary function of the thanksgiving period, I now turn my attention to five key motifs introduced in 1.3-11 that are further developed throughout the letter.

a) *Suffering*. The first motif relates to suffering. Πάθημα, usually translated 'suffering', appears three times (1.5, 6, 7) in 1.3-11. It is found 16 times in the NT, of which 7 times occur in the undisputed letters of Paul. Interestingly, in 2 Corinthians, this word only appears in 1.3-7 and nowhere else. Its verbal cognate, πάσχω, appears once in 1.6. A closely related word usually translated 'affliction', θλῖψις, including its verbal cognate θλίβω, appears a total of 3 times (1.4 [twice], 8) and once (1.6) respectively. Θλῖψις and its cognate occur 55 times in the NT but are mentioned more often by Paul (22 times in the undisputed letters), with the most frequent use found in 2 Corinthians compared to his other letters.[15] Even though πάθημα is not used subsequently in 2 Corinthians, the theme of suffering is developed throughout the letter in 2.14-16; 4.7-12; 6.1-10; 11.23–12.10 and finally recapitulated in 13.4.[16] This strongly affirms the motif of suffering as the basis for the thrust of the argument in the letter.

b) *Comfort and Deliverance*. The theme of suffering is matched by its counterpart, the motif of comfort in 1.3-7 and deliverance in 1.8-11. In this section, παράκλησις (1.3, 4, 5, 6 [twice] and 7) and its cognate παρακαλέω (1.4 [three times], 6) appear a total of ten times.[17] The frequent repetition of the theme of comfort is unmistakable: God is the Comforter (1.3) who continuously comforts Paul in every affliction; and such comfort is bound up in Christ. Closely related to the notion of comfort is the motif of God delivering Paul from mortal danger. This is found three times in 1.10 itself.

---

14. Hafemann puts it well by noting that these verses 'introduce the main themes of the letter, express Paul's key perspective on them, and contain an implicit appeal to his readers to join him in his outlook' ('The Comfort and Power of the Gospel: The Argument of 2 Corinthians 1–3', *RevExp* 86/3 [1989]: 325–45 [327]).

15. Apart from 1.3-11, θλῖψις appears six times elsewhere in 2.4; 4.17; 6.4; 7.4; 8.2, 13 while θλίβω twice in 4.8 and 7.5.

16. See also 2.4; 7.4; 8.2.

17. Παράκλησις appears five times elsewhere in 7.4, 7, 13; 8.4, 17; while παρακαλέω 14 times in 2.7, 8; 5.20; 6.1; 7.6 (twice), 7, 13; 8.6; 9.5; 10.1; 12.8, 18; 13.11.

The notion of God as comforter and deliverer and the frequent use of παράκ λησις/παράκλησις in 2 Corinthians is derived from the Scriptures. Barnett argues that this notion contains eschatological and messianic overtones deeply embedded particularly in Deutero-Isaiah (e.g., Isa. 40.1; 49.13; 51.2-3, 12, 19; 52.9; 61.2; 66.13).[18] That Paul has in mind Deutero-Isaiah is further reinforced by his frequent references to it in 2 Corinthians.[19] Furthermore, the identification of comfort with salvation makes the eschatological notion significantly clear.[20] For Paul, the eschatological comfort experienced is not only a present reality, but it is also a guarantee of the fulness of this salvation in future (1.9-10).

c) *Life and Death.* The motif of life and death occupies central place in this section (1.8, 9 and 10) and further developed in 2.14-16; 4.10-12; 5.14-15; 6.9; and 13.4. That Paul has in mind Jesus' death and resurrection is evident, especially in the close parallel between 1.9-10 and 4.10-11.

Closely related to this motif is Paul's understanding of eschatology. The Christ-event is seen as the inauguration of the new age.[21] Pao argues that in Paul, thanksgiving not only looks back to God's faithfulness, it also exhorts Paul and his readers to live their present lives in the light of the past, and provides hope in anticipation of the final fulfilment of God's promises in the future.[22] This thought may very well be present in 1.10, 'He who rescued us from so deadly a peril [looking into the past] will continue to rescue us [present]; on him we have set our hope that he will rescue us again [future].'

d) *Solidarity.* Through his suffering, the solidarity between Paul and Christ, and between Paul, the Corinthians and Christ, are interwoven. This triangular interconnectedness can be seen in God who comforts Paul through Christ and, as a result, Paul is equipped to comfort the Corinthians. Further in 1.11, Paul's appeal to the Corinthians to be in partnership with him by interceding for him is

18. Paul W. Barnett, *The Second Epistle to the Corinthians*, NICNT (Grand Rapids: Eerdmans, 1997), 68–73. It is also striking that Deutero-Isaiah begins with God's command, 'Comfort, comfort my people' (Isa. 40.1). For a detailed discussion on the notion of comfort/consolation in the Scriptures and other Jewish writings, see Alary, 'Good Grief', 59–217.

19. Paul cites Isa. 49.8 in 2 Cor. 6.2. In addition, the theme of new creation and restoration that are prominently found in Isa. 40.28-31; 41.17-20; 42.5-9; 44.21-8; 45.1-20; 49.8-13; 51.1-3, 9-16; 54.1-10; 55.6-13 is featured in 2 Cor. 5.17-21. See Barnett, *Second Epistles*, 46–7, and my discussion in Chapters 4 and 6.

20. See Alary, 'Good Grief', 281–2; Barnett, *Second Corinthians*, 69–70, 74–7; John Howard Schütz, *Paul and the Anatomy of Apostolic Authority*, SNTSMS 26 (Cambridge: Cambridge University Press, 1975), 243; Robert C. Tannehill, *Dying and Rising with Christ: A Study in Pauline Theology* (Berlin: Verlag Alfred Topelmann, 1967), 91–3.

21. Cf. Johan Christiaan Beker, *Paul the Apostle: The Triumph of God in Life and Thought* (Philadelphia: Fortress Press, 1980), 135–212.

22. Pao, *Thanksgiving*, 57–8.

another illustration of how this interconnectedness is demonstrated within the thanksgiving period.

Hafemann has pointed out that the relationship between Paul and his church is not reciprocal when it comes to Paul's sufferings.[23] Paul is called to suffer for the sake of the Corinthians but they are not called to suffer for him and neither do they administer comfort for Paul's sake. Like a fountain, the comfort of God overflows (περισσεύω) through Christ to Paul, and spills over into the lives of the Corinthians.[24] This can be further illustrated in the following diagram.

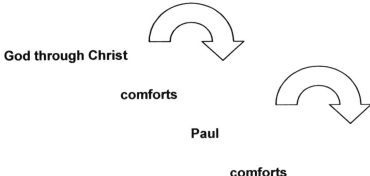

God through Christ

comforts

Paul

comforts

Corinthians

The emphasis of Paul's interconnectedness with the Corinthians in Christ is found within the context of his suffering for the benefit of the Corinthians, his appeal for reconciliation with them, and his description of their shared narrative in the story of Jesus (1.24; 2.2-3, 10; 3.2-3; 4.12, 15; 5.12-13; 6.11-13; 7.2-3, 12; 12.19; 13.4, 9).

e) *Hyberbolic Language.* Finally, the use of hyperbolic language in describing Paul's suffering is another feature in the thanksgiving section. For Paul, the sufferings of Christ περισσεύει ... εἰς ἡμᾶς, so that through Christ, the comfort also περισσεύει in Paul (1.5). Out of 35 times in the NT (of which 24 times are in the undisputed letters of Paul), περισσεύω occurs a total of 10 times in 2 Corinthians (1.5 [twice]; 3.9; 4.15; 8.2, 7 [twice]; 9.8 [twice], 12). The cognates of περισσεύω appear a total of 15 times.[25] In the context of 2 Corinthians, this word

---

23. Hafemann, *2 Corinthians*, 63, aptly describes this relationship as a 'one-way street' from God to Paul to the Corinthians.

24. See Alary, 'Good Grief', 263, and Harvey, *Renewal through Suffering*, 121 n. 20.

25. See Table 8.1 in Fredrick, J. Long, *Ancient Rhetoric and Paul's Apology: The Compositional Unity of 2 Corinthians*, SNTSMS 131 (Cambridge: Cambridge University Press, 2004), 151.

is distinctly used to describe Paul's ministry as a channel for the pouring out of eschatological blessings by God through Christ.

Paul also uses hyperbolic language elsewhere in the thanksgiving period. In recounting the mortal danger he faced in Asia, Paul describes being weighed down 'beyond measure' (καθ' ὑπερβολὴν ὑπὲρ δύναμιν ἐβαρήθημεν), beyond his strength (1.8). The use of hyperbolic language runs throughout the letter, especially in passages related to Paul's suffering. The noun and the cognates of ὑπερβολή are particularly characteristic in describing Paul's suffering in 2 Corinthians, and appear a total of eight times in 1.8; 3.10; 4.7, 17 (twice); 9.14; 11.23; and 12.7.[26] Paul's paradoxical language in emphasising the intense nature of his sufferings in 4.8-9 and the notion of power-in-weakness culminating in 12.10 further highlights the use of hyperbolic language.

2. The Story of Jesus in Paul's Sufferings as the Unifying Theme of 2 Corinthians
From the various motifs highlighted above, we can detect several important clues to the significance and importance of Paul's sufferings within the thanksgiving period. First, any of these motifs by themselves would not contribute significantly to Paul's overall argument in 2 Corinthians. The full impact of these motifs can only be completely realized if Paul's argument is grounded in the story of Jesus.[27] Paul affirms that he experiences the reality of suffering and comfort in abundance. However, by claiming that both these experiences are intimately connected with the story of Jesus, Paul demonstrates that his suffering is not meaningless; it is directly related to his apostolic mission in proclaiming the gospel. As Paul risks his life in his apostolic commission, the prospect of imminent death is no longer viewed as an end in itself. On the contrary, life and death are now reinterpreted in the light of the climactic drama of the death and resurrection of Christ that secures the foundation of Paul's hope of final deliverance.

The story of Jesus also binds Paul and the Corinthians to each other. The interconnectedness of Jesus Christ, Paul and the Corinthians in relation to Paul's suffering and his apostolic mission is clearly reflected in Paul's claims that he suffers for the sake of the Corinthians. By assigning missiological significance to his suffering, Paul is thus asserting that his mediatory suffering is not to be viewed negatively in light of his apostleship; on the contrary, it affirms his role as the herald of salvation.[28] The interconnectedness of Paul and the Corinthians is also reflected in his inviting them to be partners with him in intercessory prayers (1.11).

---

26. It is also interesting to note that ὑπερβολή and its cognates appears only six times elsewhere in the NT in Rom. 7.13; 1 Cor. 12.31; Gal. 1.13; Eph. 1.19; 2.7; 3.19.

27. As adequately argued by Wiles, *Paul's Intercessory Prayers*, 294, Paul's thanksgivings and prayers are grounded in and directed by the gospel of Christ.

28. See Chapter 6 below.

Therefore, the story of Jesus is the narrative that not only unites all these motifs in a coherent manner but also gives fresh meaning to Paul's understanding of his apostolic suffering. It is through this narrative that Paul's mediatory suffering, the comfort and deliverance he experienced, his view of his apostolic existence and ministry, and the shared narrative with the Corinthians find their fullest expression. Seen from this perspective, 2 Corinthians is primarily hortatory in character while apology or polemics only plays a secondary role.[29]

While it has been generally acknowledged that Paul's epistolary thanksgiving section introduces major themes that are developed in the body of the letter, insufficient attention has been paid to the epistolary function in 2 Corinthians. The theme of suffering introduced in this section is subsequently expanded in 2.14-16; 4.7-12; 6.1-11; 11.23–12.10 and finally recapitulated in 13.4. The thematic unity of Paul's suffering grounded in the story of Jesus throughout 2 Corinthians is too strong to be ignored and appears further to support the unity of the letter, even though a change in tone is acknowledged in sections of this letter.[30] This has rightly led Gorman to note that what unifies the shifting tones in 2 Corinthians is its 'ultimate focus on the cruciform shape of life in Christ'.[31] It is the Christ-event that lies behind Paul's apostolic commission and ministry, and it is this story that governs Paul's understanding of his apostolic suffering. It is this story that Paul wants his life and ministry to tell, and it is this story that Paul wants his community to embrace. As such, the story of Jesus appears to be the master story behind Paul's understanding of his suffering in 2 Corinthians.[32]

---

29. Cf. Barrett, 'Paul's Opponents', 246, who argues that Paul is not defending himself, his integrity or his position and authority in 2 Corinthians. So Young and Ford, *Meaning and Truth*, 15; Regina Plunkett-Dowling, 'Reading and Restoration: Paul's Use of Scripture in 2 Corinthians 1–9' (PhD dissertation, Yale University, New Haven, 2001), 22.

30. See David A. DeSilva, 'Measuring Penultimate against Ultimate Reality: An Investigation of the Integrity and Argumentation of 2 Corinthians', *JSNT* 52 (1993): 41–70. DeSilva argues that Paul's suffering is one of the thematic connections that strengthens the unity of 2 Cor. 1–9. Unfortunately, DeSilva does not extend his investigation to include chapters 10–13 as he maintains a two-letter fragment theory of 2 Corinthians (41). If chapters 10–13 are to be included in DeSilva's argument, one would discover that Paul's suffering not only plays a crucial role in the argument there but also functions as one of the main thematic connections throughout the entire canonical 2 Corinthians. However, cf. DeSilva's slightly altered position in his recent *An Introduction to the New Testament: Contexts, Methods & Ministry Formation* (Downers Grove: InterVarsity, 2004), 575–86, where he concludes: 'The points at issue [in 2 Corinthians 1–9 and 10–13] are substantially the same, indicated in the use of the same significant terms and topics in both' (584).

31. Michael J. Gorman, *Apostle of the Crucified Lord: A Theological Introduction to Paul and His Letters* (Grand Rapids: Eerdmans, 2003), 291.

32. Cf. Gorman's thesis that the cross of Christ is the master story in Paul's narrative patterns (see his *Cruciformity*). See also Stegman, *Character of Jesus*, who argues that the character of Jesus is the linchpin to understanding 2 Corinthians.

When 2 Corinthians is approached with this understanding of Paul's suffering, it becomes evident that each section of the letter is bound to the other by the notion of suffering grounded in the story of Jesus. That Paul developed the notion of suffering at crucial junctures either at the beginning or end of a particular argument within the letter is illuminating, and further reinforces the importance and significance of this theme in 2 Corinthians. As we have seen, the notion of suffering is prominent in the epistolary thanksgiving section (1.3-11). Then, in 1.12–2.13, Paul addresses his stormy relationship with the Corinthians by clarifying his change of travel plans and the issue with the offending member in the community. Moving on to a new section, Paul turns to his apostolic ministry and decisive role in God's grand narrative. He describes himself as being led in God's triumphal procession where, through him, the aroma of the knowledge of Christ spreads 'among those who are being saved and those who are perishing' (2.15). After declaring the life-and-death consequences of his apostolic ministry, Paul raises the question, 'Who is equal to such a task?' (2.16) which introduces his extended discussion on his ministry in comparison to that of Moses (3.1-18). As a minister of a new covenant (3.6), Paul preaches 'Jesus Christ as Lord' and himself as the servant of the Corinthians for Jesus' sake (4.5).

The manner in which Paul conducts himself as a minister of the glorious ministry is through weakness and suffering (4.7-15). Paul's suffering is not only the manifestation of the dying of Jesus but also a participation in the resurrection of Jesus (4.10). In keeping his focus on the shared narrative with the Corinthians, Paul declares that 'death is at work in us, but life in you' (4.12). By saying that 'the one who raised the Lord Jesus from the dead will also raise us with Jesus and present us with you to himself' (4.14) and 'all this is for your benefit' (4.15) Paul is further expressing his desire for the partnership of the Corinthians in this shared narrative.

After looking to the future by indicating that his continued suffering will one day come to an end (4.16–5.10), Paul provides a theological justification of his ministry of reconciliation grounded in the story of Jesus (5.11–6.2) by using the language of compulsion in 5.14 (ἡ γὰρ ἀγάπη τοῦ Χριστοῦ συνέχει ἡμᾶς). Here, as elsewhere (4.7-12), Paul returns to his own story by giving details of his ministry as an ambassador of Christ (5.20) and by enumerating his suffering (6.3-10). Therefore, Paul's suffering should not be seen as a stumbling block to anyone (6.3) but instead it is integral to his suffering as a servant of God. Again, by focusing on Paul's shared narrative with the Corinthians, Paul issues the invitation to the Corinthians to accept him (6.11-13).

Moving on, Paul continues to deal with issues affecting the Corinthians (7.14–9.15) before returning to an extended exposition concerning the nature of his apostolic ministry and his urgent appeal to them to be reconciled to him in chapters 10–13. At the height of his argument to win the Corinthians over to him from the interlocutors, Paul again boasts of his suffering and weakness by providing the most intense and descriptive catalogue of suffering not only in 2 Corinthians but also throughout the Pauline canon (11.23–12.10). To recapitulate his argument, Paul locates his ministry of power-in-weakness within the story of Jesus (13.3-4). His ultimate concern for the Corinthians is once again clearly demonstrated in his final warning: 'Examine yourselves to see whether you are in the faith; test yourself. Do you not realize that Christ Jesus is in you?' (13.5-6).

As I have established above, in each of Paul's presentations of his sufferings (1.3-11; 2.14-16; 4.7-12; 6.1-10; 11.23–12.10; and 13.4), the mediatory role of his apostolic mission grounded in the story of Jesus is unmistakably evident. Paul's suffering is not without purpose – it is a proclamation of his crucified Lord and for the sake of the Corinthians. Despite the shifting tones and rhetoric of 2 Corinthians, the theme of suffering not only occupies centre stage throughout Paul's argument but also unifies the letter. As Paul has earlier decided in his first visit to Corinth, his message of the gospel is nothing except 'Jesus Christ and him crucified' (1 Cor. 2.2). In 2 Corinthians, Paul continues to argue compellingly that the story of Jesus is the hallmark of his ministry, with its 'ultimate focus on the cruciform shape of life in Christ'.[33]

My argument thus far can be further summarized and illustrated in Table 2.1.

Table 2.1. *The Story of Jesus in Paul's Suffering and Mission in 2 Corinthians*

Passage	Paul's Mediatory Sufferings	Paul's Mediatory Role in his Mission
1.3-11	Christ's sufferings are abundant in Paul; the mortal danger in Asia and its resulting effects.	Paul's suffering for the benefit of the Corinthians, resulting in their comfort and salvation.
2.14-16	As conquered slave in God's triumphal procession in Christ.	Through Paul is spread the fragrance of the knowledge of Christ leading to life for those who believe and death for those who do not.
4.7-12	Paul's suffering listed in a catalogue.	Carrying in Paul's body the dying of Jesus so that the life of Jesus may be revealed; death is at work in Paul but life is at work in the Corinthians.
6.1-10	Paul's suffering listed in a catalogue.	Paul as ambassador and co-worker of Christ, making his appeal grounded in the story of Jesus and putting no obstacle in anyone's way, so that no fault is found in his ministry as the Servant of the Lord.

33. Gorman, *Cruciformity*, 291. Cf. idem, *Apostle of the Crucified Lord*, 291.

11.23–12.10	Paul's weaknesses enumerated through a catalogue, a humiliating escape from Damascus, a failed heavenly ascent and a thorn in the flesh, climaxed in a power-in-weakness statement.	Paul's appeal grounded in the meekness and gentleness of Christ; his boasting of his weaknesses and sufferings as a better servant of Christ; and his suffering on the account of Christ.
13.4	Paul's weakness in Christ.	Paul's confidence in living with Christ by God's power for the Corinthians' sake.

III. *Concluding Summary*

While it has been generally acknowledged that Paul's epistolary thanksgiving section introduces major themes of the letter, insufficient attention has been paid to the epistolary function in considering Paul's overall argument in 2 Corinthians. By taking this seriously, we notice that the introduction of the theme of suffering at the strategic position in 2 Corinthians strongly suggests the importance and dominance of this theme throughout the letter. The thanksgiving period introduces five key motifs closely related to the theme of suffering that are subsequently developed in the letter, appearing almost entirely in passages on Paul's suffering and his apostolic ministry. The full impact of the motifs identified in the thanksgiving period can only be fully appreciated if Paul's argument is grounded in the story of Jesus – a narrative that not only unites these motifs in a coherent manner but also provides fresh meaning to Paul's understanding of his suffering in 2 Corinthians. That Paul developed the notion of suffering at crucial junctures either at the beginning or end of a particular argument within the letter is illuminating, and further reinforces the importance and significance of this theme and the crucial role the story of Jesus plays in Paul's understanding of suffering with regard to his missionary framework in 2 Corinthians.

Chapter 3

SECOND CORINTHIANS 1.3-11

I. *Introduction*

In the previous chapter, I highlighted that the epistolary thanksgiving in 2 Cor. 1.3-11 contains five major motifs closely related to Paul's suffering. In this chapter, I shall analyse the story of Jesus in 1.3-11 by focusing my attention on the meaning of περισσεύει τὰ παθήματα τοῦ Χριστοῦ εἰς ἡμᾶς, and investigating how this is worked out in Paul's understanding of his suffering and his relationship with the Corinthians.

II. *Structure and Line of Thought*

There are two issues that need to be addressed concerning the structure of 2 Cor. 1.3-11. First, it is generally noted that instead of beginning the introductory section with the more familiar εὐχαριστέω-formula, Paul uses a εὐλογητός-formula. O'Brien argues that, while there is no distinction in the function of the use of these words, there is a difference in the objective of the thanksgiving formula. The former suggests Paul giving thanks for God's works in the lives of the addressees while the latter suggests that he gives thanks for the blessings in which he himself participated as the instrument of God.[1] Lambrecht has questioned this argument since the distinction between the objectives of these formulae remains unconvincing.[2] It is highly doubtful that, in using the εὐλογητός-formula, Paul's focus is entirely on himself and on the blessings he received. Even if it is true that Paul is drawing attention to himself, it is the realities of his suffering and God's comfort and deliverance that take centre stage. On the contrary, this passage emphasizes that the sufferings of Paul are

---

1. O'Brien, *Introductory Thanksgivings*, 239.
2. Jan Lambrecht, *Second Corinthians*, SP (Collegeville: Liturgical, 1999), 22. Note also the critique of O'Brien's thesis by Margaret Thrall, 'A Second Thanksgiving Period in II Corinthians', *JSNT* 16 (1982): 101–24 (119); and Pao, *Thanksgiving*, 31 n. 68. See also Fitzgerald, *Cracks in an Earthen Vessel*, 154–5, where he argues that the εὐλογητός-formula is 'a well-established vehicle for self-congratulations' (155). It is difficult to see how Paul is congratulating himself here unless he solely claims that the survival from his afflictions is the result of his complete reliance on his personal strength and power and not on God.

not for his own sake but for the Corinthians' sake. Even though Paul is pronouncing benediction to God, this does not necessarily mean that the thought of the Corinthians is far removed from his mind.

The other issue is the extent of the thanksgiving period. Should 1.8-11 describing Paul's traumatic Asian experience be considered as the introductory section or the body of the letter? While the majority see 1.3-11 forming a coherent unit, some argue that 1.8-11 belongs to the body of the letter.[3] The debate hinges on the disclosure formula (οὐ γὰρ θέλομεν ὑμᾶς ἀγνοεῖν) found in the beginning of 1.8, whether it functions to indicate the beginning of the letters body.[4] Both Thrall and Furnish have convincingly argued that the disclosure formula need not necessarily indicate the beginning of the body of the letter.[5] The presence of the conjunction (γάρ) clearly indicates that 1.8 is closely connected to the preceding section. The description of the sufferings of Paul and his co-workers in 1.3-7 is further exemplified in the disastrous experience narrated in 1.8-11. By using the disclosure formula, Paul is in fact drawing attention to the connection between what is in 1.8-11 and the foregoing section in 1.3-7. As such, the theme of suffering and comfort in 1.3-7 not only anticipates 1.8-11 but also serves as an illustration of how this theme is worked out in Paul's life in the devastating Asian experience. In view of this, it is best to view 1.3-11 as a coherent unit belonging to the epistolary thanksgiving section.[6]

In 1.3-11, Paul speaks of the reality of suffering in his apostolic ministry. He begins by expressing his benediction to God and calls God the God of all comfort who continues to comfort him (as seen in the present participle, ὁ παρακαλῶν) and his fellow co-workers in all their afflictions (1.3-4).[7] This action of God, reflected in the construction of the articular infinitive functioning as a purpose clause in 1.4 (εἰς τὸ δύνασθαι) enables Paul to comfort those in affliction with the same comfort he receives from God. Following this in 1.5-7, Paul identifies his continuous experience of suffering with Christ

---

3. So Linda L. Belleville, 'A Letter of Apologetic Self-commendation: 2 Cor 1:8–7:16', *NovT* 31 (1989): 142–63; Ben Witherington III, *Conflict & Community in Corinth: A Socio-Rhetorical Commentary on 1 and 2 Corinthians* (Grand Rapids: Eerdmans, 2004), 335; Garland, *2 Corinthians*, 72.

4. See John L. White, 'Introductory Formulae in the Body of the Pauline Letter', *JBL* 90 (1971): 91–7.

5. Thrall, *II Corinthians*, I:100; and Victor Paul Furnish, *II Corinthians*, AB (New York: Doubleday, 1984), 122.

6. See Innasimuthu, 'Comfort in Affliction', 265–81, for a defence of 1.3-11 as the thanksgiving period.

7. Paul's use of plural personal pronouns is most likely to be the literary plural and may have included his co-workers. It is unlikely he would have included the recipients of the letter. For further discussion, see Hafemann, *2 Corinthians*, 60. Cf. C. E. B. Cranfield, 'Changes of Person and Number in Paul's Epistles', in *Paul and Paulinism*, ed. M. D. Hooker and S. G. Wilson (London: SPCK, 1982), 280–9.

(1.5) where the Corinthians serve as both the beneficiaries and partners in this shared narrative of suffering (1.6-7).

This passage is characterized by a series of parallel statements with the presence of correlative conjunctions: καθὼς – οὕτως; εἴτε – εἴτε; and ὡς – οὕτως. The use of parallel structures is a fine demonstration of a similar thematic paralleling of suffering and comfort.[8] The first correlative conjunction, καθὼς – οὕτως, together with the chiastic περισσεύει τὰ παθήματα τοῦ Χριστοῦ εἰς ἡμᾶς and διὰ τοῦ Χριστοῦ περισσεύει καὶ ἡ παράκλησις ἡμῶν, serves not only to contrast 'sufferings' with 'comfort' but also to emphasize the notion of 'overflowing' (περισσεύει) which is repeated, as can be seen in the following schematic structure.

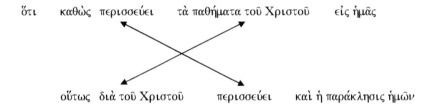

In his experience of suffering, the story of Jesus is central to Paul's thought; he is both the source from which sufferings overflow to Paul and the channel through which comfort overflows to him.[9] Furthermore, τὰ παθήματα τοῦ Χριστοῦ is first mentioned in the series of three parallel thoughts and this suggests the crucial function and role of the story of Jesus not only in Paul's thought but also in his argument in the thanksgiving period.

In 1.6 where the second pair of correlative conjunctions appears, Paul again begins with the theme of suffering before balancing it with the notion of comfort. He clearly identifies the Corinthians as the beneficiaries as indicated in the use of the preposition ὑπέρ. This can be further depicted in the following sentence diagram.

εἴτε δὲ θλιβόμεθα,
        ὑπὲρ τῆς ὑμῶν παρακλήσεως καὶ σωτηρίας
εἴτε παρακαλούμεθα,
        ὑπὲρ τῆς ὑμῶν παρακλήσεως
                τῆς ἐνεργουμένης
      ἐν ὑπομονῇ τῶν αὐτῶν παθημάτων
            ὧν
          καὶ ἡμεῖς πάσχομεν.

8.   Daniel B. Wallace, *Greek Grammar beyond the Basics: An Exegetical Syntax of the New Testament* (Grand Rapids: Zondervan, 1996), 657: 'The use of correlative conjunctions is intended as an analogy or comparison between the connected ideas.'

9.   Barnett, *Second Epistle*, 74.

Moving on to the final pair of correlative conjunctions in 1.7, Paul now turns his attention to the Corinthians. After clearly communicating his mediatory sufferings for their benefit, Paul now expresses his deep desire for reciprocity in his relationship within the shared narrative in Christ. By means of a ὡς – οὕτως construction, Paul conveys his confidence that the Corinthians will be partners (κοινωνοί) with him by sharing in his sufferings and comfort.

In 1.8-11, Paul continues with the theme of suffering by recalling the mortal danger he encountered in Asia as a result of his apostolic mission. Though he 'despaired of life itself' (1.8), Paul experienced the comfort that comes through the deliverance of God. By alluding to the resurrection of Christ, Paul is able to place his confidence in God to deliver him not only in the past and in the present but also in the future. As in 1.3-7, while Paul's emphasis is on his suffering, his concern for the Corinthians is never far from his mind. By appealing for the Corinthians' help and soliciting their prayers to God, Paul not only stresses the reciprocity, partnership and also his desire for reconciliation with them but also invites them to participate in his apostolic ministry by supporting him not only spiritually (1.11) but also in contributing financially to the collection for Jerusalem (2 Cor. 8–9).

Therefore, the main thrust of 1.3-11 can be expressed as follows: grounded in the story of Jesus, Paul interprets his apostolic sufferings as mediatory and beneficial for the Corinthians. On this basis, Paul invites the Corinthians to be part of this narrative of his apostolic ministry of suffering and the story of Jesus. With this established, I now turn to a closer examination of the story of Jesus in Paul's epistolary thanksgiving.

III. *The Story of Jesus in Paul's Epistolary Thanksgiving:*
2 Corinthians 1.3-11

A. *'The Sufferings of Christ are Abundant in Us': 2 Corinthians 1.3-7*

1. *Problems in Interpretation*

Two words are used to describe the idea of suffering in 1.3-11, θλῖψις and πάθημα. In the NT, θλῖψις refers to adverse circumstances, 'trouble that inflicts distress, oppression, affliction, tribulation'.[10] Its verbal cognate, θλίβω, means 'to cause to be troubled, oppress, afflict someone'.[11] Πάθημα, which means 'that

---

10. BDAG, s.v. See further Heinrich Schlier, 'θλίβω, θλῖψις', *TDNT* 3: 139–48; J. Kremer, 'θλῖψις, εως, ἡ; θλίβω', *EDNT* 2: 152–3. Cf. Karl Theodor Kleinknecht, *Der leidende Gerechtfertigte: Die alttestamentlich-jüdische Tradition vom 'leidenden Gerechten' und ihre Rezeption bei Paulus*, WUNT 2/13 (Tübingen: Mohr, 1984), 244; and Thrall, *II Corinthians*, I:104, who see θλῖψις as part of the vocabulary with eschatological connotations, especially that of the tradition of the suffering righteous.

11. BDAG, s.v.

which is suffered or endured, suffering, misfortune',[12] except for once (Heb. 2.9), always occurs in the plural in the NT.

Together, these two words appear a total of seven times in 1.3-11. In 1.4, Paul uses θλῖψις twice in reference to his afflictions and the afflictions of others. In 1.5, Paul makes reference to the παθήματα of Christ. Moving on to 1.6-8, Paul first uses the verbal cognate, θλίβω to describe his sufferings (1.6a), then switches to πάθημα and its verbal cognate πάσχω (1.6d), followed by πάθημα (1.7a) again. In 1.6d, Paul uses πάθημα to refer to the same suffering that the Corinthians patiently endured with him. In 1.7, both the idea of suffering and comfort appear together, and in this instance Paul uses πάθημα in reference to his suffering. Subsequently in 1.8, Paul returns to use θλῖψις to refer to the unbearable afflictions he suffered in Asia. In all these instances, it is clear that Paul uses both θλῖψις and πάθημα and their verbal cognates interchangeably to describe both his and his readers' sufferings. As such, any significant semantic difference or nuance in the meanings of these words and their usage is best avoided.[13]

As we have suggested above, the fact that τὰ παθήματα τοῦ Χριστοῦ (1.5a) is first mentioned in a series of three parallel thoughts in 1.5-7 strongly suggests the importance of this notion in Paul's understanding of his sufferings. This phrase is not only the crux of our interpretation but also indicates the central role the story of Jesus has in Paul's thought. Unfortunately, it has not been given sufficient attention in recent years.[14] Admittedly, trying to make sense of what Paul is intimating here is not without difficulty, as clearly demonstrated in the debates on the interpretations of this phrase.

The difficulty in understanding this passage centres on the nature of the sufferings in question. These παθήματα are qualified as the τὰ παθήματα τοῦ Χριστοῦ which is an unusual expression. Its parallels where sufferings are related to Christ in the NT are found only in Col. 1.24, τῶν θλίψεων τοῦ Χριστοῦ,[15] and

---

12. BDAG, s.v. See further W. Michaelis, 'πάσχω, παθητός, κτλ.', *TDNT* 5: 904–39, especially 931–4.

13. So Michaelis *TDNT* 5:933. See Innasimuthu, 'Comfort in Affliction', 203–6, for the meaning and uses of θλῖψις and πάθημα. He concludes by maintaining a doubtful distinction between θλῖψις and πάθημα; the former indicates human afflictions while the latter specifically refers to the sufferings of Christ. However, in his subsequent discussion, Innasimuthu might have contradicted himself when he remarks that the πάθημα of Christ has a reference to θλῖψις in 1.4 (245). Cf. Hafemann, *2 Corinthians*, 62, for a different nuance in his definitions of θλῖψις and πάθημα.

14. The debates on the meaning of 'sufferings of Christ' in 1.5a have been limited almost entirely to commentaries and briefly referred to in several monographs, often without substantial justification of the position being adopted. The most detailed discussion is probably that of Thrall. *II Corinthians*, I:107–10. To the best of my knowledge, any significant detailed exploration of the full significance of τὰ παθήματα τοῦ Χριστοῦ in relation to Paul's suffering remains forthcoming.

15. See Henry A. Gustafson, 'Afflictions of Christ: What Is Lacking?', *BR* 8 (1963): 28–42; Roy Yates, 'Note on Colossians 1:24', *EvQ* 42 (1970): 88–92; L. Paul Trudinger, 'Further Brief

Phil. 3.10, τὴν κοινωνίαν τῶν παθημάτων αὐτοῦ, where Christ is the antecedent for αὐτοῦ.[16]

In order to understand the passage, several issues need to be addressed. What is the precise meaning of τὰ παθήματα τοῦ Χριστοῦ, and what do we make of the genitive τοῦ Χριστοῦ? How exactly are τὰ παθήματα τοῦ Χριστοῦ said to overflow abundantly in Paul? What then is the function of this passage in view of the prominent theme of Paul's suffering in 2 Corinthians and in relation to his relationship with the Corinthians?

2. *Options in Interpretation*

Several views have been put forward in interpreting the phrase τὰ παθήματα τοῦ Χριστοῦ[17] and these can be broadly classified according to the following categories: (a) messianic woes; (b) mystical union; and (c) imitation of Christ.

a) *Messianic Woes.* Receiving the majority support,[18] this interpretation takes Χριστός as referring to the title of 'Messiah' and the genitive τοῦ Χριστοῦ as a descriptive genitive. As such, the sufferings are messianic because they are associated with the advent of the Messiah. Mark Dubis provides us with a helpful definition of messianic woes as a

> tumultuous period of eschatological distress and tribulation that, according to early Judaism, was to precede the coming of the Messiah. Characteristic features include apostasy, war, earthquakes, drought, famine, pestilence, familial strife and betrayal, cosmic signs, increasing wickedness, and the scarcity of truth and wisdom. Otherwise known in the rabbinic literature as the 'birth pangs of the Messiah', these woes

Note on Colossians 1:24', *EvQ* 45 (1973): 36–8; Richard Bauckham, 'Colossians 1:24 Again: The Apocalyptic Motif', *EvQ* 47 (1975): 168–70; W. F. Flemington, 'On the Interpretation of Colossians 1:24', in *Suffering and Martyrdom in the New Testament: Studies Presented to G. M. Styler*, ed. William Horbury and Brian McNeil (Cambridge: Cambridge University Press, 1981), 84–90; Andrew Perriman, 'The Pattern of Christ's Sufferings: Colossians 1:24 and Philippians 3:10-11', *TynBul* 42/1 (1991): 62–79; Michael Cahill, 'The Neglected Parallelism in Col 1:24-25', *ETL* 68 (1992): 142–7; Hanna Stettler, 'An Interpretation of Colossians 1:24 in the Framework of Paul's Mission Theology', in *The Mission of the Early Church to Jews and Gentiles*, WUNT 127, ed. Jostein Ådna and Hans Kvalbein (Tübingen: Mohr, 2000), 185–208.

16. See also 1 Pet. 1.11; 4.13; 5.1.

17. See Thrall, *II Corinthians*, I:107–10, for seven possible meanings. However, Thrall's classifications are not mutually exclusive.

18. Ralph P. Martin, *2 Corinthians*, WBC (Waco: Word Books Publishers, 1986), 9; O'Brien, *Introductory Thanksgivings*, 245; A. Plummer, *A Critical and Exegetical Commentary on the Second Epistle of St. Paul to the Corinthians*, ICC (Edinburgh: T&T Clark: 1915), 11–12; Furnish, *II Corinthians*, 118–19; C. K. Barrett, *The Second Epistle to the Corinthians*, BNTC (London: A. & C. Black, 1973), 61–2; Dale C. Allison, *The End of the Ages Has Come: An Early Interpretation of the Passion and Resurrection of Jesus*, SNTW (Edinburgh: T&T Clark, 1985), 66.

lead inexorably to the birth of the final state of blessedness ... In early Judaism, the
messianic woes were 'messianic' not because the Messiah suffered them, but because
these woes were the necessary prelude to the Messiah's arrival. In light of the Cross,
however, early Christians understood that the messianic woes had indeed fallen upon
the Messiah himself. As the messianic community, these Christians anticipated that
just as the Messiah had suffered eschatological tribulation prior to his resurrection,
they also would suffer the messianic woes until their own resurrection at the Messiah's second coming (Acts 14.22; Phil. 3.10; 1 Pet. 4.12-13).[19]

Proponents of this view note that messianic woes are closely analogous to
the Jewish doctrine of חֶבְלוֹ שֶׁל מָשִׁיחַ where the sufferings are borne not by
the Messiah himself, but by the people of the Messiah in the eschatological
period preceding the climax of history.

While this view has received overwhelming support, it is probably the most
problematic. This is mainly owing to the frequent reference to this concept
without any sustained analysis of the subject.[20] Scholars who argue against
this view often highlight that the usual term used in the LXX to describe the
messianic woes is either ὠδίν or ὠδίνω and not θλῖψις or πάθημα as used
in 2 Cor. 1.5a.[21] While the semantic argument by itself may not necessarily
negate the notion of messianic woes, there are other overwhelming considerations that appear to work against this interpretation of τὰ παθήματα τοῦ
Χριστοῦ here.

First, a closer investigation of the context reveals that Paul has in mind the
totality of Christ's suffering. This, not the period of apocalyptic sufferings, is
indicated in Paul's argument. Interpreters usually impose the readings of Phil.
3.10 and Col. 1.24 onto this text[22] by arguing that if Christ suffered the great
eschatological tribulation, then those who suffer with Christ also suffer the
messianic woes.

Second, a recent extensive study on the concept of messianic woes by Dubis
has pointed out that the nature and character of messianic woes include famine,
war, disease, family strife, earthquake, calamity and natural disaster that are

19. Mark Dubis, 'Messianic Woes', in *Eerdmans Dictionary of the Bible*, ed. David Noel
Freedman (Grand Rapids: Eerdmans, 2000), 890–1. See also his 'First Peter and the "Sufferings
of the Messiah"', in *Looking into the Future: Evangelical Studies in Eschatology*, ed. David W.
Baker (Grand Rapids: Baker, 2001), 85–96; and *Messianic Woes in First Peter: Suffering and
Eschatology in 1 Peter 4:12-19*, SBL 33 (New York: Peter Lang, 2002).

20. Dubis, *Messianic Woes*, 5: 'This neglect ... is especially surprising given that modern
scholars have suggested this concept as the background for numerous NT passages.' In his study,
Dubis attempts to provide a detailed analysis of the notion of messianic woes in the Scriptures and
other Jewish and Rabbinic writings. Apart from Dubis's work, studies that give this notion some
attention include Allison, *End of the Ages* and Conrad Gempf, 'The Imagery of Birth Pangs in the
New Testament', *TynBul* 45 (1994): 119–35.

21. See Thrall, *II Corinthians*, I:108.

22. See Allison, *End of the Ages*, 66.

universal in scope.[23] This is seen in the use of the metaphor ὠδίνω or ὠδίν in the eschatological discourse in the Synoptic Gospels (Mt. 24.8; and Mk 13.8). However, Paul's detailed description of his suffering in 2 Corinthians is highly personal as a direct result of his preaching the gospel and does not reflect any of those universal catastrophic elements. It is inconceivable that Paul should have supposed that his sufferings would have made any significant difference to the eschatological universal tribulation.[24]

Third, the understanding of the doctrine of messianic woes in this passage is further complicated by the late attestation of this doctrine after 135 CE.[25] Allison further notes that the evidence of the parallel of חֶבְלוֹ שֶׁל מָשִׁיחַ with ὠδίν is only apparent in second-century rabbinic sources.[26] However, both N. T. Wright and Barry Smith, while acknowledging late attestation of the notion of messianic woes, nevertheless maintain that this idea can still be confidently postulated.[27] Such ready acceptance of rabbinic materials has been subjected to intense criticism in recent years. In particular, Tom Holland not only sharply criticizes but strongly cautions against the use of rabbinic literature in interpreting biblical texts.[28] As such, the certainty that the full

---

23. Dubis, *Messianic Woes*, 5–36, especially his summary in 35–6. See Allison, *End of the Ages*, 5–25, 62–9 for discussion on the great tribulation in Jewish literature and Paul respectively.

24. Cf. Kenneth Grayston, *Dying, We Live: A New Inquiry into the Death of Christ in the New Testament* (New York: Oxford University Press, 1990), 52.

25. Beker, *Paul the Apostle*, 146. According to Beker, the Jewish doctrine of the messianic woes is a 'concept not documented in Jewish literature until 135 CE'. Beker's assertion is picked up subsequently by E. P. Sanders, *Jesus and Judaism* (London: SCM Press, 1985), 124. See also Michaelis, *TDNT* 5: 933 n. 20: 'The idea of a fore-ordained amount of suffering which has to be met is present neither in Paul ... nor elsewhere in the NT, nor is it suggested by contemporary assumptions.'

26. Allison, *End of the Ages*, 6 n. 6. Allison notes that the technical term, חֶבְלוֹ שֶׁל מָשִׁיחַ, does not occur until the late second century. However, Allison also expresses the possibility that the attestation of this phrase might be pushed back to approximately 90 CE based on the use of the term by Eliezer in *b. Sanh.* 98b and *Mek.* on Exod. 16.25. This suggestion can only be sustained if the Eliezer mentioned is the first-century Eliezer ben Hyrcanus.

27. Wright, *New Testament and the People of God*, 277–9; idem, *Jesus and the Victory of God*, COQG 2 (London: SPCK, 1996), 577–8; Smith, *Paul's Seven Explanations*, 1–3. Cf. Dubis, *Messianic Woes*, 6–7.

28. Tom Holland, *Contours of Pauline Theology: A Radical New Survey of the Influences on Paul's Biblical Theology* (Fearn: Christian Focus, 2004), 51–68. Cf. Holland's review of Smith, *Paul's Seven Explanations*: 'The method of collecting texts from a range of independent Second Temple documents and from them constructing a theological argument that supposedly represents the Jewish understanding of that era is theologically irresponsible. To do so denies these texts the voices of their own authors and their theological view points' (90–1). Note also Robert L. Plummer, *Paul's Understanding of the Church's Mission: Did the Apostle Paul Expect the Early Christian Communities to Evangelize?*, PBM (Milton Keynes: Paternoster, 2006), 132: 'it is noteworthy that in Paul's frequent references to suffering and hardship he never explicitly speaks of "Messianic Woes", as some Jewish sources arguably do'.

expression of messianic woes was already widely in use in the first century remains doubtful.

Fourth, the idea of messianic woes does not carry with it the notion of redemptive benefits. It is difficult to understand how Paul could claim to be enduring the messianic woes when he says that his suffering is for the benefit of the Corinthians.[29]

Finally, in the Corinthian passage, the sufferings of Christ are matched by the comfort that overflows through Christ. Perriman is right to point out that there is no concept of 'messianic comfort' alongside the notion of messianic woes.[30]

b) *Mystical Union.* This view argues that by sharing in the 'sufferings of Christ' believers participate in Christ's historical sufferings and Christ likewise participates in the sufferings of the Church. The genitive τοῦ Χριστοῦ is taken to be a subjective genitive which carries the nuance 'the sufferings that Christ experiences'. Ahern is representative of this view where he argues that the bond between the sufferings of Paul and Christ is based on intimate inner union.[31]

Those who attempt to argue for the understanding of mystical union explicitly connect it with the rite of baptism by way of reference to Rom. 6.3-11 where believers are united with Christ in his death and resurrection.[32] As a result of this relationship, Proudfoot argues,

> The sufferings of Christ are the Christians' sharing in the historical sufferings (or death) of Jesus, as these are mediated to them through their spiritual connection with the risen Christ – just as 'comfort' is their sharing in the resurrection of Christ through the somatic union with him.[33]

The allusion to baptism would appear to be more convincing if it can be clearly established that a baptism liturgy or thought lies behind 2 Cor. 1.3-11 and 2 Corinthians as a whole, which is highly unlikely.

Furthermore, the mystical union view does not explain the distinction Paul makes in 2 Cor. 1.3-11 between apostolic suffering and that of general suffering of the Christ-believers. Paul clearly declares that his sufferings result in

---

29. Cf. Alary, 'Good Grief', 17.

30. Perriman, 'Pattern of Christ's Sufferings', 64.

31. Ahern, 'Fellowship of His Sufferings', 1–32, especially 20–1. Other interpreters who share a similar view of mystical union include Furnish, *II Corinthians*, 120; Garland, *2 Corinthians*, 66–7; Proudfoot, 'Imitation or Realistic Participation'; Stettler, 'Interpretation of Colossians 1:24', 196–8. Note that Smith, *Paul's Seven Explanations*, 174–83, prefers to use 'spiritual union' because of the negative connotation attached to the phrase 'mystical union'. Cf. Schweitzer, *Mysticism of Paul*, 101–59.

32. Ahern, 'Fellowship of His Sufferings', 21, 31. Cf. Proudfoot, 'Imitation or Realistic Participation', 146–7; Thrall, *II Corinthians*, I:108–9.

33. Proudfoot, 'Imitation or Realistic Participation', 147.

comfort and salvation among the Corinthians, and this relationship does not have a reciprocal effect on Paul. The Corinthians are not so much sharers in Paul's sufferings as they are witnesses and beneficiaries of them. In view of this, O'Brien persuasively argues against this line of interpretation.[34]

c) *Imitation of Christ.* E. J. Tinsley argues that the genitive construction of τοῦ Χριστοῦ is understood as a genitive of source, indicating that Paul's suffering is like that of Christ, or that it has its origin in his service to Christ, the model of suffering.[35] Another proponent, Morna Hooker, argues that suffering is the necessary way to participation in glory. For her, the gospel is not merely an objective fact to be believed in but also a way of life to be lived out by embracing the suffering and humiliation it brings. Modelling Christ's suffering is an expression of faith that leads to righteousness.[36]

A major critique of this interpretation is that the sufferings of Paul simply do not resemble the sufferings of Christ. The idea of imitation should also not be read as an invitation to suffering, glorification in suffering, or as a path that leads to a closer communion with Christ. Neither should it be read in line with the martyr theology where martyrdom is viewed as the highest form of witness in following Christ.[37] While the notion of the imitation of Christ existing in Paul's thought cannot be doubted (1 Cor. 4.16; 11.1; 2 Cor. 8.9; 13.4),[38] it must be noted that this concept finds its expression in the ethical dimensions of a missionary lifestyle grounded in the cruciform life of the gospel,[39] and not in the desire to subject oneself to suffering or glorification in suffering.

34. O'Brien, 'Mysticism', *DPL*, 623–5. Cf. Tan, 'Idea of "Suffering"', 164.

35. E. J. Tinsley, *The Imitation of God in Christ: An Essay on the Biblical Basis of Christian Spirituality* (Philadelphia: Westminster, 1960), 138–40. Cf. Willis P. de Boer, *The Imitation of Paul: An Exegetical Study* (Kampen: Kok, 1962), 212–15, where Paul's idea of the imitation of Christ is based on participatory union with Christ.

36. Morna Hooker, 'Interchange and Suffering', in *Suffering and Martyrdom in the New Testament: Studies Presented to G. M. Styler*, ed. William Horbury and Brian McNeil (Cambridge: Cambridge University Press, 1981), 71–83.

37. Cf. Paul Middleton, *Radical Martyrdom and Cosmic Conflict in Early Christianity*, LNTS 307 (London: T&T Clark, 2006), 136–46, who argues that Paul is not a radical martyr – one who intentionally seeks out arrest and martyrdom – nor does he advocate radical martyrdom although his writings contain many of the concepts that enable subsequent development of martyr theology. 'Nowhere does Paul unambiguously refer to anyone martyred for the faith' (143).

38. For the notion of imitation in relation to Paul's sufferings, see Boykin Sanders, 'Imitating Paul: 1 Cor 4:16', *HTR* 74 (1981): 353–63; Robert L. Plummer, 'Imitation of Paul and the Church's Missionary Role in 1 Corinthians', *JETS* 44 (2001): 219–35; idem, *Paul's Understanding of the Church's Mission*, 81–96; Kathy Ehrensperger, '"Be Imitators of Me as I am of Christ": A Hidden Discourse of Power and Domination in Paul?', *LTQ* 38 (2003): 241–61.

39. See Peter O'Brien, *Gospel and Mission in the Writings of Paul: An Exegetical and Theological Analysis* (Grand Rapids: Baker, 1995), 83–7, for Paul's idea of imitation in missiological context.

d) *Evaluation*. Attempts to understand the phrase τὰ παθήματα τοῦ Χριστοῦ thus far appear to locate Paul's suffering within a particular model or tradition of suffering. This approach suffers from several deficiencies. First, a recurrent peculiarity of the exegetical history of this phrase is to analyse it independently, that is, without taking into account the immediate and wider context and the thrust of Paul's argument in 2 Corinthians. Most commentators have largely ignored the prepositional phrase εἰς ἡμᾶς that comes immediately after τὰ παθήματα τοῦ Χριστοῦ, which strongly suggests that this phrase needs to be interpreted in the light of Paul's sufferings. Furthermore, how τὰ παθήματα τοῦ Χριστοῦ εἰς ἡμᾶς functions within the epistolary thanksgiving section and 2 Corinthians has not been given adequate attention. That Paul continues to return to the subject of suffering subsequently in 2.14-16; 4.7-12; 6.1-10; 11.23–12.10; and 13.4 indicates his intention to further develop his understanding of the phrase περισσεύει τὰ παθήματα τοῦ Χριστοῦ εἰς ἡμᾶς. Those who argue for the traditions of mystical union or messianic woes completely miss Paul's emphasis on suffering/ weakness and power that exist simultaneously in his apostolic experience as reflected in these passages, a notion that is alien to these traditions.

In view of the fact that these sufferings are a direct result of Paul's apostolic mission, his mission theology within his eschatological framework as inaugurated by the story of Jesus needs to be taken into account as well. Therefore, the phrase τὰ παθήματα τοῦ Χριστοῦ cannot be understood in itself according to any of the interpretations discussed above, but can only be fully appreciated if we closely consider the story of Jesus in the wider context of 2 Corinthians in particular and Paul's mission theology in general. It is to this that I now turn my attention.

3. *The Story of Jesus in Paul's Understanding of His Suffering*
In what sense are Paul's sufferings designated as the sufferings of Christ? Schweitzer insists that they are to be connected only to the death of Christ.[40] However, this view appears to be narrowly construed, as Paul never uses τὰ παθήματα τοῦ Χριστοῦ in his letters to refer to the death or resurrection of Christ. Instead, Paul always uses the imagery of the cross or crucifixion and the language of dying and being raised to life to refer to Jesus' death and resurrection.[41] This can be further illustrated in Table 3.1 highlighting references to the death and/or resurrection of Christ in the undisputed letters of Paul.

---

40. Schweitzer, *Mysticism of Paul*, 141–59. See also Schütz, *Paul and the Anatomy of Apostolic Authority*, 242–3, where 'sharing Christ's sufferings means sharing Christ's death' (243).

41. For a detailed treatment of death and resurrection of Christ in Pauline thought, see Grayston, *Dying, We Live*, 8–130; N. T. Wright, *The Resurrection and the Son of God*, COQG 3 (Minneapolis: Fortress Press, 2003), 209–398; David A. Brondos, *Paul on the Cross: Reconstructing the Apostle's Story of Redemption* (Minneapolis: Fortress Press, 2006), 63–149.

Table 3.1 *References to the Death and/or Resurrection of Christ in Paul's Letters*

Passage	Reference to Christ's Death	Reference to Christ's Resurrection	Reference to both Christ's Death and Resurrection
Romans	5.6-8; 8.3; 14.15	1.4; 8.11; 10.9	4.24-5; 5.10; 6.3-10; 7.4; 8.34; 14.9
1 Corinthians	1.17-18, 23; 2.2, 8; 5.7; 8.11; 10.16; 11.23-7	6.14; 15.12-23, 29, 32, 35-57	15.3-4
2 Corinthians		1.9; 4.14	4.10-12; 5.14-15; 13.4
Galatians	1.4; 3.1; 5.11; 6.12-14	1.1	
Philippians	3.18		2.8-9; 3.10-11
1 Thessalonians		1.10	4.14; 5.10

In this respect, Paul most probably does not narrowly limit himself to refer to Christ's death and resurrection when he uses τὰ παθήματα τοῦ Χριστοῦ. Willert echoes this when he argues that Paul's suffering must also be viewed in the light of the passion tradition, and not merely the crucifixion of Jesus.[42] Similarly, Furnish also emphasizes that the background of Paul's idea of τὰ παθήματα τοῦ Χριστοῦ is to be found within the Son of Man tradition in the Synoptic Gospels,[43] where that Jesus the Messiah must suffer and overcome death through resurrection is deeply embedded.[44] This leads Furnish to his conclusion: 'that this same tradition is at work in 2 Cor. 1.5-7 cannot be doubted'.[45] Furnish's suggestion may be open to objection as the title 'Son of Man' is never used by Paul. But even if the tradition of the Son of Man is removed, there remains sufficient evidence that the sufferings of Jesus have been interpreted by the early Christ-believing movement as divine necessity and that the death and resurrection of Jesus are also part of God's grand narrative (Rom. 4.25; 5.8; 8.23; 1 Cor. 15.3-4; Gal. 1.4. Cf. Acts 2.23-4, 36; 3.18; 4.28; 17.3; 26.22). As such, Furnish's argument cannot be completely set aside.

Both Willert and Furnish are essentially correct to argue for the passion tradition in Paul's thought. However, it is more likely that Paul is thinking beyond the cross, death and resurrection to the story of Jesus in the idea of τὰ παθήματα τοῦ Χριστοῦ. When Paul refers to the story of Jesus including the death and resurrection of Jesus as depicted in the table above, he is concerned with bringing out the significance of this story interpreted according

---

42. Willert, 'Catalogues of Hardships', 218.

43. Furnish, *II Corinthians*, 119. Cf. Barnett, *Second Epistle*, 75.

44. See Mt. 16.21, par. Mk 8.31 and Lk. 9.22; Mt. 17.12, par. Mk 9.12, 31; Lk. 17.25, 24.7. Cf. Mk 10.32-4; Mt. 10.37-9, par. Lk. 14.25-7; and Mt. 16.24, par. Mk 8.34-5; Lk. 9.23; 24.25.

45. Furnish, *II Corinthians*, 119.

to the Scriptures. As Belleville rightly notes, 'The theological implication of describing Jesus' earthly ministry in this way is that the incarnate life of Jesus – and not just the crucifixion – becomes the locus of God's redemptive activity.'[46]

If my argument that Paul has in mind the story of Jesus in his understanding of suffering is correct, then he most likely interprets τὰ παθήματα τοῦ Χριστοῦ εἰς ἡμᾶς as the sufferings he experienced in his apostolic ministry. It is said to be 'of Christ' because Paul views his suffering of every kind as an expression of the same kind of sufferings Christ experienced in his mission.[47] As such, the genitive τοῦ Χριστοῦ can be seen as a genitive of relationship. As an apostle called by Christ, it is not surprising that Paul would ground the reflection of his sufferings in that of his crucified Lord. As Christ had to suffer persecution and rejection in his mission, so Paul is not exempted from suffering in his ministry of the gospel. Therefore, Hafemann rightly comments that the 'identification of the suffering of Paul with Christ is best explained in view of the missiological (not ontological) identity between Paul's own suffering as an apostle and the cross of Christ'.[48] As such, there is no need to go beyond this understanding by appealing to the doctrine of messianic woes, the traditions of the suffering righteous, mystical union, or the imitation of Christ.

This perspective makes better sense if we were to take it as the thrust of Paul's argument throughout 2 Corinthians where he clearly has in mind the story of Jesus in the passages listing his sufferings (2.14; 4.10-11; 6.3-10; 11.23-33; 12.10; 13.4) as well as in the overall argument of 2 Corinthians (5.14-15, 20-1; 8.9; 10.1).[49] When he calls attention to the story of Jesus, especially in the depiction of Jesus' character, Paul appears to have in mind the whole drama of the incarnation, life, death and resurrection, rather than any specific event in Jesus' life. And it is also probably significant that in referring to Christ's sufferings in his life and ministry, Paul refers not to any words or deeds of Jesus but to the depiction of the Suffering Servant in Deutero-Isaiah, an argument that I shall pursue in Chapter 6. Paul is also concerned to establish this truth to the Corinthians that Jesus is indeed the promised Messiah in fulfilment of

---

46. Linda L. Belleville, 'Gospel and Kerygma in 2 Corinthians', in *Gospel in Paul: Studies on Corinthians, Galatians and Romans for Richard N. Longenecker*, JSNTSup 108, ed. L. Ann Jervis and Peter Richardson (Sheffield: Sheffield Academic Press, 1994), 134–64 (142). Cf. Brondos, *Paul on the Cross*, 76: 'for Paul, Jesus' coming, ministry, death, and resurrection are a unified whole and had a single objective: the redemption of God's people'. See Brondos's wider argument in 63–102. See also my definition of the story of Jesus in Chapter 1.

47. Hafemann, *2 Corinthians*, 62. Cf. Brondos, *Paul on the Cross*, 169–73.

48. Scott J. Hafemann, 'The Role of Suffering in the Mission of Paul', in *The Mission of the Early Church to Jews and Gentiles*, ed. Jostein Ådna and Hans Kvalbein (Tübingen: Mohr, 2000), 165–84 (174). So Brondos, *Paul on the Cross*, 172.

49. See Stegman, *Character of Jesus*. Stegman's thesis is that the character of Jesus is the linchpin to understanding 2 Corinthians.

the Scriptures (1 Cor. 15.3-4). All this seems to tend strongly towards Willert's argument that, for Paul, 'the earthly life of Jesus Christ is much more important than often assumed'.[50]

4. *The Story of Jesus in Paul's Mission Theology*

Having established the story of Jesus in 2 Cor. 1.5, we now need to see it in the wider context of Paul's understanding of his mission to the gentiles and how this is further deliberated in relation to the theme of suffering in 2 Corinthians.

It was not until Schweitzer's *The Mysticism of Paul the Apostle* that Paul's mission was taken into account as part of a systematic exposition of his theology.[51] According to Schweitzer, the driving force behind Paul's mission to the gentiles is the eschatological conviction that the Parousia would only take place when the elected number of gentiles was fulfilled. Being alone in recognizing this urgent task, Paul felt himself 'under compulsion to carry the knowledge of Christ into the whole world'.[52]

In following Schweitzer, Cullman further took into account the relationship between Paul's mission and eschatology.[53] Cullmann argued that for Paul the eschatological task which must be fulfilled is no longer the preaching of the gospel in general but, more precisely, the preaching of the gospel to the gentiles, and that Paul was convinced that he himself had a pivotal role to play in this mission leading up to the Parousia.

Cullmann's insights have been taken up, in particular, by Munck in his *Paul and the Salvation of Mankind*.[54] In his treatment on Paul's mission to the gentiles, Munck investigates a series of Pauline texts (2 Thess. 2.6; Rom. 9–11; 15.14-19; 2 Cor. 3.7-18; Gal. 2.1-10) to substantiate his argument that Paul took his gentile mission to be connected with the events leading to the Parousia. Munck argues that Paul's pivotal role in the eschatological mission is seen as 'more important than all of the figures in the OT redemptive history, because he had been appointed by God to fill this key position in the last great

---

50. Willert, 'Catalogues of Hardships', 225. Cf. Michaelis, *TDNT* 5:932; Belleville, 'Gospel and Kerygma'; David Wenham, *Paul: Follower of Jesus or Founder of Christianity?* (Grand Rapids: Eerdmans, 1995), especially 338–410; John M. G. Barclay, 'Jesus and Paul', *DPL*, 492–503; and the compilation of essays in Todd Still, ed., *Jesus and Paul Reconnected: Fresh Pathways into an Old Debate* (Grand Rapids: Eerdmans, 2007).

51. Schweitzer, *Mysticism of Paul*, 177–87.

52. Schweitzer, *Mysticism of Paul*, 183.

53. Oscar Cullmann, 'Le caractère eschatologique du devoir missionaire et de la conscience apostolique de S. Paul: Étude sur le κατέχον (-ων) de 2. Thess. 2:6-7', *RHPR* 16 (1936): 210–45, reprinted with a different title as 'Der eschatologische Charakter des Missionsauftrags und des apostolischen Selbstbewusstseins bei Paulus', in *Oscar Cullmann: Vorträge und Aufsätze, 1925–1962*, ed. Karlfried Fröhlich (Tübingen: Mohr, 1966), 305–36.

54. Johannes Munck, *Paul and the Salvation of Mankind*, trans. Frank Clarke (London: SCM Press, 1959), 36–68.

drama of salvation'.[55] The completion of the gentile mission would then hasten the coming of the Parousia and it is within this eschatological framework that Paul's mission is to be conceptualized.

Stettler takes this argument further by examining the relationship of Paul's suffering to his mission within this eschatological framework. By closely analysing Col. 1.24, she proposes that Paul's 'completing of what is lacking in Christ's afflictions' needs to be interpreted within the framework of Paul's mission theology and eschatology.[56] Stettler holds that the preaching of the gospel and suffering belong together as characteristics of the times of the messianic woes. Just as the number of gentiles must be filled up through Paul's gentile mission, there is also a corresponding amount of suffering that needs to be fulfilled as well.[57] In this respect, Stettler argues that, as the Servant of the Lord in completing the gentile mission, Paul is helping to shorten the time before the Parousia, the messianic woes and the suffering of the Church.[58]

While it is right to see Paul's gentile mission as an eschatological event, the formulation that Paul saw himself as the pivotal figure in ushering in the Parousia, which in turn explains the motivation for Paul's apostolic mission, is defective in several ways. Bowers is right to point out that there are two areas that need correction.[59] First, such a formulation ignores other numerous clear indications that Paul recognized the limitation and interdependency of his vocation. Paul's mission was regularly described as a collaboration with his co-workers rather than an individual effort (e.g., 1 Cor. 3.4-9; Phil. 2.22, 25).[60]

Second, this formulation is seen from the perspective that Paul is moving towards an eschatological event and assumes a uniformly future orientation for the eschatological dimension of hiss missionary understanding. This interpretive framework sees Paul's call as fulfilling the OT eschatological ingathering of the gentiles and as the pivotal figure in ushering in the eschatological drama. His suffering is seen as the quota that needed to be fulfilled, as part of the messianic woes that afflict the righteous before the final eschatological age. Based on this interpretation, Paul's eschatological understanding of his missionary vocation appears to be intimately connected with the events surrounding the Parousia.

For Paul, however, the most decisive event of the End had already taken place in Christ and this recognition was forcefully impressed upon Paul in his

---

55. Munck, *Paul*, 43.

56. Stettler, 'Interpretation of Colossians 1:24'. While Stettler's argument follows Munck's fairly closely, it is surprising that she does not make any reference to Munck.

57. Stettler, 'Interpretation of Colossians 1:24', 205.

58. Stettler, 'Interpretation of Colossians 1:24', 191, 206.

59. Paul Bowers, 'Mission', *DPL*, 617–18. Cf. idem, 'Studies in Paul's Understanding of His Mission' (PhD dissertation, University of Cambridge, Cambridge, 1977). For further critique on Munck's position, see Eckhard Schnabel, *Early Christian Mission: Paul and the Early Church*, Vol. 2 (Downers Grove: InterVarsity, 2004), 1002, 1458.

60. For further discussion on Paul's co-workers, see E. Earle Ellis, 'Paul and His Co-Workers', *NTS* 17 (1971): 437–52; Schnabel, *Early Christian Mission*, 2: 1425–45.

personal Damascus encounter. That Jesus was the Messiah could only mean for Paul, a Jew, that the final age had indeed begun,[61] and that the eschatological ingathering of the nations was now being fulfilled.[62] Hence, Paul conceived of his gentile mission not merely in connection with a future event but primarily in connection with the past event reflected in the Christ-event and the inauguration of the new age by Christ. Therefore, contrary to Munck and Stettler, Bowers is right to argue that Paul's mission 'is much more demonstrably working *from* an eschatological event than *toward* one'.[63]

If Bowers is right in his critique and subsequently in providing the above corrective measures for Paul's mission within the eschatological framework, then the shape of Paul's mission takes on a new direction. What drives Paul in his mission is not the conviction of alleviating the sufferings of the Church and bringing the period of the messianic woes to a faster conclusion, but it is the conviction of the story of Jesus as the climax of God's salvation drama. In other words, Paul primarily grounds his understanding of suffering as a result of his apostolic ministry in the eschatological drama of the story of Jesus and not in the Parousia.[64] Paul's conceiving of his gentile mission as eschatological in nature is not disputed, but it is not primarily connected to a future event. Instead, it is linked with a past one – the Christ-event. Bosch is right to comment that one of the basic errors of much apocalyptic understanding of Paul lies in the fact that it 'minimizes the central significance of Christ'.[65]

In this way, the story of Jesus determines Paul's understanding of God and reconciliation with God on the one hand and of the nature of faithful apostolic existence demonstrated through suffering on the other. Barclay forcefully asserts that Paul does not simply

> recall the story of Jesus as an event to be remembered, a chapter now past … Rather, the crucifixion of Jesus is a *present* reality for Paul, present … also in the continuing experiences and sufferings of his life … Paul both *lives from* the story of Jesus (it happened, crucially, once in history) and *lives in* it: it happens again, time and again, inasmuch as Christ lives in him.[66]

---

61. Cf. David Bosch, *Transforming Mission: Paradigm Shifts in Theology of Mission* (Maryknoll: Orbis, 1991), 127; Donald Senior and Carroll Stuhlmueller, *The Biblical Foundations for Mission* (Maryknoll: Orbis, 1983), 169.

62. See Chapter 4 for further discussion.

63. Bowers, 'Mission', 618, emphasis his. Cf. O'Brien, *Gospel and Mission*, 40–1.

64. While Paul may have the Parousia in view (e.g., 2 Cor. 1.10-11; 4.17-18), it is not the only and primary factor that establishes his understanding of his suffering in the light of his mission theology.

65. Bosch, *Transforming Mission*, 142. Cf. J. Paul Sampley, *Walking between the Times: Paul's Moral Reasoning* (Minneapolis: Fortress Press, 1991), 7: 'The death and resurrection of Jesus Christ is the primary reference point in Paul's thought world. Paul sees past, present, and future in light of that pivotal event.' See also Grams, 'Gospel and Mission', 267–90.

66. John M. G. Barclay, 'Paul's Story: Theology as Testimony', in *Narrative Dynamics in*

While Barclay is essentially right in his insightful remarks, he misses the fact that having been grounded in the story of Jesus, Paul continues to look forward to live in Christ in the future (cf. 2 Cor. 5.1-10). While the resurrection has inaugurated the new age and grounds the eschatological hope, the period between the 'first fruits' (1 Cor. 15.20, 23; cf. Rom. 8.29) and the 'full harvest' (1 Cor. 15.54-5) is marked fundamentally by the cross of Christ.[67] Thus Paul can assert that while he was among the Corinthians he had 'resolved to know nothing … except Jesus Christ and him crucified' (1 Cor. 2.2). In this respect, Paul's mission works within a framework of eschatological events that is understood to be grounded in the past Christ-event and the future Parousia. Therefore, Bosch rightly asserts that Paul's mission theology is not *unifocal* in nature as demonstrated by the argument of Cullmann, Munck and Stettler but *bifocal* in focusing both on God's past and future acts in Christ.[68] Paul's bifocal framework is powerfully expressed in his retelling of the story of the Lord's Supper to the Corinthians, 'For as often as you eat this bread and drink the cup, you proclaim the Lord's *death* until he *comes*' (1 Cor. 11.26).[69] This can be further illustrated in the following diagram.

Unifocal Nature of Paul's Mission Theology

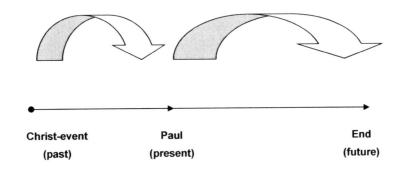

Christ-event	**Paul**	**End**
(past)	**(present)**	**(future)**

Paul: A Critical Assessment, ed. Bruce W. Longenecker (Louisville: Westminster/John Knox, 2002), 133–56 (155, emphasis his).

67. Joel B. Green, 'Paul's Theology of the Cross', in *The Death of Jesus in Early Christianity*, ed. John T. Carroll and Joel B. Green (Peabody: Hendrickson, 1995), 113–32 (115–16).

68. Bosch, *Transforming Mission*, 143.

69. It is also interesting to note that the bifocal framework essentially supports Pao's investigation of Pauline thanksgiving – that thanksgiving is not only an act of remembrance in the past but also a call to live one's life in the light of the past that provides hope for the future in anticipation of the fulfilment of God's promises. Cf. Pao, *Thanksgiving*, 143–4; and my discussion in Chapter 2. See also Beker's discussion on the bifocal nature of Paul's thought comprising the dynamic tension between the Christ-event and the Parousia (*Paul the Apostle*, 135–81, particularly 159–63).

Bifocal Nature of Paul's Mission Theology

The Story of Jesus

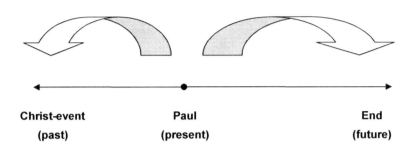

Christ-event	Paul	End
(past)	(present)	(future)

Seen from a bifocal framework, Paul's perspective concerning his mission in some respects takes on a radically new direction. In the confidence of the resurrection of Christ (cf. 1 Cor. 15.12-56), Paul is able to look forward to the new era being inaugurated, a 'new creation' (2 Cor. 5.17) that not only comprises the Jews but also the gentiles. Yet Paul also sees the life and death of Jesus characterized by a life of service and obedience (2 Cor. 8.9; cf. Rom. 15.3; Phil. 2.5-11). This paradoxical reality grounded in the story of Jesus and the gospel as a manifestation of weakness and power (cf. 13.3-4) becomes the paradigmatic framework in Paul's argument.[70]

As a servant of the Corinthians for Christ's sake, Paul is subjected to intense sufferings in his apostolic ministry which he interprets as τὰ παθήματα τοῦ Χριστοῦ. Through his sufferings, he receives the comfort of God. There is a corresponding parallel between the sufferings and the comfort received. The comfort overflows abundantly from God and reaches Paul through Christ, and it then overflows abundantly from Paul into the lives of the Corinthians. The parallelism allows us to see that the identification of Paul's sufferings with the sufferings of Christ is a means of mediating the comfort of God to the Corinthians. This reveals that Paul unequivocally considered his suffering as an apostle to be a divinely ordained vehicle for mediating God's presence in the lives of his people. As Stanley rightly observes, 'the two most important relationships in [Paul's] apostolic career' were 'that to Christ and that to his communities'.[71] Therefore, Paul's experience of suffering, far from disquali-

70. Cf. Schütz, *Paul and the Anatomy of Apostolic Authority*, 244–5.

71. David M. Stanley, 'Imitations in Paul's Letters: Its Significance for His Relationship to Jesus and to His Own Christian Foundations', in *From Jesus to Paul: Studies in Honour of Francis Wright Beare*, ed. Peter Richardson and John C. Hurd (Waterloo: Wilfrid Laurier University Press, 1984), 127–41 (131). Cf. Tannehill, *Dying and Rising*, 98: 'The sufferings which (Paul) endures in fulfilling his mission are for the sake of the church. Both the suffering which he undergoes and the comfort he receives work to the church's benefit.'

fying his apostleship and ministry, works on the contrary towards the comfort and salvation of the Corinthians, as long as they remain partners with Paul.

Grounded in the story of Jesus, Paul's suffering takes on missiological significance. This is demonstrated throughout Paul's argument related to his suffering in 2 Corinthians. Paul describes himself as the conquered slave of Christ by using the imagery of a Roman triumphal procession. Through Paul, the fragrance of the knowledge of Christ is spread, resulting in an aroma of life and death. He also views himself as Christ's ambassador, a vehicle through whom God makes the appeal for reconciliation. As a servant of the Corinthians for the sake of Christ, Paul commends himself through sufferings and hardships. He conducts his ministry in service and obedience, as a reflection of the story of Jesus, so that it is not discredited.

In summary, Paul, an apostle and servant of Christ, places the pattern of death and new life, suffering and hope, service and obedience, at the very heart of his gospel. Paul's life as an apostle focuses on 'the Son of God who loved me and gave himself for me' (Gal. 2.20). His motivation is based on the universal implications of the story of Jesus, 'For the love of Christ urges us on, because we are convinced that one has died for all; therefore all have died' (2 Cor. 5.14). His ministry is characterized by the powerful image of 'always carrying in the body the dying of Jesus, so that the life of Jesus may also be made visible in our bodies' (2 Cor. 4.10). By itself, Paul's story of his own suffering is of no ultimate significance. Only when it is grounded in the story of Jesus and the final victory of God does Paul's suffering find its significance. Here, we see that the story of Jesus and Paul's presentation of himself especially in his suffering cannot be separated in any way.[72]

B. *Paul's Afflictions in Asia: 2 Corinthians 1.8-11*

1. *The Nature and Effects of Paul's Afflictions in Asia*
In 1.8-11, Paul continues his theme of suffering by reminding the Corinthians of his Asain tribulations. He offers no details of his suffering and thus it is difficult to ascertain the precise character of his affliction.[73] Commentators have speculated about the nature of Paul's suffering, ranging from severe persecution,[74] through imprisonment[75] to some kind of severe chronic illness.[76]

---

72. Cf. Belleville, 'Gospel and Kerygma'.

73. See Roy Yates, 'Paul's Affliction in Asia: 2 Corinthians 1:8', *EvQ* 53 (1981): 241–5 and Innasimuthu, 'Comfort in Afflictions', 281–99, for various suggestions.

74. Martin, *2 Corinthians*, 16, suggests that the tribulation is some form of hardship or physical violence leading to exposure to death. Wan, *Power in Weakness*, 35, thinks it is some form of real peril encountered. Yates sees it as Jewish opposition ('Paul's Affliction in Asia'). So John. E. Wood, 'Death at Work in Paul', *EvQ* 54 (1983): 151–5.

75. So Furnish, *II Corinthians*, 123; Thrall, *II Corinthians*, I:116–17; Nigel Watson, *The Second Epistle to the Corinthians*, EC (London: Epworth, 1993), 6–7.

76. Harris, *Second Corinthians*, 164–82; Barrett, *Second Corinthians*, 64; Harvey, *Renewal through Suffering*, 20.

While precise identity is not necessary for our understanding of Paul's suffering,[77] his language and description seem to suggest some forms of devastating dangers from without, rather than chronic illness. First, the disclosure formula in 1.8, οὐ γὰρ θέλομεν ὑμᾶς ἀγνοεῖν, requires that the Asian experience be understood in the light of what precedes in 1.3-7. In this respect, Paul's mortal danger is not any form of natural disaster or human illness but sufferings that he encountered in association with his ministry. Second, Paul does not list illness in any of his catalogues of suffering.[78] If the devastating Asian experience is indeed some form of chronic illness that so severely affected Paul, we would naturally expect it to be listed in the catalogues.

Paul's silence on the precise *nature* and *character* of his afflictions in this passage may be significant,[79] especially in view of his detailed recitals of his sufferings elsewhere in the letter (2.14-16; 4.7-12; 6.3-10; 11.23-33; 12.10). Thus Paul's primary focus here is on the *effects* of this experience which are described in a very dramatic and overwhelming manner. Paul was completely[80] weighed down (ἐβαρήθημεν) to such a great extent that he despaired (ἐξαπορηθῆναι) even of life itself. By using such hyperbolic language in describing his experience, Paul is emphasizing the dangers and hardships he underwent for the Corinthians' benefit (cf. 4.8-12, 15). This desperate situation drove Paul to place his complete trust and hope in the God 'who raises the dead' (1.9). This description not only foreshadows the subsequent reference in 4.14 to 'the one who raised the Lord Jesus' but is also strongly suggestive of Paul having the story of Jesus in mind.

Harvey argues that Paul's Asian experience caused him to evaluate his understanding of suffering and death. It is through this traumatic experience of a crisis of faith that Paul finds positive value in suffering.[81] While Harvey's argument appears attractive, it needs to be reiterated that this is not the first time Paul has experienced, or mentioned, his extreme suffering.[82] It can hardly be claimed that the issue of suffering and possible death is something

---

77. Cf. F. F. Bruce, *1 & 2 Corinthians*, NCB (London: Oliphants, 1971), 179, who cautions that 'the task of identifying it calls for speculation beyond the exegete's province'. Wood's conjecture that Paul's sentence of death in 1.9 echoes the cries of the crowd in calling for the death of Jesus is an example of ignoring Bruce's caution ('Death at Work in Paul', 152).

78. Peter H. Davis, 'Why Do We Suffer? Suffering in James and Paul', in *The Missions of James, Peter and Paul: Tensions in Early Christianity*, NovTSup 115, ed. Bruce D. Chilton and Craig A. Evans (Leiden: Brill, 2005), 435–66 (446 n. 22).

79. See Harvey, *Renewal through Suffering*, 11–20. Harvey suggests that to ask the question of the exact nature of the Asian experience is to ask the wrong question.

80. Note the superlative and redundant description of the effects of the Asian tumultuous experience, καθ' ὑπερβολὴν ὑπὲρ δύναμιν.

81. See Harvey, *Renewal through Suffering*, 8–31.

82. On Paul's suffering prior to the traumatic Asian experience, see the discussion below. Cf. Hall, *Unity of the Corinthian Correspondence*, 159–61, for a critique of Harvey's position.

new to Paul, either doctrinally or personally, that required him to alter his theological position.[83]

2. *The Story of Jesus in Paul's 'Sentence of Death'*

In 2 Cor. 1.9a, Paul declares ἀλλὰ αὐτοὶ ἐν ἑαυτοῖς τὸ ἀπόκριμα τοῦ θανάτου ἐσχήκαμεν. This clause has often been interpreted as a reinforcement of the effects of the devastating Asian experience by taking ἀλλά in 1.9 as supporting what was said earlier in 1.8 and by seeing ἐσχήκαμεν as functioning in the aoristic perfect.[84] This reading then takes the incident in 1.8 as tantamount to τὸ ἀπόκριμα τοῦ θανάτου received by Paul.[85] While this is plausible, Stegman has suggested an alternative reading of the text. He argues that Paul might have intended more in 1.9a if ἐσχήκαμεν is taken as a true perfect, giving the force of the ongoing ramifications for the present of something received in the past.[86] Stegman suggests reading τὸ ἀπόκριμα τοῦ θανάτου in light of the wider context of 1.1-7, and not solely in light of the Asian incident expressed in 1.8. If Stegman is right, then Paul's understanding of τὸ ἀπόκριμα τοῦ θανάτου here is not merely limited to recounting a singular incident but also including the larger reality of his apostolic existence, a reality that entailed 'both suffering and embodying Jesus' self-emptying mode of existence'.[87]

---

83. Cf. Fredrik Lindgård, *Paul's Line of Thought in 2 Corinthians 4:16–5:10*, WUNT 2/189 (Tübingen: Mohr Siebeck, 2005). Lindgård argues that 2 Corinthians does not support the view that Paul changed or developed his eschatology over the course of time prior to writing the letter.

84. So Furnish, *II Corinthians*, 113; Martin, *2 Corinthians*, 14; Plummer, *Second Epistle*, 18.

85. The word ἀπόκριμα is a hapax legomena in the NT. Literally, it carries the meaning of official report or decision (BDAG). For further discussion on the meaning and use of this word, see Colin J. Hemer, 'A Note on 2 Corinthians 1:9', *TynBul* 23 (1972): 103–7. Hemer is basically right to question the forensic interpretation of this passage where Paul literally receives the judicial sentence of death. However, his own interpretation that Paul received the answer of 'death' from God in his petition while in great danger and that he would not live until the Parousia remains highly doubtful. See the critique by Thrall, *II Corinthians*, I:118. Cf. Witherington, *Conflict and Community*, 361–2, who speculates that the sentence and verdict was some form of chronic illness that Paul pronounced upon himself. See also David E. Fredrickson's proposal that the 'sentence of death' should be taken as Paul's rhetoric in expressing regrets ('Paul's Sentence of Death [2 Corinthians 1:9]', in *God, Evil and Suffering: Essays in Honor of Paul R. Sponheim*, ed. T. Fretheim and C. Thompson, WWSup 4 [St Paul: Word & World, 2000], 99–107). Fredrickson's argument that Paul pronounced his own sentence by condemning himself to death as a result of his guilt of writing the letter of grief (2 Cor. 2.4) appears too speculative. Other conjectures include Wood's suggestion that the sentence of death echoes the cries of the crowd in calling for the death of Jesus ('Death at Work in Paul', 152) and Michael Goulder's proposal that the severe trial is Paul's failed mission in Ephesus (*Paul and the Competing Mission in Corinth* [Peabody: Hendrickson, 2001], 45–6).

86. Stegman, *Character of Jesus*, 260. Cf. Belleville who also takes ἐσχήκαμεν as true perfect: 'we received and still experience' (*2 Corinthians*, IVPNTC [Downers Grove: InterVarsity, 1996], 58). So Barnett, *Second Epistle*, 86; Garland, *2 Corinthians*, 78–9.

87. Stegman, *Character of Jesus*, 260.

While Stegman's proposal appears attractive, he does not develop this idea further. He is basically right to suggest that Paul could not have developed the notion of 'τὸ ἀπόκριμα τοῦ θανάτου from a singular Asian incident as depicted in 1.8. There are at least six other references in the Corinthian correspondence where the metaphorical notion of death is developed, two of which occurred prior to the Asian experience (cf. 1 Cor. 4.9; 15.31; 2 Cor. 4.11; 6.9; 11.22-3; 13.4). It is also interesting to note that all these allusions and references to death all occur either within Paul's catalogues of suffering or in the context of his mission. The clear parallel between 1 Cor. 15.31, 2 Cor. 4.11, and 11.26 as highlighted by Hafemann indicates that Paul is using 'death' as a metonymy for his life of suffering as an apostle.[88] Therefore, it is highly implausible that in 1.9a, τὸ ἀπόκριμα τοῦ θανάτου that Paul received is narrowly limited to the single incident in Asia. Furthermore, since Paul considers the devastating experience as θλίψεως (1.8), it makes better sense to locate it within the same category of τὰ παθήματα τοῦ Χριστοῦ in 1.5a,[89] that is, suffering associated with the ministry of the gospel for Christ's sake. As supported by the perfect tense of ἐσχήκαμεν, Paul received and still experiences the sentence of death in his apostolic mission.

It is within this context of Paul's apostolic mission that the following 1.9b is to be understood. Paul's intense suffering is not without any pedagogical purpose[90] – 'so that we would rely not on ourselves but on God who raises the dead'. Here, Paul makes it clear that he is able to fulfil his apostolic mission which involves intense suffering and sacrificial giving of himself for the sake of others only because of God, and not by his own means. The ongoing experience of hardships has taught Paul that his only assurance of survival in his mission is to place his complete trust in God to preserve him and to raise him from the dead at the End of days. In characterizing God in such a manner, Paul clearly has the story of the death and resurrection of Jesus in mind. The bifocal missionary framework of Paul as suggested earlier is once more replicated here – Paul looks back to the Christ-event and looks forward to his own final deliverance in the final victory of God.[91]

The bifocal framework is further supported in Paul's threefold use of ῥύομαι in 1.10. Structurally, 1.10 contains two relative clauses that further supplement Paul's depiction of God in 1.9b. The 'One who raises the dead' (1.9b) is also

---

88. Hafemann, 'Role of Suffering', 179.

89. Cf. Plummer, *Second Epistle*, 16: the mortal danger in Asia 'would fitly be compared with "the sufferings of the Messiah"'. So Hooker, 'Interchange and Suffering', 78.

90. Smith, *Paul's Seven Explanations*, 172–4.

91. Nigel Watson takes 1.9b to be the clearest expression of the centre of Paul's theology. See his '"To Make us Rely not on Ourselves but on God who Raises the Dead": 2 Corinthians 1.9b as the Heart of Paul's Theology', in *Die Mitte des Neuen Testaments: Einheit und Vielfalt neutestamentlicher Theologie: Festschrift für Eduard Schweizer zum siebzigsten Geburtstag*, ed. Ulrich Luz and Hans Weder (Göttingen: Vandenhoeck & Ruprecht, 1983), 384–98.

the 'One who delivered [note the aorist ἐρρύσατο] us from so deadly a peril and will deliver [note the future ῥύσεται] us'; and 'on him we have set our hope [note the perfect ἠλπίκαμεν] that he will yet deliver [note the future ῥύσεται] us again'. Rooted in this confidence, Paul demonstrates his faithfulness in his apostolic mission by setting his hope on God who will deliver him yet again as he endures painful and intense suffering in his apostolic mission. This faithfulness is in turn a demonstration of his embodying the faithfulness of Christ in Christ's earthly mission.

3. *Paul's Shared Narrative with the Corinthians*
Paul brings his thanksgiving period to an end by appealing to the continuous partnership (note the present συνυπουργούντων) of the Corinthians in praying for him (1.11), which will not only remain beneficial for both parties but will extend to others as well, who will continue to be thankful for Paul's ministry. By inviting the Corinthians to share with him in his suffering through their prayer, Paul is essentially pleading with them to be in partnership in his apostolic ministry and also to participate in the story of Jesus that Paul so clearly embraced in his life and ministry.

Paul understands that his gospel grounded in Christ is embodied in his own experience as Christ's apostle so that, even in authenticating the legitimacy of his own apostleship, he is fighting for the salvation of the Corinthians (see Chapter 4). Rather than rejecting Paul based on the nature of his suffering (cf. 6.3-10 and Chapter 6), the Corinthians should be partners with Paul in praising God for the suffering that Paul suffers and continues to suffer for the sake of Christ. If O'Brien is right to suggest that one of the reasons Paul begins 2 Corinthians with a blessing instead of the usual thanksgiving formula is that Paul feels the Corinthians are not progressing in their faith,[92] then Paul's invitation to the Corinthians to participate in the story of Jesus is seen as Paul's final appeal to align the Corinthians not only to himself but also to Christ. This fellowship involves shared activity: they receive comfort and salvation, and in return they are to enter into this fellowship and offer their prayers on behalf of Paul.

The alternative, never openly stated by Paul, is that rejecting Paul's invitation to be participants in this shared narrative is essentially to reject Paul based on the nature of his suffering. This is to deny recognizing Paul as Christ's mediator, thereby cutting off the flow of comfort channelled to them through Paul. In other words, if the Corinthians refused to accept Paul's suffering, they were in fact rejecting Christ's suffering and his redemptive works in their lives as well, a theme to which we shall return in Chapters 4, 6 and 7.

---

92. O'Brien, *Introductory Thanksgiving*, 257.

IV. *Concluding Summary*

Our analysis of 2 Cor. 1.3-11 has thrown light on Paul's understanding of his sufferings. By turning our attention to the story of Jesus in 1.3-11, we argued that the phrase τὰ παθήματα τοῦ Χριστοῦ is the crux of our interpretation. We suggested that this phrase cannot be understood in itself according to any of the categories of messianic woes, mystical union, or the imitation of Christ, but can only be fully appreciated if we consider the story of Jesus in the wider context of 2 Corinthians in particular and Paul's mission theology in general. In the light of this, Paul most likely interprets the phrase τὰ παθήματα τοῦ Χριστοῦ εἰς ἡμᾶς as the sufferings he experienced in his apostolic ministry for Christ. In 1.8-11, Paul not only locates his devastating Asian experience within the story of Jesus but also highlights the pedagogical purpose of this experience. In bringing the thanksgiving period to an end, Paul appeals to the partnership of the Corinthians, not only to share in his suffering but also to participate in the story of Jesus that Paul so embraced in his life and ministry.

Chapter 4

SECOND CORINTHIANS 2.14-16

I. *Introduction*

In this chapter, we will advance our argument that the rationale for Paul's apostolic suffering and his mission theology grounded in the story of Jesus is further established in 2 Cor. 2.14-16. Here, Paul creatively employs two strikingly sensual images to give a theological support for the legitimacy of his apostleship and also to depict his relationship with God, Christ and the Corinthians.

II. *Structure and Line of Thought*

2.14a	Τῷ δὲ θεῷ χάρις

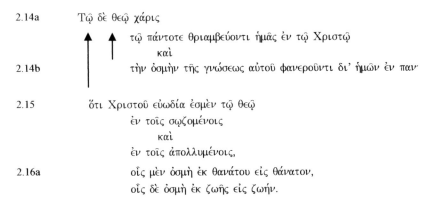

	τῷ πάντοτε θριαμβεύοντι ἡμᾶς ἐν τῷ Χριστῷ
	καὶ
2.14b	τὴν ὀσμὴν τῆς γνώσεως αὐτοῦ φανεροῦντι δι' ἡμῶν ἐν παν·
2.15	ὅτι Χριστοῦ εὐωδία ἐσμὲν τῷ θεῷ
	ἐν τοῖς σῳζομένοις
	καὶ
	ἐν τοῖς ἀπολλυμένοις,
2.16a	οἷς μὲν ὀσμὴ ἐκ θανάτου εἰς θάνατον,
	οἷς δὲ ὀσμὴ ἐκ ζωῆς εἰς ζωήν.

Paul begins this section by expressing his thanksgiving to God (2.14a). The distinctive word order in the sentence construction places special emphasis on God,[1] the subject of the sentence. As such, the primary focus is on God's decisive actions in the drama of salvation in Christ where Paul is portrayed as the agent through whom God's purpose is achieved.

God's actions are further elaborated as twofold, demonstrated in two participial clauses, θριαμβεύοντι ... φανεροῦντι, bound by the connecting conjunction καὶ (2.14). These dual actions of God, leading Paul in triumphal

---

1. As in 1 Cor. 15.57, the unusual word order is τῷ δὲ θεῷ χάρις instead of the more common word order, χάρις δὲ τῷ θεῷ, as seen in Rom. 6.17; 7.25; 2 Cor. 8.16; 9.15.

procession and displaying the fragrance of the knowledge of Christ, are seen as constant, as reflected in the present participles. They are further qualified by the adverbial modifier, πάντοτε, and the prepositional phrase, ἐν παντὶ τόπῳ, respectively, with the former depicting temporal action and the latter representing spatial dimension. As such, these two participial clauses are parallel, each having the same subject, denoting the action of God; and in each case, Paul has a functional role in God's action.

That these two actions of God *collectively* form the basis of Paul's thanksgiving has been overlooked. Most commentators perceive the first participial clause in 2.14a as the basis for Paul's thanksgiving at the expense of neglecting the force of the second clause in 2.14b. Martin is representative of this view: 'God is praised for one special reason: θριαμβεύοντι ἡμᾶς ἐν τῷ Χριστῷ'.[2]

The rationale for Paul's thanksgiving to God is grounded in the subsequent ὅτι clause (2.15), which is subordinate to the main thanksgiving clause of 2.14a.[3] By applying the OT cultic imagery, Paul declares himself as the aroma of Christ to God and further expands on the decisive role his apostolic mission plays in God's drama of salvation in the following two chiastic parallel clauses, highlighting the implications of those who respond positively or negatively to his message of the gospel: either they are saved or they perish. The chiastic construction continues until 2.16, placing emphasis on the final state of those who respond to Paul's aroma of Christ, either from death to death or from life to life.

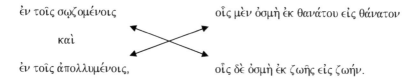

III. *The Story of Jesus and Paul's Apostolic Ministry*

A. *The Function of Paul's Thanksgiving in 2 Corinthians 2.14*

Several initial observations can be made at this point concerning Paul's thanksgiving, τῷ δὲ θεῷ χάρις. First, the elliptical construction is a unique Pauline expression. In the NT, it is found only in the Corinthian correspondence (1 Cor. 15.57; 2 Cor. 8.16)[4] and Romans (Rom. 6.17; 7.25).

---

2. Martin, *2 Corinthians*, 46. Cf. the logical structure in Hafemann, *Suffering and the Spirit*, 43. Hafemann takes the second participial clause (2.14b) as a logical progression from the first participial clause (2.14a), rendering the flow of Paul's argument as follows: 'Thanks be to God *because* he always leads me as his conquered slave to death *and in so doing* reveals through me as an apostle the fragrance of the knowledge (ὀσμή) of him in every place' (emphasis his).

3. Contra Hafemann who takes the ὅτι as modifying 2.14b instead of 2.14a (*Suffering and the Spirit*, 43). Similarly, Harris takes ὅτι to be associated with δι' ἡμῶν in 2.14b (*Second Corinthians*, 248). However, Thrall, *II Corinthians*, I:199 takes 2.15 as explanatory of 2.14.

4. In 2 Cor. 9.15, the elliptical construction, χάρις τῷ θεῷ, appears without δέ.

Second, whenever the conjunction δέ which denotes continuation and further thought development is used, its function is to highlight contrast in the argument.[5] This can be noticed in Rom. 6.17-18 where sin is set against righteousness; Rom. 7.25, the law of God against the law of sin; 1 Cor. 15.57, death against victory in death; and in 2 Cor. 8.16, the delay in the completion of the Jerusalem collection contrasted with the enthusiasm of Titus. It is also interesting to note that Paul's expressions of thanksgivings to God in the preceding examples always occur at crucial points of his argument. Therefore, it seems very likely that the inclusion of δέ in 2.14 also indicates some sort of contrast in what comes before and after Paul's argument, as my argument below demonstrates.[6]

Third, the ground for Paul's thanksgiving is established within negative circumstances, with the tone of despair being detected in all the aforesaid passages. In the context of 2.13-14, Paul's thought flows from despair and agony (over not being able to find Titus) to thanksgiving and hope about his apostolic ministry, and from the negative circumstances of his suffering to the positive effects of his ministry despite the setbacks in Troas and Asia (1.8-11).[7] It is only after recounting these circumstances that Paul subsequently introduces the character of his ministry exemplified in suffering.

Finally, Paul's expression of thanksgiving is grounded in the story of Jesus, a factor that has often been overlooked by commentators. That the story of Jesus functions in heightening the intervention of God is particularly true in passages like Rom. 6.17; 7.25; and 1 Cor. 15.57 where the helplessness of human predicaments can only be reversed by the intervention of God through the redemptive work of Christ.[8] Such a contrast is set to bring forth the greatness of God. As such, Sampley correctly notes that τῷ δὲ θεῷ χάρις is a 'Pauline expression that he evokes when he wants to honor the great power of God to transform and redeem; so the phrase appears in passages where Paul is recognizing transformation'.[9]

---

5.   Cf. BDAG, s.v.

6.   Cf. Andrew Perriman, 'Between Troas and Macedonia: 2 Cor 2:13-14', *ExpT* 101 (1989–90): 39–41. Contra the doubtful position of Rudolf Bultmann, *The Second Letter to the Corinthians* (Minneapolis: Augsburg, 1957), 62: 'Usually (δέ) refers to what directly precedes, by introducing a contrast or a new element organically attached to what precedes ... Here there is no such reference. The context is lost.'

7.   The sudden shift of tone from 2.13 to 2.14 is well noted. See Chang, 'Integrity of 2 Corinthians', 174–6; Harris, *Second Corinthians*, 14–25; Thrall, *II Corinthians*, I:25–36. Cf. Roger D. Aus, *Imagery of Triumph and Rebellion in 2 Corinthians 2:14-17 and Elsewhere in the Epistle: An Example of the Combination of Greco-Roman and Judaic Traditions in the Apostle Paul*, SJ (Lanham: University Press of America, 2005), 4–41, for his creative suggestion that Paul is comparing his apostolic ministry to that of the military victory of Paulus Macedonicus.

8.   So Barnett, *Second Epistle*, 147 n. 8, where the conjunction δέ indicates 'the greatness of God in contrast to human predicament'.

9.   J. Paul Sampley, *The Second Letter to the Corinthians*, NIB 11 (Nashville: Abingdon Press, 2000), 57.

Hafemann, in closely following O'Brien's thesis, argues for a twofold function of the thanksgiving formula in 2 Cor. 2.14: (1) a thesis-like statement that encapsulates the main themes of 2.14–7.4; and (2) Paul thanking God for the blessing in which he participated.[10] In this respect, Hafemann appears to regard Paul's thanksgiving formula here as functioning within the epistolary framework, a position that may have been influenced by Thrall who regards 2.14 as Paul's second thanksgiving period that introduces 2.14–7.4.[11] This is doubtful. Lambrecht rightly notes that in the context of 2.14, Paul uses the 'non-epistolary formula' characterized by χάρις instead of the epistolary εὐχαριστέω/εὐλογητός formula.[12]

The recent carefully executed work of Pao in attempting to establish Paul's thanksgiving expressions within the covenantal traditions of the Hebrew Bible lends strong support to my argument that Paul's thanksgiving in 2.14 should not be narrowly construed as functioning within the epistolary framework.[13] It also further supports my suggestion above that Paul's thanksgiving is firmly grounded in the story of Jesus. According to Pao, Paul draws on the OT covenantal traditions in his expression of thanksgiving to God in remembering the past acts of God (in delivering his people through Christ), celebrating the present relationship with God (as reflected in ethical living in Christ), and anticipating the future acts of God (with the return of Christ).[14] Rather than seeing the thanksgiving expression as a liturgical expression,[15] an unexpected emotional outburst,[16] a homiletical discourse,[17] or simply a rhetorical device,[18] Pao's study helpfully points us to a 'central Pauline theme that salvation comes only from God',[19] which I shall develop below. As such, Paul's thanksgiving

---

10. Hafemann, *Suffering and the Spirit*, 10–12. Cf. O'Brien, *Introductory Thanksgiving*.

11. Thrall, 'Second Thanksgiving Period'. Cf. Harris, *Second Corinthians*, 243, who takes 2.14 as the first thanksgiving period in 2 Corinthians by considering 1.3-11 a doxology.

12. Lambrecht, *Second Corinthians*, 37. See also J. D. H. Amador, 'Revisiting 2 Corinthians: Rhetoric and the Case for Unity', *NTS* 46 (2000): 92–111 (105–6).

13. See Pao, *Thanksgiving*.

14. Pao, *Thanksgiving*, 58.

15. So Bultmann, *Second Corinthians*, 62; Jean-François Collange, *Enigmes de la deuxième épître de Paul aux Corinthiens: Étude exégétique de 2 Cor. 2:14–7:4*, SNTSMS 18 (Cambridge: Cambridge University Press, 1972), 22; Furnish, *II Corinthians*, 186; Martin, *2 Corinthians*, 45; Plummer, *Second Epistle*, 67.

16. So Barnett, *Second Epistle*, 147; Matera, *II Corinthians*, 70; Victor Bartling, 'God's Triumphant Captive, Christ's Aroma for God', *CTM* 22 (1951): 883–94 (886).

17. James I. H. McDonald, 'Paul and the Preaching Ministry: A Reconsideration of 2 Cor 2:14-17 in Its Context', *JSNT* 17 (1983): 35–50 (43–4, 48–9).

18. Paul Brooks Duff, 'Metaphor, Motif, and Meaning: The Rhetorical Strategy behind the Image "Led in Triumph" in 2 Corinthians 2:14', *CBQ* 53/1 (1991): 79–92 (80); J. D. H. Amador, 'The Unity of 2 Corinthians: A Test Case for a Rediscovered and Re-invented Rhetoric', *Neot* 33 (1999): 411–32.

19. Pao, *Thanksgiving*, 38 n. 86. Cf. Sampley, *Second Corinthians*, 57: 'All of these "thanks to God" formulations ... are therefore eschatological acknowledgements of God's great power to deliver in Christ.'

to God in 2.14 is significant and cannot be lightly dismissed in the light of his subsequent exposition of his apostolic ministry[20] grounded in the story of Jesus, as reflected in the use of the triumphal procession and cultic metaphors.

B. *Two Metaphors Related to the Story of Jesus as Paul's Grounds for Thanksgiving*

Two governing metaphors are used to describe Paul's role in God's drama of salvation: triumphal procession (θριαμβεύω) and the fragrance from sacrificial offering (ὀσμή and εὐωδία). The combination of these two images is striking and has generated much discussion, primarily focusing on the background of these images – whether the imagery is borrowed exclusively from the Roman triumph or the Hellenistic context;[21] a mixture of Roman triumph and the OT cultic sacrificial imagery;[22] or solely from the OT background.[23] I shall briefly examine these two images before proposing my reading.

1. *The Triumphal Procession Metaphor*
The triumphal procession of the Roman world is widely documented.[24] Approximately 350 triumphs are recorded in Greco-Roman literature and triumphal

---

20. Cf. Lambrecht, who misses the significance of Paul's thanksgiving by arguing that, since 2.14-16 is a long sentence, 'the thought of thanksgiving is no longer in Paul's mind' when he reaches the end of 2.15 (*Second Corinthians*, 40). However, Lambrecht seems to contradict himself in his subsequent comments: 'The pericope 2:14-17 opens with a thanksgiving to God and dwells on the reasons why Paul should thank God: Paul and his co-workers are the aroma of Christ, spreading in every place the knowledge of God (2:14-16b)' (44).

21. Peter Marshall, 'A Metaphor of Social Shame: ΘΡΙΑΜΒΕΥΕΙΝ in 2 Cor 2:14', *NovT* 25/4 (1983): 302–17; Cilliers Breytenbach, 'Paul's Proclamation and God's "Thriambos" (Notes on 2 Corinthians 2.14-16b)', *Neot* 24 (1990): 255–71; Duff, 'Metaphor'; and recently, Harold W. Attridge, 'Making Scents of Paul: The Background and Sense of 2 Cor 2:14-17', in *Early Christianity and Classical Culture: Comparative Studies in Honor of Abraham J. Malherbe*, NovTSup 110, ed. John T. Fitzgerald, Thomas H. Olbright and L. Michael White (Leiden: Brill, 2003), 71–88.

22. Aus, *Imagery of Triumph and Rebellion*; Bartling, 'God's Triumphant Captive'; Lamar Williamson Jr., 'Led in Triumph: Paul's Use of *Thriambeuo*', *Int* 22/3 (1968): 317–32; McDonald, 'Paul and the Preaching Ministry'; Hafemann, *Suffering and the Spirit*, 12–83; Jan Lambrecht, 'The Defeated Paul, Aroma of Christ: An Exegetical Study of 2 Corinthians 2:14-16b', *LS* 20 (1995): 170–86; Thrall, *II Corinthians*, I:207.

23. William J. Webb, *Returning Home: New Covenant and Second Exodus as the Context for 2 Corinthians 6:14–7:1*, JSNTSup 85 (Sheffield: JSOT, 1993), 75–84; James M. Scott, 'The Triumph of God in 2 Cor 2.14: Additional Evidence of Merkabah Mysticism in Paul', *NTS* 42 (1996): 260–81; idem, 'Throne-Chariot Mysticism in Qumran and in Paul', in *Eschatology, Messianism, and the Dead Sea Scrolls*, ed. Craig A. Evans and Peter W. Flint, SDSSRL (Grand Rapids: Eerdmans, 1997), 101–19.

24. For a detailed investigation of Roman triumph, see H. S. Versnel, *Triumphus: An Inquiry into the Origin, Development and Meaning of the Roman Triumph* (Leiden: Brill, 1970); Mary

motifs can be found on arches, statues, columns, coins, cups, medallions and paintings.[25] The triumphal metaphor, then, would not have been alien to the Corinthians, living as they did in a Roman city.

Θριαμβεύω in 2 Cor. 2.14 can be used both intransitively and transitively, and its precise meaning has been variously understood.[26] Breytenbach's extensive lexical analysis of θριαμβεύω in *corpus hellenisticum* demonstrates that when used intransitively it carries the meaning 'to celebrate a prior victory by means of a triumph'.[27] When θριαμβεύω is used transitively with a personal object, as in 2.14, the sense of a celebration of a prior victory remains and it carries the meaning 'to lead as a conquered enemy in a victory parade' with the connotation 'to celebrate (by means of a triumph) a victory over'.[28]

While Breytenbach's conclusion is persuasive, there have been attempts to make the meaning of θριαμβεύω fit within the theological framework reflecting the triumphant nature of the gospel. When applied to 2.14, this popular interpretation indicates that Paul pictures himself not as the conquered enemy but as part of God's victorious army, as seen in the translation of θριαμβεύω in KJV: 'causeth us to triumph'.[29] Even though Breytenbach's analysis has clearly ruled out this possibility,[30] it continues to find wide and unwavering support. Barrett is representative when he states that Paul is 'describing himself and his colleagues as collaborating with God, and not as exposed by him to disgrace. *Notwithstanding the lack of supporting lexical evidence it is right ... in taking Paul to represent himself as one of the victorious general's soldiers sharing in the glory of his triumph.*'[31]

Beard, *The Roman Triumph* (Cambridge: Belknap Press of Harvard University Press, 2007). On the Roman triumph as the exclusive privilege of the emperor since 20 BCE, see T. E. Schmidt, 'Mark 15.16-32: The Crucifixion Narrative and the Roman Triumphal Procession', *NTS* 41 (1995): 1–18 (3–4).

25. For some of these images, see Beard, *Roman Triumph*, 11, 19, 20, 48, 90–1.

26. For possible meanings of θριαμβεύω, see Thrall, *II Corinthians* I:191–5; Hafemann, *Suffering and the Spirit*, 18–21; Aus, *Imagery of Triumph and Rebellion*, 40–6. See also Lambrecht, 'Defeated Paul', for his extensive reviews of the various meanings of θριαμβεύω.

27. Breytenbach, 'Paul's Proclamation', 259–65 (quotation from 260). Cf. BDAG, s.v. See also Hafemann, *Suffering and the Spirit*, 22–39, for a survey on the nature and purpose of the Roman triumph.

28. Breytenbach, 'Paul's Proclamation', 261–2, 268–9. So Hafemann, *Suffering and the Spirit*, 34.

29. Cf. the translation of Tyndale's NT; NJB; and BBE. See also the comments on 2.14-17 in the NIV Study Bible, 1765.

30. Breytenbach, 'Paul's Proclamation', 265. So Thrall, *II Corinthians*, I:192.

31. Barrett, *Second Corinthians*, 98 (emphasis mine). See also John Calvin, *Commentary on the Epistles of Paul the Apostle to the Corinthians*, 2 vols., trans. John Pringle (Edinburgh: Calvin Translation Society, 1848), 2:157–8; Aus, *Imagery of Triumph and Rebellion*, 17–20; Jean Héring, *The Second Epistle of Saint Paul to the Corinthians* (London: Epworth, 1967), 18. Cf. Belleville,

If Paul's use of θριαμβεύω in 2.14a accords with the meaning as established by Breytenbach, then he does not present himself as part of the victorious army of God sharing in the glory of the triumph. Instead, Paul is describing God's celebration of a prior victory over him, signifying himself as a captive who is led in the Conqueror's train, one that has been captured by Christ's love to be his slave.[32] Barnett rightly notes that this image captures the meaning of 'triumphal yet antitriumphal'[33] – triumphal because God is leading and antitriumphal because for Paul it means suffering. The NLT captures this nuance well: 'But thank God! He has made us his captives and continues to lead us along in Christ's triumphal procession.'

What remains uncertain is whether Paul pictures himself as a conquered prisoner being led to execution. Hafemann argues that since all captives in the Roman triumph were led to execution, this naturally demands that we picture the same fate for Paul.[34] This position has been rightly challenged[35] in light of the evidence that not all Roman triumphs terminated with the execution of the prisoners.[36] As such, it is best to avoid the danger of pressing the metaphor too far.

While the metaphorical use of the triumphal procession has been firmly established, there are also attempts to deny this reading. In his study, Egan notes the lack of attestation for the Roman triumph metaphor in Greek literature until well after Paul's time. According to Egan, whenever the triumph is mentioned, its reference is literal, pointing to actual triumph. Based on this finding, Egan rejects any connection with the Roman triumph and argues that θριαμβεύω carries the alternate meaning of 'manifest, publicize, display, divulge, noise abroad'.[37] Egan's proposal has not gone without any challenge, especially in the

---

who suggests Paul has in mind that God overcomes 'ministerial weaknesses and ineffectiveness' (*2 Corinthians*, 81–2). This proposal seems unlikely as it is alien to the context of 2 Corinthians. If God has triumphed over Paul's weaknesses, why does Paul continue to focus on these realities throughout 2 Corinthians?

32. Cf. Lambrecht, 'Defeated Paul', 185–6.

33. Barnett, *Second Epistle*, 146–7.

34. Hafemann, *Suffering and the Spirit*, 25–34.

35. So Lambrecht, 'Defeated Paul', 186; Goulder, *Paul and the Competing Mission*, 79; Beard, *Roman Triumph*, 128–32. Cf. Barnett's critique on Hafemann's position (*Second Epistle*, 147–8 n. 10): '[T]o see in this one word the whole Story of God's triumph over Paul in his conversion and God's subsequent leadership of him as his minister may be to prove too much from that single word' (148).

36. See Beard, *Roman Triumph*, 107–42. For additional sources where prisoners of Roman triumph are not executed, see Frederick W. Danker, *II Corinthians*, ACNT (Minneapolis: Augsburg, 1989), 50; Harris, *Second Corinthians*, 245–6.

37. R. B. Egan, 'Lexical Evidence on Two Pauline Passages', *NovT* 19 (1977): 34–62 (quotation from 40). So Frederick Field, *Notes on the Translation of the New Testament* (Cambridge: Cambridge University Press, 1899), 181. While not denying the metaphorical use of θριαμβεύω, Bultmann also supports this interpretation. *Second Corinthians*, 63; G. Dautzenberg, 'θριαμβεύω',

critique where he attaches too much weight to the meaning of ἐκθριαμβίζω for illuminating the meaning of θριαμβεύω.[38] As such, the metaphorical use of the triumphal procession in 2.14a is beyond doubt.

2. *The Fragrance Metaphor*

Like the triumphal procession imagery, the fragrance metaphor has also been variously interpreted. Interpreters who argue for the Hellenistic background of the imagery see coherence developed around the triumphal procession. Likewise, they also see the background of the fragrance metaphor as being related to the incense diffused to the deity during the triumphal march.[39] Others, however, argue that Paul shifts his imagery from a Hellenistic Roman triumph in 2.14a to an OT cultic sacrificial metaphor in 2.14b-15.[40] A minority maintains that throughout Paul's argument in 2.14-16 he is using images that have their roots in the Scriptures.[41]

The fragrance metaphor is represented by two words related to cultic celebration: ὀσμή and εὐωδία. These appear frequently in the LXX and are the standard translations of רֵיחַ and נִיחוֹחַ respectively.[42] By itself, ὀσμή appears 79 times while εὐωδία appears 57 times. Out of these occurrences, ὀσμή and εὐωδία appear juxtaposed against each other a total of 50 times, with εὐωδία functioning in a genitival relationship without exception, as in the construction of ὀσμή εὐωδίας.

It is also interesting to note that when used independently, ὀσμή can denote both positive and negative effects of the scent,[43] while εὐωδία always denotes positive effects of the fragrance. When these two words are intimately connected with each other, they carry with them the positive effects of the aroma as pleasing to God, and are used in association with cultic experience without exception. This leads Hafemann to argue that when these two words are combined, they merge in meaning, take on 'the nature of a *terminus technicus*', and function as a metonymy for the idea of sacrifice.[44] This phenomenon is also seen in the combined construction of the two Hebrew words רֵיחַ and נִיחוֹחַ, where both lose their usual meanings and take on the meaning of a

---

EDNT 2: 155–6; Williamson, 'Led in Triumph'. Cf. John Chrysostom who went for the meaning of 'who maketh us renowned unto all' (*Homiliae in epistulam ii ad Corinthios* 5:1).

38. See Hafemann, *Suffering and the Spirit*, 36–9. Cf. Marshall, 'Metaphor', 303–4.

39. See n. 21 above.

40. See n. 22 above.

41. See n. 23 above.

42. The only exceptions are where רֵיחַ is otherwise translated by ὀσφρασία in Hos. 14:7 and נִיחוֹחַ by θυσία (sacrifice) in Lev. 26.31.

43. The negative effects of ὀσμή are reflected in Exod. 5.21; Isa. 34.3; 2 Macc. 9.9-10, 12; Tob. 8.3.

44. Hafemann, *Suffering and the Spirit*, 46–8.

'soothing, tranquillizing odour of sacrifices acceptable to YHWH'.[45] This construction is found primarily in Genesis, Exodus, Leviticus, Numbers and Ezekiel.[46]

This same meaning is picked up in the use of ὀσμή εὐωδία in the NT. The occurrences of these two words are rare and are found almost exclusively in the Pauline literature in 2 Cor. 2.14-15; Phil. 4.18; and Eph. 5.2.[47] In these passages, neither word appears without the other and in the last two passages the combined usage of these two words is connected in a genitival construction, ὀσμὴν εὐωδίας, as in all the fifty occurrences in the LXX, carrying the meaning 'fragrant offering' (RSV) or, more literally, 'fragrance of aroma'. In the Philippians context, Paul describes the gift sent to him by the Philippians not only as ὀσμὴν εὐωδίας but also θυσίαν δεκτήν, εὐάρεστον τῷ θεῷ. In the Ephesians context, the same sacrificial imagery is used in the description of the death of Christ as θυσίαν τῷ θεῷ εἰς ὀσμὴν εὐωδίας.[48]

In drawing further on the use of ὀσμή and εὐωδία in wisdom sayings found in Sir. 24.15; 35.5; and 38.11, Hafemann asserts that ὀσμή εὐωδίας

> as a metonymy for sacrifice seems to have been so well established by the post-exilic period that not only could the term εὐωδία be used alone to dignify the odor of the acceptable sacrifice, but when used in the same context, the two terms could also be *separated* and used as *synonyms*. In contrast, when ὀσμή was used alone it retained its usual meaning of 'scent'.[49]

Based on this observation, Hafemann argues that a similar pattern is found in 2 Cor. 2.14-16 where the *terminus technicus* of ὀσμή εὐωδίας has been split up, but both terms retain their sacrificial meaning. However, this cultic interpretation of ὀσμή and εὐωδία in 2.14-16 has not gone unchallenged, based on the premise that the idea of sacrifice is either alien to the context or that both ὀσμή and εὐωδία are not connected in a genitival relationship, as in the case of Eph.

45. BDB, 629, 926. Cf. Diana Edelman, 'The Meaning of *Qiṭṭēr*', *VT* 35 (1985): 395–404. for a discussion on the Hebrew language of sacrifice; and Menahem Haran, 'Uses of Incense in the Ancient Israelite Ritual', *VT* 10 (1960): 113–29, on the practice of sacrifices with regard to incense.

46. For the use of ὀσμή and εὐωδία in the Second Temple texts, see Hafemann, *Suffering and the Spirit*, 48–51; Plunkett-Dowling, 'Reading and Restoration', 41–5. See also T. W. Manson, '2 Cor 2:14-17: Suggestions towards an Exegesis', in *Studia Paulina*, ed. J. Sevenster and W. C. van Unnik (Haarlem: Erven F. Bohn, 1953), 155–62, for their use in Rabbinic literature.

47. Apart from Pauline literature, the only other time ὀσμή appears in the NT is in Jn 12.3 while εὐωδία is not found elsewhere. In Jn 12.3, it is interesting to note that where ὀσμή occurs outside the *terminus technicus* ὀσμή εὐωδίας it reverts back to the usual meaning of 'fragrance' referring to the smell of the perfume Mary used to anoint the feet of Jesus. Cf. Hafemann, *Suffering and the Spirit*, 48.

48. While many scholars have questioned Pauline authorship of Ephesians, there is hardly any dispute that the letter itself reflects the teachings of Paul.

49. Hafemann, *Suffering and the Spirit*, 48 (emphasis his).

5.2; Phil. 4.18, and in the LXX.[50] If we were to take Hafemann's already persuasive argument further and consider the combined usage of ὀσμή and εὐωδία by Paul elsewhere in Phil. 4.18, the dominant usage of these terms in the LXX, the recipient of the aroma identified in the dative as τῷ θεῷ in 2 Cor. 2.15, and the Christological content as depicted in 2.14 (τὴν ὀσμὴν τῆς γνώσεως αὐτοῦ) and 2.15 (Χριστοῦ εὐωδία), these arguments not only reinforce but collectively point to the OT cultic sacrifices as the background for the ὀσμή and εὐωδία imagery.[51] In this regard, it makes any serious attempt to deny the cultic interpretation in 2.14-16 lose all its force.[52]

C. *A Proposal for a Fresh Reading of 2 Corinthians 2.14-16*

I have established the meaning of the metaphorical use of the triumphal procession and fragrance metaphors, and I now turn to consider how these metaphors are expressed in 2 Cor. 2.14-16.

1. *Paul's Thanksgiving: God as the Triumphator in the Messianic Procession*

To the best of my knowledge, almost all interpreters appeal to the imagery of the Roman triumphal procession as the controlling motif of 2 Cor. 2.14-16.[53] As has been firmly established, the primary purposes of the triumphal procession were to be an act of worship and thanksgiving to the deity who grants the victory, and to serve as a vehicle to honour and glorify the victorious general

---

50. So Bultmann, *Second Corinthians*, 63–4. Bultmann's main objection to the notion of sacrificial imagery is that the aroma of the sacrifices of Israel is directed to God, whereas Paul's use of aroma in 2.14 is directed to persons. Instead, Bultmann suggests that the notion of fragrance should be located within the ancient idea that it is 'a sign of the divine presence and the divine life' (64), citing Sir. 24.12-15. See also the critique by Plunkett-Dowling, 'Reading and Restoration', 38 n. 80, 40; David A. Renwick, *Paul, the Temple and the Presence of God*, BJS 224 (Atlanta: Scholars Press, 1991), 85. Others who object to the cultic reading include Plummer, *Second Epistle*, 71; Héring, *Second Corinthians*, 18–19; McDonald, 'Paul and Preaching Ministry', 40; Furnish, *II Corinthians*, 176–7.

51. Cf. Hafemann, *Suffering and the Spirit*, 49: 'For there is no compelling reason to interpret the meaning of ὀσμή and εὐωδίας against any other background than that of the cultic sacrifice of the Old Testament.' So Albert L. A. Hogeterp, *Paul and God's Temple: A Historical Interpretation of Cultic Imagery in the Corinthian Correspondence*, BTS 2 (Leuven: Peeters, 2006), 364–5; Smith, *Paul's Seven Explanations*, 131. See also H. L. Goudge, *The Second Epistle to the Corinthians*, WC (London: Methuen, 1927), 19: 'Paul was a Jew, and his language should nearly always be interpreted by its Jewish rather than its Gentile associations. Thus the thought is probably of the sacrifices, or sweet savour offerings of the O.T.'

52. Cf. Barnett, *Second Epistle*, 151–2, who seems to be confused. Initially, he supports Hafemann's suggestion that, when used separately, both ὀσμή and εὐωδία carry sacrificial overtones (151 n. 21). However, he later argues that ὀσμή 'is continuous with the Roman victory parade, in particular the use of incense' (152 n. 25).

53. The only possible exception is Egan, 'Lexical Evidence'.

leading the conquest.[54] This would further strengthen the triumphator's already great might that enabled him to conquer his enemies. In this respect, it is evident that the primary focus of the triumph is on the display of the power and might of the triumphator, the *subject* of the triumph, and not on the spoils of war, the *object* of the triumph. However, the thrust of the discussion in recent years has centred on the *object* of the triumph by focusing on the role and function of Paul as God's defeated captive in the triumphal procession. This investigation of the *object* instead of the *subject* of the triumph can be largely attributed to Hafemann's influential monograph that takes this line of interpretation.[55] While Hafemann and those who closely follow his argument have made significant contributions to our understanding of the role of Paul in the triumphal imagery and the nature of his apostolic ministry, this narrow interpretation, unfortunately, suffers from at least three deficiencies: (1) the failure to appreciate the subject of θριαμβεύω; (2) the function of the prepositional phrase, ἐν τῷ Χριστῷ; and (3) the use of metaphor by Paul in making his theological argument.

a) *The Subject of* θριαμβεύω. The first shortcoming is that the rightful emphasis on triumphator as *subject* of the triumphal procession has been relegated to the periphery in the treatment of 2 Cor. 2.14-16. That the purpose of every Roman triumph is to flaunt the power of the victorious army and the nations and gods cannot be more emphatically demonstrated than in the Roman victory ideology during the time of Augustus.[56] The celebration of the Roman triumph reinforced the mythology of 'the ruler as the invulnerable victor and guarantor of the world order', thus giving '"proof" of the unique and godlike nature of the ruler'.[57] This victory reaffirmed that the gods of the triumphators were on their side.[58]

My earlier argument has established that Paul clearly has in mind God as the primary subject of his thanksgiving in 2.14-16, as seen in the emphatic position he accords to God in the beginning of the sentence construction. This can be further validated in Paul's rationale for expressing thanksgiving to God in 2.15 where he depicts himself as the Χριστοῦ εὐωδία rising up τῷ θεῷ. With the dative expression τῷ θεῷ in 2.15, it forms a neat inclusio where he begins his thanksgiving to God (Τῷ δὲ θεῷ χάρις) in 2.14 and ends with the subject of God in 2.15.

Therefore, seen from this perspective, the primary focus should rightly be centred on God as the subject, while Paul as the object of the triumphal proces-

54. Hafemann, *Suffering and the Spirit*, 31–2.

55. Hafemann, *Suffering and the Spirit*.

56. Paul Zanker, *The Power of Images in the Age of Augustus*, translated by Alan Shapiro (Ann Arbor: University of Michigan Press, 1988), 183–92.

57. Zanker, *Power of Images*, 184–5.

58. Versnel, *Triumphus*, 1.

sion, at best, plays a secondary role in God's triumphal procession. To the best of my knowledge, with the only possible exception of Scott, almost all interpreters of this passage essentially emphasize Paul's role in the triumphal procession imagery by completely discounting God's role.[59] Hafemann's monograph, though important and significant, is representative of how the entire argument is focused on the role of Paul as a captive to the unfortunate neglect of the role of God.[60]

b) *The Function of the Prepositional Phrase, ἐν τῷ Χριστῷ.* Another shortcoming is that the prepositional phrase, ἐν τῷ Χριστῷ, has not been appropriately dealt with. The significance of this prepositional phrase is evident in Paul's placement of it in the prominent position towards the end of the clause in 2.14a. However, the function of this phrase is almost naturally neglected once our energy is directed towards ascertaining Paul's role as the object of θριαμβεύοντι. Therefore, it is not surprising that, to the best of my knowledge, other than Plummer who devoted considerable space to his treatment of ἐν τῷ Χριστῷ, recent commentators tend either to neglect or skim over it completely without attaching any significance to this phrase.[61]

The ἐν Χριστῷ formula appears almost exclusively in Pauline literature, with the only exceptions found in 1 Pet. 3.16; 5.10, 14.[62] This phrase appears a total of 84 times in the Pauline corpus (57 times in the undisputed Pauline letters and 27 times in Deutero-Pauline literature).

This prepositional phrase plays a crucial function in determining the nature and characteristic of the triumphal procession in Paul's argument. This can be seen in at least three aspects. First, to Paul, Χριστός could mean nothing else but

---

59. Cf. Scott, 'Triumph of God'. Scott rightly points out that most interpreters consider the metaphor only with respect to Paul, and 'no interpretation has so far considered the metaphor with respect to *God as the acting subject*' (263, emphasis mine).

60. Hafemann, *Suffering and the Spirit*, 23: 'Our purpose is ... to present the role of the captives who were led in these processions ... since ... Paul pictured himself in II Cor 2:14a as the object (ἡμᾶς) of θριαμβεύειν'. Cf. Lambrecht, *Second Corinthians*, 37–47. While acknowledging that in 2.14-17 'God is the subject; the verbs describe the actions of God' (37), Lambrecht strangely states a few pages later that '[t]he whole of 2:14-17 clearly deals with Paul's own apostolic status, his ministry' (44).

61. Plummer, *Second Epistle*, 69–70. Cf. Harris, *Second Corinthians*, 246, and his surprisingly brief treatment of the prepositional phrase in one short sentence as part of the ancillary discussion on the question of the identity of the triumphator in the triumph. The only possible exception is Thrall, *II Corinthians*, I:196, who gives some emphasis to the prepositional phrase.

62. Cf. Plummer, *Second Epistle*, 69, who argues that the Petrine ἐν Χριστῷ expression 'may be due to Pauline influence'. See also Dunn, *Theology of Paul*, 396. For further discussion on the statistics of prepositional phrases including Χριστός in Pauline literature, see N. T. Wright, *The Climax of the Covenant: Christ and the Law in Pauline Theology* (Minneapolis: Fortress Press, 1993), 41–55.

the title Messiah.[63] There are numerous passages in which Paul unambiguously speaks of Jesus as ὁ Χριστός, the Messiah,[64] and Dunn rightly notes that 'It would be surprising if Paul the Jew showed no interest whatsoever in the messiahship of Jesus'.[65] Furthermore, early apostolic proclamation of the gospel clearly demonstrated that Jesus was the promised Messiah (cf. Acts 2.36; 8.5; 9.22; 17.3; 18.5, 28).[66] This significance cannot be downplayed in any way, especially with Paul's threefold references to Χριστός in 2.14-16.

Second, the presence of the definite article before Χριστῷ lends further support to the significance of the prepositional phrase. This is a very rare construction in Pauline literature as almost all ἐν Χριστῷ formula phrases are anarthrous. Apart from the passage under consideration, the only other place where a similar articular construction of ἐν τῷ Χριστῷ in Pauline literature is found is in 1 Cor. 15.22; and in Eph. 1.10, 12, 20; 3.11.[67] It is also interesting to note that in each of these articular occurrences it is used not only within the context of emphasizing the story of Jesus within God's redemptive act but also to amplify the eschatological significance of this story. In the context of 1 Cor. 15, Paul is narrating the implications of the story of the resurrection of Christ – 'For as in Adam all die, so also in the Messiah (ἐν τῷ Χριστῷ) shall all be made alive' (1 Cor. 15.22) – followed by the story of the eschatological enthronement of Christ (1 Cor. 15.23-8). Turning to Eph. 1, the author praises God for revealing the mystery 'to unite all things … in the Messiah (ἐν τῷ Χριστῷ)' (Eph. 1.10; cf. 3.11) and that the early Christ-believers are the first to hope 'in the Messiah' (ἐν

---

63. For a rigorous defence of reading Χριστός as 'Messiah', see Wright, *Climax of the Covenant*, 41–9; idem, *Resurrection of the Son of God*, 553–83. Cf. Dunn, *Theology of Paul*, 197–9; Larry W. Hurtado, *Lord Jesus Christ: Devotion to Jesus in Earliest Christianity* (Grand Rapids: Eerdmans, 2003), 98–101. See also Craig Blomberg, 'Messiah in the New Testament', in *Israel's Messiah in the Bible and the Dead Sea Scrolls*, ed. Richard S. Hess and M. Daniel Carroll R. (Grand Rapids: Baker, 2003), 111–41, and the response by Willian W. Klein, '*Christos*: Jewish Title or Hellenistic Name? A Response to Craig L. Blomberg', 143–50. Contra those who take Christ as the proper name of Jesus, including Martin Hengel, *Between Jesus and Paul: Studies in the Earliest History of Christianity*, trans. John Bowden (London: SCM Press, 1983), 65–77; idem, *Studies in Early Christology* (Edinburgh: T&T Clark, 1995), 58–63, 384–6; Werner Kramer, *Christ, Lord, Son of God*, SBT 50 (London: SCM Press, 1966), 203–14; George E. Ladd, *A Theology of the New Testament*, rev. Donald A. Hagner (Grand Rapids: Eerdmans, 1993), 139–41; Helmut Koester, 'Suffering Servant and Royal Messiah: From Second Isaiah to Paul, Mark and Matthew', *TD* 51 (2004): 103–24 (111). For a survey of the emergence of messianic hopes from the OT to the NT, see Joseph Fitzmyer, *The One Who Is to Come* (Grand Rapids: Eerdmans, 2007).

64. E.g., Rom. 7.4; 8.35; 9.5; 14.18; 15.3; 16.16; 1 Cor. 1.23; 10.4; 2 Cor. 5.10; 11.2-3; Gal. 3.16; 5.2, 4, 24; 6.12; Phil. 1.15, 17. In these passages, the messiahship of Jesus is significant for Paul.

65. Dunn, *Theology of Paul*, 199.

66. See Belleville, 'Gospel and Kerygma'.

67. For an argument about Pauline tradition in Ephesians, see Ernest Best, *A Critical and Exegetical Commentary on Ephesians*, ICC (Edinburgh: T&T Clark, 1998), 6–40.

τῷ Χριστῷ) (Eph. 1.12). Moving on further, in Eph. 1.20, the author provides a narrative of the resurrection and enthronement of Christ as a result of the great power of God working 'in the Messiah' (ἐν τῷ Χριστῷ).[68]

That Jesus is the Messiah, the one who is victorious over death and is now making himself known among both Jews and gentiles through his mediatory agents, appears to be the theme that is reinforced in these passages. If my observation of the uniqueness of this construction is correct (which is further reinforced by the emphatic position of the phrase in 2.14), I can conclude with certainty that at the heart of this motif is the story of Jesus, the risen and living Messiah. As Dunn rightly argues: 'The fact that it is used in reference to the objective saving work of Christ is certainly of major significance.'[69]

This leads me to my final consideration, the function of ἐν τῷ Χριστῷ.[70] Interpreters have variously interpreted it as incorporative union,[71] sphere of reference,[72] and causal[73] among others. As I have earlier pointed out, most interpreters have either neglected or glossed over the significance of this phrase and, as such, have not taken the overall flow of Paul's argument into serious consideration. Thrall has rightly suggested: 'There may be more emphasis on the … ἐν τῷ Χριστῷ.'[74]

By assigning proper emphasis to the phrase ἐν τῷ Χριστῷ, Thrall has made a compelling case to take it as functioning instrumentally:

---

68. Cf. Stegman, *Character of Jesus*, 264. However, it has been argued that the use of χριστός with the definite article may not necessarily denote any particular significance. See Best, *Ephesians*, 143; Kramer, *Christ, Lord, Son of God*, 207–12; Hengel, *Between Jesus and Paul*, 65–77; Nils Alstrup Dahl, 'The Messiahship of Jesus in Paul', in *The Crucified Messiah and Other Essays*, ed. Nils Alstrup Dahl (Minneapolis: Augsburg, 1974), 37–47. This line of argument may be true if the articular construction is to be considered solely by itself. But taken collectively with other factors in this case, the evidence seems to tip the scale that the presence of the definite article is indeed significant and cannot be simply discounted.

69. Dunn, *Theology of Paul*, 399. See also Dunn's wider argument in 396–401.

70. See Wallace, *Greek Grammar beyond the Basics*, 372–5, for uses of the preposition ἐν. Cf. BDAG, s.v. See also Murray J. Harris, 'Prepositions and Theology in the Greek New Testament', *NIDNTT* 3: 1192–3.

71. Charles Hodge, *An Exposition of the Second Epistle to the Corinthians*, 6th edn (London: James Nisbet, 1883), 44; Harris, *Second Corinthians*, 246; Stegman, *Character of Jesus*, 264–5. This interpretation is questionable as it remains to be seen how God would lead Paul in union with Christ in the light of the overall argument of 2.14-16.

72. Bultmann, *Second Corinthians*, 63; Matera, *II Corinthians*, 69; Plummer, *Second Epistle*, 69. Cf. James Denney, who takes ἐν τῷ Χριστῷ as functioning both as sphere and agency/instrumentality and argues that these two meanings 'are not inconsistent; and practically they coincide' (*The Second Epistle to the Corinthians* [London: Hodder & Stoughton, 1894], 87).

73. While Harris, *Second Corinthians*, 246, argues for 'through (our union) with Christ', he does not discount the possibility of the causal notion as well. But this is to be doubted as it makes Paul's flow of argument awkward: God always leads Paul in triumphal procession *because* of Christ.

74. Thrall, *II Corinthians*, I:196.

> God's display of his power in the apostolic proclamation comes about through the
> agency of Christ. It is the victory over death achieved through the death and resur-
> rection of Christ that is both proclaimed in the apostle's preaching and dramatically
> illustrated in his continual experience of suffering and delivery (4.7-11).[75]

Taking Thrall's argument further, coupled with the presence of the definite
article in the prepositional phrase, it only serves to reinforce Paul's argument that
the triumphal procession is none other than *the* triumphal procession carried out
through the agency of the Messiah. This is *God's messianic triumphal procession*
where God is leading Paul and spreading the fragrance of the knowledge of Christ
through him. Seen from this perspective, it carries not only Christological claim
but also strong eschatological connotations. Such amplification of the messianic
overtones could not be more emphatically, forcefully and powerfully stated in
Paul's argument,[76] and this will be further expanded in the following argument.

c) *The Use of Metaphors*. The third deficiency in previous interpretations of the
triumphal procession concerns Paul's use of metaphors. Paul frequently uses
images drawn from agricultural, social, economic, religious and political life as
illustrations and these metaphors are widely distributed in all of his writings.[77]
They are seldom mere metaphors, for they function as aids to understanding.
They 'must always be distinguished in some degree from the truth to which
(they are) pointing ... (and) beyond the metaphor, there lies a reality that is
more than the metaphor'.[78] While Paul's metaphors may be drawn from the
Hellenistic world, more often than not, their theological concepts are deeply
rooted in the Scriptures.[79]

   In recognizing this, Webb has challenged the narrowly construed line of interpretation by limiting the metaphor θριαμβεύω specifically to a *Roman* triumph.

---

75. Thrall, *II Corinthians*, I:196.

76. Danker, *II Corinthians*, 47. Cf. Stegman, *Character of Jesus*, 264–5.

77. For Paul's use of metaphors, see David J. Williams, *Paul's Metaphors: Their Context and Character* (Peabody: Hendrickson, 1999).

78. Williams, *Paul's Metaphors*, 1. See David M. Park, 'Interpretative Value of Paul's Metaphors', *SEAJT* 18 (1977): 37–40; idem, 'The Value of Biblical Metaphor: 2 Cor 2:14-17', in *Metaphor and Religion (Theolinguistics 2)*, ed. Jean-Pierre Van Noppen (Brussels: Vrije Universitiet, 1983), 253–68; and Scott's discussion on the notion of vehicle and tenor in the use of metaphor in his 'Triumph of God'. See also Dunn, *Theology of Paul*, 231–3.

79. Common metaphors used by Paul that are given theological interpretation include justi-fication, redemption, reconciliation and adoption. For further discussion on usage of Hellenistic metaphors that exemplify theological concepts rooted in the Scriptures, see John Byron, *Slavery Metaphors in Early Judaism and Pauline Christianity: A Traditio-Historical and Exegetical Examination*, WUNT 2/162 (Tübingen: Mohr Siebeck, 2003); Stephen Finlan, *The Background and Contents of Paul's Cultic Atonement Metaphors*, AcBib 19 (Leiden: Brill, 2004); James M. Scott, *Adoption as Sons of God: An Exegetical Investigation into the Background of YIOTHESIA in the Pauline Corpus*, WUNT 2/48 (Tübingen: Mohr Siebeck, 1992).

According to Webb, Paul's use of θριαμβεύω could also refer to other triumphal processions.[80] He suggests there could be another 'theological category which may be *equally* operational in Paul's thought, namely, the *Old Testament triumphal procession* developed especially by the prophets'.[81] Webb's suggestion that Paul 'has obviously *imported* theological meaning into the picture of the Roman triumph with the use of God, Christ, sacrificial imagery'[82] is not only attractive but warrants further investigation. It is unfortunate that Webb does not further develop his suggestion, resulting in its failure to receive careful consideration by commentators.

2. *The Divine Warrior in the Isaianic New Exodus as Background of 2 Corinthians 2.14-16*

I have highlighted three deficiencies of previous scholarship in interpreting 2.14-16 and have suggested that the rightful focus in understanding this passage is on God as the main actor leading his apostle in the triumphal procession through Christ the Messiah. In doing so, a new perspective in reading the text emerges.[83]

To take Webb's suggestion further in his use of θριαμβεύω, Paul has in mind not only the imagery of God as the Divine Warrior leading a triumphal procession through the agency of Christ the Messiah, but also the paradigm of the triumphal procession of the Isaianic new exodus. Several lines of evidence highlighted below reinforce this thought.

First, the depiction of God as a warrior not only dominates the entire Hebrew Bible in a variety of Divine Warrior hymns but also gains prominence in the exilic and post-exilic literature. The early literature recording Israel's military success attributes the victory to divine activity where God is introduced in explicit warfare terminology in leading his people (e.g., Exod. 15; Deut. 33; Judg. 5; 2 Sam. 22).

While the earlier Divine Warrior hymns generally depict God as involved in historical conflicts between Israel and her enemies, the setting of the conflict appears to shift towards a cosmic dimension inaugurating a new era particularly in the exilic and post-exilic literature (e.g., Isa. 26.16–27.6; 42.13; 51.4-11;

---

80. Webb, *Returning Home*, 78, to whom I owe some of my observations here. Similarly, both Duff ('Metaphor', 83) and Attridge ('Making Scents of Paul', 79) also recognize the possible wider meaning of the metaphor θριαμβεύω.

81. Webb, *Returning Home*, 79, emphasis his.

82. Webb, *Returning Home*, 84, emphasis his. For Webb's justifications for the use of the OT triumphal procession imagery, see 79–84.

83. Cf. Scott, 'Triumph of God', 263, who interestingly raises the question: 'What do we "see" when we think of God as leading his apostle in triumphal procession?' While Scott sets his discussion in the correct direction, his suggestion that the triumphal procession is to be located within the Merkabah mysticism tradition is questionable.

59.15-20; 63.1-6; Zech. 9.1-17; 14.1-21).[84] This apocalyptic appearance of the Divine Warrior is understood as an attack of the heavenly forces on existing political empires oppressing the people of God in order to establish a new world order heralded by the coming Day of the Lord.[85] The extensive use of this motif is not only limited to the OT but continues to emerge in the early Christ-believing communities.[86]

Second, it cannot be doubted that Paul's theological thought is deeply rooted in Isaiah, in particular the new exodus motif, as rightly argued by Hays:

> Isaiah offers the clearest expression in the Old Testament of a universalistic, eschatological vision in which the restoration of Israel in Zion is accompanied by an ingathering of Gentiles to worship the Lord; that is why the book is both statistically and substantively the most important scriptural source for Paul.[87]

84. For treatment of God as Divine Warrior from ancient Israel up to the monarchy period, see Frank Moore Cross, *Canaanite Myth and Hebrew Epic: Essays in the History of the Religion in Israel* (Cambridge: Harvard University Press, 1973); H. Fredrikson, *Jahwe als Krieger* (Lund: C. E. K. Gleerup, 1945); Sa-Moon Kang, *Divine War in the Old Testament and in the Ancient Near East*, BZAW 177 (Berlin: Walter de Gruyter, 1989); Millard C. Lind, *Yahweh Is a Warrior: The Theology of Warfare in Ancient Israel* (Scottdale: Herald, 1980); Patrick D. Miller Jr., *The Divine Warrior in Early Israel* (Cambridge: Harvard University Press, 1973). For post-exilic treatment on this motif, see Paul D. Hanson, *The Dawn of Apocalyptic: The Historical and Sociological Roots of Jewish Apocalyptic Eschatology*, rev. edn (Philadelphia: Fortress Press, 1979). For the use of Divine Warrior in Psalms, see Marc Brettler, 'Images of YHWH the Warrior in Psalms', *Semeia* 61 (1993): 135–65; Martin Klingbeil, *Yahweh Fighting from Heaven: God as Warrior and as God of Heaven in the Hebrew Psalter and Ancient Near Eastern Iconography*, OBO 169 (Göttingen: Vandenhoeck & Ruprecht, 1999); Tremper Longman III, 'Psalm 98: A Divine Warrior Victory Song', *JETS* 27 (1984): 267–74.

85. For historical development of the Divine Warrior motif in the Hebrew Bible, see Theodore Hiebert, 'Warrior, Divine', *ABD* 6: 876–9. Bruce A. Stevens, '"Why 'Must' the Son of Man Suffer?" The Divine Warrior in the Gospel of Mark', *BZ* 31 (1987): 101–10, provides a succinct discussion on the development of the Divine Warrior during the post-exilic period where there is a re-interpretation of the enthronement psalms, and the hope being now transferred to the coming Messiah.

86. It has generally been recognized that the Divine Warrior motif is prevalent in Revelation. However, its use in Pauline literature and the Gospels has been recently explored. See Tremper Longman III, 'The Divine Warrior: The New Testament Use of an Old Testament Motif', *WTJ* 44 (1982): 290–307; Timothy Gombis, 'Ephesians 2 as a Narrative of Divine Warfare', *JSNT* 26 (2004): 403–18; idem, 'The Triumph of God in Christ: Divine Warfare in the Argument of Ephesians' (PhD dissertation, University of St Andrews, St Andrews, 2005); Paul Brooks Duff, 'The March of the Divine Warrior and the Advent of the Greco-Roman King: Mark's Account of Jesus' Entry into Jerusalem', *JBL* 111 (1992): 55–71; Bruce A. Stevens, 'Jesus as the Divine Warrior', *ExpT* 94 (1983): 326–9; idem, ' "Why 'Must' the Son of Man Suffer?" '. For a general survey of the theme of Divine Warrior as a controlling motif in the OT and NT, see Tremper Longman III and Daniel G. Reid, *God Is a Warrior* (Grand Rapids: Zondervan, 1995); Tom Yoder Neufeld, *Put on the Armour of God: The Divine Warrior from Isaiah to Ephesians*, JSNTSup 140 (Sheffield: Sheffield Academic Press, 1997).

87. Hays, *Echoes of Scripture*, 162. See also Barnett, *Second Epistle*, 46–7. The strong

Throughout 2 Corinthians, this strong influence is indicated by a number of overwhelming allusions to the central themes related to the new exodus motif of Isa. 40–66, including the notions of comfort (1.5), restoration, new creation (5.17), reconciliation (5.18-19) and the Servant of Isa. 40–55, as well as by Paul's quotation of Isa. 49.8 in 2 Cor. 6.2. In addition, recent scholarship has also recognized and firmly established the Isaianic influence in 2 Corinthians.[88]

Third, the image of God the Divine Warrior leading the triumphal procession is reminiscent of the Isaianic new exodus with the expectation of the return of God to Zion. This image should not surprise us, as one significant aspect that characterizes the Divine Warrior hymns is the portrayal of God's processional march to Zion where he establishes his temple. Taken together, these two motifs of Divine Warrior and the Isaianic new exodus undoubtedly evoke the triumphal march in Isa. 40.1-10.[89] In this passage, the prophet envisions the building of a great highway for the Divine Warrior to lead his people in a procession back from exile to Zion. This connection between the Divine Warrior and the exilic return has been firmly established, since the way God will restore his people is

influence of Isaiah in Paul's thought has gained prominence in the recent works of Shiu-Lun Shum, *Paul's Use of Isaiah in Romans: A Comparative Study of Paul's Letter to the Romans and the Sibylline and Qumran Sectarian Texts*, WUNT 2/156 (Tübingen: Mohr Siebeck, 2002); and J. Ross Wagner, *Heralds of the Good News: Isaiah and Paul 'in Concert' in the Letter of Romans*, NovTSup 101 (Leiden: Brill, 2002). See also Richard B. Hays, ' "Who Has Believed Our Message?": Paul's Reading of Isaiah', *SBLSP* 37/1 (1998): 205–25, reprinted in his *The Conversion of the Imagination: Paul as Interpreter of Israel's Scripture* (Grand Rapids: Eerdmans, 2005), 25–49 (subsequent reference is taken from the reprinted edition); Douglas A. Oss, 'A Note on Paul's Use of Isaiah', *BBR* 2 (1992): 105–12. For a list of quotations and possible allusions to the OT in Paul's epistles, see Hans Hübner, *Vetus Testamentum in Novo Band 2: Corpus Paulinum* (Göttingen: Vanderhoeck & Ruprecht, 1997).

88. In particular, see Gregory K. Beale, 'The Old Testament Background of Reconciliation in 2 Corinthians 5–7 and Its Bearing on the Literary Problem of 2 Corinthians 6:14–7:1', *NTS* 35 (1989): 550–81; Jan Lambrecht, 'The Favourable Time: A Study of 2 Cor 6,2a in Its Context', in *Vöm Urchristentum zu Jesus: Für Joachim Gnilka*, ed. Hubert Frankemölle and Karl Kartelge (Freiberg: Herder, 1989), 377–91; Webb, *Returning Home*; James M. Scott, 'The Use of Scripture in 2 Corinthians 6.16c-18 and Paul's Restoration Theology', *JSNT* 56 (1994): 73–99; Scott J. Hafemann, 'Paul's Argument from the Old Testament and Christology in 2 Cor 1–9', in *The Corinthian Correspondence*, BETL 125, ed. R. Bieringer (Leuven: Leuven University Press, 1996), 277–303; idem, 'Paul's Use of the Old Testament in 2 Corinthians', *Int* 52/3 (1998): 246–57; Plunkett-Dowling, 'Reading and Restoration'; Mark Gignilliat, *Paul and Isaiah's Servants: Paul's Theological Reading of Isaiah 40–66 in 2 Corinthians 5.14–6.10*, LNTS 330 (London: T&T Clark, 2007); idem, '2 Corinthians 6:2: Paul's Eschatological "Now" and Hermeneutical Invitation', *WTJ* 67 (2005): 147–61. For Paul's citation of Isa. 49.8 in 2 Cor. 6.2, see Chapter 6 below.

89. On the return of God to Zion, see the list described as 'impressive in its range and scope' in Wright, *Jesus and the Victory of God*, 616–21. Cf. Holland, *Contours of Pauline Theology*, 20–30, 293–300, for reviews on the new exodus motif in Second Temple writings and the NT respectively.

often set in a military context. [90] Isaiah 40.10-11 declares that God will come with power and he will rule with his right arm. This language evokes the exodus paradigm in which God restores and delivers his people from the bondage of Egypt. God will do again in the Isaianic new exodus what he did at the Exodus, and will dwell in the midst of his people once more (cf. Exod. 13.21-2; 14.19; 19.9-11). The combination of the triumphal procession image and the imagery of the strength of the arm of God in Isa. 40.1-11 is also found in Isa. 51.9-10, where the exodus tradition is clearly evoked. God as the mighty warrior that appeared in the Song of Moses in Exod. 15 is declared as אִישׁ מִלְחָמָה. Similarly, the God of Isa. 40–55 who is going to deliver and gather his people is also described as one that is כְּאִישׁ מִלְחָמוֹת (Isa. 42.13). As God delivers his people from exile, they become his booty (e.g., Isa. 40.10), and this image conforms to the triumphal procession of 2 Cor. 2.14, where God is envisioned as the subject of the triumphal procession, leading his people as his booty back from exile.

Fourth, the eschatological triumphal procession imagery focused on the gathering of the people of God from all corners of the earth (Isa. 49.11-12; 43.5-6; 45.22; 49.11-12, 22) leading to the restoration of Israel that includes the gathering of the gentiles/nations (Isa. 56.1-8; 60.4-11; 66.18; cf. Isa. 2.2-4; 25.6-10; 42.6; 49.6; Zech. 8.20-3; 14.16-19; Mic. 4.1-4; cf. *Pss. Sol.* 17.30-5; *2 Apoc. Bar.* 68.5; Tob. 13.11; *1 En.* 90.30-6).[91] That God will come to save his people is now fulfilled through Jesus the Messiah (as supported by my argument concerning the instrumental function of the prepositional phrase ἐν τῷ Χριστῷ in 2.14 above), as God the Divine Warrior leads the triumphal procession. This explains Paul's understanding of his call as an apostle to the gentiles/nations. His description of the universal implications of his apostolic mission as reflected in the use of πάντοτε and ἐν παντὶ τόπῳ in 2.14 is based on this universal triumph. By applying this image to God, Paul is also reinforcing God's sovereignty not only over Israel but also over the gentile nations. Paul has now become an instrument that witnesses the ingathering of the gentiles to Zion, based on the completed work of Jesus the Messiah.[92]

Fifth, the Zion that would be restored is not strictly defined in terms of narrow geographical boundaries, but also includes the restoration of God's

---

90. For the thematic connection between the motif of Divine Warrior and Isaianic new exodus, see Rikki E. Watts, 'Consolation or Confrontation? Isaiah 40–55 and the Delay of the New Exodus', *TynBul* 41 (1990): 31–59; idem, *Isaiah's New Exodus and Mark*, WUNT 2/88 (Tübingen: Mohr Siebeck, 1997), 140–4, 296–304; David W. Pao, *Acts and the Isaianic New Exodus*, WUNT 2/130 (Tübingen: Mohr Siebeck, 2000), 51–9; Wright, *Jesus and the Victory of God*, 612–53; Robert L. Webb, *John the Baptizer and Prophet: A Socio-Historical Study*, JSNTSup 62 (Sheffield: JSOT Press, 1991), 219–60.

91. For further discussion, see J. Daniel Hays, *From Every People and Nation: A Biblical Theology of Race*, NSBT 14 (Downers Grove: InterVarsity Press, 2003),

92. Cf. Schnabel, *Early Christian Mission*, 2:1317, where the prophecy of the pilgrimage of the nations to Zion is specifically fulfilled in Paul's gentile mission.

presence and power on earth. Hanson rightly notes that the focus of the Divine Warrior's saving act is to form a new eschatological community.[93] Paul sees the gospel he proclaims as redefining the community formed by the story of Jesus as heirs to the covenant promise of God. This is reflected in the formation of the new eschatological community consisting of both Jews and gentiles. This new community becomes the 'living evidence of God's eschatological purposes and of his restoring power that calls his creation together from all nations of the earth under his kingship'.[94] It is with this understanding that Paul is able to describe the Corinthians themselves as 'a letter of Christ, prepared by us, written not with ink but with the Spirit of the living God' (3.3). This naturally explains why Paul does not need letters of recommendation (3.1) for his apostolic ministry. If the Corinthians insist on these letters from Paul to substantiate his ministry, then they are denying their very existence as the eschatological community formed by the story of Jesus, and thus as heirs to the covenant promise of God.

Sixth, an important theme within the Isaianic new exodus motif is the appearance of the Servant of the Lord. Hugenberger rightly points out that within the context of each of the four Servant Songs in Deutero-Isaiah the new exodus motif is evidently present.[95] While the triumphal procession as envisioned by the writer of Isaiah is led by God, this is nevertheless done through the agency of his Servant.[96] This human agent is generally understood to be a messianic figure in the Second Temple writings (*Tg. Isa.* 42.1-7; 52.13–53.12; cf. *Pss. Sol.* 17.21, 32). The agency of the Servant should not surprise us, as Paul repeatedly identifies Jesus as the Isaianic Servant of the Lord and the royal messianic figure (e.g., Rom. 4.25/Isa. 53.12; Rom. 15.8-12/Isa. 11.1-2; Rom. 15.20-1/Isa. 52.15; 1 Cor. 15.3/Isa. 53.5).[97] Hence for Paul, God's triumphal procession

93. Hanson, *Dawn of Apocalyptic*, 159.

94. C. Marvin Pate, J. Scott Duvall, J. Daniel Hays, E. Randolph Richards, W. Dennis Tucker Jr. and Preben Vang, *The Story of Israel: A Biblical Theology* (Downers Grove: InterVarsity Press, 2004), 151.

95. Gordon P. Hugenberger, 'The Servant of the Lord in the "Servant Songs" of Isaiah: A Second Moses Figure', in *The Lord's Anointed: Interpretation of Old Testament Messianic Texts*, ed. Philip E. Satterthwaite, Richard S. Hess and Gordon J. Wenham (Grand Rapids: Baker, 1995), 105–40. Cf. Mark Gignilliat, 'Who Is Isaiah's Servant? Narrative Identity and Theological Potentiality', *SJT* 61 (2008): 125–36.

96. Webb, *Returning Home*, 80.

97. Morna D. Hooker (*Jesus and the Servant: The Influence of the Servant Concept of Deutero-Isaiah in the New Testament* [London: SPCK, 1959]), among others, challenges the use of servant passages, in particular Isa. 53, in Christological reflections. Hooker argues that Jesus never saw himself as the Deutero-Isaiah Servant and this reflection cannot be dated to before 1 Peter. But recently, Hooker has altered her position by accepting that the evidence could now be traced to Paul. See her 'Did the Use of Isaiah 53 to Interpret His Mission Begin with Jesus?' in *Jesus and the Suffering Servant: Isaiah 53 and Christian Origins*, ed. William H. Bellinger Jr. and William R. Farmer (Harrisburg: Trinity, 1998), 88–103. Cf. Fitzmyer, *The One Who Is to Come*, 39–43.

would have occurred because of Jesus the Messiah.[98] This further supports my earlier argument of the titular sense of Χριστός as Messiah and the instrumental function of the prepositional phrase ἐν τῷ Χριστῷ in 2.14.

Seventh, the triumphal march as depicted by the various Deutero-Isaianic passages (e.g., Isa. 49.7; 50.4-7; 53.3, 12) not only involves the agency of the Servant but also parallels the suffering–exaltation paradox of the Servant of the Lord. It is not surprising that Paul would have the nature of this paradox in mind as he reflects on his apostolic suffering in bringing in the gentiles, and also the final restoration of Israel in fulfilment of God's covenant promise. This picture conforms to what Paul says of himself earlier in 1 Cor. 4.9-13 and subsequently in 2 Cor. 3.6. In view of this, Barnett is probably right to argue that God is leading Paul in Christ as a Suffering Servant, thereby legitimizing his ministry.[99] As Paul identifies himself with Jesus the suffering Servant of the Lord, the story of Jesus is therefore reproduced in the life of Paul.[100] The continuity of suffering shared by the obedient Christ and his faithful servant is therefore a necessary precondition of Paul's apostolic calling. This not only fits into Paul's wider exposition of his suffering earlier in 1.5, 'the sufferings of Christ are abundant for us', but also anticipates 4.7-12 where Paul describes himself as 'always carrying in the body the dying of Jesus, so that the life of Jesus may also be manifested in our bodies' (4.10), as well as his citation of Isa. 49.8 in 2 Cor. 6.2 in declaring God's favour and salvation to the Corinthians.[101] Paul's role as God's servant can be further substantiated in conceiving of his gentile mission in prophetic terms[102] where the Servant image of Isa. 49.1 is referenced to his being set apart in his mother's womb (Gal. 1.15) in defending his apostolic call (cf. Jer. 1.5). Concerning Paul's use of the Servant passage, William S. Campbell argues:

---

98. See B. J. Oropeza, 'Echoes of Isaiah in the Rhetoric of Paul: New Exodus, Wisdom, and the Humility of the Cross in Utopian-Apocalyptic Expectations', in *The Intertexture of Apocalyptic Discourse in the New Testament*, ed. Duane F. Watson, SBLSymS 14 (Atlanta: Society of Biblical Literature, 2002), 87–112 (92–7). Cf. Wright in his *New Testament and the People of God* and *Jesus and the Victory of God*, where he strongly argues for the failure of the fulfilment of the new exodus as Israel remains under the bondage of foreign powers. However, Oropeza's argument that the new exodus 'is not really the end but the beginning of the end' (96) appears to be a better perspective and in coherence with our argument.

99. Barnett, *Second Epistle*, 150. According to Barnett, the triumphal procession imagery is critical 'both to the sovereignty of God and to his servants' sufferings "in Christ" as they proclaim him; it is "*in Christ*" that God leads (Paul)'.

100. Cf. Barnett, *Second Epistle*, 150.

101. See discussion in Chapters 5 and 6 below.

102. This has been rigorously and persuasively defended by Karl Olav Sandnes, *Paul – One of the Prophets? A Contribution to the Apostle's Self-Understanding*, WUNT 2/43 (Tübingen: Mohr Siebeck, 1991). See further discussion in Chapter 6.

> The Servant's call in this passage ties together the twin aspects of his universal work – to be an agent of Israel's restoration and a light to the Gentiles ... It is more fitting to see him as the apostle to the Gentiles *for the sake of Israel*, so that there is a necessary connection between Paul's Gentile mission and the restoration of Israel.[103]

Campbell's position finds further support in my reading of 2.14-16 – the Isaianic new exodus in bringing Israel to restoration also entails the bringing in of the gentiles on this eschatological pilgrimage, and Paul is precisely fulfilling this role. In presenting himself as a minister of the new covenant (2 Cor. 3), Paul not only employs the vocabulary of Isa. 40–66 for the restoration of Israel, he also portrays his relationship with the Corinthians in terms analogous to the relationship of the Isaianic Servant of the Lord with Israel, a point I shall further develop below.

Finally, deeply woven into the theme of the Isaianic new exodus is the pattern of new things that constitutes the new acts of deliverance that God will perform (e.g., Isa. 9.1; 22.11; 25.1; 37.26; 41.22-7; 42.9; 43.9-19; 44.6-8; 46.9-10; 48.3-6; 65.16-17).[104] Barnett points out that the themes of 'new creation' and 'reconciliation', arise out of Isaiah's twin themes of 'new creation' and 'restoration'.[105] While the motif of the new covenant that immediately follows (2 Cor. 3.1-6) is not explicitly found in Isaiah, it is significant that the background of the concept of the new covenant is found in texts like Jer. 31.31-4; Ezek. 11.19; and 36.26-7, where the notions of exodus/exilic return are interwoven together like a tapestry. These background texts collectively refer to God's promises for a new covenant at the time of restoration.[106] Similarly, the background of the theme of new creation and reconciliation in 2 Cor. 5–7 (in particular 5.17-21) as convincingly argued by Beale are deeply rooted in Isa. 43.18-19 and 65.17, two passages that place strong emphasis on God's promise of restoration.[107] Beale goes on to suggest that, for Paul, reconciliation in Christ is the evidence that 'Isaiah's promises of "restoration" from the alienation of exile have begun to be fulfilled by the atonement and forgiveness of sins in Christ'.[108] My argument that Christ the Messiah is the agent, the Servant of

---

103. William S. Campbell, 'Israel', *DPL*, 441–6 (445), emphasis his.

104. For excellent treatment of the 'old things' and 'new things' in Isa. 40–55, see D. H. Odendaal, 'The "Former" and the "New Things" in Isaiah 40–48', *OTWSA* 10 (1967): 64–75; Christopher R. North, 'The "Former Things" and the "New Things" in Deutero-Isaiah', in *Studies in Old Testament Prophecy*, ed. H. H. Rowley (New York: Charles Scribner's Sons, 1950), 111–26. See also Webb, *Returning Home*, 113–28.

105. Barnett, *Second Epistle*, 46. See also the scriptural citations in n. 168.

106. See Scott J. Hafemann, *Paul, Moses and the History of Israel: The Letter/Spirit Contrast and the Argument from Scripture in 2 Corinthians 3* (Peabody: Hendrickson, 1996), 92–186. Cf. Barnett, *Second Epistle*, 46–7, who sees 'reconciliation' as bearing similarity to 'restoration' in Deutero-Isaiah.

107. Beale, 'Old Testament Background', 550–81.

108. Beale, 'Old Testament Background', 556.

the Lord, in the eschatological triumphal procession further supports Beale's position.

It will be helpful at this point to summarize my argument. I have argued that the Isaianic new exodus triumphal procession better accounts for the natural flow and progression from the triumphal procession imagery to the sacrificial aroma metaphor. This reading places God the subject as the primary focus of the imagery. To overemphasize Paul as the captive in God's triumphal procession is to miss the force of the metaphor.[109]

I have highlighted that concentrating solely on the provenance of Paul's imagery fails to appreciate the dynamic role that the allusion to the Isaianic new exodus paradigm plays in providing meaning and coherence for Paul's argument in 2 Corinthians. My proposed reading resolves the difficulty of the supposed switch from the Hellenistic triumphal procession imagery to the OT cultic metaphor. As such, Attridge's call in serving a 'yellow, if not red flag' to those seeing this switch to the cultic notion of sacrificial language can be confidently set aside.[110]

3. *Paul's Thanksgiving: God Manifesting the Fragrance through His Servant*

Once it has been established that Paul has in view the Isaianic new exodus triumphal procession in 2 Cor. 2.14a, the remainder of his argument in 2.14b-16 flows naturally. In 2.14b, Paul continues the second ground for his thanksgiving to God: τὴν ὀσμὴν τῆς γνώσεως αὐτοῦ φανεροῦντι δι' ἡμῶν ἐν παντὶ τόπῳ. Since the participle φανεροῦντι is coordinated with θριαμβεύοντι as is evident in the use of the connecting conjunction καί, and both are present participles expressing God's continuous action in and through Paul, it is best to take the object of the action of 2.14b (τὴν ὀσμὴν τῆς γνώσεως αὐτοῦ) as coming from the same background of the triumphal procession imagery of 2.14a.[111]

As Harris notes, the move from ἡμᾶς in 2.14a to δι' ἡμῶν in 2.14b is significant, and he sees this shift as describing Paul's dual function of the passive captive and the active evangelist.[112] While Harris's observation of the dual function is essentially correct, Paul's role should not be narrowly restricted to that of a mere active evangelist. Sufficient attention should also be given to the prepositional phrase, δι' ἡμῶν, which shares a similar function as instrument or agency[113] with the prepositional phrase ἐν τῷ Χριστῷ in 2.14a. As in the

---

109. Thrall, *II Corinthians*, I:195.

110. Attridge, 'Making Scents of Paul', 83.

111. Harris, *Second Corinthians*, 246, among others, maintains that diffusion of the fragrance continues the Roman triumph imagery. Cf. Hafemann, *Suffering and the Spirit*, 43–51; Thrall, *II Corinthians*, I:198–9, who find a transition from the Hellenistic Roman triumph to Hebraic cultic language of sacrifice. If my argument that Paul has in mind the triumphal procession of the Isaianic new exodus is correct, then this shift of imagery is unnecessary. See my argument below.

112. Harris, *Second Corinthians*, 247.

113. BDAG, s.v.; Wallace, *Greek Grammar beyond the Basics*, 368–9.

prepositional phrase in 2.14a, almost all commentators miss the significance of the similar function of δι' ἡμῶν in 2.14b and thus fail to notice the emphasis that is being underscored. Just as Christ the Messiah is God's agent in the triumphal procession, Paul is now seen as God's instrument in manifesting the fragrance of the knowledge of Christ.[114] As such, Paul is not highlighting himself merely as an active evangelist. Rather, Paul now establishes himself as functioning in the role analogous to the Servant of the Lord in manifesting the fragrance of Christ's knowledge, as depicted in Table 4.1.[115]

Table 4.1. *The Relationship between the Subject, Action and Agent in 2 Corinthians 2.14*

Passage	Subject	Action	Agent
2.14a. First Ground for Thanksgiving	God	leading in triumphal procession	Christ the Messiah
2.14b. Second Ground for Thanksgiving	God	spreading the fragrance of the knowledge of Christ	Paul the servant

As God's servant, how and where is this fragrance of the knowledge of Christ to be diffused? It would be natural and logical to expect a verbal form related to smell such as εὐωδιάζω being used to describe the spreading of the ὀσμὴν τῆς γνώσεως αὐτοῦ.[116] Instead, a verbal form related to sight, φανερόω, is used.[117] The choice of φανερόω is not only unusual but also significant. It contributes to the surprising twist in the manner the fragrance of the knowledge of Christ is to be diffused.

Φανερόω carries the meaning 'to cause to become known, disclose, show, make known'[118] and within this context it most likely functions in two ways. First, it suggests that this fragrance is something that appeals not only to the olfactory senses but also to sight. Second, it indicates the manner in which the fragrance is diffused through Paul.

---

114. The question of the antecedent of αὐτοῦ has generated much debate. See Thrall, *II Corinthians*, I:199. The antecedent can either refer to Christ (so Harris, *Second Corinthians*, 246–7; Fitzgerald, *Cracks in an Earthen Vessel*, 161) or to God (so Garland, *2 Corinthians*, 147; Hafemann, *2 Corinthians*, 110; Matera, *II Corinthians*, 69; Scott, *2 Corinthians*, 64; Thrall, *II Corinthians*, I:199). What seems to further complicate the matter is that Paul uses both phrases 'knowledge of Christ' (Phil. 3.8) and 'knowledge of God' (Rom. 11.33; 2 Cor. 4.6; and 10.5) elsewhere. In view of Paul's use of φανερόω here and also elsewhere in describing the life of Jesus as manifested in Paul (4.10 and 11), and that Christ is the image of God (4.4), it tips the scale to take αὐτοῦ as referring to Christ.

115. Cf. the table in Jeffrey A. Crafton, *The Agency of the Apostle: A Dramatistic Analysis of Paul's Responses to Conflict in 2 Corinthians*, JSNTSup 59 (Sheffield: JSOT Press, 1991), 77.

116. Cf. Sir. 39.14.

117. NIV, NLT, NRSV and RSV translate φανεροῦντι as 'spread'. This misses the nuance and force of Paul's argument. KJV and NASB correctly capture the nuance by translating it as 'manifest'.

118. BDAG, s.v.

How then can the ὀσμὴν τῆς γνώσεως αὐτοῦ not only be *smelled* but also *seen*? According to Bultmann, the fragrance is spread through the preaching of the gospel.[119] While this is no doubt right, it appears to be too narrowly construed within the immediate and wider context of this passage and 2 Corinthians respectively.

In 2 Corinthians, φανερόω is an important term[120] and this word appears twice in 4.10-11: 'always carrying in the body the dying of Jesus, so that the life of Jesus may also be made visible (φανερωθῇ) in our bodies. For while we live, we are always being given up to death for Jesus' sake, so that the life of Jesus may be made visible (φανερωθῇ) in our mortal flesh'. The strongest indication as to how the fragrance of the knowledge of Christ may be manifested according to 4.10-11 is through the story of Jesus. As I have argued, Paul is positioning himself and his ministry as analogous to the Isaianic Servant of the Lord and, as such, I can confidently establish that he models himself after the story of Jesus as the Servant of the Lord par excellence.[121] Hence, his whole embodiment of the calling of the Servant and the story of Jesus is reflected in the manner in which the fragrance is manifested – primarily through his life of suffering (1.5-11; 4.7-12; 6.3-10; 11.23-9; cf. Phil. 3.10-11) and his carrying in his body 'the marks of Jesus' (Gal. 6.17) as he bears witness to the gospel.

Finally, the prepositional phrase ἐν παντὶ τόπῳ provides yet another strong indication as to the extent of the manifestation of the fragrance of the knowledge of Christ. The modifier παντί strongly suggests the universal character of Paul's apostolic mission without temporal or national boundaries. It is through his apostolic ministry that Paul sees the eschatological ingathering of Israel and the gentiles as a present reality in Christ.

After establishing the dual purpose of Paul's thanksgiving to God, I shall consider the rationale for this in 2.15-16a.

4. *Paul's Rationale for Thanksgiving: He is the Aroma of Christ*
In 2.15, Paul proceeds to substantiate the rationale for his thanksgiving. As indicated earlier, ὅτι should be rightly connected to χάρις in 2.14a. As such, the thought of thanksgiving continues to be in operation,[122] and ὅτι should be more appropriately translated as 'because', functioning as a 'marker of causality',[123] instead of 'for' as in most translations (e.g., KJV, NASB, NIV,

---

119. Bultmann, *Second Corinthians*, 63.

120. Φανερόω appears a total of nine times in 2 Corinthians. Furnish's suggestion that this is part of the vocabulary used by Paul's opponents against him is questionable (*II Corinthians*, 175).

121. For Paul's embodiment of the story of Jesus, see Gorman, *Cruciformity*.

122. Contra Lambrecht, *Second Corinthians*, 40, who believes thanksgiving is no longer in operation in Paul's thought in 2.15.

123. BDAG, s.v. So Bonnie Bowman Thurston, '2 Corinthians 2:14-16a: Christ's Incense', *ResQ* 29/2 (1987): 65–9; Scott, 'Triumph of God', 274; Attridge, 'Making Scents of Paul', 84. See also the translation of YLT.

NRSV, RSV). Paul's rationale is now being spelt out in 2.15-16a in cultic terms: Χριστοῦ εὐωδία ἐσμὲν τῷ θεῷ ἐν τοῖς σῳζομένοις καὶ ἐν τοῖς ἀπολλυμένοις, οἷς μὲν ὀσμὴ ἐκ θανάτου εἰς θάνατον, οἷς δὲ ὀσμὴ ἐκ ζωῆς εἰς ζωήν.

Closely related to the image of God as a Divine Warrior leading the triumphal procession back from exile is the motif of cultic celebration. The Isaianic new exodus reaches its climax in the glorious return and joyful enthronement of God in a gloriously restored Jerusalem, with the declaration, 'Your God reigns!' (Isa. 52.7; cf. 41.21; 43.15. Cf. Ezek. 20.33). This gives occasion for praise and joy as the people respond to God's saving intervention (Isa. 56.7; 60.5-6; 61.2-11; cf. Isa. 35.10). The triumphal procession climaxes in musical and cultic celebrations and this can be seen from the Divine Warrior victory songs in Psalms (e.g., Pss. 18; 21; 24; 46; 68; 76; 96-8; 114; 124-5; 136).[124] Furthermore, while the triumphal procession is not explicitly stated, Ezekiel portrays the eschatological return to Zion with sacrificial language (e.g., Ezek. 20.41).

As such, there is no need to account for Paul's sudden shift from Hellenistic imagery to OT imagery, as both the triumphal procession images and cultic metaphors fit in tightly in Paul's argument. Stumpff's objection to linking the notion of aroma of Christ to triumphal procession on the basis that this 'has the disadvantage that it makes the expression purely metaphorical and dispenses with any concrete or material sense (and that) it does not adequately explain the plainly stated power of the εὐωδία to salvation or perdition' can now be set aside.[125] In addition, it is not necessary to argue for a dichotomy in Paul's use of the triumphal procession and fragrance metaphors here.[126]

In this instance, Paul continues to use the OT cultic metaphor in emphasizing the decisive nature of his apostolic ministry. As God's servant in the universal diffusion of the fragrance of the knowledge of Christ, Paul, through his apostolic suffering and ministry, constitutes the sweet-smelling fragrance of Christ the Messiah (Χριστοῦ εὐωδία ἐσμὲν τῷ θεῷ). The genitive Χριστοῦ is most likely possessive,[127] signifying Paul's role as an instrument and emissary of Christ.[128]

---

124. See Longman, 'Psalm 98: A Divine Warrior Victory Song'.

125. Albrecht Stumpff, 'εὐωδία', *TDNT* 2:810. Cf. Webb, *Returning Home*, 79–80.

126. Plunkett-Dowling, 'Reading and Restoration', 37–8. Following Bultmann and Allo, Plunkett-Dowling argues that too much weight should not be given to the triumph imagery, as Paul 'immediately drops it in favour of another metaphor' (37) of fragrance. This is because Plunkett-Dowling perceives that 'the thought of aroma first occurred to Paul, it is the metaphor he chose to develop' (38).

127. So Harris, *Second Corinthians*, 248. Cf. Barrett, *Second Corinthians*, 99; Matera, *II Corinthians*, 69, who argues for a subjective genitive reading. If this is the case, Paul would be seen as the sacrificial offering here. While this notion is expressed elsewhere (e.g., Rom. 12.1), there is difficulty in accepting it here. It leaves the phrase without connection to the following statement about the decisive effects of the aroma.

128. Attridge, 'Making Scents of Paul', 84.

Paul's implicit intention in using ὀσμή and εὐωδία in their cultic sense to indicate that his suffering evokes the story of Jesus is significant, more so in that Paul places Χριστοῦ in the emphatic first position. In both instances, ὀσμή and εὐωδία, which have their background in the OT cultic practices, are now applied to life and action pleasing to God. Paul's interest in expressing the intimate association of his life with cultic activity centres on the story of Jesus, particularly the death of Jesus 'for others' (5.14-15) which effects reconciliation and salvation. The emphasis on the story of Jesus, particularly on his sacrificial death in shaping Paul's apostolic suffering and ministry, cannot be simply regarded as only of passing significance for Paul,[129] for he refers to the theme on numerous occasions throughout the letter, as I have noted earlier in Chapters 1 and 3 (cf. 1.5; 4.7-12; 5.14-15, 16, 21). Furthermore, Paul's interest in cultic activity is not only confined to 2 Corinthians but seen also elsewhere (e.g., 1 Cor. 5.1-8, 21; 16.15; Rom. 3.25; 8.3, 23; 12.1; 15.16; 16.5; Gal. 3.13; Phil. 2.17; 25).[130] In this regard, Renwick rightly argues that it is

> quite conceivable that in 2:14-16, where the connection between Paul's existence and Christ's salvific work is also clearly in view, Paul's implicit intention in employing the words ὀσμή and εὐωδία was to use them in their cultic sense, as indicative of the intimate connection between his own life and the life of Christ given in sacrifice (as it were, on the cultic altar in the presence of God) for himself and for others.[131]

My argument can be further supported from 4.7-12, which highlights the connection between the character of Paul's existence and the life of Jesus and also displays a remarkable similarity of vocabulary with that of 2.14-17. Key words like φανερόω (2.14/4.10, 11), ἀπόλλυμι (2.15/4.9), θάνατος (2.16/4.11, 12) and ζωή (2.16/4.10, 11, 12) all appear in both passages. As noted by commentators, this close overlap of vocabulary cannot be regarded as merely coincidental, but further supports my earlier argument that there is a progressive development on the theme of Paul's suffering in 2 Corinthians. Furthermore, this is not the first time that Paul links his apostolic mission to the story of Jesus. As we have seen earlier in Chapter 3, the 'sufferings of Christ are abundant for us' (1.5a), and such afflictions teach Paul to rely on God who raises the dead (1.8-11). The story of Jesus again emerges in 4.10-11 where it serves as a template for Paul's apostolic experience. As Steven Kraftchick rightly notes, Jesus' death

---

129. Renwick, *Paul, The Temple*, 87–8. Cf. Finlan, *Background and Contents*, 60, who argues that Paul's use of cultic metaphors are used to describe 'the death of Christ and also the suffering and rejection undergone by the apostles'.

130. See Finlan, *Background and Contents*, for an excellent detailed treatment on Paul's use of cultic atonement metaphors.

131. Renwick, *Paul, The Temple*, 80. So Collange, *Enigmes*, 33; Barrett, *Second Corinthians*, 99–100.

and resurrection serve as a generative metaphor in 2 Corinthians.[132] As such, Paul's use of the OT sacrificial imagery in 2.14-16 naturally presses the Corinthians to see in the 'aroma of Christ' a picture of the story of Jesus as it is reflected in the Christ hymn in Phil. 2.5-11,[133] and it is to this story that Paul's life is conformed. Paul's life is an embodiment of the gospel he proclaims, for he proclaims the gospel not by his word alone, but by his life of suffering – and this apostolic existence is, metaphorically, the aroma of Christ that rises up to God (τῷ θεῷ),[134] the recipient of the sacrificial aroma.

At the same time, Paul's use of cultic metaphors is also closely related to his apostolic ministry to the gentiles. The sacrificial imagery is reminiscent of Paul's apostolic ministry which he categorizes in cultic terms: 'a minister of Christ Jesus to the gentiles in the priestly service of the gospel of God, so that the offering of the gentiles may be acceptable (ἵνα γένηται ἡ προσφορὰ τῶν ἐθνῶν εὐπρόσδεκτος), sanctified by the Holy Spirit' (Rom. 15.16). Although much debate has taken place over the precise meaning of the phrase ἡ προσφορὰ τῶν ἐθνῶν εὐπρόσδεκτος, it makes better sense to take this as Paul's task as a servant in bringing the gentiles as a sacrifice that would be acceptable to God.[135] This cultic element can most likely be traced to Isa. 66.20 where Paul now sees it as a prophecy for the inclusion of gentiles within restored Israel and as the fulfilment of God's covenant faithfulness. It also looks forward to Paul's citation of Isa. 49.8 in 2 Cor. 6.2 immediately preceding his detailed description of his suffering (2 Cor. 6.3-11): 'At the acceptable time I have listened to you,

---

132. Steven J. Kraftchick, 'Death in Us, Life in You: The Apostolic Medium', in *Pauline Theology*, Vol. 2, ed. David M. Hay (Minneapolis: Fortress Press, 1993), 156–81.

133. Cf. Stegman, *Character of Jesus*, 266, where he suggests that Paul uses the metaphor of fragrance/aroma to 'signify his embodiment of Jesus' character and mode of self-emptying existence'.

134. The dative should be taken as locative, in line with the dative κυρίῳ that accompanies the cultic expression in the LXX denoting sacrifice acceptable to God. This also agrees with the Pauline usage elsewhere where the aroma of sacrifice is said to be well-pleasing to God (Phil. 4.18). So Harris, *Second Corinthians*, 249. Cf. NAB's translation as the dative of advantage, 'we are the aroma of Christ for God'. Similarly, Moffatt: 'I live for God (as the fragrance of Christ)'.

135. The phrase ἡ προσφορὰ τῶν ἐθνῶν is interpreted to mean: (1) the gentiles themselves as the offering to God, signifying the inclusion of gentiles in restored Israel; or (2) the material gifts brought in by the gentiles, referring to Paul's collection from the gentiles to Jerusalem. Most commentators support the former position; see Artland J. Hultgren, *Paul's Gospel and Mission* (Philadephia: Fortress Press, 1985), 125–50; Richard J. Dillon, 'The "Priesthood" of St Paul, Romans 15:15-16', *Worship* 74 (2000): 156–68; Steve Strauss, 'Missions Theology in Romans 15:14-33', *BibSac* (2003): 457–74; Bert Jan Lietaert Peerbolte, 'Romans 15:14-29 and Paul's Missionary Agenda', in *Persuasion and Dissuasion in Early Christianity, Ancient Judaism, and Hellenism*, ed. Pieter W. van der Horst, Maarten J. J. Menken, Joop F. M. Smit and Geert Van Oyen, CBET 33 (Leuven: Peeters, 2003), 143–59. For a defence of the second position, see O'Brien, *Gospel and Mission*, 27–51; Roger D. Aus, 'Paul's Travel Plans to Spain and the "Full Number of the Gentiles" of Rom. 11:25', *NovT* 21 (1979): 232–62.

and helped you on the day of salvation'. This leads Paul to declare, in eschatologically loaded terminology to the Corinthians: 'Behold, now is the acceptable time; behold, now is the day of salvation.' It is beyond doubt that such language finds its root in the tradition of the exilic return/restoration to God.

Paul's use of cultic metaphor also functions to highlight the decisive effects it has on those who smell and see the aroma, as demonstrated through several distinctive literary features of 2.15-16 in Table 4.2.

Table 4.2. *Literary Features of 2 Corinthians 2.15-16*

Parallelism 2 Cor. 2.16	οἷς μὲν ὀσμὴ ἐκ θανάτου εἰς θάνατον	οἷς δὲ ὀσμὴ ἐκ ζωῆς εἰς ζωήν.
Repetition 2 Cor. 2.16	θανάτου ζωῆς	θάνατον ζωήν.
Contrast 2 Cor. 2.15-16	ἐν τοῖς σῳζομένοις μὲν οἷς μὲν ὀσμὴ ἐκ θανάτου εἰς θάνατον	ἐν τοῖς ἀπολλυμένοις δὲ οἷς δὲ ὀσμὴ ἐκ ζωῆς εἰς ζωήν.
Progression 2 Cor. 2.16	ἐκ θανάτου εἰς θάνατον	ἐκ ζωῆς εἰς ζωήν.

These literary features clearly demonstrate that the final outcomes of those who respond to Paul's apostolic ministry are to be decisively cast into two distinct and mutually exclusive categories: those who are being saved and those who are perishing. The decisive factor hinges on how one responds to the gospel of Christ: life resulting from a positive response to the apostolic message, and death resulting from a negative response.[136] Harvey states that such a claim asserts Paul's crucial assumption that:

> [E]verything the person says and does is entirely motivated by God. If people react adversely to the message, may it not be because of the personal bias of the messenger? If people do not accept the testimony, may it not be because of the dubious character of the witness? To speak of oneself in terms of being an agent of God for life and death ... is to make an enormous claim – that one's motives are perfectly clear, that one is totally transparent to the purposes of God.[137]

This is precisely what Paul claims to be doing here; he puts no obstacle in anyone's way, so that no fault may be found with his ministry, including his sufferings (2.17; 6.3-10). This will be further explored in Chapter 6.

The vocabulary of σῴζω, ἀπόλλυμι, θάνατος and ζωή in 2.15b-16a carries strong eschatological overtones, announcing that the day of God's promised deliverance for Israel has arrived.[138] With the arrival of the eschatological

---

136. Cf. 1 Cor. 1.18. See also 1 Pet. 2.6-8.

137. Harvey, *Renewal through Suffering*, 46.

138. Cf. Martin, *2 Corinthians*, 48. See Plunkett-Dowling, 'Reading and Restoration', 45–50, for a discussion on the eschatological overtones in the use of ὀσμή and εὐωδία.

age, the expectation of eschatological judgement is also anticipated. In portraying his apostolic mission as delivering 'life to life', Paul is proclaiming the arrival of the promised eschatological restoration and reconciliation to God in Christ. At the same time, this also evokes the image of eschatological judgement to those who refuse to accept the eschatological message as 'death to death'.

This leads us to the final consideration in this section: who are those being saved and those perishing? Is Paul making a general statement describing the resulting effects of his ministry to the gentiles in general, or is Paul more specific here?

Before we can propose an answer, a brief survey of the Corinthians' acquaintance with cultic fragrance might be illuminating. The city of Corinth was a centre of cultic worship graphically attested to by its many magnificent and imposing temples, statues and shrines dedicated to both Greek and Roman gods such as Apollo, Athena, Tyche, Aphrodite, Pantheon, Demerter, Kore, Dionysus, Neptune, Asklepios, Venus, Octavia and Poseidon. Pausanias listed at least 24 sanctuaries and temples for Corinth.[139] In addition, there were also temples dedicated to the Roman imperial cult and the Egyptian cults of Isis and Sarapis. Such juxtaposition clearly defined not only the varieties of deities that are well represented here but also the extent to which religion penetrated every sector of life in Corinth. The strong religious attitudes of Corinth were reflected in coins, terracotta and marble statues, mosaic flooring and other daily household wares.[140] When travellers arrived in Corinth from the port of Cenchreae or left the city to head west to Sicyon, they would be greeted by the temples of Aphrodite and Isis and the temple of Apollo, respectively. The imposing Acrocorinth that rises 575 metres high would also have reminded the Corinthians of the sanctuary of Aphrodite on the summit. As such, the Corinthians literally lived continually in the presence of the gods with the smell of fragrant offerings wafting out of the temples. Paul himself was keenly aware of this, having stayed there for more than a year (cf. Acts 18.11).

---

139. See Pausanias, *Description of Greece*, Book II on Corinth. For further discussion, see Donald Engels, *Roman Corinth: An Alternative Model for the Classical City* (Chicago: University of Chicago Press, 1990), 92–107; John R. Lanci, *A New Temple for Corinth: Rhetorical and Archaeological Approaches to Pauline Imagery*, SBL 1 (New York: Peter Lang, 1997), 25–43, 89–113; Daniel N. Schowalter and Steven J. Friesen, eds, *Urban Religion in Roman Corinth: Interdisciplinary Approaches*, HTS 53 (Cambridge: Harvard University Press, 2005), in particular the article by Nancy Bookidis, 'Religion in Corinth: 146 B.C.E. to 100 C.E.', 141–64. On textual and archaeological evidence on social, political and religious activities in Corinth, consult Jerome Murphy-O'Connor, *St. Paul's Corinth: Texts and Archaeology*, 3rd edn (Collegeville: Liturgical Press, 2002).

140. For images of some of these statues now housed in the Corinth Museum at ancient Corinth, see Nicos Papahatzis, *Ancient Corinth: The Museums of Corinth, Isthmia and Sicyon* (Athens: Ekdotike Athenon, 1977), 88–97.

Hence here lies the force of Paul's use of cultic metaphor. As I have argued earlier, the vocabulary of ὀσμή and εὐωδία evokes the scriptural image of cultic sacrifice acceptable to God, and this serves as a reminder of Israel's right relationship with God. Deeply embedded in this loaded cultic metaphor is a reflection not only on God's attitude toward the sacrifice but also on the attitude of the sacrificing community itself towards God. Of all the offerings, only one that is offered by Israel for the atonement of sins according to the Law of Moses remains acceptable to God. As such, Paul is reminding the Corinthians that the gods of Corinth could never be their saviours. The sacrifices of the gods only lead from 'death to death'. Having turned from the worship of idols, the Corinthians are 'sanctified in Christ Jesus' (1 Cor. 1.1) and now serve and worship the living God. But if they refuse to accept Paul and continue to shun suffering and weakness, mistaking Paul's apostolic suffering as stench rather than fragrance, then they should be numbered among those who are perishing. But if they are not to be found among those who are perishing, then they must be firmly established in the worship of the living God, together with his servant, Paul, who offers his life of cruciformity as the aroma of sacrifice acceptable to God.

Therefore, it is not surprising that Paul has the Corinthians in mind and specifically warns them in 2.15-16a when he mentions the two distinct categories. To the Corinthians, the dangers of defection are real, whether this is caused by another gospel (11.4-5), idols (1 Cor. 10.6-12) or the opponents of Paul.[141] In 1 Corinthians, the story of Israel's exodus, her failure, and the direct consequences of doing likewise have been clearly told to the Corinthians (1 Cor. 10; cf. 2 Cor. 3.12-16). By comparing the Corinthians to the Israelites, it seems quite clear that Paul considers the followers of Christ to have embarked on the Isaianic new exodus where 'the fulfilment of the ages has come' (1 Cor. 10.11).[142] Since both the triumphal possession and sacrificial offering are actions witnessed by the multitudes and directly related to the worship of God, the Corinthians can hear Paul's message very clearly. As the instrument of God, Paul is the aroma of Christ through which the Corinthians have come to faith in Christ; hence, they are included in those who are being saved. To turn their backs on Paul is to turn their backs on not only Paul's apostolic preaching and gospel but also ultimately Christ. If this is the case, the alternative – being numbered among the perishing – is the tragedy that awaits them.

---

141. So Plunkett-Dowling, 'Reading and Restoration', 50–60. Cf. Attridge, 'Making Scents of Paul', 87–8; Collange, *Enigmes*, 34–5; Thrall, *II Corinthians*, I:202, who, among others, take Paul's categorization as referring to believers and unbelievers in general. Scott, *2 Corinthians*, 64, dubiously suggests that the category of those who are perishing is a reference to Paul's opponents.

142. Cf. Oropeza, 'Echoes of Isaiah in the Rhetoric of Paul', 92–3. Contra the questionable suggestion of Bruce, *1 & 2 Corinthians*, 188, where those being saved refer to the soldiers while those perishing refer to the captives of the triumph.

Finally, seen in this perspective, the tone of 2.14-16a is no longer primarily apologetic, as suggested by almost all commentators, but parenaetic. While Paul no doubt defends the nature of his apostleship to those who challenge him concerning his weaknesses (10.10), I agree with Plunkett-Dowling that these apologetic elements throughout 2 Corinthians are best treated as 'subordinated to the main goal of the letter'.[143] Furthermore, in the light of the Isaianic new exodus motif that I suggested above, Paul may even have the Deuteronomic covenant (Deut. 30.12-20) in mind, where the radical choice between obedience and disobedience is in fact a choice for life or for death.[144] In this respect, Sampley is right on target:

> Although interpreters of this extended section understandably often mine it for its profound and rich theological claims, every portion of it is aimed by Paul not only at enhancing the Corinthians' understanding of his ministry among and for them, but also especially at binding them more closely to himself as their apostle.[145]

Hence, we can confidently conclude that the primary purpose here is parenaetic, exhorting and awaking the Corinthians to be part of the narrative of God's reconciliation effected through the story of Jesus. Paul is extending this invitation to the Corinthians to be part of the new eschatological community that God is establishing among the gentile nations and to be part of the narrative of the story of Jesus. Barnett notes: 'It seems likely that (Paul) meditated on Isaiah 40–55 in light of the crisis in Corinth and, as it were, prophesied from it, exhorting the Corinthians – in particular the wayward groups – to align themselves with God's "day of salvation", which Paul had heralded.'[146]

To summarize the argument: Paul substantiates his rationale for his thanksgiving in 2.15-16a. As bearer of the aroma of Christ, Paul's apostolic life and proclamation of the gospel characterized by suffering plays a decisive role in God's redemptive narrative, resulting in a twofold effect for the Corinthians: to those who accept the gospel and its messenger, it brings life; and to those who refuse, it brings death. This is Paul's urgent plea, inviting the Corinthians to be part of, and remain in, God's narrative effected through the story of Jesus. As such, 2.14-16 is to be read not merely as Paul's defence of his apostleship but primarily as parenaetic.

---

143. Plunkett-Dowling, 'Reading and Restoration', 22.

144. Cf. James M. Scott, 'Paul's Use of Deuteronomic Tradition', *JBL* 112 (1993): 645–65. Cf. Aus, *Imagery of Triumph and Rebellion*, 47–79, 83, who argues that Paul has in mind the notorious rebellion of LXX Num. 17.6-15 in the fragrance metaphor (2.14-16). With this warning, the Corinthians 'must now react to Paul and his fellow missionaries, those who speak as persons of sincerity (and authority), who stand in God's presence'.

145. Sampley, *Second Corinthians*, 56.

146. Barnett, *Second Epistle*, 47.

IV. *Concluding Summary*

The rationale for Paul's apostolic suffering and his mission theology grounded in the story of Jesus is now further established in 2.14-16a. Paul begins this section by expressing thanksgiving to God for God's dual decisive actions in the salvation drama: (1) in leading the triumphal procession through Christ the Messiah; and (2) in displaying the fragrance of the knowledge of Christ through him. I have highlighted that previous scholarship has narrowly focused on Paul, the object of the triumph, instead of God, the subject of the triumph. By rightly focusing on God, a new perspective in reading the text emerges. I suggest that Paul has in mind the image of God as a Divine Warrior leading the triumphal procession through Christ the Messiah and this reading evokes the tradition of the Isaianic new exodus. In using the cultic metaphor (2.14b), Paul establishes himself as God's servant in manifesting the fragrance of the knowledge of Christ, and the manner of this manifestation is through his cruciformed life of suffering and proclamation of the gospel grounded in the story of Jesus.

Paul further substantiates the rationale of his thanksgiving (2.15) by continuing to employ the OT cultic metaphor in emphasizing the decisive nature of his apostolic ministry, resulting in a twofold effect for the Corinthians: to those who accept Paul and his preaching of the gospel, it brings life; and to those who refuse, it brings death (2.15-16a). Hence, 2.14-16 is to be primarily read as parenaetic in which Paul's urgent plea is not merely to defend his apostleship but also to invite the Corinthians to be part of God's narrative so that they will not be tragically numbered among those who are perishing.

Chapter 5

SECOND CORINTHIANS 4.7-12

I. *Introduction*

In Chapter 3, I argued that Paul's exposition of his sufferings takes place at crucial junctures of his argument throughout 2 Corinthians; and this will be further reinforced in 4.7-12 where Paul presents the first of his *peristasis* catalogues at the beginning of a larger literary unit of 4.7–5.10. In this chapter, I shall continue to investigate what I established in Chapter 4: that the rationale for Paul's apostolic suffering and his mission theology is grounded in the story of Jesus.

Second Cor. 4.7-12 is a well-studied passage on the theme of Pauline suffering.[1] The common key approach is to focus on the religious[2] and the literary

---

1. See, among others, Michael Byrnes, *Conformation to the Death of Christ and the Hope of Resurrection: An Exegetico-Theological Study of 2 Corinthians 4,7-15 and Philippians 3,7-11*, TGST 99 (Rome: Editrice Pontificia Universita Gregoriana, 2003); Paul Brooks Duff, 'Apostolic Suffering and the Language of Processions in 2 Corinthians 4.7-10', *BTB* 21 (1991): 158–65; Susan R. Garrett, 'The God of This World and the Affliction of Paul: 2 Cor 4:1-12', in *Greeks, Romans, and Christians: Essays in Honor of Abraham J. Malherbe*, ed. David L. Balch, Everett Ferguson and Wayne A. Meeks (Minneapolis: Fortress Press, 1990), 99–117; Joyce Kaithakottil, '"Death in Us, Life in You" Ministry and Suffering: A Study of 2 Cor 4,7-15', *BiBh* 28 (2002): 433–60; Jan Lambrecht, 'The *Nekrōsis* of Jesus: Ministry and Suffering in 2 Cor 4:7-15', in *L'Apôtre Paul: Personnalité, style et conception du ministère*, ed. A. Vanhoye, BETL 73 (Leuven: Leuven University Press, 1986), 120–43; idem, 'The Eschatological Outlook in 2 Cor 4:7-15', in *To Tell the Mystery: Essays on New Testament Eschatology in Honor of Robert H. Gundry*, ed. Thomas E. Schmidt and Moisés Silva, JSNTSup 100 (Sheffield: JSOT Press, 1994), 122–39; idem, 'Brief Anthropological Reflections on 2 Corinthians 4:6–5:10', in *Paul and the Corinthians: Studies on a Community in Conflict, Essays in Honour of Margaret Thrall*, ed. Trevor J. Burke and J. K. Elliott, NovTSup 109 (Leiden: Brill, 2003), 259–66; Alexander Mak, '2 Corinthians 4:7-12: Life Manifesting in Death', *CMSJ* 3 (2003): 109–35; Frank J. Matera, 'Apostolic Suffering and Resurrection Faith: Distinguishing between Appearance and Reality (2 Cor 4,7–5,10)', in *Resurrection in the New Testament: Festschrift J. Lambrecht*, ed. R. Bieringer, Veronica Koperski and B. Lataire, BETL 165 (Leuven: Leuven University Press, 2002): 387–405; Jerome Murphy-O'Connor, 'Faith and Resurrection in 2 Cor 4:13-14', *RB* 95 (1988): 543–50; Pate, *Adam Christology*.

2. E.g., see Duff, 'Apostolic Suffering'; Fitzgerald, *Cracks in an Earthen Vessel*; and Pate, *Adam Christology*.

and rhetorical[3] background of the *peristasis* catalogue. While these approaches yield informative results, they rely heavily on word studies and formal parallels to background materials at the expense of Paul's theological interpretation of his own suffering as is evident in 4.10-11.[4] It needs to be emphasized that Paul's catalogue of suffering in this passage cannot be interpreted by itself or by merely depending on background materials.

In this passage, Paul grounds the understanding of his apostolic ministry in the story of Jesus and it is this story that becomes the interpretive lens through which Paul understands his suffering in three aspects: (1) in relation to himself (4.7-11); (2) in relation to his apostolic mission (4.12a); and; (3) in relation to the Corinthians (4.12b, cf. 4.15). These aspects of Pauline suffering have been overlooked by most commentators,[5] and it is the aim of this chapter to correct this imbalance.

II. *Structure and Line of Thought*

Paul begins his argument in a new paragraph (as indicated by δέ) with a thesis-like statement in 4.7, declaring that, as an earthen vessel, he carries τὸν θησαυρὸν τοῦτον in order to demonstrate that the exceeding greatness of power in his ministry of the gospel has its source from God and not from any human. This is further followed by a catalogue of hardships embodied in what can be regarded as the most powerful series of four antithetical statements that Paul bequeaths to his readers that further anticipates his other catalogues of sufferings in 6.3-10 and 11.23-33. This is then followed by a series of interpretive statements grounded in the story of Jesus, demarcating how this story functions in relation to himself (4.10-11), his mission theology (4.12) and the Corinthians (4.12b, cf. 4.15).

As a summary, the structure of Paul's flow of thought can be summarized as follows:

---

3. See Mak, '2 Corinthians 4:7-12', 109; Norbert Baumert, *Täglich sterben und auferstehen: Der Literalsinn von 2 Kor 4,12–5,10*, SANT 34 (München: Kösel-Verlag, 1973); Byrnes, *Conformation to the Death of Christ*.

4. Some studies that have emphasized word studies in the *peristasis* catalogue result in dubious suggestions that Paul is using warfare or wrestling terminology (see C. Spicq, 'L'image sportive de II Corinthians', *ETL* 14 [1937]: 209–29) or the language of manhunt (see Philip E. Hughes, *Paul's Second Epistle to the Corinthians*, NICNT [Grand Rapids: Eerdmans, 1962], 139) in the description of his suffering.

5. Most commentators see Paul's understanding of his sufferings as for his own benefit such as in defending the legitimacy of his apostleship or to present himself as a virtuous sage. The only two possible exceptions are Matera and Grams. Matera suggests that Paul interprets his suffering in relation to himself and the Corinthians (*II Corinthians*, 109) and seems to miss out the missiological dimension of Paul's suffering. Grams discusses the importance of suffering in terms of Pauline mission but his primary focus is on ethics instead of Paul's relationship to the Corinthians ('Gospel and Mission', 383–97, see also 278–87).

4.7   Thesis statement: earthen vessel and power from God

4.8-11   The story of Jesus in relation to Paul's understanding of his suffering

4.12a   The story of Jesus in relation to Paul's understanding of his mission theology

4.12b   The story of Jesus in relation to the Corinthians

There are several interesting stylistic and literary features in 4.7-12. Apart from the series of four antithetical statements in 4.8-9, the paradox between life and death is juxtaposed three times in 4.10-12. Second, this passage is loaded with four ἵνα clauses that highlight the divine purpose revolving around the story of Jesus within Paul's experience of suffering.

Third, it is also interesting to note that there is a strikingly close similarity in terms of theme and vocabulary in 4.7-12 compared to 1.3-11 and 2.4-16 as earlier discussed in Chapters 3 and 4 respectively. In terms of theme, I note the following: (1) Paul's sufferings are linked to the sufferings of Christ (1.5; 2.14; and 4.8-9); (2) the motif of Paul as the mediator of salvation is evident (1.6; 2.15-16a; and 4.12); (3) the motifs of life and death are juxtaposed with each other (1.8-9; 2.15-16; and 4.10-12); (4) the intended human response as a result of Paul's apostolic ministry is emphasized (1.11; 2.15-16; and 4.12); and (5) a close similarity between the structure of 2.14 and 4.11 is detected and highlighted in Table 5.1.[6]

Table 5.1. *A Comparison of the Structure of 2 Corinthians 2.14 and 4.11*

	2 Cor. 2.14	2 Cor. 4.11
1.	Thanks be to God	divine passive
2.	always	always
3.	us	we who are living
4.	lead in triumphal procession	being handed over to death
5.	in the Messiah	on account of Jesus
6.	through us	in our mortal body
7.	reveals the fragrance of the knowl-edge of him	his life may be revealed
8.	everywhere	implied in 4.10, always

The similarity of vocabulary can be further illustrated in Table 5.2. This overwhelming similarity in both vocabulary and theme not only further enforces my earlier argument on the epistolary function of 1.3-11, but also strongly indicates that the narrative that binds Paul's argument in a coherent manner is the story of Jesus.

---

6.   Cf. Hafemann, *Suffering and the Spirit*, 73, where he highlights the parallel structure of 1 Cor. 4.9; 2 Cor. 2.14; and 4.11. See below for further discussion on 4.11.

Table 5.2. *Distribution of Similar Vocabulary in 2 Corinthians 1.3-11; 2.14-16; and 4.7-12*

Vocabulary	2 Cor. 1.3-11	2 Cor. 2.14-16	2 Cor. 4.7-12
ὑπερβολή	1.8	–	4.7
δύναμις	1.8	–	4.7
θλίβω	1.6	–	4.8
ἐξαπορέομαι	1.8	–	4.8
ἀπόλλυμι	–	2.15	4.9
ζωή	–	2.16 (twice)	4.10, 11, 12
φανερόω	–	2.14	4.10, 11
ζάω	1.8	–	4.11
θάνατος	1.9, 10	2.16 (twice)	4.11, 12
ἐνεργέω	1.6	–	4.12
περισσεύω	1.5 (twice)	–	cf. 4.15

Finally, in describing his apostolic sufferings, Paul clearly has himself in view,[7] as indicated by the distinction of the first person and second person personal pronouns. This sharp contrast is clearly spelt out in 4.12 (ἐν ἡμῖν ... ἐν ὑμῖν); 4.14 (ἡμᾶς σὺν Ἰησοῦ ... σὺν ὑμῖν); and 4.15 (δι' ὑμᾶς). This striking distinction serves the purpose of highlighting Paul's apostolic ministry and its beneficiaries, the Corinthians.

III. *The Story of Jesus and Paul's Ministry of Suffering as Treasure in an Earthen Vessel: 2 Corinthians 4.7-12*

A. *The Thesis Statement: The Earthen Vessel and the Power of God*

1. *Treasure in an Earthen Vessel*

In 2 Cor. 4.7, Paul declares: ἔχομεν ... τὸν θησαυρὸν τοῦτον ἐν ὀστρακίνοις σκεύεσιν. However, Paul does not specify what is the θησαυρός he carries.[8] In addition, the antecedent of τοῦτον that modifies θησαυρός is not entirely clear. This has led to various suggestions that Paul could have in mind: (1) 'the light of the knowledge of the glory of God in the face of Christ' (4.6);[9] (2) 'the light

---

7.   While the use of first person plurals (cf. ἔχομεν and ἡμῶν) primarily refers to Paul, it cannot be discounted that his co-workers are also in view. However, our discussion will be predominantly focused on Paul.

8.   In the NT, θησαυρός appears only once elsewhere, in Col. 2.3.

9.   So Barnett, *Second Epistle*, 229; Fitzgerald, *Cracks in an Earthen Vessel*, 168; Hughes, *Second Corinthians*, 135; Raymond Pickett, *The Cross in Corinth: The Social Significance of the Death of Jesus*, JSNTSup 143 (Sheffield: Sheffield Academic Press, 1997), 130; Scott, *2 Corin-*

of the gospel of the glory of Christ' (4.4);[10] (3) the gospel;[11] or (4) his apostolic ministry (4.1).[12]

It is to be noted that Paul's metaphorical reference to τὸν θησαυρὸν τοῦτον closely follows his earlier discussion in 4.1-6, and as such the metaphor is to be understood against this background.[13] In view of this, it is best to take τὸν θησαυρὸν τοῦτον as a reference to Paul's apostolic ministry. Several lines of evidence seem to further support this reading. First, in 4.1-6, Paul is essentially deliberating on his ministry of the proclamation of the gospel. No matter how one identifies τὸν θησαυρὸν τοῦτον, whether it be 'the light of the knowledge of the glory of God in the face of Christ', 'the light of the gospel of the glory of Christ' or 'the gospel', Paul is making a reference that is ultimately connected to his apostolic ministry of the gospel. Second, 4.2-6 is an expansion of Paul's argument in 4.1, and Paul's apostolic ministry would naturally incorporate all the above proposals which are further expressions of his thoughts concerning his ministry. Third, Paul's subsequent description of his apostolic suffering in 4.8-9 further addresses the nature of his apostolic ministry. Finally, taking into account that the verb ἔχομεν in 4.7 occurs a number of times in finite and participial verbal forms in the immediate and wider context where Paul is reflecting on the nature of the new covenant ministry,[14] it further supports the reading that τὸν θησαυρὸν τοῦτον most likely refers to Paul's apostolic ministry.

Paul further says that τὸν θησαυρὸν τοῦτον is contained in ὀστρακίνοις σκεύεσιν (4.7). The use of pottery imagery would resonate well with the Corinthians as Corinth was well known for its pottery.[15] Earthen vessels in antiquity were inexpensive and fragile, thus having no enduring value by themselves (cf. LXX Lev. 6.21; 15.12; Ps. 31.12 [LXX Ps. 30.13]; Isa. 30.14; Jer. 19.11).[16]

thians, 103. Cf. Pate, *Adam Christology*, 77–106, who dubiously suggests that the 'treasure' is the divine glory lost by Adam but now restored by Christ inwardly through righteous suffering.

10. Thrall, *II Corinthians*, I:321–32.

11. Barrett, *Second Corinthians*, 138; Mak, '2 Corinthians 4:7-12', 113.

12. Bultmann, *Second Corinthians*, 112; Byrnes, *Conformation to the Death of Christ*, 48; Collange, *Enigmes*, 146; Petrus J. Gräbe, *The Power of God in Paul's Letters*, WUNT 2/123 (Tübingen: Mohr Siebeck, 2000), 148; Hafemann, *2 Corinthians*, 182; Lambrecht, *Second Corinthians*, 71; Jerry W. McCant, *2 Corinthians*, Readings (Sheffield: Shefield Academic Press, 1999), 42; Savage, *Power through Weakness*, 164.

13. Furnish, *II Corinthians*, 279.

14. See the uses of ἔχομεν and ἔχοντες in 3.4, 12; 4.1, 7, 13; 5.1, which all point to Paul's apostolic ministry.

15. On pottery in Corinth, see John W. Hayes, 'Roman Pottery from the South Stoa at Corinth', *Hesperia* 42 (1973): 416–70; Kathleen W. Slane, *The Sanctuary of Demeter and Kore: The Roman Pottery and Lamps*, Corinth 18.2 (Princeton: American School of Classical Studies at Athens, 1990); idem, 'Corinth's Roman Pottery: Quantification and Meaning', in *Corinth: The Centenary, 1896–1996*, ed. Charles K. Williams II and Nancy Bookidis, Corinth 20 (Princeton: American School of Classical Studies at Athens, 2003), 321–36.

16. Fitzgerald, *Cracks in an Earthen Vessel*, 167, takes the earthen vessels as 'disposable

The only entity that gives them their worth is their contents and, as such, the outward appearance of the vessels cannot be taken as representative of or a guide to the contents.[17]

Applied to Paul, the focus of this striking metaphor is on the weakness and fragility of a human vessel bearing the treasure of the ministry of the gospel.[18] Hence the metaphor functions as a fitting description of Paul's apostolic ministry characterized by sufferings, apparent lack of credentials and unimposing appearance in contrast to the powerful treasure contained within the vessel.[19] It is the weak and suffering apostle who people see and this brings to mind what Paul had earlier reminded the Corinthians. 'God chose what is low and despised in the world, things that are not, to reduce to nothing things that are, so that no one might boast in the presence of God' (1 Cor. 1.28-9; cf. 2.1-5).

At the same time, the metaphor of earthen vessels also has a deeper significance. The nuance of instrumentality[20] should not be discounted, as this metaphor also alludes to the imagery of God as the potter who shapes the clay (Isa. 29.16; 41.25; 45.9; 64.8; Jer. 18.1-6; 22.8; cf. Wis. 15.7; Lam. 4.2; Sir. 33.10-13; Rom. 9.20-1) and underscores the divine intention for Paul as God's servant (cf. Acts 9.15, where Paul is described as 'a chosen vessel').

This is another clear demonstration of Paul's creativity in integrating familiar metaphors drawing from both the Hellenistic context and the Scriptures to illustrate his point. This provides him with a platform to articulate a powerful theological statement reflected in the following purpose clause in 2 Cor. 4.7b.

2. *Power from God, Not from Us*
Syntactically, the main clause in 2 Cor. 4.7 provides the basis for the following purpose clause, ἵνα ἡ ὑπερβολὴ τῆς δυνάμεως ᾖ τοῦ θεοῦ καὶ μὴ ἐξ ἡμῶν.

---

bottles of antiquity'. But within the context of 4.7-12, it is not the *disposability* of the vessels that Paul has in mind but their *fragility* or *cheapness*. Cf. Schnabel, *Early Christian Mission*, 2: 966: 'Clay jars that contain a valuable treasure are *quantité négligeable*, insignificant, undeserving of much attention or excitement.'

    17. Kraftchick, 'Death in Us, Life in You', 172.

    18. Cf. Savage, *Power through Weakness*, 166. Earthen vessels are '*both* weak *and* inferior, fragile *and* expendable' (emphasis his).

    19. Cf. the teachings of the rabbis who emphasized that the Torah only resides in those who are like humble vessels, *Sipre Deut* 48.2.7; *Pesiq. Rab Kah.* 24.5. See also Isa. 66.2. Other less-secure views of 'treasure in earthen vessels' include: (1) Barrett, *Second Corinthians*, 138, who argues that the focal point of the metaphor is on the treasure of the contents rather than the cheapness of the one who carries it; (2) Scott, *2 Corinthians*, 103–4, who sees this metaphor as God's creation of humans from dust by alluding to Gen. 2.7; (3) Manson, '2 Cor 2:14-17', 156, who suggests that Paul draws his analogy from small pottery lamps where their frail mortal bodies exhibit the light of Christ; (4) Collange, *Enigmes*, 146, who suggests that σκεῦος carries a title of honour and dignity; and (5) Duff, 'Apostolic Suffering', who proposes that the imagery is drawn from pagan triumphal processions.

    20. Lambrecht, *Second Corinthians*, 71.

This divine purpose is stated both positively and negatively (ἴνα ... ᾖ ... καὶ μὴ) to convey two basic ideas. First, the all-surpassing power is from God who appoints the bearer of the treasure;[21] and second, this power cannot and must not come from Paul as the bearer of the treasure. In emphasizing God's power, Paul employs the term hyperbole, ὑπερβολή, a word that is highly concentrated in 2 Corinthians.[22] By juxtaposing the all-surpassing power from God and the weakness and frailty of the apostle, it not only heightens the extent and nature of the contrast but also makes this section an imposing argument. Paul is the vehicle through which the power of God is strongly exhibited. As such, one should not mistake the vessel for the treasure.[23]

The theme of God's power being demonstrated in Paul's ministry is a recurring notion throughout the Corinthian correspondence. First, the greatness of God's power is closely associated with the proclamation of the gospel. In 1 Cor. 1.18, Paul declares that 'the message about the cross is foolishness to those who are perishing, but to us who are being saved it is the power of God'. Further on, Paul declares that his apostolic ministry to the Corinthians is marked with weakness, fear and trembling and that his proclamation of the gospel is not done with eloquence or superior wisdom (1 Cor. 2.1, 4) but with a demonstration of the Spirit with the result that their faith might rest not on human wisdom but on the power of God (1 Cor. 2.1-5; cf. Rom. 1.16).

Second, the reality of the greatness of God's power is experienced through Paul's weakness and suffering. Further on in 2 Cor. 12.7, Paul echoes Jesus' words to him, 'My power is made perfect in weakness', and in 13.4, which is probably the best commentary on Paul's statement here: 'For (Jesus) was crucified in weakness, but lives by the power of God. For we are weak in him, but in dealing with you we will live with him by the power of God.'[24]

The dynamics of God working through those who are weak is also well attested in the OT. The examples of Moses ('Who am I that I should go to Pharaoh, and bring the Israelites out of Egypt?', Exod. 3.11), Gideon ('My clan is the weakest in Manasseh, and I am the least in my family', Judg. 6.15) and David ('I am a poor man and of no repute', 1 Sam. 18.23) most likely resonated

21. Τοῦ θεοῦ functions as the genitive of source. See Wallace, *Greek Grammar beyond the Basics*, 110.

22. In the NT, ὑπερβολή appears a total of eight times, out of which five are found in 2 Corinthians. See Chapter 3 for a brief treatment of the use of hyberbolic language in 2 Corinthians.

23. Cf. Scott J. Hafemann, '"Because of Weakness" (Galatians 4:13): The Role of Suffering in the Mission of Paul', in *The Gospel to the Nations: Perspectives on Paul's Mission*, ed. Peter Bolt and Mark Thompson (Downers Grove: InterVarsity Press, 2000), 131–46 (137).

24. For further discussion on the notion of power, see Gräbe, *Power of God in Paul's Letters*, especially 86–119; idem, 'The All-Surpassing Power of God through the Holy Spirit in the Midst of Our Broken Earthly Existence: Perspectives on Paul's Use of *Dýnamis* in 2 Corinthians', *Neot* 28/1 (1994): 147–56; idem, '*Dýnamis* (Power) in Paul's Ministry as Portrayed in His Main Letters', *NGTT* 32/2 (1991): 201–13.

in Paul's mind. At the same time, Paul's idea here also corresponds with the OT tradition that God dwells with the humble, contrite and lowly in spirit (e.g., Ps. 34.18; Isa. 57.15; 66.22). As such, for Paul, weakness is *never* seen as a hindrance in God's service.

In summary, Paul's argument in 4.7 serves to highlight two fundamental truths in his apostolic ministry: power from God is demonstrated through his weakness and suffering; and his sufferings are not a barrier to the progress of the gospel.

B. *The Interpretive Statements Grounded in the Story of Jesus*

Through the imagery of treasure in an earthen vessel, Paul not only declares that his suffering is fundamental to his apostolic ministry but also prepares his readers for his interpretation of his sufferings in 4.8-12. Grounded in the story of Jesus, Paul's interpretive statements can be seen in three aspects – in relation to himself, to his mission theology and to the Corinthians.

1. *In Relation to Paul's Understanding of His Sufferings*

a) *Antithetical Statements.* Paul's first *peristasis* catalogue in 4.8-9 consists of four pairs of balanced antitheses as seen in the following construction.

ἐν παντὶ

θλιβόμενοι	ἀλλ' οὐ	στενοχωρούμενοι,
ἀπορούμενοι	ἀλλ' οὐκ	ἐξαπορούμενοι,
διωκόμενοι	ἀλλ' οὐκ	ἐγκαταλειπόμενοι,
καταβαλλόμενοι	ἀλλ' οὐκ	ἀπολλύμενοι

i) *Stylistic Features.* Several interesting stylistic features heighten the rhetorical effects of the description of Paul's suffering. First, these antitheses are parallels, and each pair consists of two participles separated by ἀλλά and the negating adverbial modifier οὐ(κ).[25] This gives the effect that the first set of participles highlights Paul's apostolic suffering while the second set demonstrates the reversal of the anticipated consequences of the first. Second, grammatically these participles most likely function as indicative where they are syntactically absolute.[26] Third, each of these four antitheses is an asyndeton, a stylistic and rhetorical feature that generates the element of surprise in the readers.[27] Finally,

---

25. The second set of participial clauses is negated by οὐκ, instead of the usual μή. In this context, οὐκ negates the single concept of Paul's sufferings contained within these parallel clauses. See Harris, *Second Corinthians*, 342–3.

26. Harris, *Second Corinthians*, 342; Thrall, *II Corinthians*, 1:326. Contra Byrnes, *Conformation to the Death of Christ*, 53, who takes the participles as subordinate to the main verb ἔχομεν in 4.7.

27. For further discussion on the effects of asyndeton see Aida Besançon Spencer, *Paul's Literary Style: A Stylistic and Historical Comparison of II Corinthians 11:16–12:13, Romans*

since all of these participial clauses are constructed in the present tense, they not only indicate the present reality of Paul's hardship but also, coupled with the stylistic feature of asyndeton, they would have caused the Corinthians to be amazed at God's power working in Paul. Taken together, their cumulative effect of surprise would have been heightened. Despite Paul's being constantly afflicted, perplexed, persecuted and struck down, God's power is, at the same time, working in him so that he is not crushed, driven to despair, forsaken or destroyed. The emphasis here is not merely on Paul's survival but on a wider divine purpose where sufferings do not impede his apostolic mission. On the contrary, they serve to advance his mission.

ii) *The Reality of Paul's Sufferings.* Most interpreters syntactically relate Paul's *peristasis* catalogue to his earlier thesis statement in 4.7, arguing on the basis of God's power sustaining Paul in his hardships. While this is no doubt right, it does not provide the overall picture of Paul's train of thought. What most commentators miss is that Paul's list of sufferings is not only connected to 4.7 but also syntactically connected to the interpretive statement in 4.10, as is evident in the following participial clause, πάντοτε τὴν νέκρωσιν τοῦ Ἰησοῦ ἐν τῷ σώματι περιφέροντες.[28] The starting point for understanding Paul's flow of thought is not to see the catalogue of sufferings of 4.8-9 merely in relation to 4.7, but to see it in relation to 4.10-12, and then see how this entire passage of 4.8-12 relates to Paul's thesis statement in 4.7.

The *peristasis* catalogue begins with the prepositional phrase, ἐν παντί. It is placed in the beginning of 4.8 for emphasis and should be taken as modifying all the four participial clauses rather than merely the first participial clause.[29] It can be rendered locally (i.e., on every side, in every way, as in most translations)[30] or temporally (i.e., always, at all times).[31] If we take both

8:9-39 and Philippians 3:2–4:13 (Lanham: University of America Press, 1998), 34–7, 282–3; Eberhard W. Guting and David L. Mealand, *Asyndeton in Paul: A Text-Critical and Statistical Enquiry into Pauline Style*, SBEC 39 (Lewiston: Queenston, 1998), 1–23.

28. While 2 Cor. 4.8-9 comprises a series of participial clauses, they are syntactically absolute, functioning as indicative. However, in 4.10, the participle περιφέροντες most likely functions temporally as indicated by the adverbial modifier πάντοτε and is subordinated to the participial clauses in 4.8-9.

29. So Byrnes, *Conformation to the Death of Christ*, 55; Garland, *2 Corinthians*, 228; Lambrecht, *Second Corinthians*, 72; Thrall, *II Corinthians*, I:327. However, this nuance is not captured by most translations, giving the impression that ἐν παντί only modifies the first participle (e.g., NIV: 'We are hard pressed on every side, but not crushed').

30. Byrnes, *Conformation to the Death of Christ*, 55; Savage, *Power through Weakness*, 169; Thrall, *II Corinthians*, I:327. However, note the mistranslation of TEV: 'We are *often* troubled, but not crushed, *sometimes* in doubt, but never in despair.' See the critique by Roger L. Omanson and John Ellington, *A Handbook on Paul's Second Letter to the Corinthians* (New York: United Bible Societies, 1993), 79.

31. Bultmann, *Second Corinthians*, 113, correctly emphasizes that 'the temporal aspect in the ἐν παντί is thus dominant'.

the πάντοτε in 4.10 and ἀεί in 4.11 as functioning temporally (as reflected in the translation 'always' and 'constantly' respectively), this strongly indicates that Paul's train of thought is directed towards the constant nature of his afflictions. It also serves to reinforce the idea of the continuous reality of his sufferings as reflected in all the present participles in 4.8-9. As such, the evidence seems to favour ἐν παντὶ in 4.8 as functioning in the temporal sense.[32]

In speaking of the reality of his suffering, Paul is not minimizing the effects of the hardships on him, nor does he suggest that the power of God negates the hardships imposed on him. As mentioned earlier, the cumulative effect of the asyndetic construction in 4.8-9 is to highlight the element of surprise. Anyone reading the experience of Paul as recounted in the first set of antitheses would have anticipated him to have succumbed completely to the devastating adversities he faced. But the opposite is true. The afflictions were real, but they were not mortal; perplexity was certain but Paul was not completely lost; persecutions were daily occurrences, but God did not abandon his servant; the most overwhelming forces may have knocked Paul down, but they were not fatal.

Therefore, these four antitheses do not serve to highlight Paul's virtuous character, his self-sufficiency or his steadfast courage amid adversity,[33] or even his endurance in the midst of hardships.[34] Nor do they merely demonstrate the power of God in rescuing Paul from the hardships.[35] God's power is not divine power revealing itself as weakness and thereby replacing human weakness, but divine empowerment experienced by Paul in his weakness so that he is able to continue his missionary activities and to serve as a living embodiment of the story of Jesus in the manifestation of the resurrection power of God. The very reason that Paul is ἀλλ᾽ οὐ στενοχωρούμενοι ... ἀλλ᾽ οὐκ ἐξαπορούμενοι ... ἀλλ᾽ οὐκ ἐγκαταλειπόμενοι ... ἀλλ᾽ οὐκ ἀπολλύμενοι is that these hardships fail to impede the progress of the proclamation of the gospel. As Paul would have subsequently made it clear, suffering can be a vehicle that God can use to bring glory to himself (4.15).

As such, this catalogue strongly suggests that Paul regards suffering as intrinsic to his apostolic ministry (cf. Gal. 6.17; Acts 9.16).[36] This is further confirmed in 2 Cor. 4.10-11 where Paul explicitly connects his sufferings with the story of Jesus, a point I shall consider in greater depth in the following discussion.

---

32. See Barrett, *Second Corinthians*, 136 and 138, where he combines both local and temporal ideas.

33. This is the thesis of Fitzgerald, *Cracks in an Earthen Vessel*.

34. Schrage, 'Leid, Kreuz und Eschaton'.

35. Thrall, *II Corinthians*, I:324.

36. Harris, *Second Corinthians*, 342.

b) *The Name of Jesus*. One of the striking features of 4.10-11 is the unusually concentrated use of the absolute name of 'Jesus' without associating it with the messianic title 'Christ' or the Christological title 'Lord' within a short span of a few verses. Six of the 17 instances of 'Jesus' in Paul's writings appear within the immediate context, once each in 4.5 and 4.11 and twice each in 4.10 and 4.11.[37] Such a high concentration is found nowhere else in other Pauline letters.[38]

It has generally been noted that when Paul refers to the personal name of Jesus his emphasis is on the human identity of Jesus or the earthly Jesus.[39] While this observation is generally true, it does not give us the big picture that Paul has in mind here. Pryor's detailed analysis of the use of Jesus in Pauline writings leads him to conclude that 'where Iēsous is used absolutely, there is a clear reference to the events of his life, chiefly to his death and resurrection, and often in a confessional and kerygmatic framework'.[40] This 'confessional and kerygmatic framework' establishes Paul's use of Jesus as more than merely referring to the earthly Jesus as simply another human being. It also evokes and points to the significance of the story of Jesus as the Messiah – his faithfulness (Rom. 3.26), his sufferings (Gal. 6.17) and his salvific acts climaxing in his death and resurrection (Rom. 8.11; 10.9; 2 Cor. 4.14; 1 Thess. 1.10; 4.14). Thus it is doubtful that Paul's purpose in his frequent reference to Ἰησοῦς is to repeat the use of slogans from his opponents in order to combat the false understanding of Jesus' earthly life, as suggested by Georgi.[41] Nor is the suggestion by Denney that it is to bring consolation to Paul tenable.[42]

---

37. There is a minor textual dispute with the inclusion of κύριον in 4.14 rendering the reading τὸν κύριον Ἰησοῦν. However, strong manuscript evidence supports the shorter reading. See Bruce M. Metzger, *A Textual Commentary on the Greek New Testament*, 2nd edn (Stuttgart: United Bible Society, 1994): 510–11.

38. For the remaining 11 references to 'Jesus', see Rom. 3.26; 8.11; 10.9; 1 Cor. 12.3 (twice); 11.4; Gal. 6.17; Phil. 2.10; 1 Thess. 1.10; 4.14 (twice). In Deutero-Pauline literature, it appears only once in Eph. 4.21.

39. Murphy-O'Connor, 'Faith and Resurrection', 545–6 argues that the use of the name of Jesus is to evoke the earthly Jesus. See also his '"Another Jesus" (2 Cor. 11:4)', *RB* 97 (1990): 238–51, where he argues that the use of 'Jesus' 'carries the connotation, not only of an earthly, historical existence, but of one marked by weakness, humiliation and suffering. This is true for ... *all the instances in the Corinthian correspondence*' (248, emphasis his).

40. John W. Pryor, 'Paul's Use of Iēsous: A Clue for the Translation of Romans 3:26?', *Colloquium* 16 (1983): 31–45, quotation taken from 40–1. See also Michel Bouttier, 'La souffrance de l'apôtre: 2 Cor 4:7-18', in *The Diakonia of the Spirit (2 Co 4:7–7:4)*, ed. Lorenzo De Lorenzi, Benedictina 10 (Rome: Benedictina, 1989), 47, where the use of Jesus seems suited for kerygmatic or confessional contexts.

41. Georgi, *Opponents of Paul*, 274–5.

42. Denney, *Second Corinthians*, 164.

It is surprising that in the absolute use of Jesus in 2 Corinthians the relationship between the story of Jesus (in particular the sufferings of Jesus) and Paul's suffering has not been given adequate attention. The only possible exceptions are Lambrecht and Fitzgerald, who give a brief suggestion of this relationship without further elaboration.[43] In order to determine the function of the story of Jesus in this passage, we now turn to examine the phrase πάντοτε τὴν νέκρωσιν τοῦ Ἰησοῦ ἐν τῷ σώματι περιφέροντες.

c) *Carrying the νέκρωσις of Jesus.* I have argued earlier that it makes better sense to connect the paradoxical nature of Paul's suffering to the story of Jesus in 2 Cor. 4.10-11. Therefore, 4.10-11 is the crux of interpreting 4.7-12, the relationship of Paul's suffering and the sufferings of Christ.[44] What is clear thus far is how God's power is at work in Paul, but how the story of Jesus functions in this passage is not explicit.

There are several striking features in 4.10-11. First, the grammatical construction of this passage reveals much of Paul's understanding of his own suffering. Πάντοτε is placed at the beginning of the phrase for emphasis, strongly suggesting the temporal reference of 4.10 (see 1 Cor. 15.30; Rom. 8.36). This correlates with the prepositional phrase ἐν παντὶ in 4.8 and anticipates the emphatic adverb ἀεί at the beginning of 4.11. The participle περιφέροντες and the main verb παραδιδόμεθα in 4.10 and 11 respectively are both in the present tense. The connecting conjunction καί in the ἵνα clause of both 4.10 and 11 highlights a contemporaneous aspect between the dying of Jesus and the life of Jesus across these clauses.[45] All these features collectively point to the present, ongoing and essential characteristic of Paul's apostolic ministry. Byrnes is right to suggest that, in this respect, there is 'a kind of inevitability: apostolic preaching necessarily involves one in suffering'.[46]

It is interesting that Paul uses νέκρωσις instead of the more common θάνατος in reference to Jesus' death.[47] What then does Paul mean by τὴν νέκρωσιν τοῦ Ἰησοῦ? This phrase has been used to support various arguments such as the mystical union with Christ's suffering,[48] the imitation of Christ's

---

43. Lambrecht, *Second Corinthians*, 73, suggests that Paul presents his own suffering as a continuation of the suffering of Jesus. So Fitzgerald, *Cracks in an Earthen Vessel*, 176.

44. Mak, '2 Corinthians 4:7-12', 124.

45. Byrnes, *Conformation to the Death of Christ*, 62.

46. Byrnes, *Conformation to the Death of Christ*, 63. Cf. Savage, *Power through Weakness*, 181.

47. Νέκρωσις appears only once elsewhere in Rom. 4.19. Colin G. Kruse, *The Second Epistle of Paul to the Corinthians: An Introduction and Commentary*, TNTC (Leicester: InterVarsity, 1987), 107, suggests that the use of νέκρωσις should be taken as 'stylistic rather than substantial'. Kruse's position is debatable in view of the discussion below.

48. Proodfoot, 'Imitation or Realistic Participation', 156. So Plummer, *Second Epistle*, 130.

suffering,[49] the epiphany of Christ in Paul's weakness,[50] the power of the old aeon at work in Paul,[51] and the extension of the sufferings of Christ.[52]

The word νέκρωσις can either denote: (1) death as a process, putting to death; or (2) cessation of a state or activity, state of deadness.[53] Applied to 4.10, the former can be rendered as either the process of putting to death or the process of the dying of Jesus and is usually translated as 'dying of Jesus'.[54] The latter can be taken to signify Jesus' state of deadness, and is usually translated as 'death of Jesus'.[55]

As we have highlighted above, since Paul has in mind the present, ongoing and essential characteristic of his apostolic ministry (as established by the use of the present περιφέροντες[56] and the prominent placement of πάντοτε at the beginning of the clause), it would be 'bizarre, to say the least, for Paul to claim that he always carried about Jesus' "state of being dead"'.[57] As such, the first reading, the process of dying, is to be preferred.[58] This reading is also in tandem with Paul's earlier declaration to the Corinthians in 1 Cor. 15.31: 'I die every day'. Moffatt captures this well: 'wherever I go, I am being killed in the body as Jesus was'.

---

49. Lambrecht, '*Nekrōsis* of Jesus', 137–40, sees both categories of ontological union (i.e. mystical union) and imitation at work in this passage.

50. Erhardt Güttgemanns, *Der leidende Apostel und sein Herr: Studien zur paulinischen Christologie*, FRLANT 90 (Göttingen: Vandenhoeck & Ruprecht, 1966), 122–3.

51. Tannehill, *Dying and Rising*, 85–6. Tannehill's reading appears to depend on Rom. 5.12-21 instead of 2 Cor. 4.10. See the critique by Stegman, *Character of Jesus*, 148 n. 408; and Mak, '2 Corinthians 4:7-12', 125.

52. Byrnes, *Conformation to the Death of Christ*, 64.

53. BDAG, s.v. See also Fitzgerald's analysis of νέκρωσις in *Cracks in an Earthen Vessel*, 177–80.

54. E.g., NASB, 'always carrying about in the body the dying of Jesus'. Cf. KJV and NKJV. See also Barrett, *Second Corinthians*, 139–40; Harris, *Second Corinthians*, 346; Lambrecht, '*Nekrōsis* of Jesus'; Martin, *2 Corinthians*, 87; McCant, *2 Corinthians*, 45; Stegman, *Character of Jesus*, 147–8; Witherington, *Conflict and Community in Corinth*, 387.

55. E.g., RSV, 'always carrying in the body the death of Jesus'. Cf. NRSV, NIV, and JB. See also Ahern, 'Fellowship of His Sufferings', 22; Collange, *Enigmes*, 154–5; Güttgemanns, *Der leidende Apostel*, 114–17; Tannehill, *Dying and Rising*, 85–90; Thrall, *II Corinthians*, I:331–2.

56. Plummer, *Second Epistle*, 131, suggests that περιφέροντες alludes to Paul's missionary activities. So Furnish, *II Corinthians*, 255; Schrage, 'Leid, Kreuz und Eschaton', 158 n. 44. This suggestion is doubtful as it appears to overload the term.

57. Stegman, *Character of Jesus*, 148. See also Omanson and Ellington, *Handbook*, 80, where it is impossible to have death as the grammatical object of the participle περιφέροντες.

58. Byrnes, *Conformation to the Death of Christ*, 64, suggests that there is a need to hold both aspects of dying and death in balanced tension. As such, he sees τὴν νέκρωσιν τοῦ Ἰησοῦ as 'a subjective participation in the death of Jesus and an objective proclamation of that death'. So Fitzgerald, *Cracks in an Earthen Vessel*, 177–80.

Paul's expression πάντοτε τὴν νέκρωσιν τοῦ Ἰησοῦ ἐν τῷ σώματι περιφέροντες can be understood on two levels.[59] The first level is the experiential level where Paul uses this phrase to interpret his ongoing experiences of being afflicted, perplexed, persecuted and struck down, as highlighted in 4.8-9. There is no doubt that Paul has in mind the reality of the constant sufferings and persecutions that are inherent in his apostolic ministry. The point that Paul seems to emphasize strongly is that he draws upon the story of Jesus in his understanding of his apostolic existence. By comparing his own ongoing suffering with the νέκρωσις of Jesus, Paul seems to view the putting to death of Jesus as including his whole life,[60] rather than merely the passion and crucifixion, as our reading of 1.5 in Chapter 3 demonstrates.[61] As such, Paul would have viewed the 'whole course of Jesus' life as a "dying", a being given up to death, just as he is thinking of the whole of the apostolic life in that way'.[62] For Paul, it is the entire incarnate life of Jesus, and not just the crucifixion, that becomes God's redemptive activity.[63] While the event of the cross no doubt takes centre stage, Paul seems constantly to have the whole course of the life of Jesus in view. This is in agreement with Paul's earlier declaration to the Corinthians that he is determined 'to know nothing among you except Jesus Christ, *and* him crucified' (1 Cor. 2.2; cf. Phil. 3.10). The language here also echoes the narrative pattern of the crucified Christ as seen in Gal. 2.20.[64]

At the same time, by declaring that he always carries in his body the νέκρωσις of Jesus, Paul also understands his suffering as an outward and visual proclamation of that death. This is the second level. For Paul, carrying the νέκρωσις of Jesus is a reality that has a revelatory character, as suggested by Güttgemanns.[65]

---

59. Byrnes, *Conformation to the Death of Christ*, 66–7. See also Thrall, *II Corinthians*, I:334–5.

60. Belleville, *2 Corinthians*, 122, rightly suggests that Paul has in mind 'the hardships, troubles and frustrations that Jesus faced during his ... ministry – the loneliness, the disappointments with his disciples, the exhaustion, the constant harassments by opponents, the crowd's continuous demands, the incredulity of his family, the mocking and jeers of his foes, the flight of his friends, the hours on the cross, the thirst and then the end'. Cf. Harvey, *Renewal through Suffering*, 59; Brondos, *Paul on the Cross*, 172–3.

61. Byrnes, *Conformation to the Death of Christ*, 63, narrowly suggests that τὴν νέκρωσιν τοῦ Ἰησοῦ is Paul's identification with the process of Jesus' passion and death. See also H. L. Goudge, *The Second Epistle to the Corinthians*, WC (London: Methuen, 1927), 41; Savage, *Power through Weakness*, 174–5.

62. Furnish, *II Corinthians*, 283. Cf. Barrett, *Second Corinthians*, 139–40; Stegman, *Character of Jesus*, 148; Plummer, *Second Epistle*, 130.

63. See Brondos, *Paul on the Cross*, 76–7.

64. See also the discussion by Gorman, *Cruciformity*, 285.

65. Güttgemanns, *Der leidende Apostel*, 106–23. However, I disagree with Güttgemanns' view that Paul's paradox is to be seen in an absolute sense in which Paul's suffering becomes the literal epiphany of the risen Christ. Against Güttgemanns, Lambrecht has emphasized that Paul's paradoxical language intends to be provocative and not literal (see his '*Nekrōsis* of Jesus', 128–32). In addition, see also the critique by Kaithakotill, 'Death in Us', 455.

The sufferings he endures are a 'reiteration of the suffering of Jesus – God's saving activity – carried around and displayed for the salvation of humanity'.[66] It is precisely in this manner that Paul's ministry exhibits the paradox between weakness and power and lowliness and exaltation that is found in the story of Jesus; and this is the very message about Christ crucified that Paul proclaims to the Corinthians (1 Cor. 1.23). For Paul, suffering not only accompanies his proclamation of the gospel but also *is* a proclamation of the gospel. 'The *con-veyer* of the message pictures the *content* of the message.'[67] As such, Furnish is right to suggest that 2 Cor. 4.10a is Paul's 'theological resumé' where sufferings are not merely casual happenings but are 'the essential and continuing characteristic of apostolic service'.[68]

d) *Manifesting the ζωή of Jesus*. In 2 Cor. 4.10a and 4.11a, Paul clearly under-scores the common purpose (as demonstrated by the ἵνα clauses) for his τὴν νέκρωσιν τοῦ Ἰησοῦ ἐν τῷ σώματι περιφέροντες (4.10a) and his εἰς θάνατον παραδιδόμεθα διὰ Ἰησοῦν (4.11a) is that ἡ ζωὴ τοῦ Ἰησοῦ, might be φανερωθῇ.[69]

To what then does ἡ ζωὴ τοῦ Ἰησοῦ refer? This has been interpreted either existentially or eschatologically. Murphy-O'Connor has vigorously defended the understanding of ἡ ζωὴ τοῦ Ἰησοῦ in the existential sense as a mode of human existence.[70] He argues that, in using the phrase 'life of Jesus', Paul is evoking the same existential life that was in the earthly Jesus.[71] This position has been rightly critiqued by Lambrecht.[72] The major problem with Murphy-O'Connor's interpretation is that he reduces the notion of eschatological life completely to a future reality. This position seems unbalanced. Paul elsewhere speaks of the eschatological life both in terms of the present (1.20; 3.18) and future reality (4.14; 5.1-10). As I have argued in Chapter 3, for Paul the decisive eschatological event has been inaugurated by the Christ-event, and the period

66. Duff, 'Apostolic Suffering', 162. While I basically agree with Duff that Paul's sufferings are revelatory, I differ from his understanding that the νέκρωσις of Jesus is the sacred object carried in an earthen vessel used in a Greco-Roman epiphany procession.

67. Plummer, *Paul's Understanding*, 130.

68. Furnish, *II Corinthians*, 283. Cf. Gorman, *Cruciformity*, 285–8.

69. Note that the use of φανερωθῇ in 4.11b and 4.12b echoes τὴν ὀσμὴν τῆς γνώσεως αὐτοῦ φανεροῦντι δι' ἡμῶν ἐν παντὶ τόπῳ in 2.14. See the discussion on the notion of 'being handed over' below.

70. Murphy-O'Connor, 'Faith and Resurrection'. See also his *Theology of the Second Letter to the Corinthians* (Cambridge: Cambridge University Press, 1991), 46–8. 'This is certainly an accurate description of the consistent attitude both of the historical Jesus and Paul' (quotation from 47).

71. Murphy-O'Connor, 'Faith and Resurrection', 545–6.

72. Lambrecht, 'Eschatological Outlook in 2 Cor 4:7-15'. Cf. Stegman, *Character of Jesus*, 151–2 n. 416. See also Gordon D. Fee, *God's Empowering Presence: The Holy Spirit in the Letters of Paul* (Peabody: Hendrickson, 1994), 323 n. 118, who suggests that if Jesus' earthly life is in view the proper term to use is βίος and not ζωή.

between the Christ-event and the future Coming of Christ should be rightly seen
as the eschatological age. The inaugurated eschatology, the 'now-and-not-yet'
understanding, would dictate that we be careful in making such a strict distinction between the existential and eschatological-as-future event argument, which
is best avoided.[73] Instead, ἡ ζωὴ τοῦ Ἰησοῦ in both 4.10b and 4.11b refers to
the resurrected life of Jesus, not the earthly life of Jesus.[74] It is the power of
the risen Jesus that enables Paul to live in the present life, and this power corresponds with what Paul has earlier identified in 4.7 as the all-surpassing power
of God.[75]

In what manner can ἡ ζωὴ τοῦ Ἰησοῦ be made manifest in Paul? This power
is explicitly said to be at work ἐν τῷ σώματι and ἐν τῇ θνητῇ σαρκὶ (4.10-11;
cf. ἐν ὀστρακίνοις σκεύεσιν in 4.7) of Paul through his sufferings. It is this
power that enables Paul to live a life after the manner of Jesus as described in
4.8-9 and, as such, manifest the power of the resurrection at work in him in the
present (cf. 4.7).[76]

Still, there is another question that is left unanswered. Why is Paul so concerned about the manifestation of the life of Jesus in that he repeats this as
the purpose of his suffering twice, in 4.10 and 4.11? At one level, as I have
indicated above, it is to demonstrate God's power at work in him through his
sufferings. But, at a deeper level, Paul wants the Corinthians fully to comprehend that his apostolic life experiences mirror the message of the gospel
that centres on the death and resurrection of Christ. Paul is emphasizing here
that the life of Jesus can only be fully manifested against the background
of death, as demonstrated in the order of words used where there is death
first, then only life. This indicates that Paul has the story of Jesus in mind
and the ζωὴ τοῦ Ἰησοῦ can only be made manifest by Paul incarnating Jesus'

---

73. Byrnes proposes that Paul presents 4.7-12 as his existential argument, 4.13-14 as eschatological argument, and returns to 4.15 as existential argument (*Conformation to the Death of
Christ*, 45–99). In view of my discussion, a caveat on Byrnes's analysis needs to be placed. For
further discussion on the 'now' and 'future' argument of Paul in 2 Corinthians, see John Koenig,
'The Knowing of Glory and Its Consequences (2 Corinthians 3–5)', in *The Conversation Continues: Studies in Paul and John in Honor of J. Louis Martyn*, ed. Robert T. Fortna and Beverly R.
Gaventa (Nashville: Abingdon, 1990), 158–69.

74. So Byrnes, *Conformation to the Death of Christ*, 68–9; Harris, *Second Corinthians*, 347;
Matera, *II Corinthians*, 107. However, Barrett, *Second Corinthians*, 140, argues that ἡ ζωὴ τοῦ
Ἰησοῦ refers to believers' future bodily resurrection. This is misguided.

75. So Scott, *2 Corinthians*, 105; Tannehill, *Dying and Rising*, 84–5; Thrall, *II Corinthians*,
I:225.

76. Furnish, *II Corinthians*, 256: 'The phrase as used here does not refer to the course of
Jesus' earthly life and ministry, but to the power of his resurrection life as that is manifested in the
present.' See also Savage, *Power through Weakness*, 175–7. Cf. the doubtful argument of Kaithakottil, 'Death in Us', 441, where she argues for both existential (the sufferings of the earthly
Jesus) and eschatological (the resurrection life of Jesus) experience. This appears to overload the
phrase ζωὴ τοῦ Ἰησοῦ.

self-emptying mode of existence, a manner of living that brings life to others (4.12; cf. Phil. 2.5-11; 3.10).[77] Paul cannot manifest the ζωή of Jesus apart from carrying the νέκρωσις of Jesus.

Hence, the thesis that Paul's apostolic suffering is grounded in the story of Jesus and his suffering as an essential constituent part of his apostolic ministry is reinforced. Through his hardships, Paul demonstrates that he is the living manifestation and public demonstration of the gospel, the revelation of Jesus Christ who was crucified and raised to life. This paradigm of the gospel is clearly visible to the Corinthians.

e) *Being Handed Over, παραδίδωμι, on Account of Jesus.* In 2 Cor. 4.11a, Paul declares, ἀεὶ γὰρ ἡμεῖς οἱ ζῶντες εἰς θάνατον παραδιδόμεθα διὰ 'Ιησοῦν. While 4.11 begins a new sentence, it supports and joins 4.10 as indicated by the postpositive γάρ. It has generally been noted that 4.10 and 4.11 are parallel in both structure and thought.[78] Both begin with an adverb in the prominent position emphasizing the temporal notion of 'always', a reference related to death in Paul and an allusion to the story of Jesus. But at the same time, the differences of these two verses should also be given due attention, as indicated below.

[10] πάντοτε τὴν <u>νέκρωσιν</u> τοῦ 'Ιησοῦ   ἐν τῷ σώματι   <u>περιφέροντες,</u>
      ἵνα καὶ ἡ ζωὴ τοῦ 'Ιησοῦ   <u>ἐν τῷ σώματι ἡμῶν</u> φανερωθῇ.

[11] ἀεὶ γὰρ <u>ἡμεῖς οἱ ζῶντες</u>   εἰς <u>θάνατον</u>   <u>παραδιδόμεθα διὰ 'Ιησοῦν,</u>
      ἵνα καὶ ἡ ζωὴ τοῦ 'Ιησοῦ   φανερωθῇ <u>ἐν τῇ θνητῇ σαρκὶ ἡμῶν.</u>

First, in 4.10, Paul declares that τὴν νέκρωσιν τοῦ 'Ιησοῦ ... περιφέροντες while in 4.11a Paul describes himself as εἰς θάνατον παραδιδόμεθα διὰ 'Ιησοῦν. Second, while both verses make reference to death, as I have indicated earlier, νέκρωσις in 4.10 and θάνατος in 4.11 carry different nuances. Third, in 4.11, there is the added emphasis on the subject of the participle οἱ ζῶντες as demonstrated by the presence of the first personal plural pronoun ἡμεῖς. Fourth, in the ἵνα clause of 4.11, instead of using the phrase ἐν τῷ σώματι ἡμῶν as in 4.10, Paul changes it to ἐν τῇ θνητῇ σαρκὶ ἡμῶν. Finally, the most significant difference is the actions of Paul in these two verses. In 4.10, Paul is said to be involved in the *active action of carrying in the body the dying of Jesus*, while in 4.11 he is engaged in the *passive action of being handed over to death on account of Jesus*. This significant difference of the active and passive actions in 4.10 and 11 has been almost completely missed by commentators. As such,

77. Cf. Garland, *2 Corinthians*, 219: 'Paul reads the cross into all his experiences and interprets the ups and downs of his ministry theologically as carrying around in his body the death of Jesus to manifest the life (the resurrection) of Jesus.'

78. Harris, *Second Corinthians*, 346, describes these two verses as 'precise parallelism'. So Fitzgerald, *Cracks in an Earthen Vessel*, 180; Thrall, *II Corinthians*, I:336.

while both 4.10 and 4.11 may at the first glance appear to be parallel, close scrutiny reveals that they are not exact parallels.

The syntax of 4.11a is striking. The presence of the personal pronoun, ἡμεῖς, as the subject for the substantive participle οἱ ζῶντες places additional emphasis on Paul as the one being given over to death. This participle does not merely refer to the physical life, emphasizing contrast between life and death. It most likely also indicates the kind of life lived by Paul that serves as an embodiment of the self-emptying life of Jesus who died so that others might live.

It is significant that Paul should use the terminology παραδίδωμι in the passive voice.[79] Paul's usage of this word elsewhere strongly suggests that he is aware of the tradition of Jesus being handed over to death.[80] In 1 Cor. 11.23, Paul indicates that he has clearly passed on the tradition of the story of Jesus in the Lord's Supper to them (cf. ἐν τῇ νυκτὶ ᾗ παρεδίδετο). In Rom. 4.25, Paul again evokes the tradition of the story of Jesus as ὃς παρεδόθη διὰ τὰ παραπτώματα ἡμῶν καὶ ἠγέρθη διὰ τὴν δικαίωσιν ἡμῶν. Then in Rom. 8.32, Paul declares τοῦ ἰδίου υἱοῦ οὐκ ἐφείσατο ἀλλὰ ὑπὲρ ἡμῶν πάντων παρέδωκεν αὐτόν.

It is interesting to note that only in Rom. 8.32 does Paul name the agent or subject of the act of παραδίδωμι as God. Elsewhere, the agent who handed over Jesus is not identified.[81] However, in Gal. 2.20, where the active voice of παραδίδωμι is used, Paul interestingly names Jesus as the subject of the verb in a reflexive sense where the active act of Jesus giving up himself is seen as an act of love: τοῦ ἀγαπήσαντός με καὶ παραδόντος ἑαυτὸν ὑπὲρ ἐμοῦ.[82]

---

79. Contra the questionable suggestion of the use of middle voice by Fitzgerald, *Cracks in an Earthen Vessel*, 180.

80. Byrnes, *Conformation to the Death of Christ*, 73–4; Lambrecht, *Second Corinthians*, 73; Martin, *2 Corinthians*, 88. Contra Furnish, *II Corinthians*, 256–67, where παραδίδωμι does not necessarily carry the technical sense of the handing over of Jesus. Cf. Mak's argument against the synoptic tradition ('2 Corinthians 4:7-12', 129–31). However, the evidence in support of the relationship with the Passion seems to be overwhelming, particularly within the context of 2 Cor. 4 where it has to do with Paul's sufferings and the death and resurrection of Christ. So McCant, *2 Corinthians*, 45; Matera, *II Corinthians*, 111.

81. In 1 Cor. 11.23 almost all translations render παρεδίδετο as 'betrayed', suggesting Judas as the implied agent (e.g., ESV, KJV, NASB, NIV, NRSV and RSV). BBE even names Judas as the agent. See Gordon D. Fee, *The First Epistle to the Corinthians*, NICNT (Grand Rapids: Eerdmans, 1987), 549, where the 'treachery of Judas' is the primary sense here. However, in line with the tradition used in Rom. 4.35 and 8.32, it makes better sense to translate παρεδίδετο as 'handed over' with God as the implied agent. See Raymond F. Collins, *First Corinthians*, SP (Collegeville: Liturgical, 1999), 431; C. K. Barrett, *The First Epistle to the Corinthians*, BNTC, 2nd edn (London: A. & C. Black, 1992), 266; Richard B. Hays. *First Corinthians*, IBC (Louisville: John Knox Press, 1997), 198. Cf. the translations of NAB ('handed over').

82. Cf. Eph. 5.2, 25. For other passages where other variants of παραδίδωμι are used, see Gal. 1.4; 1 Tim. 2.6; Tit. 2.14. See also *1 Clem.* 21.6; 49.6.

All the above passages highlight one common theme whenever παραδίδωμι is used: the death of Jesus is to be understood as a narrative of selfless love in giving up himself for others.[83] Thus, grounded in the story of Jesus, it is this same love that motivates Paul in his experience of apostolic suffering, 'For the love of Christ urges us on, because we are convinced that one has died for all; therefore all have died' (2 Cor. 5.14).[84]

As I have drawn attention to the passive action of Paul in 4.11, who then is the agent of παραδιδόμεθα, the one who handed Paul over? It makes good sense to take this as a divine passive with God as the agent who hands Paul over to death, as in the tradition of Jesus being handed over to death.[85] This corresponds with Paul's earlier statement to the Corinthians: 'For I think that *God* has exhibited us apostles as last of all, as though sentenced to death, because we have become a spectacle to the world, to angels and to mortals' (1 Cor. 4.9; cf. Phil. 1.29-30).

At the same time, it is highly possible that Paul may have alluded to LXX Isa. 53.12 as spelled out below.[86] This is not surprising since the Isaianic context is significantly mirrored in Paul's wider argument.[87]

διὰ τοῦτο αὐτὸς κληρονομήσει πολλοὺς καὶ τῶν ἰσχυρῶν μεριεῖ σκῦλα ἀνθ' ὧν παρεδόθη εἰς θάνατον ἡ ψυχὴ αὐτοῦ καὶ ἐν τοῖς ἀνόμοις ἐλογίσθη καὶ αὐτὸς ἁμαρτίας πολλῶν ἀνήνεγκεν καὶ διὰ τὰς ἁμαρτίας αὐτῶν <u>παρεδόθη</u>

---

83. For further treatment on Paul's use of παραδίδωμι, see Victor Paul Furnish, '"He Gave Himself (Was Given) Up ..."': Paul's Use of a Christological Assertion', in *The Future of Christology: Essays in Honor of Leander E. Keck*, ed. Abraham J. Malherbe and Wayne A. Meeks (Minneapolis: Fortress Press, 1993), 109–21. Furnish focuses on Rom. 4.25; 8.32; Gal. 1.4; 2.20 and concludes that 'Jesus' death is to be understood as an act of utterly selfless love for others' (120). It is unfortunate that Furnish omits 2 Cor. 4.11 in his otherwise excellent treatment.

84. Cf. Grams, 'Gospel and Mission', 402: 'The mission is *motivated* by love; its *content* entails proclaiming the love of God in Jesus Christ; and it *results* in a community of love' (emphasis his).

85. Harris, *Second Corinthians*, 348. So Bouttier, 'La souffrance', 35; Byrnes, *Conformation to the Death of Christ*, 74; Hafemann, *2 Corinthians*, 184; Thrall, *II Corinthians*, 1:336. In the Passion predictions (see Mk 8.31; 9.31; 10.33-4 and parallels), παραδίδωμι underscores the tradition that Jesus was going to the cross in accordance with God's plan as revealed in the Scriptures. The OT background for this is often attributed to LXX Isa. 53 where παραδίδωμι occurs three times (once in 53.6 and twice in 53.12). The use of παραδίδωμι in the Synoptic Gospels is often in reference to Jesus' death (e.g., Mt. 10.4; 17.22; 20.18-19; 26.24-5; 27.2-4, 26; Mk 3.19; 14.10; 15.1, 10, 15; Lk. 9.44; 18.32; 20.20; 24.7).

86. Cf. Florian Wilk, 'Isaiah in 1 and 2 Corinthians', in *Isaiah in the New Testament: The New Testament and the Scriptures of Israel*, ed. Steve Moyise and Maarten J. J. Menken (New York: T&T Clark, 2005), 133–58 (149). See also Hays, *First Corinthians*, 198; Webb, *Returning Home*, 104.

87. E.g., 2 Cor. 4.3 (Isa. 53.1); 4.4 (Isa. 52.14); 4.5 (Isa. 52.11, 15); 4.9 (54.6); 5.6 (Isa. 52.13). See also 2.14 in Chapter 4. Elsewhere in Paul's writings, see Phil. 2.7 (Isa. 53.3, 11-12); Rom. 4.25 (Isa. 53.5); 1 Cor. 15.3 (Isa. 53.5-6, 8, 12); Rom. 5.15, 19 (Isa. 53.11-12); Rom. 4.24 (Isa. 53.12). Outside Pauline literature, see also Heb. 9.28 and 1 Pet. 2.21-5, which echo Isa. 53.12.

If Paul's allusion to Isa. 53.12 is correct, then this is the background against which 2 Cor. 4.11 must be understood. If Paul takes the context of Isa. 53.12 as a prophecy of Christ's suffering and its vicarious effects, it is not surprising that Paul in his identification with the role of Servant of the Lord interprets his suffering as intrinsic to his apostolic ministry, bringing its benefits to those who believe, the Corinthians.[88] As Paul views the suffering of Jesus the Messiah as part of the divine plan, so it is in his apostolic ministry.[89] It is precisely because Jesus is a suffering Messiah that Paul can claim to be a suffering apostle. By employing the traditional materials concerning the death of Jesus to interpret the significance of his apostolic suffering, Paul is placing himself within the framework of the story of Jesus (cf. Rom. 4.25). By being handed over to death, Paul participates in the pattern of Jesus giving himself in love for the sake of others.

Finally, the use of the divine passive in παραδίδωμι can be further supported by Paul's frequent use of divine passives in 4.8-9, 10-11 and 12. What has been consistent throughout is that God is seen as the acting subject through Paul as the vehicle, and the implied indirect object is without exception the Corinthians.

Following his declaration that εἰς θάνατον παραδιδόμεθα, Paul continues to express that this is done διὰ Ἰησοῦν. Διά is used in a causal sense here and signifies the reason something happens, results or exists.[90] It is usually translated 'for the sake of', 'on account of', or 'because of'. Applied to the context of 4.11, I prefer the translation 'on account of Jesus' rather than 'for the sake of Jesus' as found in most translations. This is because 'for the sake of' may denote that Paul's being handed over to death occurs for the benefit of Jesus which is alien in this context.[91]

The prepositional phrase διὰ Ἰησοῦν functions as the cause and motivational factor behind Paul's suffering.[92] Commitment to the gospel of Jesus requires that one also embraces the hardships that come with it; as Byrnes

88. Similarly, Danker, *II Corinthians*, 66, suggests that the picture of the Suffering Servant in Isaiah 53 may be in operation in Paul's thought. See also Webb, *Returning Home*, 105, and the further discussion in Chapter 6.

89. Cf. Acts 17.1-3 where Paul is said to argue from the Scriptures, 'explaining and demonstrating that the Christ had to suffer and rise again from the dead' (Acts 17.3). See also his defence before King Agrippa, 'that the Messiah must suffer, and that, by being the first to rise from the dead, he would proclaim light both to our people and to the Gentiles' (Acts 26.23).

90. BDAG, s.v. Cf. Wallace, *Greek Grammar beyond the Basics*, 369.

91. Cf. Furnish, *II Corinthians*, 267, where διὰ Ἰησοῦν is not to be understood as 'for Jesus' sake' but as 'on account of Jesus'.

92. Cf. 2 Cor. 4.5 where Paul presents himself as the Servant for the Corinthians on account of Jesus (διὰ Ἰησοῦν). See Paul's use of διὰ Ἰησοῦν or διὰ Χριστὸν elsewhere in 1 Cor. 4.10; 9.23; 2 Cor. 10.10; and Phil. 3.7-8, which are closely related to his suffering and preaching of the gospel.

rightly puts it: 'Preaching the gospel of Jesus necessarily entails suffering, and the love of Jesus motivates the apostle to give of himself the same way that Jesus did.'[93] At the same time, the prepositional phrase also serves to underscore the character of Jesus that is foundational to Paul's apostolic mission. Paul as servant of Jesus is no exception, and he must share the self-emptying character of Jesus. In this respect, Paul is motivated by the same dynamics at work in the story of Jesus which is ultimately directed towards otherness. As such, the real beneficiaries of Paul's apostolic mission are the Corinthians themselves (4.12-15; cf. 1.8-11). Therefore for Paul, εἰς θάνατον παραδιδόμεθα διὰ Ἰησοῦν clearly specifies that, grounded in the story of Jesus, Paul views his whole apostolic life as a 'life lived in service of Jesus and in conformity to the gospel'.[94] Paul's hardship is not to prove himself as a sage, to fill up the set quota of apocalyptic afflictions, or merely to establish the legitimacy of his apostleship, but as 'the sign that his life is being conformed to the pattern of Christ crucified'.[95] He is the suffering apostle of the suffering Messiah; 'like Master, like servant'.[96]

After considering how the story of Jesus functions in Paul's suffering, we now turn our attention to how this story relates to Paul's mission theology.

2. *In Relation to Paul's Mission Theology*

Second Corinthians 4.12 begins with a conjunction ὥστε that introduces the idea of consequence in the flow of Paul's thought, where the focus is on the results rather than the purpose or intention of the prior action.[97] Paul restates and sums up his earlier statements (4.7-11) by asserting that ὁ θάνατος ἐν ἡμῖν ἐνεργεῖται, ἡ δὲ ζωὴ ἐν ὑμῖν, establishing that the life that is being made operative in the Corinthians is the direct result of the apostolic activity earlier described in 4.7-11.[98]

---

93. Byrnes, *Conformation to the Death of Christ*, 75. Cf. Martin, *2 Corinthians*, 87; Stegman, *Character of Jesus*, 150; Murphy-O'Connor, *Theology*, 46.

94. Sampley, *Second Corinthians*, 81.

95. See also Nigel Watson, '"The Philosopher Should Bathe and Brush His Teeth": Congruence between Word and Deed in Graeco-Roman Philosophy and Paul's Letters to the Corinthians', *ABR* 42 (1994): 1–16 (12).

96. Barnett, *Second Epistle*, 237. Cf. Pobee's mistaken argument that Paul's use of παραδίδωμι corresponds to the exhortation to martyrdom (*Persecution and Martyrdom*, 48–9). See my critique in Chapter 1.

97. Wallace, *Greek Grammar beyond the Basics*, 673, defines ὥστε as an inferential conjunction that gives '*deduction, conclusion*, or *summary* to the preceding discussion' (emphasis his).

98. Byrnes, *Conformation to the Death of Christ*, 77; Hafemann, *2 Corinthians*, 186. Güttgemanns, *Der leidende Apostel*, 99, suggests that this is Paul's polemics directed towards his opponents. This is unlikely, as ἐν ὑμῖν, a dative of advantage, is directed towards the Corinthians.

The crux of Paul's argument in 4.12 hinges on the treatment of ἐνεργεῖται. Grammatically, ἐνεργεῖται may be interpreted as a passive (translated as 'made operative in us') or an intransitive deponent (translated as 'at work in us'). Most commentators prefer the latter position.[99] However, Furnish, following Baumert, argues persuasively that the passive form would fit the context better.[100] This reading is in accord with the other three passive verbs used earlier in 4.10-11 (φανερωθῇ [twice] and παραδιδόμεθα [once]) and flows with the following clause ἡ δὲ ζωὴ ἐν ὑμῖν, as I shall argue below.

If Furnish is right that the passive form is intended here, it gives rise to the next question: who then is the implied subject? Mak argues that there are two different agents at work in 4.12.[101] In 4.12a, the implied agents are the enemies of the gospel with reference to θάνατος; and in 4.12b, the implied agent is God in reference to ζωή. As such, Mak translates 4.12 as 'life is said to be at work among the Corinthians by the hand of God while death in Paul by the enemies of the gospel'.[102] While Mak's proposal is attractive, there is a serious grammatical flaw in his argument. Syntactically, both the phrases ὁ θάνατος ἐν ἡμῖν and ἡ ... ζωὴ ἐν ὑμῖν are subordinated to the same main verb ἐνεργεῖται. This asyndetic construction grammatically demands that the implied agent of ἐνεργεῖται in 4.12a should also be the same for 4.12b as seen below.

ὥστε	ὁ θάνατος	ἐν ἡμῖν	ἐνεργεῖται,
	ἡ δὲ ζωὴ	ἐν ὑμῖν	(ἐνεργεῖται implied)

There is good reason to see ἐνεργεῖται as a divine passive with God as the intended agent. Several lines of evidence strongly support this reading. First, since the life that Paul has in view in 4.12b is certainly the new life in Christ (cf. my earlier argument on ἡ ζωὴ τοῦ Ἰησοῦ above), and this new life that the Corinthians receive can only be from God, it is therefore appropriate to consider God as the implied agent.[103]

Second, 4.12 is a concluding statement of Paul's earlier argument on his understanding of his suffering grounded in the story of Jesus where the comparison and contrast between the notions of death and life are made. The argument that Paul seeks to establish thus far can be schematically illustrated as follows.

---

99. Barnett, *Second Epistle*, 238; Byrnes, *Conformation to the Death of Christ*, 78; Garland, *2 Corinthians*, 234; Thrall, *II Corinthians*, I:337. Cf. KJV, NASB, NIV, NKJV, NRSV and RSV.

100. Furnish, *II Corinthians*, 257. See also Baumert, *Täglich sterben und auferstehen*, 72–3, and his Excursus A, Ἐνεργεῖσθαι, 267–83.

101. Mak, '2 Corinthians 4:7-12', 131–2.

102. Mak, '2 Corinthians 4:7-12', 132.

103. Kraftchick, 'Death in Us', 176.

4.10 Always

> carrying the *dying* of Jesus in the body
>> so that
> the *life* of Jesus might be made manifest (φανερωθῇ) in our body.

4.11 For constantly

> we who are living are being handed over (παραδιδόμεθα) to *death* on account of Jesus,
>> so that
> the *life* of Jesus might be made manifest (φανερωθῇ) in our mortal flesh.

4.12 Consequently,

> *death* is made operative in us
>> but
> *life* in you.

From the above, the use of the divine passive in 4.12a would conform to the earlier divine passives φανερωθῇ and παραδιδόμεθα.

The significance of the divine passive in 4.12a is that, grounded in the story of Jesus, Paul sees God at work in his life characterized by suffering. It is through the death of Jesus that God brings new life, and as such God uses the 'dying' apostle to bring life to the Corinthians. In this respect, 4.12 powerfully underscores the missiological significance of Paul's suffering,[104] assuring Paul that his present suffering is not the final result that marks the outcome of his apostolic ministry. In contrast, with God as the implied subject of ἐνεργεῖται, apostolic sufferings are not 'liabilities' that would discount Paul's apostolic status but rather 'potential assets'[105] because they provide the occasion for the manifestation of the life of Jesus in the Corinthians. As such, apostolic suffering is a necessary element of the divine strategy in God's drama of salvation (cf. Acts 9.15-16). Just as Paul views Jesus' suffering climaxed in his death as a necessity, Paul also considers his suffering as a constituent part of his ministry.[106] The conviction of seeing his apostolic mission bearing fruit in the formation of the Christ-believing community in Corinth remains a motivating factor for Paul in bearing his load of suffering. This makes it worthwhile to continue his apostolic ministry despite his immense sufferings and apostolic

---

104. For further discussion, see Mark J. Cartledge, 'A Model of Hermeneutical Method: An Exegetical Missiological Reflection upon Suffering in 2 Corinthians 4:7-15', *ERT* 17 (1993): 472–83.

105. Pickett, *Cross in Corinth*, 135.

106. *Pace* Charles B. Cousar, 'Paul and the Death of Jesus', *Int* 52/1 (1998): 32–52 (48), who sees suffering as a *consequence* and not *constituent* of Paul's apostolic ministry.

ministry that invites little appreciation and gratitude from the Corinthians. Outwardly, Paul's apostolic mission seems to be everything but successful, and discouragement seems much more of a reality (see 2 Cor. 4.1, 16). Yet, for Paul, this life of Jesus that is made available through the power of the Spirit (as in 2 Cor. 3) in the Corinthians becomes for him the fruit of his labour and the eschatological fulfilment of the Scriptures, where the ingathering of the gentiles is now a reality (cf. the discussion in Chapter 4). Bauckham articulates this well: 'If God's definitive salvific act occurred through the weakness of the crucified Jesus, then it should be no surprise that the saving gospel of the crucified Jesus should reach the Gentiles through the weakness of his apostle.'[107] As such, this passage again reinforces the thesis that Paul's suffering is intrinsic and integral to his missionary task in bringing in the gentiles to Christ. Far from impeding the progress of Paul's mission, Paul's sufferings actually enhance it.[108] Hence, the missionary motif in Paul's sufferings is now clearly established. It is through Paul's weakness that the power of Christ is particularly potent, a theme that I shall expand on in Chapter 7.

Finally, in claiming that his sufferings effect life in the Corinthians, Paul is not substituting himself or his sufferings for Christ; for Paul is aware that it was Christ who suffered and died for humanity (cf. Rom. 5.8; 1 Cor. 15.3-4; 2 Cor. 5.14-15). At the same time, there is also no suggestion in Paul's argument that the Corinthians will be spared from the hardships and persecutions in following Christ because of the sufferings of Paul (cf. 2 Cor. 1.6-7).[109]

With the story of Jesus in relation to Paul's understanding of his sufferings and his mission theology established, I now turn to the final section to consider this story in relation to the Corinthians.

3. *In Relation to the Corinthians*

In 2 Cor. 4.7-11, Paul has been speaking of his apostolic suffering with the Corinthians as the background, but in 4.12 the tone shifts and the Corinthians now take centre stage. Paul changes the recipients of the manifestation of life from 'us' in 4.10-11 to 'you' in 4.12b. This makes the contrast between ἐν ἡμῖν and ἐν ὑμῖν in 4.12 even more striking and obvious: ὥστε ὁ θάνατος ἐν ἡμῖν ἐνεργεῖται, ἡ δὲ ζωὴ ἐν ὑμῖν.

This reflects the orientation of Paul's apostolic ministry. Paul's assertion in 4.12 as a conclusion of the discourse that begins in 4.7 suggests that the treasure in earthen vessels and the Christological interpretation of his sufferings are all directly oriented to the Corinthians. This is not the first time that Paul

---

107. Richard Bauckham, 'Weakness – Paul's and Ours', *Themelios* 7/3 (1982): 4–6 (5).

108. Garland, *2 Corinthians*, 219, who correctly suggests that Paul's suffering is 'part of God's design to spread the gospel'.

109. Witherington, *Conflict and Community*, 389, argues that Paul is suffering the messianic woes so that the Corinthians would suffer less. See Chapter 3 for my critique of this view.

intimates this line of thought. Earlier in 1.6-7, Paul makes clear that the ultimate beneficiaries of his apostolic suffering are the Corinthians. A similar case is also made in 2.14-16. Now, in 4.12, Paul again identifies the Corinthians as the real beneficiaries of his apostolic suffering.[110] As such, the apostolic ministry characterized by suffering is always missionary in its purpose (as indicated by ἵνα in 4.7, 10-11) and consequence (as indicated by ὥστε in 4.12). Paul's apostolic ministry characterized by suffering results in the formation of the Christ-believing community in Corinth, and through this the messenger and the community are now drawn together in a tight relationship within the dynamics of Paul's narrative.

The story of Jesus as demonstrated through the manifestation of the death and life of Jesus, which is the very essence of the gospel message that Paul is proclaiming, is to be reflected in his life as a witness of the gospel to the Corinthians. Paul has become the locus of the story of Jesus encapsulating both the dying and rising of Jesus, and it is through this that the message of the gospel of Christ crucified and risen is replicated and re-enacted in Paul's life.

Paul is not merely talking about being preserved in the midst of his hardships for the sake of his survival. Stegman interestingly suggests that Paul's ongoing experience of being preserved in the midst of suffering in and of itself does not benefit the Corinthians. What really benefits them is Paul embodying the story of Jesus for their sake.[111] This is the fundamental and crucial difference between Paul and the Hellenistic virtuous sage whose perseverance in suffering benefits and enhances his status while Paul's embodiment of the story of Jesus benefits the Corinthians.[112]

For Paul, the story of Jesus is not to be merely understood as narrative which is purely external to the Christ-believers, and one that is simply informed. Rather, the story of Jesus is the narrative of which believers became an integral part and through which the community of cruciformity is formed.[113]

This is precisely where the story of Jesus becomes normative for Paul in his life and ministry. 'To suffer for the gospel of the cross is to extend the life-giving, loving death of Jesus on that cross to those who do not yet know its benefits.'[114] Christology for Paul has a normative impact upon his life and

---

110. This is indicated by the prepositional phrase ἐν ὑμῖν functioning as dative of advantage. See Martin, *2 Corinthians*, 89. *Pace* Duff, 'Apostolic Suffering', 161, where he argues that Paul is using the description of his suffering for his advantage.

111. Stegman, *Character of Jesus*, 255. Cf. Garland, *2 Corinthians*, 234.

112. On the differences between Paul and the Hellenistic sage, see Roy A. Harrisville, *Fracture: The Cross as Irreconcilable in the Language and Thought of the Biblical Writers* (Grand Rapids: Eerdmans, 2006), 84–91; Ulrich Heckel, *Kraft in Schwachheit: Untersuchungen zu 2. Kor 10–13*, WUNT 2/56 (Tübingen: Mohr Siebeck, 1993), 279–84. See also Schrage, 'Leid, Kreuz und Eschaton', 142–60; L. E. Woods, 'St. Paul's Apostolic Weakness' (PhD dissertation, University of Manchester, Manchester, 1986), 131–2.

113. See Gorman, *Cruciformity*, 349–67; Grams, 'Gospel and Mission', 416–34.

114. Gorman, *Cruciformity*, 203.

this is reflected no more clearly than in the way the story of Jesus becomes the interpretive key to unlock his understanding of his apostolic experiences of sufferings. This story that informs Paul concerning the life of Jesus being laid down for others and for the glory of God becomes for him an anchor to his apostolic call. The self-emptying and self-sacrificial character of Jesus becomes operative in Paul's life and ministry. Through this, he proclaims the gospel and suffers for it so that the Corinthians may experience the life of Jesus and give glory to God by their thanksgiving (4.15). With this interpretation of his sufferings drawn from the story of Jesus, Paul is again inviting the Corinthians to reconsider his sufferings in the service of the gospel, not sufferings as punishment by God or sufferings as misfortune[115] but as sufferings of one who carries the reconciling power of God to the Corinthians.

As such, Paul again issues the invitation to the Corinthians to participate in the story of Jesus (4.13-15). By their participation in this story they will in turn be witnesses for the gospel to other people that will ultimately cause 'thanksgiving to overflow to the glory of God' (4.15; cf. 1.11). This is the ultimate result of the Pauline mission – that Jews and gentiles would glorify God (cf. Rom. 15.5-13) – and this coincides with the message of Deutero-Isaiah as has been earlier presented in Chapter 4.[116]

IV. *Concluding Summary*

In 2 Cor. 4.7-12, Paul gives his suffering the most profound Christological interpretation expressed in one of the sharpest and most paradoxical formulations. Paul begins this section with a thesis-like statement by declaring that the power of God is demonstrated through his weakness and suffering, and that his sufferings are not a hindrance to the progress of the gospel. Following this, Paul provides the interpretive statements grounded in the story of Jesus, and these statements can be seen in three aspects: in relation to his sufferings, in relation to his understanding of mission, and in relation to the Corinthians. Through these three aspects, Paul sees his sufferings as intrinsic and integral to his apostolic commission. He further claims that suffering has positive missiological benefits for the Corinthians where life is being awakened in those who believe his gospel. As a result, Paul once more invites the Corinthians to participate in the story of Jesus and be witnesses for the gospel.

---

115. On suffering as misfortune, see Jerome H. Neyrey, *Paul, in Other Words: A Cultural Reading of His Letters* (Louisville: Westminster/John Knox, 1990), 167–80.

116. It is surprising that this fact is almost neglected by most commentators. One possible exception is Scott, *2 Corinthians*, 106 who gives a very brief mention of the possibility of the relationship with the Deutero-Isaianic message.

Chapter 6

SECOND CORINTHIANS 6.1-10

I. *Introduction*

In this chapter, I shall investigate whether 2 Cor. 6.1-10 can further substantiate my thesis that Paul's understanding of his apostolic suffering is grounded in the story of Jesus. While most studies on this passage focus primarily on the extended hardship list in 6.3-10 and treat it as an independent unit in Paul's argument, I shall argue that it cannot be detached from the wider literary unit of 5.11–6.10. I shall also pay special attention to Paul's citation of Isa. 49.8 as the foundational key to unlock Paul's understanding of his apostolic suffering.

II. *Structure and Line of Thought*

Second Corinthians 5.11–6.10 is generally considered as a self-contained unit within the larger division of 2.14–7.4.[1] Within this unit, a concentric structure can be detected, as follows:[2]

> *a* (5.11-13) – Paul's apostolic ministry
> > *b* (5.14-21) – The rationale for Paul's apostolic ministry
> *a'* (6.1-10) – Paul's apostolic ministry

The close connection between the *a* and *a'* units can be illustrated by the first person plural appeals at the beginning of each unit (ἀνθρώπους πείθομεν in 5.11 and παρακαλοῦμεν ... ὑμᾶς in 6.1). Equally striking is that both units contain Paul's description of his apostolic experience and his attitude towards the Corinthians as seen in the use of second person plurals (a total of four times in 5.11-13 and once in 6.1). In addition, both units also share similar themes and vocabulary as indicated by ἑαυτοὺς συνιστάνομεν in 5.12 and συνιστάντες ἑαυτούς in 6.4; and διδόντες in both 5.12 and 6.3. Finally, Paul's response to

---

1. So Bultmann, *Second Corinthians*, 109–10; Harris, *Second Corinthians*, 464; Lambrecht, *Second Corinthians*, 102; Matera, *II Corinthians*, 8.

2. For similar structural outlines, cf. Lambrecht, *Second Corinthians*, 102; Chris Ukachuku Manus, 'Apostolic Suffering (2 Corinthians 6.4-10): The Sign of Christian Existence and Identity', *AJT* 1 (1987): 41–54 (42).

'those who boast in outward appearance and not in the heart' (5.12) is further elaborated through the hardship list contained in 6.4-10.

In 5.11-13, Paul begins by affirming that he is already known to God and expresses his hope that he is also known to the conscience of the Corinthians so that they may be able to answer others who question them. Paul's response to the interlocutors who seem to place much emphasis on outward appearance will be followed through subsequently in 6.1-10.

In the *b* unit, Paul grounds his apostolic ministry in the story of Jesus (5.14-21). He begins by relating God's act of redeeming and reconciling the world through Christ in a series of formulaic statements (5.14-17), followed by recounting the inauguration of his ministry of reconciliation as an ambassador of Christ (5.18-21).

Paul continues to locate his apostolic existence within God's salvation drama and in relation to the story of Jesus in *a'* (6.1-10). The participle συνεργοῦντες and the phrase τὴν χάριν τοῦ θεοῦ in 6.1 clearly point back to his earlier argument in 5.18-21.[3] At the same time, it is also worthwhile noting that apart from 5.10-13, 6.1-10 also shares similar vocabulary with 5.14-21 (παρακαλέω in 5.20 and 6.1; ἰδού in 5.17 and 6.2, 9; νῦν in 5.16 and 6.2; διακονία in 5.18 and 6.3 [cf. διάκονος in 6.4]; and δικαιοσύνη in 5.21 and 6.7). Before presenting his catalogue of suffering (6.3-10), Paul grounds his appeal in the Scriptures by quoting LXX Isa. 49.8 and providing the contemporary significance of this passage (6.2) in his apostolic ministry and suffering.

In this section, Paul's description of his suffering appears strategically towards the end of the wider unit of 5.11–6.10, further reinforcing my earlier argument that the theme of his suffering appears at crucial junctures in 2 Corinthians.[4]

III. *The Story of Jesus and Paul's Self-Commendation through Suffering in the Ministry of Reconciliation*

How does the story of Jesus function in Paul's ministry of reconciliation? How does the citation of LXX Isa. 49.8 in 2 Cor. 6.2 relate to the story of Jesus, Paul's understanding of his apostolic ministry, his suffering and his mission to the gentiles? These are the questions to which I aim to respond in this section.

A. *The Story of Jesus and Paul's Ministry of Reconciliation*

1. *Paul, the Ambassador of Christ in the Ministry of Reconciliation*
Paul categorically states that it is precisely because of the story of Jesus that God's divine plan of reconciliation can now take effect (5.18). This divine plan

---

3.   Jan Lambrecht, ' "Reconcile Yourselves ..." ': A Reading of 2 Cor. 5,11-21', in *The Diakonia of the Spirit (2 Co 4:7–7:4)*, ed. Lorenzo De Lorenzi, Benedictina 10 (Rome: Benedictina, 1989), 163–4.

4.   Cf. my earlier discussion in Chapters 3–5 of how the theme of Paul's apostolic suffering strategically appears at the beginning of a new section or unit within Paul's argument.

is spelled out in two parallel participial clauses. καταλλάξαντος ἡμᾶς ἑαυτῷ διὰ Χριστοῦ and δόντος ἡμῖν τὴν διακονίαν τῆς καταλλαγῆς. The first clause makes it clear that God reconciled Paul to himself through Christ while the second demonstrates the inauguration of the ministry of reconciliation. This divine plan is further elaborated in 5.19 on a much grander scale. While 5.18 speaks of Paul as the object of God's reconciliatory deed, 5.19 expands the scope to include the κόσμος. God is now reconciling the world to himself through Christ by entrusting the message of reconciliation to Paul. As such, Paul emphatically asserts that his apostolic ministry, grounded in the story of Jesus, is not only solidly based on divine commission but is also integral to the divine plan of salvation.

Paul's apostolic ministry is further spelt out by using political terminology in declaring that he is an ambassador (πρεσβεύομεν) for Christ (ὑπὲρ Χριστοῦ) (5.20). The word πρεσβεύω carries the meaning 'be an ambassador/envoy',[5] while the phrase ὑπὲρ Χριστοῦ in this context carries the meaning 'on behalf of Christ'.[6] An ambassador represents the political entity that commissions the person to speak and act not only on behalf of but also in place of itself.[7] As such, as an ambassador not appointed by any human authorities (cf. Gal. 1.1, 12) but by Christ himself, Paul serves as a channel for God to speak through him to the Corinthians on behalf of Christ (ὑπὲρ Χριστοῦ): 'Be reconciled to God' (5.20b). It is striking that in 5.20b, a second ὑπὲρ Χριστοῦ is used in Paul's appeal. Paul is not only an ambassador ὑπὲρ Χριστοῦ but his proclamation of the gospel is also carried out ὑπὲρ Χριστοῦ[8] and the content of Paul's gospel is the story of Jesus as expressed in 5.21.[9] This twofold use of ὑπὲρ

5.   BDAG, s.v.

6.   So Barrett, *Second Corinthians*, 178; Plummer, *Second Epistle*, 184; Scott, *2 Corinthians*, 140. Note that ὑπὲρ Χριστοῦ is placed in the beginning of 5.20 for added emphasis.

7.   Harris, *Second Corinthians*, 446, argues that the phrase includes both notions of representation, 'on behalf of Christ', and substitution, 'in the place of Christ'. So Thrall, *II Corinthians*, I:437. On the mediatorial role of ambassadors in the ancient world, see Cilliers Breytenbach, *Versöhnung: Eine Studie zur paulinischen Soteriologie*, WMANT 60 (Neukirchen-Vluyn: Neukirchener Verlag, 1989), 64–6; Margaret M. Mitchell, 'New Testament Envoys in the Context of Greco-Roman Diplomatic and Epistolary Conventions: The Example of Timothy and Titus', *JBL* 111 (1992): 641–62.

8.   Cf. 2 Cor. 12.10; Phil. 1.29. See also Eph. 3.1. Paul not only speaks but suffers as well for Christ.

9.   Second Corinthians 5.21 constitutes a statement that conforms to the traditional expectation of the Messiah as well as the description of the Suffering Servant in Isa. 53. See Beale, 'Old Testament Background'; Hafemann, *2 Corinthians*, 246–8; Harris, *Second Corinthians*, 456; Hendrikus Boers, '2 Corinthians 5:14–6:2: A Fragment of Pauline Christology', *CBQ* 64 (2002): 527–47; William H. Bellinger Jr. and William R. Farmer, eds, *Jesus and the Suffering Servant: Isaiah 53 and Christian Origins* (Harrisburg: Trinity, 1998); Bernd Janowski and Peter Stuhlmacher, eds, *The Suffering Servant: Isaiah 53 in Jewish and Christian Sources* (Grand Rapids: Eerdmans, 2004). On the striking parallels of 5.21 with Isa. 53.9-11, see W. Hulitt Gloer, *An*

Χριστοῦ is a clear indication that Paul sees his ambassadorial role as continuing the story of Jesus.[10]

2. *Paul, the Co-Worker of Jesus Christ in the Ministry of Reconciliation*

After declaring his ambassadorial role, Paul continues to assert his role by identifying himself as a co-worker (συνεργοῦντες) in the ministry of reconciliation and appealing (παρακαλοῦμεν) to the Corinthians not to accept God's grace (τὴν χάριν τοῦ θεοῦ) in vain (2 Cor. 6.1). However, there is no object immediately following συνεργοῦντες and this raises the question, 'With whom is Paul working?' Most commentators and English translations assume that Paul is a co-worker with God.[11] In favour of this reading, it is often argued that since God is the subject of παρακαλοῦντος in 5.20, God must also be in view in 6.1. Still others suggest that Paul has the Corinthians[12] or other apostles and leaders[13] in mind as his co-workers.

However, there is another possibility of seeing Paul as the co-worker of Jesus Christ.[14] Several lines of evidence support this reading. First, this makes better sense in the flow of Paul's argument since in the immediate context Paul is talking about him being the ambassador of Christ. In continuation of

---

Exegetical and Theological Study of Paul's Understanding of New Creation and Reconciliation in 2 Cor 5:14-21, MBPS 42 (Lampeter: Edwin Mellen, 1996), 155–7.

10. Stegman, *Character of Jesus*, 273.

11. So Barnett, *Second Epistle*, 316; Beale, 'Old Testament Background', 560; Belleville, *2 Corinthians*, 162; Furnish, *II Corinthians*, 341; Garland, *2 Corinthians*, 303–4; Lambrecht, 'Favourable Time', 382–3; Matera, *II Corinthians*, 149; Scott, *2 Corinthians*, 142; Thrall, *II Corinthians*, I:451. See NIV, TEV and NLT. Cf. the ambiguous translations of KJV, NKJV, RSV and NRSV which insert 'with him/Him' after συνεργοῦντες.

12. So E. B. Allo, *Saint Paul: Seconde Épître aux Corinthiens*, 2nd edn, EB (Paris: J. Gabala, 1956), 173. Cf. the translation of NAB. Sampley, *Second Corinthians*, 96, argues that Paul is both working together with God and hoping for the cooperation of the Corinthians. This view is less likely as Paul is addressing the Corinthians and not expressing his cooperation with them. In addition, whenever Paul refers to 'co-workers' he always has ministers of the gospel in mind, not his readers (e.g., Rom. 16.3, 9, 21; 1 Cor. 3.9; 2 Cor. 8.23; Phil. 2.25; 4.3; 1 Thess. 3.2; Phlm. 1, 24). See also John P. Dickson, *Mission-Commitment in Ancient Judaism and in the Pauline Communities: The Shape, Extent and Background of Early Christian Mission*, WUNT 2/159 (Tübingen: Mohr Siebeck, 2003), 86–132.

13. Cf. Bruce, *1 & 2 Corinthians*, 211.

14. H. A. W. Meyer, *Critical and Exegetical Hand-Book to the Epistles to the Corinthians* (New York: Funk and Wagnalls, 1884), 544–5; and Stegman, *Character of Jesus*, 273–4, argue for Jesus. Others like Bultmann, *Second Corinthians*, 166; Harris, *Second Corinthians*, 457; and Plummer, *Second Epistle*, 189, suggest that Jesus or Christ could be intended here. Cf. Danker, *II Corinthians*, 84, where Paul is taken to be in partnership with both God and Christ. Note Héring, *Second Corinthians*, 46, who appears to be contradictory. In his translation of 6.1, Héring explicitly states, 'As co-workers (with Christ)', but in his subsequent comments he names God as the one with whom Paul is collaborating. A similar confusion is detected in Schütz, *Paul and the Anatomy of Apostolic Authority*, 181, 205.

this argument, it would thus be fitting to see the object of συνεργοῦντες as Jesus Christ. Second, this also corresponds with Paul's subsequent appeal to the Corinthians (6.1) and this action makes sense only if we see that Paul is further carrying out his mediatorial role as an ambassador of Christ. Third, Paul appeals to the Corinthians not to receive τὴν χάριν τοῦ θεοῦ in vain. If God is the intended object of both συνεργοῦντες and τὴν χάριν, we would naturally expect the construction of the subsequent phrase to be τὴν χάριν αὐτοῦ and not τὴν χάριν τοῦ θεοῦ, as τοῦ θεοῦ would be rendered redundant.[15] The fact that God is explicitly mentioned as the object of τὴν χάριν suggests that συνεργοῦντες may have a different object in view. Finally, it is interesting to note that in Rom. 15.8 Paul attributes Christ as a διάκονος to the περιτομῆς (referring to the Jews) on behalf of the truth of God. If Christ is the διάκονος of the Jews and Paul the διάκονος (2 Cor. 6.4; cf. Rom. 15.16-17) of the gentiles, it seems logical to consider that Paul and Jesus are both at work together in bringing about the reconciliation of God for the κόσμος (5.19), comprising Jews and gentiles.

After establishing himself as a co-worker with Jesus Christ, Paul once again appeals to the Corinthians 'not to accept the grace of God in vain' (6.1).[16] But in what ways can the Corinthians be said to receive God's grace in vain? Talbert argues that it refers to the Christ-believers behaving in a manner inconsistent with their experience of grace.[17] But the problem with this position is that there is no suggestion of moral laxity or inappropriate behaviour here. More probable in this context is the Corinthians' failure to recognize Paul's apostleship for what it is – a mission from God as an ambassador of Christ in effecting reconciliation.[18] As Paul has already argued, his apostolic ministry cannot be separated from God's act of reconciliation and, as such, to reject the ambassador is to reject the one who sends him, and to renounce Paul because of his suffering is to renounce Christ, on whose behalf Paul is speaking and with whom he is working. In other words, the Corinthians are at risk of rejecting the very gospel they earlier embraced through Paul.

---

15. Cf. Stegman, *Character of Jesus*, 274.

16. Paul's earlier appeals are found in 5.11 and 5.20.

17. Charles H. Talbert, *Reading Corinthians: A Literary and Theological Commentary*, rev. edn (Macon: Smyth & Helwys, 2002), 202. Talbert's position is a reflection of the majority view. See Plummer, *Second Epistle*, 189, for a similar view that Paul is addressing those 'who were in danger of a lapse into heathen laxity' after failing to reach 'a Christian standard of holiness'. So Murphy-O'Connor, *Theology*, 63; Thrall, *II Corinthians*, I:452. Cf. Hans Windisch, *Der zweite Korintherbrief*, 9th edn, KEK (Göttingen: Vandenhoeck & Ruprecht, 1924), 200.

18. Judith M. Gundry-Volf, *Paul and Perseverance: Staying in and Falling Away*, WUNT 2/37 (Tübingen: J. C. B. Mohr, 1990), 278, maintains that the only fault of the Corinthians in this context 'has to do with resistance to the apostle'. See also her discussion on receiving God's grace in vain in 277–80. Cf. Hafemann, *2 Corinthians*, 248; Matera, *II Corinthians*, 150.

In order to drive home the point that his suffering should not be considered an offence but integral to and embedded in his calling as a servant of God (6.3-10), Paul now appeals to the Scriptures in his argument.

3. *Paul, the Servant and the Citation of Isaiah 49.8 in 2 Corinthians 6.2*

In 2 Cor. 6.2, Paul grounds the authority of his appeal to the Corinthians not to receive God's grace in vain by quoting verbatim from LXX Isa. 49.8[19] which in turn is a word-for-word translation of the MT.[20]

However, it is interesting to note that Paul's quotation of Scripture here has been neglected in the treatment of 2 Cor. 6 and this can most likely be attributed to the problems surrounding the interpretation of the Isaianic citation.[21]

a) *Problems in Interpreting the Citation of Isaiah 49.8 in 2 Corinthians 6.2.* Paul's citation of Isa. 49.8 in 2 Cor. 6.2 appears to break his flow of argument in 5.11–6.10. Grammatically in 6.3-4 Paul employs two participles (διδόντες and συνιστάντες in 6.3a and 4a respectively), and these participles are often taken to be syntactically dependent on the main verb (παρακαλοῦμεν) in 6.1a.[22] As such, this has given rise to the problems accounting for the citation of Isa. 49.8 in

19. The quotation is preceded by the introductory formula λέγει γάρ. The subject of λέγει could either be God or Scripture. In favour of the former, it is the Lord, κύριος, who speaks within the context of LXX Isa. 49.8; so Barrett, *Second Corinthians*, 183; Furnish, *II Corinthians*, 342; Harris, *Second Corinthians*, 459. However, Hughes, *Second Corinthians*, 219, makes a case for taking the Scripture as the subject of λέγει. Contra the dubious suggestion of Goudge who thinks that the subject of λέγει is the Servant, identified by Paul with the 'glorified Christ' (*Second Corinthians*, 67).

20. For a comparison between the LXX and MT of Isa. 49, see Eugene Robert Ekblad Jr., *Isaiah's Servant Poems according to the Septuagint: An Exegetical and Theological Study*, CBET 23 (Leuven: Peeters, 1999), 122–4.

21. To the best of my knowledge, apart from Lambrecht's article dealing specifically with Paul's quotation of Isa. 49.8 ('Favorable Time'), there has not been any serious attempt to locate this Isaianic citation within Paul's argument in 2 Cor. 6, particularly in the understanding of his suffering that follows in 6.3-10. In his recent work, Gignilliat's primary concern is to locate the quotation of Isaiah as the hermeneutical key to understand Paul's theological reading of the redemptive drama of Isa. 40–66, and not how the Isaiah passage influences Paul's understanding of his mission and suffering (*Paul and Isaiah's Servants*, 55–107). Sections of Gignilliat's work are earlier published with slight variations as 'A Servant Follower of the Servant: Paul's Eschatological Reading of Isaiah 40–66 in 2 Corinthians 5:14–6:10', *HBT* 26 (2004): 98–124; and '2 Corinthians 6:2'.

22. E.g., Hafemann, *Suffering and the Spirit*, 77; Lambrecht, *Second Corinthians*, 109; Plummer, *Second Epistle*, 191. Cf. Gräbe, *Power of God*, 121, who takes διδόντες as a true participle and observes that 2 Cor. 6.1-2 'seemingly does not fit well into this context'. However, these participles in 6.3a and 4a could also possibly function as absolute participles and carry the force of the indicative. So Harris, *Second Corinthians*, 468; and Furnish, *II Corinthians*, 342. If this is correct, then it is not necessary to take 6.3-10 as dependent on 6.1, and subsequently to treat 6.2 as an interpolation. But this does not mean that while 6.3-10 begins with a new sentence its thought is not related to 6.1-2, as I shall argue below.

2 Cor. 6.2 that appears to be interjected between 6.1 and 6.3-4. This difficulty is reflected in the first and second editions of UBS Greek text which frame 6.2 with dashes, giving a strong impression of the parenthetical nature of Paul's Isaianic citation.[23] The translations of KJV, BBE, ASV and Moffatt also place the Isaianic citation in brackets while NASB puts it in dashes, further reinforcing this impression.

Most commentators regard Paul's Isaianic citation as an interruption. Plummer suggests that it can be considered as equivalent to the modern-day 'foot-note' because Paul 'remembers an OT saying which will drive home' his point and, as such, he inserts it into his argument.[24] This view is also echoed by Harvey, who takes the Isaianic quotation to be 'simply a preacher's gambit for stressing the urgency of the appeal'.[25] Therefore, Martin unsurprisingly concludes that the Isaianic quotation results in 'breaking Paul's train of thought'.[26] Similarly, others claim that Paul's quotation not only 'does not fit well into' the context of his argument in light of the catalogue of sufferings that follows in 6.3-10,[27] but is also done 'without regard to its original application'.[28] Still others dismiss any significance of Paul's citation of Scripture in his argument. This is reflected in Christopher Stanley's work where he argues that all of Paul's citations of Scripture in 2 Corinthians, including 6.2, do not play 'a significant role in his argumentation' as far as Paul's apostolic authority is concerned.[29]

---

23. It is interesting to note that subsequent third and fourth editions of UBS Greek text omit the dashes.

24. Plummer, *Second Epistle*, 190. Danker, *II Corinthians*, 85, also picks up the 'footnote' idea. However, note A. T. Hanson's critique of Plummer's view as an 'artless suggestion' (*Jesus Christ in the Old Testament* [London: SPCK, 1965], 151).

25. Harvey, *Renewal in Suffering*, 74. See also those who consider the Isaianic citation as either a parenthesis or interpolation: Harris, *Second Corinthians*, 459; Hughes, *Second Corinthians*, 219, 221; R. V. G. Tasker, *The Second Epistle of Paul to the Corinthians: An Introduction and Commentary*, TNTC (London: Tyndale Press, 1958), 92.

26. Martin, *2 Corinthians*, 160, 167. Cf. R. H. Strachan, *The Second Epistle of Paul to the Corinthians*, MNTC (London: Hodder & Stoughton, 1935), 123, who maintains that the connection between 6.2 and 6.3 'is not at once obvious'.

27. Gräbe, *Power of God*, 121.

28. Hodge, *Second Corinthians*, 155. So Denney, *Second Corinthians*, 228.

29. Christopher D. Stanley, *Arguing with Scripture: The Rhetoric of Quotations in the Letters of Paul* (New York: T&T Clark, 2004), 97–8. Stanley identifies the OT quotations in 4.6, 13; 6.2; 8.15; 9.9; and possibly in 10.17. Cf. D. Moody Smith who holds that, in comparison to Romans, Galatians and to a certain extent 1 Corinthians, Paul's use of the OT in 2 Corinthians is 'if anything more incidental, and even casual ... and the use of Scripture is not basic to Paul's argument' ('The Pauline Literature', in *It Is Written: Scripture Citing Scripture: Essays in Honour of Barnabas Lindars*, ed. D. A. Carson and H. G. M. Williamson [Cambridge: Cambridge University Press, 1988], 265–91 [275]).

As such, it is not surprising that most commentators fail to pay serious attention to Paul's quotation of Isa. 49.[30] How Paul's quotation of Isa. 49.8 functions within the wider context of his ministry of reconciliation and apostolic suffering is almost completely ignored. A good example is Hafemann's extensive study on Paul's suffering and use of the OT in 2 Corinthians, where he merely acknowledges the Isaianic quotation without further elaboration on its significance in Paul's thought.[31] This omission is striking as Hafemann has strongly argued that Paul's use of Scripture centres around the traditions associated with the exodus (as evidenced in Paul's frequent use of Exodus and Deuteronomy) and the prophetic hope of the new covenant/new exodus/new creation motifs (as supported by the frequent allusion to and citations of Deutero-Isaiah and Jeremiah).[32] Hafemann's tabulation of OT allusions and quotations in 2 Cor. 1–9 clearly demonstrates that the influence of the OT in Paul's thought is not only impressive but is also an indication of his focus on the new exodus motif.[33] This strange neglect of Paul's quotation in 6.2 is even more remarkable, as I shall demonstrate in the following discussion, to the effect that the context of Isa. 49.1-13 clearly contains the motif of the new exodus, a central idea in Paul's thought as I earlier articulated in my treatment of 2.14-17 in Chapter 4.

As a consequence, any serious neglect of Paul's citation of Isa. 49.8 is tantamount to missing the force of his argument. Therefore, it is imperative to recognize that this scriptural citation is not merely a 'plunder from random raids on Israel's sacred texts' as eloquently argued by Wagner.[34] Rather, it reveals the

---

30. E.g., see Martin Ebner, *Leidenslisten und Apostelbrief: Untersuchungen zu Form, Motivik und Funktion der Peristasenkataloge bei Paulus*, FB 66 (Wurzburg: Echter Verlag, 1991), 244; Furnish, *II Corinthians*, 342, 353; Garland, *2 Corinthians*, 304–5; Matera, *II Corinthians*, 150; Thrall, *II Corinthians*, I:452–3.

31. See his *Suffering and the Spirit*, 77; 'Paul's Argument', 277–303; 'Paul's Use of the Old Testament', 246–57; and his *2 Corinthians*. In his 'Paul's Argument', Hafemann pays special attention to 3.7-18 even though he recognizes that 5.11–6.2 is one of the four passages that most significantly feature Paul's use of the OT (286–7). See also his 'Paul's Use of the Old Testament', 252; and *2 Corinthians*, 249, where the Isaianic citation is only briefly mentioned. Cf. John B. Polhill, 'Reconciliation at Corinth: 2 Corinthians 4–7', *RevExp* 86 (1989): 345–57 (353), where he merely mentions the citation without assigning any particular significance to Paul's argument.

32. Hafemann, 'Paul's Argument'.

33. See the tabulation in Hafemann, 'Paul's Argument', 283–6. The influence of Scripture, particularly Isaiah, on Paul's thought is very clear and significant. Hays has detected at least 31 quotations and 50 allusions taken from Isaiah within the 7 undisputed letters of Paul. The results yield significant clusters of quotations and allusions taken from Isa. 28–9 and 49–55 ('Who Has Believed Our Message?', 25–6). See also Holland, *Contours of Pauline Theology*, 31–4; Alexander Kerrigan, 'Echoes of Themes from the Servant Songs in Pauline Theology', in *Studiorum Paulinorum Congressus Internaionalis Catholicus 1961*, Vol. 2, AnBib 17–18 (Rome: Pontificio Instituto Biblico, 1963), 217–28; Oss, 'A Note on Paul's Use of Isaiah'.

34. Wagner, *Heralds of the Good News*, 356. Cf. Schütz, *Paul and the Anatomy of Apostolic Authority*, 181.

deep influence that Scripture has on Paul's thought. As such, Paul's citation of Isaiah in 6.2 is not only a key verse in 5.11–6.10, but also a central focus for the entire letter.[35] As I have earlier argued, Paul's thought in 2 Corinthians is very much influenced by Deutero-Isaiah; the citation of Isa. 49.8 is thus the key to unlock and guide our understanding of Paul's ministry of reconciliation (5.14-21) and apostolic suffering (6.3-10).

b) *Echoes of Isaiah 49 in 2 Corinthians and other Pauline Writings.* The fact that Isa. 49 had a significant influence on Paul is clearly demonstrated by the numerous allusions and citations to it. Within 2 Corinthians, apart from the citation of Isa. 49.8, there are several allusions to the Servant passage of Isa. 49.1-13. In the immediate context, the thought of the Corinthians receiving God's grace in vain in 2 Cor. 6.1 echoes the lament of the Servant in Isa. 49.4.[36] Furthermore, there are also reflections of the nature of suffering described as being 'deeply despised, abhorred by the nations' in Isa. 49.7 within Paul's list of hardships in 6.4-10. In the wider context of 2 Corinthians, the call of the Servant to be a light to the gentiles in Isa. 49.6, 8 seems to inform Paul's ministry of unveiling the darkness (3.14, 18; 4.4) to reveal 'the light of the knowledge of the glory of God in the face of Christ' (4.6) through 'the message of reconciliation' (5.19). The Servant's task to bring God's salvation to the ends of the earth (Isa. 49.6, 12) is also reflected in Paul's ministry of reconciliation to the world (5.18-19). The promise that God will make the Servant to be a covenant for the people in Isa. 49.8 is seen to be fulfilled in Paul as he is made a minister of the new covenant of the Spirit (3.6). As such, in the context of 2 Corinthians, both the allusions and quotations of Isaiah are of particular significance in Paul's thought.

In the other undisputed letters of Paul, his allusions to Isa. 49 are reflected in at least three categories: (1) Paul's call as one set apart from birth (Gal. 1.15 = Isa. 49.1, 5); (2) his mission to Israel and the gentiles (Rom. 11.13, 25; 15.16; Gal. 1.16; 2.2, 8-9 = Isa. 49.6b); and (3) Paul's anxiety over his ministry being in vain and the misunderstanding/misgiving about the outcome of his mission (e.g., 1 Cor. 9.15; 15.10, 58; Gal. 2.2; 4.11; Phil. 2.16; 1 Thess. 2.1; 3.5 = Isa. 49.4). From the above evidence, it is clear that Paul sees the prophetic declarations of Isaiah as prefiguring his own apostolic ministry to the gentiles.[37]

---

35. Cf. Barnett who fittingly takes the Isaianic citation as the 'critical eschatological text' in 2 Corinthians (*Second Epistles*, 46, cf. 318). See also Hanson, *Jesus Christ in the Old Testament*, 148; Kerrigan, 'Echoes of Themes', 217.

36. So Hanson, *Jesus Christ in Old Testament*, 149; Webb, *Returning Home*, 128–31.

37. See the important works of Hays, 'Who Has Believed Our Message?'; Sandnes, *Paul – One of the Prophets?*; and Wagner, *Heralds of the Good News*. Cf. also Alary, 'Good Grief', 222–30; C. J. A. Hickling, 'Paul's Reading of Isaiah', in *Studia Biblica 1978 III: Papers on Paul and Other New Testament Authors*, JSNTSup 3, ed. E. A. Livingstone (Sheffield: JSOT Press, 1980), 215–23; Kerrigan, 'Echoes of Themes'; D. M. Stanley, 'The Theme of the Servant of Yahweh in Primitive Christian Soteriology, and Its Transposition by St. Paul', *CBQ* 16 (1954): 385–425.

The early Christ-movement tradition also attributes the Isaiah passage to Paul. In Acts 13.47, Isa. 49.6 is applied in the testimony of Paul and Barnabas as a command from the Lord for the justification of the gentile mission. In Acts 26.17-18, Isa. 49 is used as a scriptural foundation for Paul's commission from Jesus to the gentiles. As such, according to this tradition, Paul closely identifies his ministry with the Servant figure in Isa. 49.[38]

From the impressive evidence above, it is unmistakably clear that the significant influence of Isa. 49 on Paul's thought is undeniable since it has been alluded to or cited in six of Paul's undisputed letters.[39]

c) *The Context of Isaiah 49.8.* Isaiah 49.8 forms part of the second Servant passage in Isa. 49.1-13.[40] The address is given to the Servant of the Lord, describing his special election prenatally, his mission of restoring Israel back to God and his empowerment to carry out this task (Isa. 49.1-3). However, the result of this task is far from being a success. According to the Servant, his labour is in vain and he responds to the divine mission with discouragement and failure (Isa. 49.4, 5b). Despite this, the Servant is given a further mission with a much broader scope beyond Israel. He is called to be a light to the gentiles in bringing the salvation of Yahweh to the nations of the world (Isa. 49.5a, 6). This dual commission of bringing both Israel and the gentile nations to God signifies the divine plan in using the Servant for reconciling the whole of humanity. Within the context of Isaiah, this mission involves the notion of new exodus depicted in the imagery of the eschatological triumph of Yahweh (Isa. 49.8-13; cf. Isa. 45.23; 60.3, 10-11; 62.2). Yet, this mission will only be achieved in Yahweh's appointed time (Isa. 49.8). Although the exact time for God's favourable response is not stated, it will surely come and God will be faithful to his promises spoken through the prophets (cf. Isa. 41.8-9; 43.10; 44.1-2; 45.4).

During the time of God's favour and the hour of salvation (Isa. 49.8), God will appoint the Servant to carry out the tasks of restoring the land, apportioning the heritage and calling the prisoners to be set free to enjoy the benefits of

38. For further discussion on Paul's appropriation of Isa. 49 in Acts, see Schnabel, *Early Christian Mission*, 2: 942–4.

39. In addition, other Servant passages (Isa. 42.1-9/1-12; Isa. 50.4-11; and 52.13–53.12) are also alluded to or cited elsewhere in Paul's letters as prefiguring his apostolic ministry. E.g., Isa. 52.15 in Rom. 15.21; and Isa. 53.1 in Rom. 10.16. See also the significant parallels between Isa. 53.9-11 and 2 Cor. 5.21 highlighted above, and Isa. 42.7 in Acts 26.18. For further treatment of the Servant Songs in Paul's thought, see Kerrigan, 'Echoes of Themes'.

40. Although the extent of the second Servant passage is debatable, with some scholars limiting the passage to Isa. 49.1-6, it is undeniable that Isa. 49.7-13 contains a similar theme on the task of the Servant and the restoration of Israel. As such, Isa. 49.7-13 can be read in conjunction with Isa. 49.1-6 without much difficulty. In addition, the theme of universal joy in 49.13, a dominant feature of the new exodus motif, makes it logical to extend the second Servant Song to 49.13. For literary links between Isa. 49.1-6 and 49.7-13 in the LXX, see Kerrigan, 'Echoes of Themes', 218 n. 1.

the blessings of the Lord (Isa. 49.8-10). This task strongly echoes the familiar language of the Year of Jubilee (Lev. 25.8-10; Isa. 61.1-4).

The Servant's task is to make it possible for God's people to return to God by removing all obstacles hindering this pilgrimage. Mountains which proved to be insurmountable are now approachable and highways will be raised up so that the pilgrims cannot go astray in this journey (Isa. 49.11. Cf. 40.3-4; 62.10). When this eschatological pilgrimage returns, it is not limited to Israel returning from exile, but also involves people from every corner of the earth (Isa. 49.12; see also 43.6; 49.22). The emphasis in Isa. 49.11-12 is that neither obstacle nor uncertainty, distance ('from afar') nor location ('north … west … the region of Aswan') will prevent the return of the pilgrims.[41]

This eschatological pilgrimage, in response to God's mighty work through the Servant, will result in universal praise and joy (Isa. 49.13; see also 42.10-13; 44.23; 45.8; 52.8-9; 55.12-13; and chapters 60–6. Cf. the discussion in Chapter 4).

d) *Function of Paul's Citation of Isaiah 49.8 in the Light of His Ministry of Suffering*. In order to fully appreciate the significance of Paul's citation of Isa. 49.8, it should be read in the light of the wider argument of 2 Cor. 5.11–6.10.[42] With this in mind, we now proceed to consider how this citation in 6.2 relates to the story of Jesus and Paul's understanding of his apostolic ministry and his suffering.

First, the question that puzzles interpreters is to whom the Isaianic citation applies. Most take σύ in the Isaianic passage as referring to the Corinthians.[43] A strong advocate of this reading is Stanley. He argues that if the σύ is taken to mean Paul, 'the point of the verse is rendered obscure, if not lost altogether' and the 'informed audience', with some degree of familiarity with the context of Isaiah, 'would have found themselves both enlightened and confused when they referred back to the original context of Paul's quotation'.[44] However, a major grammatical problem with this line of thought is that it makes the singular pronoun to be a plural referent. If Paul had the Corinthians in mind, he could have easily altered the second personal pronoun to the plural form so that there would be no ambiguity. With the reference to the Corinthians, it makes the story of reconciliation and restoration in the Isaiah context lose its force completely.

Another position is to take σύ as referring to all Christians, as suggested by Hanson. Hanson grounds his argument by referring to the Targum where the

41. Cf. J. Alec Motyer, *The Prophecy of Isaiah: An Introduction & Commentary* (Downers Grove: InterVarsity, 1993), 392.

42. Cf. Hays, *Echoes of Scripture*, 226 n. 48. Cf. Wilk, 'Isaiah in 1 and 2 Corinthians', 151–2, who argues that 2 Cor. 5.17–6.2 corresponds to the context of Isa. 49.8.

43. So Barnett, *Second Epistle*, 318; Harris, *Second Corinthians*, 461; Lambrecht, 'Favourable Time'; Thrall, *II Corinthians*, 1:453.

44. Stanley, *Arguing with Scripture*, 103.

second person singular in Isa. 49.8 is interpreted as a second person plural, 'just as Paul does'.[45] The problem with Hanson's reasoning is that Paul cites from the LXX and not the Targum, and in Paul's citation the pronoun remains singular. In addition, the use of Targum Isaiah as evidence for Second Temple Judaism is extremely problematic due to its late dating around the fifth century CE.[46]

As such, it makes better sense to see Paul applying the Isaianic passage to himself. As the context of Isaiah refers to the Servant of the Lord, Paul similarly sees himself as an Isaianic Servant who receives help from God in working together with Jesus in the ministry of reconciliation.[47] As I have argued earlier, since Paul applies Isa. 49 to himself elsewhere in his writings, it should not surprise us that here '(i)n a radical fashion Paul applies to himself a prophecy of the Isaianic Servant'.[48] Just as the Servant of Isaiah is called to be a light to the gentiles to bring God's people back to him, Paul the ambassador and co-worker of Christ is also the one through whom God makes the appeal to the Corinthians and the gentile nations to be reconciled to him (5.18-21; Rom. 1.13; 15.16-20; Gal. 1.16; 2.2, 8-9. Cf. Eph. 3.8; 1 Tim. 2.7; 2 Tim. 4.17). Playing the role analogous to the Servant of the Lord, Paul sees himself totally dedicated to God's agenda and the interests of the Corinthians, and his gentile mission is now the living demonstration that Isaiah's vision of salvation has finally found its fulfilment.

Second, by applying the Isaianic passage to himself, Paul allows the text to guide and inform him on his apostolic mission. As we have seen, Paul would

45. Hanson, *Paradox of the Cross*, 56. Cf. Hughes, *Second Corinthians*, 219, who sees three levels of application of the Isaiah passage: (1) to the Corinthians; (2) to Paul; and (3) to Christ as Yahweh's Servant.

46. As rightly noted by James Ware, *The Mission of the Church in Paul's Letter to the Philippians in the Context of Ancient Judaism*, NovTSup 120 (Leiden: Brill, 2005), 107–12, evidence from the Targum must be used with great care.

47. So Beale, 'Old Testament Background', 562; Danker, *II Corinthians*, 85; Hafemann, 'Paul's Use of the Old Testament', 249; Webb, *Returning Home*, 128–45. Cf. Wilk, 'Isaiah in 1 and 2 Corinthians', 152: 'Paul saw his own ministry as ambassador for Christ foretold in Isa. 49:4-8.'

48. Beale, 'Old Testament Background', 562. See also Paul E. Dinter, 'Paul and the Prophet Isaiah', *BTB* 13 (1983): 48–52; Holland, *Contours of Pauline Theology*, 69–82. *Pace* Gignilliat, *Paul and Isaiah's Servants*, 108–42, who argues that Paul is not the Servant *per se* but a servant to the Servant. Gignilliat argues that since Paul applies the Isaianic Servant passages to Christ in 2 Cor. 5.14-21, it is untenable and contradictory to locate Paul as a servant in 6.2. However, if my reading that Paul is a co-worker with Jesus is correct, this would solve the apparent tension articulated by Gignilliat. Cf. Harris, *Second Corinthians*, 459–62. Although Harris spends a considerable amount of space in detailing the influence of Isa. 49 and other Servant passages on Paul's thought in which 'Paul envisaged his ministry as a continuation of the role of the Servant of Yahweh' (460), he concludes that it is a 'giant step' to move from this inference to the interpretation that the citation in 6.2 applies to Paul (461). In arguing for the application of the Isaiah passage to the Corinthians instead of Paul, Harris seems to suggest that Paul makes an exception here in his application of Scripture. This position appears to deny the impressive evidence Harris earlier provides on how Paul's ministry corresponds to Isa. 49 (cf. 460).

have been aware of the context of Isaiah and this no doubt forms the back-ground of Paul's citation. With the impressive evidence of the use of Isa. 49 here in 2 Corinthians and elsewhere, Paul is not only reflecting primarily on Isa. 49 but he is drawing from it in his understanding of his own vocation and mission to the gentiles. Paul literally finds himself and his apostolic mission in Isa. 49. As such, the paramount significance of Isa. 49.8 on Paul's thought can never be simply discounted.[49]

Paul identifies his own apostolic proclamation of the gospel to the gentile nations with the role of the Servant of Isaiah toward Israel in Isa. 49.8. But unlike the Servant in Isaiah where God's deliverance remains a future event, Paul announces that it has already arrived through the Christ-event. This con-nection in Paul's mind between the second Servant Song and his gentile mission is remarkably evident in 2 Corinthians. As we have seen in the discussion in Chapter 4, the focus of Isa. 40–55 on God's activity for the nations reaches its climax in the Servant Songs. It has also been widely recognized that the first two Servant Songs (Isa. 42.1-9; 49.1-13) in Second Temple Judaism are a major focus for exegetical reflection on the eschatological ingathering of the nations which is tantamount to gentile conversions.[50] Strikingly, Paul's use of the second Servant Song in the context of his ministry and exhortation to the Corinthians clearly reflects his deep conviction that the eschatological reign of God over the nations as envisioned in Deutero-Isaiah has now begun in Jesus the Messiah (cf. 5.16-21), and he is fulfilling this mission to the gentiles by pro-claiming the message of reconciliation that has been committed to him (5.19).

This leads us to the third function of Paul's citation of Isa. 49.8. It is the conviction of Paul that the eschatological promise in the Isaianic text finds its fulfilment now through the Christ-event. Immediately after quoting Isa. 49.8, Paul makes a declaration by repeating the theme of Isaiah, ἰδοὺ νῦν καιρὸς εὐπρόσδεκτος, ἰδοὺ νῦν ἡμέρα σωτηρίας. Paul uses the word ἰδού twice. In the LXX, it is frequently used to introduce a solemn pronouncement, particularly in incidences where divine promises are given.[51] In Paul's usage here, ἰδού empha-sizes the declaration that comes after it: 'now the favourable time ... now the day of salvation'. Paul not only repeats the Isaianic citation but also the idea of νῦν twice, thereby giving the citation its contemporary significance in which the καιρὸς and ἡμέρα mentioned in Isa. 49 have now arrived.

The language of favourable time and day of salvation clearly has in view the motif of the new exodus (cf. Isa. 49.9-12) and the ingathering of God's people.[52]

---

49. Lambrecht, 'Favourable Time', 386, seems to dismiss the context of Isaiah in Paul's quo-tation of Isa. 49.8 in 2 Cor. 6.2.

50. Pao, *Acts and the Isaianic New Exodus*, 227–48. Elsewhere in Rom. 15.15-21, Paul likens his apostolic mission to a priestly activity to the gentiles.

51. Furnish, *II Corinthians*, 315.

52. See Beale, 'Old Testament Background;' W. D. Davies, 'Paul and the New Exodus', in *The Quest for Context and Meaning: Studies in Biblical Intertextuality in Honor of James A. Sanders,*

It is God's appointed time where the restoration of the relationship between God and his people takes place,[53] and this is now being fulfilled through Paul's ministry as Christ's co-worker. The present time is the time in which both the 'new things' and 'new creation' that God promised in Isaiah (Isa. 42.9; 43.18-19; 48.6; 65.17) are now made possible because of the redemptive work of Jesus (2 Cor. 5.17; Gal. 6.15; cf. Eph. 2.15; 4.24; 2 Pet. 3.13).[54] The 'now' can be 'the favourable time' and 'the day of salvation' for the Corinthians because God has reconciled the world through Christ, and has initiated the ministry of reconciliation through his servant, Paul.[55]

Fourth, seeing his ministry as a continuation of the role of the Servant of the Lord, Paul pays particular attention to carrying out his ministry (διακονία) in order to put no obstacle whatsoever in anyone's way so that his ministry may not be discredited (2 Cor. 6.3), a theme that I shall consider in greater length below. Paul's initiative here is to ensure that the progress of the gospel is not hindered and that the Corinthians are not prevented from experiencing the full reconciliation and benefits of the blessings of God as heralded by the Christ-event.[56] On the contrary, as God's servant (διάκονος), Paul recommends himself in every way and his commendation is reflected in the following list of what is generally regarded as the second *peristasis* catalogue (6.4-10). This catalogue, explaining what makes Paul's διακονία to be (1) the glorious διακονία of the Spirit (3.8), (2) the διακονία of righteousness (3.9), and (3) the διακονία of reconciliation (5.18), is embedded in his sufferings. And this διακονία must be understood on

ed. Craig A. Evans and Shemaryahu Talmon (Leiden: Brill, 1997), 443–63; Thomas R. Schreiner, *Paul, Apostle of God's Glory in Christ: A Pauline Theology* (Downers Grove: InterVarsity, 2001), 48–9; Webb, *Returning Home*, 131–50, for an excellent discussion of the background of new exodus in Paul's thought. For further discussion on this motif, see Pao, *Acts and the Isaianic New Exodus*; and Watts, *Isaiah's New Exodus and Mark*.

53. *Pace* Plummer, *Second Epistle*, 191, who argues that the favourable time refers to the time of human's favour instead of God's. Hughes, *Second Corinthians*, 220, rightly criticizes Plummer as 'almost certainly wrong'.

54. See also Scott, *2 Corinthians*, 136. It is interesting to note that ἰδού is also found in LXX Isa. 42.9; 43.19; 65.17-18, passages which speak of the new things that God will be doing.

55. Paul's citation of Isaiah in 2 Cor. 6.2 may also be seen as a continuation of his thought in 5.17. There are parallels: (1) emphasis on eschatology; (2) use of ἰδού; and (3) both references are from Isaiah. See Beale, 'Old Testament Background', 559–66. For a discussion on the notion of reconciliation as salvation, see Stegman, *Character of Jesus*, 290–5; Garland, *2 Corinthians*, 291–2. Cf. Kruse, *Second Corinthians*, 131, who argues that if the time of the exile's return was a day of salvation then the time when God has acted in Christ to reconcile the world to himself is 'the day of salvation *par excellence*' (emphasis his). John N. Oswalt, *The Book of Isaiah: Chapters 40–66*, NICOT (Grand Rapids: Eerdmans, 1998), 298, also supports this argument by suggesting that Paul's use of Isa. 49.8 'shows that he clearly understood it to apply to the messianic age (which had come with Jesus)'.

56. Cf. Webb, *Returning Home*, 145–50; Belleville, *2 Corinthians*, 164. See 1 Cor. 9.12; cf. 1 Tim. 6.1; Tit. 2.5.

the basis of suffering which has Christological meaning and which is grounded in the story of Jesus, a fact that I shall further argue in the following section. In other words, what Paul is explicitly saying here is that his suffering is integral to his calling as a διάκονος of God in carrying out his διακονία and that his sufferings are not προσκοπή, a cause for offence, which hinders the progress of the gospel. Like the Servant in Isaiah, Paul should be known by his faithfulness to the divine task through his labours, even his sufferings.

As in the servant passage in Isaiah, no distance or location can prevent the eschatological pilgrimage from taking place. Applied to Paul, he sees himself as someone who places no obstacles, including his sufferings, in the way of this pilgrimage. For Paul his suffering remains an obstacle only from the perspective of the Corinthians.[57] Since this ingathering from the gentile nations has already taken place, Paul is now reminding the Corinthians not to allow their perception of his appearance and their estranged relationship to be a hindrance to them in taking this eschatological journey home.

Finally, in the light of the argument above, Paul is once more issuing the invitation to the Corinthians to continue to be part of the story of God that finds its fulfilment in Jesus. Paul has already made it clear that the Corinthians are now brought into the participation of the eschatological blessings and the narrative of God through the story of Jesus. In 6.1-2, Paul makes his urgent appeal to the Corinthians not to receive God's grace in vain. I earlier argued that, for Paul, receiving God's grace in vain is to accept the apostolic message only to abandon the messenger later. The Corinthians will do so if they base Paul's ministry on his weakness or suffering, suffering which Paul insists is not a cause for offence in itself. For Paul, rejecting Christ's ambassador has serious consequences as it is tantamount to rejecting the one who sent him. Paul makes it clear that his ministry to the Corinthians is a ministry of the spirit (3.8) for righteousness (3.9) and reconciliation (5.18). And his chief task is to help them to take their full part in God's redemptive story. As a letter from Christ, ministered to by the apostle, they are to be 'known and read by all' (3.2-3) and this can only be done if the Corinthians carefully discern and accept the reality of who Paul is. As such, the quotation of Isa. 49.8 rightly 'reminds the Corinthians of their acceptance of grace, made possible by Paul, in the transforming power of their Saviour'.[58] By doing so, Paul is drawing the Corinthians deeper into God's activity, and the only ones who can hinder the Corinthians from achieving this are the Corinthians themselves, not Paul.

After considering the functions of the citation of Isa. 49 in 2 Cor. 6.2, we are now in a better position to respond to probably the only article dedicated solely to the treatment of this citation. In his work, Lambrecht argues that by alter-

---

57. Cf. Crafton, *Agency of the Apostle*, 65–6: 'The only obstacle between Paul and the Corinthians is their own failure to respond to him.'

58. Martin, *2 Corinthians*, 168.

ing the theological significance of the Isaianic text to suit his purpose, Paul's primary focus is on the eschatological interpretation of the passage.[59] By doing so, Lambrecht minimizes the influence of the Isaiah passage in Paul's thought by taking the second person pronoun σύ as referring to the Corinthians. This position leads him to argue that Paul's use of the passage is to emphasize 'the extreme significance of the eschatological "now"', denoting the urgency for the Corinthians to commit themselves to God.[60] Based on this reading, the promise of God to the Servant of Isaiah has now become the promise to the Corinthians. Lambrecht's 'eschatological now' reading also leads him to argue that 'Paul does not look so much to the past salvation event' in 6.1-2.[61] This reading almost completely misses the force of Paul's argument and severs the narrative that is operative in his thought. Paul's understanding of God's saving drama is not and should not be limited exclusively to the past, or the present, or the future event. For a person who is deeply rooted in his Jewish heritage, Paul would naturally see a continuation of the story of God working through Christ and himself as the Servant in fulfilling God's grand narrative. Paul sees the fulfilment of this passage not only in the story of Jesus but also in the role he plays in bringing the story of the Corinthians to be incorporated into God's narrative. By focusing on the eschatological now and applying the Isaiah passage to the Corinthians instead of Paul, Lambrecht somehow fails to appreciate the strong influence of Isaiah in Paul's thought and his ministry.

e) *Summary*. I have argued that Paul finds in Isa. 49 not only a prefiguration of his apostolic ministry but also a justification of his gentile mission.[62] In addition, the vocabulary and imagery for expressing his apostolic identity have also been greatly influenced by Isaiah. This is clear from the way Paul interprets the relation of his gospel to the ancient story of God's covenant relationship with Israel which finds its climax in the story of Jesus. If we take the context of Isa. 49 carefully into account, we cannot but be impressed by Paul's boldness and the depth of his thought on the story of Jesus in this passage. Whatever is described in Isa. 49, Paul sees not only Christ fulfilling the role of the Servant

---

59. Lambrecht, 'Favourable Time'. So Gignilliat, *Paul and Isaiah's Servants*, 57–60.

60. Lambrecht, 'Favourable Time', 389. For a critique of this view, see Alary, 'Good Grief', 228–9 n. 41.

61. Lambrecht, 'Favourable Time', 389. Lambrecht appears to be confused in his position. Earlier on, he argues that Paul is 'interested in the salvation aspect of Is 49,8a' (390). Perhaps what Lambrecht is arguing here is that Paul is only interested in the *present* and not the *past* aspect of salvation.

62. See Hays, 'Who Has Believed Our Message?', 26, 48; J. Ross Wagner, 'The Heralds of Isaiah and the Mission of Paul', in *Jesus and the Suffering Servant: Isaiah 53 and Christian Origins*, ed. William H. Bellinger Jr. and William R. Farmer (Harrisburg: Trinity, 1998), 193–222; idem, *Heralds of the Good News*. Cf. Alary, 'Good Grief', 222–4; William Lane, 'Covenant: The Key to Paul's Conflict at Corinth', *TynBul* 33 (1982): 3–29 (8–9).

but himself as well. In other words, Paul interprets his citation of Isa. 49.8 at two levels; (1) God's reconciling activity in the Christ-event; and (2) God's institution of the ministry of reconciliation through him.

As such, Paul does not simply search the Scripture for proof-texts or dress up the Scripture to suit his argument. On the contrary, he discerns in Scripture a continuous story of God. For Paul, the meaning of Scripture is brought to light through the story of Jesus in his ministry of reconciliation. Reading the Scripture through the lens of the story of Jesus, Paul discovers himself and the Corinthians at the very centre of God's redemptive purpose. It is through this understanding that the interconnectedness between the story of Jesus, Paul and the Corinthians is once again made apparent. As such, Paul's citation and application of Isa. 49.8 makes it one of his greatest assertions of his apostolic ministry grounded in the Scriptures. This, in turn, throws his mission and suffering into sharp perspective. Not only does Paul locate the Corinthians within the story of God's redemptive act but also this community is now a constituent part of the story of God.

B. *The Story of Jesus and Paul's Self-Commendation as the True Ambassador for Reconciliation Demonstrated through Suffering*

There seems to be an abrupt transition at 2 Cor. 6.3 where Paul moves from his appeal to the Corinthians not to receive God's grace in vain (6.1-2) to his self-commendation based on his recounting of his apostolic hardships. But this transition is less awkward if it can be recognized that the overall theme of 5.11–6.10 is the nature and character of Paul's apostolic ministry grounded in the story of Jesus.[63] Paul's catalogue of suffering underscores the way he works together with Jesus in making the appeal to the Corinthians not to accept God's grace in vain.

In 6.3-10, Paul presents his second *peristasis* catalogue in a very impressive rhetorical fashion, and this has led to studies that focus on its literary and rhetorical analysis that include the meaning of individual words in the catalogue, the relationship between the list of hardships and the list of virtues, and the relationship of the first διά phrase with the following διά list. It is highly sur-

---

63. Cf. Harris, *Second Corinthians*, 464. Many commentators often discard this connection. See Collange, *Enigmes*, 282–3, who suggests that 6.3-13 and 6.14–7.4 are originally alternate endings to 2.14–6.2; Windisch, *Der zweite Korintherbrief*, 202–3, who suggests three possibilities for the arrangement of 6.3-10, but none is connected to 6.1-2. Contra those who emphasize the thematic connections here, e.g., Furnish, *II Corinthians*, 353; Güttgemanns, *Der leidende Apostel und sein Herr*, 316–17; Plummer, *Second Epistle*, 189. Interestingly, Lambrecht insists that the entire 6.1-10 should be seen as a unit (*Second Corinthians*, 110–11) but in the following paragraph he comments that, while writing 6.4b-10, 'Paul no longer has in mind the grammatical connection with vv. 1-2' (111). Cf. also the contradictory statements in Wilk, 'Isaiah in 1 and 2 Corinthians' in 151 n. 72 and 152 n. 74.

prising that there is hardly any serious consideration of Paul's Isaianic citation being taken into account in understanding this catalogue, given that the citation occurs immediately before the catalogue.

1. *The Story of Jesus in Paul's Self-Commendation*

a) *No Cause for Offence in Paul's Ministry.* Paul categorically states that he places no obstacles in anyone's way (μηδεμίαν ἐν μηδενὶ διδόντες προσκοπήν, 6.3). The word order is illuminating of Paul's constant effort in avoiding any offence. Μηδεμίαν and προσκοπήν are placed at both the beginning and end of the clause respectively, and this clearly emphasizes the *negative*: 'no offence or obstacle whatsoever' (cf. Rom. 14.13; 1 Cor. 10.32).[64] The purpose of Paul's careful effort here is clearly spelled out in the following purpose clause ἵνα μὴ μωμηθῇ ἡ διακονία. The ministry (διακονία) that Paul has in view is the ministry of a 'new covenant', 'the ministry of the Spirit', 'the ministry of righteousness' and 'the ministry of reconciliation' (3.6, 8, 9; 5.18; cf. 4.1). His preoccupation here is that his ministry will in no way be discredited.

But who will find fault with Paul's ministry? The passive μωμηθῇ seems to indicate that the Corinthians are certainly in view, but Paul's opponents should not be completely ruled out as well. In what sense can there be fault with Paul's ministry? Paul clearly understands that the message and the messenger are inseparable. To put it negatively, any inappropriate behaviour on the part of the messenger would adversely affect the message; and positively, the embodiment of the message expressed in his life experience not only enhances the credibility of the gospel but also demonstrates the power of the message. For Paul, the preaching of the cross will inevitably give offence (cf. Rom. 9.32-31; 1 Cor. 1.23; Gal. 5.11), but this is undoubtedly not what he has in view here. In this context, the stumbling block is not the message, but rather the life of the messenger which is improper and inconsistent with the message of the gospel.[65]

b) *The Basis of Paul's Self-Commendation.* Paul moves from the *negative* in 2 Cor. 6.3 to the *positive* commendation of his apostolic ministry, as indicated by the conjunction ἀλλ' in the beginning of 6.4: ἐν παντὶ συνιστάντες ἑαυτοὺς ὡς θεοῦ διάκονοι.

The manner with which Paul introduces the catalogue of suffering by self-commendation (συνιστάντες ἑαυτοὺς) in 6.4 creates a problem. Elsewhere (3.1; 5.12; 10.12, 18), Paul appears to denounce self-commendation. Here, as in 4.2 (cf. 12.11), Paul seems to revert to this practice, a move that appears to be self-contradictory, particularly so within the wider argument itself

---

64. Cf. Harris, *Second Corinthians*, 470–1; Fitzgerald, *Cracks in an Earthen Vessel*, 187–8.

65. Harris, *Second Corinthians*, 469. Cf. Gustav Stählin, 'προσκόπτω πρόσκομμά κτλ', *TDNT* 6: 754: 'According to Paul's conviction, there ought not to be anything to cause offence at his ministry in the whole sphere of apostolic life so fully described in vv 4–10.'

(5.11–6.10) where he explicitly denies that he is commending himself in 5.12. This apparent difficulty is often resolved by making the distinction between illegitimate self-commendation based on glorifying the self and legitimate self-commendation based on character and virtue in line with the message of the gospel.[66] The distinction between these two is indicated by how Paul positions the reflective pronoun ἑαυτοῦ. Whenever Paul wanted to emphasize illegitimate self-commendation, he would place ἑαυτοῦ *before* συνίστημι as in the case of 3.1; 5.12; 10.12, and 18. In the case where Paul wishes to commend himself positively, as in the case of 4.2 and 6.4 (cf. 7.11; 12.11), the order of the words is reversed with ἑαυτοῦ placed *after* συνίστημι. In this respect, the emphasis then lies on the fact of commendation rather than the self.

A careful consideration of the context of 2 Corinthians suggests that it is not the convention of self-commendation that Paul is opposing[67] but the *basis* of such commendation. Hafemann persuasively argues that Paul's opponents in Corinth are 'measuring themselves by themselves and comparing themselves by themselves' and this is done based on the prevailing social conventions.[68] If Hafemann is right, it is precisely this very *basis* of self-commendation that Paul is going against; it is one that is based on external appearances and the expectations of others (cf. 10.12). Rather than basing his commendation on prevailing expectations, Paul judges his apostleship based on the criteria and measures that God assigned and grounded in the story of Jesus. That is the reason why Paul clearly states that he is συνιστάντες ἑαυτοὺς ὡς θεοῦ <u>διάκονοι</u> and *not* συνιστάντες ἑαυτοὺς ὡς θεοῦ <u>διακόνους</u>. In the former, the nominative διάκονοι should rightly be rendered 'we, as servants of God, commend ourselves' while in the latter the accusative διακόνους carries the meaning, 'we commend ourselves as servants of God', that is, to prove ourselves as servants of God.[69]

As such, the basis of Paul's commendation here is his status as a servant (διάκονος) of God. It is never his intention to set out to prove himself as one.

---

66. On the issue of self-commendation in 2 Corinthians, see Belleville, 'Letter of Apologetic Self-Commendation'; Paul Brooks Duff, 'Glory in the Ministry of Death: Gentile Condemnation and Letters of Recommendation in 2 Cor. 3:6-18', *NovT* 46 (2004): 313–37; Scott J. Hafemann, '"Self-Commendation" and Apostolic Legitimacy in 2 Corinthians: A Pauline Dialectic?', *NTS* 36 (1990): 66–88; Jan Lambrecht, 'Dangerous Boasting: Paul's Self-Commendation in 2 Corinthians 10–13', in *The Corinthian Correspondence*, BETL 125, ed. R. Bieringer (Leuven: Peeters, 1996), 325–46. For further treatment on the Greco-Roman convention of letters of self-commendation, see Chan-Hie Kim, *Form and Structure of the Familiar Letter of Recommendation*, SBLDS 4 (Missoula: Society of Biblical Literature, 1972); Peter Marshall, *Enmity in Corinth: Social Conventions in Paul's Relationship with the Corinthians*, WUNT 2/23 (Tübingen: J. C. B. Mohr, 1987), 91–129, 259–77.

67. Marshall, *Enmity in Corinth*, 274.

68. Hafemann, 'Self-Commendation', 79. See the further discussion in Chapter 7.

69. Cf. the dubious translations of NJB ('we prove ourselves authentic servants of God') and NLT ('we show that we are true ministers of God').

Paul's self-commendation here is not a commendation of *himself*, but God's commendation of his status as a co-worker and ambassador of Jesus Christ (cf. 10.17-18).[70] This further confirms my earlier reading that Paul applies Isa. 49.8 to himself, and he sees his role as a servant of God analogous to the Isaianic Servant of the Lord. As a servant of God, Paul recognizes that this entails incarnating the very mode of existence as revealed in Jesus.[71] Here, Paul embodies Jesus' self-emptying existence for others as unmistakably reflected in 6.10 (see the argument below). In this *peristasis* catalogue, what Paul offers is simply not what is generally regarded as his so-called 'resumé of credentials' on which his ministry is based, as if Paul needed these credentials to defend himself against the opponents.[72] Instead, this list of suffering demonstrates what is integral to the life and calling of the διάκονος of the gospel that embodies the story of Jesus. Gignilliat rightly asserts: 'Suffering for Paul was part and parcel of his activity as servant of God; it defined his being as servant.'[73] It is through this perspective that the catalogue of hardships in 6.4-10 is to be understood.

Seen from this perspective, Paul's ministry of the new covenant, of the Spirit, of righteousness and of reconciliation (3.6, 8, 9; 5.18; cf. 4.1) is a διακονία of suffering, and this is a pure διακονία, a mediation without fault as the Isaianic passage makes it clear. Through his suffering, Paul as a διάκονος not only plays the role of making this revelation real to the Corinthians but, at the same time, he places no offence whatsoever in anyone's way (6.3). Thus, when Paul speaks of himself, it is not to promote self, or to enhance his status, but it is for the benefit of the Corinthians in their struggle fully to comprehend the nature of Paul's ministry, and to provide them with a basis to respond to any criticisms that may have been thrown at Paul (cf. 5.12; 10.10).[74]

---

70. Cf. Hafemann, 'Self-Commendation', 87. See also Antoinette Clark Wire, 'Reconciled to Glory in Corinth? 2 Cor 2:14–7:4', in *Antiquity and Humanity: Essays on Ancient Religion and Philosophy Presented to Hans Dieter Betz on His 70th Birthday*, ed. Adela Yarbro Collins and Margaret M. Mitchell (Tübingen: Mohr Siebeck, 2001), 263–75; John N. Collins, 'The Mediatorial Aspect of Paul's Role as *Diakonos*', *ABR* 40 (1992): 34–44.

71. Cf. Stegman, *Character of Jesus*, 217.

72. E.g., Furnish, *II Corinthians*, 353; Mak, 'Holistic View of Pauline Suffering', 188–9; Wan, *Power in Weakness*, 94. This is to misread the nominative διάκονοι as accusative. It is also interesting to note that in this context Paul never refers to himself as an apostle (ἀπόστολος) but as a servant (διάκονος) of God. In fact throughout 2 Corinthians, much emphasis is placed on Paul's role as a διάκονος (3.6; 6.4; 11.23) and his διακονία (3.8, 9; 4.1; 5.18; 6.3; 11.8). Hence, it appears that when alluding to his sufferings, it is more important for Paul to be known as a διάκονος rather than an ἀπόστολος. Collins suggests one reason for this is that the authenticity of an apostle requires credentials and therefore can be challenged, while as a διάκονος the authenticity 'speaks for itself: it is the Lord who speaks' ('Mediatorial Aspects', 44). This further confirms my reading that Paul's sufferings in 6.4-10 should not simply be considered as Paul's credentials in his defence of his apostleship.

73. Gignilliat, *Paul and Isaiah's Servants*, 140.

74. Cf. Matera, *II Corinthians*, 151.

2. *The Story of Jesus in Paul's Sufferings*

In the following investigation, I shall not rehearse the meaning of the individual words that Paul uses in the *peristasis* catalogue, as this has been done elsewhere.[75] Other than a few comments on the literary structure, my focus here is on the function of the story of Jesus in Paul's thought and two areas that have been neglected or received little attention in recent scholarship: (1) the relationship between the LXX Isa. 49.8 citation in 2 Cor. 6.2 and Paul's list of hardships; and (2) the influence of the Servant passage of Isa. 49.1-13 in Paul's understanding of his suffering.

a) *Literary Structure of 2 Corinthians 6.4-10.* The literary structure that contains the list of hardships in 6.4-10 is not only highly impressive but systematically structured, and any reader would undoubtedly recognize its powerful and eloquent rhetorical impact.[76] In addition, it must not be overlooked that this catalogue is, as rightly noted by Manus, 'very theological' and provides the framework for Paul's argument.[77]

The catalogue is introduced by the phrase ἐν ὑπομονῇ πολλῇ, and this is followed by a list of nine hardships;[78] eight virtues; three διά phrases; and finally, seven antitheses introduced by the conjunction ὡς.

The list of nine hardships can be further divided into three sets of three, ranging from general statements to specific hardships. The first triad is set in general terms describing Paul's sufferings: θλῖψις, ἀνάγκη and στενοχωρία. This is followed by the second set which provides specific examples of the sufferings inflicted on Paul in the course of his apostolic ministry: πληγή, φυλακή and ἀκαταστασία. The third triad wraps up the final set that further enumerates physical hardships that accompany Paul: κόπος, ἀγρυπνία and νηστεία. These threefold repetitions of his sufferings set out in different descriptions and varying degrees of difficulty are meant to indicate the comprehensive and

75. See Mak, 'Holistic View of Pauline Suffering', 176–204, who painstakingly and meticulously analyses the meaning of each word used in the catalogue; Barnett, *Second Epistle*, 326–34; Harris, *Second Corinthians*, 470–86.

76. See Harris, *Second Corinthians*, 465–7, for an analysis of 6.4-10 both by grammatical construction and by content.

77. Manus, 'Apostolic Suffering', 44. On the list of sufferings, Manus further suggests that Paul 'structures them in a narrative style quite consistent with his mind set on Christ's passion and death as the example par excellence'.

78. The phrase ἐν ὑπομονῇ πολλῇ is best taken as the general heading for the following nine lists of suffering that Paul puts forward in his self-commendation. Several indications seem to support this reading: (1) ὑπομονῇ is the only singular noun and one that is modified (by πολλῇ) in 6.4-5; (2) the list of nine hardships that follows is clearly structured into a triad of three sets. See Harris, *Second Corinthians*, 471. Cf. NLT where ἐν ὑπομονῇ πολλη is taken as modifying the first three hardships in the list: 'We patiently endure troubles and hardships and calamities of every kind.'

extensive nature of Paul's sufferings that he endures for the sake of the gospel, covering both external and internal distresses. In addition, all these nine items are in the plural, suggesting the intensity, fullness, totality and multiplicity of these hardships.

This list, as in the earlier catalogue in 4.8-9, speaks of Paul's hardships as a reality and those that Paul must endure as a minister of God and an ambassador of Christ. Its graphic account of Paul's intense suffering coupled with the asyndetic construction result in the rhetorical effect of increasing amplification. This would have created in the readers a sense of amazement and surprise that such a person as Paul would have to suffer so much for the sake of the gospel and the community of Christ-followers that he is establishing.[79]

It is also interesting to note that some of these words that Paul uses here appear elsewhere in Paul's catalogues of sufferings as depicted in Table 6.1.[80]

Table 6.1. *A Comparison of Vocabulary Related to Paul's Sufferings in 2 Corinthians*

Text	List of Suffering	Similar Word Used Elsewhere in 2 Corinthians
2 Cor. 6.4	θλῖψις	1.4 (twice), 8; cf. Rom. 8.35
	ἀνάγκη	12.10
	στενοχωρία	12.10; cf. Rom. 8.35
2 Cor. 6.5	πληγή	11.23
	φυλακή	11.23
	ἀκαταστασία	12.20
	κόπος	11.23, 27
	ἀγρυπνία	11.27
	νηστεία	11.27

The similarity between the vocabulary of 6.5 and 11.23, 27 is striking; the terms are all repeated, except for ἀκαταστασία (which is found in 12.20). Four of these terms (πληγή, φυλακή, ἀγρυπνία and νηστεία) are words found only in 6.5 and 11.23, 27, and not elsewhere in the Pauline corpus. The most

---

79. The technique that Paul is using here has sometimes been identified as *enargeia*, which aims to give amplification by using vivid examples and illustration in order to create a mental picture in the audience. See Mak, 'Holistic View of Pauline Suffering', 202–4. For further discussion on amplification in the Greco-Roman convention, see Duane F. Watson, 'Amplification Techniques in 1 John: The Interaction of Rhetorical Style and Invention', *JSNT* 51 (1993): 99–123 (113).

80. Cf. Martin, *2 Corinthians*, 161–2.

common word is κόπος, possibly Paul's favourite word to describe his missionary labours.[81] At the same time, the use of ἀνάγκη in 6.4 is also very
significant. This word contains the notion of necessity; and both Tasker and
Martin clearly note that these ἀνάγκαις of Paul are 'hardships of which no
mitigation was possible' and 'a destiny to which Paul the servant of God is
committed' respectively.[82]

Following this list of hardships, Paul speaks of his moral integrity, structured
in a pair of tetrads (6.6-7), all represented by singular nouns. The inclusion of
the list of virtues is surprising and has puzzled many commentators. Allo and
Collange argue that the virtue list is to be understood as power given by God
to Paul for him to resist the hardships enumerated in 6.4-5.[83] This is doubtful
as it is difficult to see how 'purity', 'knowledge' and 'love' can be understood
as powers for resisting hardship. In contrast, Schiefer Ferrari proposes that
the hardship list and the virtue list are to be seen from opposing perspectives
– with the former from the worldly perspective and the latter from that of new
creation – and these two opposing perspectives are further intensified in the
following antitheses in 6.8-10.[84] This again is doubtful, as evidence for seeing
Paul's suffering from a worldly perspective appears to be alien in the present
context. Still others like Mak suggest that this list of virtues should be seen
as a list of 'ministerial criteria', as Paul's opponents allege that Paul does not
possess the proper criteria of a servant of God. This list then serves to correct
his opponents' criteria for ministers.[85] While Mak is right that this list is not
entirely a list of virtues (e.g., 'Holy Spirit' and 'power of God' do not constitute virtues), his argument that Paul needs a list of ministerial credentials to
silence his opponents appears speculative. Mak's treatment is essentially based
on 'mirror reading' by assuming that every item listed in Paul's catalogue is
a response to the charge of his opponents, which is doubtful in this context.
Furthermore, as I have earlier argued, the basis of Paul's self-commendation is
his status as God's servant, and if my reading is right then it is difficult to see
why Paul needs to present another list of 'ministerial credentials' to substantiate the basis of his commendation.

That this virtue list is given within the context of Paul's commendation
should not be missed. Paul insists that his own conduct as God's servant and
Christ's ambassador does not constitute an occasion for causing an offence that
may have hindered the Corinthians from accepting God's grace. When put in

81. E.g., 1 Cor. 3.8; 1 Thess. 2.9, 3.5. Cf. 2 Thess. 3.8. Cf. Wood, 'Death at Work in Paul', 151.

82. Tasker, *Second Corinthians*, 93; Martin, *2 Corinthians*, 173. Cf. the use of ἀνάγκη in
1 Cor. 9.16 where Paul considers the preaching of the gospel as a necessity for him.

83. Allo, *Seconde Épître aux Corinthiens*, 176; Collange, *Enigmes*, 295.

84. Markus Schiefer Ferrari, *Die Sprache des Leids in den paulinischen Peristasenkatalogen*
(Stuttgart: Verlag Katholisches Bibelwerk, 1991), 232–3.

85. Mak, 'Holistic View of Pauline Suffering', 190.

the perspective of his own suffering and weakness, the function of the list of virtues and particularly the mention of the Holy Spirit and the power of God within the list becomes clear. Paul's list of sufferings gives substance to the list of virtues as the items listed therein are all related to Paul's preaching ministry. The inclusion of the Holy Spirit and the power of God in the midst of Paul's hardships list once more affirms that suffering is intrinsic to apostolic ministry, and this theme goes back to 1.9 and 4.7-12 (see Chapters 3 and 5) and points forward to 12.6-10 and 13.1-10 (see Chapter 7). The complete dependence on God's power in all aspects of Paul's apostolic ministry clearly forms a stark contrast to the self-sufficiency and independence of the ideal Hellenistic sage. For Paul, power lies not in the deliverance from hardships but elsewhere in the powerful working of the Holy Spirit through his sufferings in his apostolic mission.[86]

In wrapping up his hardships list, Paul presents a series of three διά phrases and seven ὡς phrases containing a series of antitheses (6.7-10) in a similar fashion to those found in 4.8-9. The first διά phrase, διὰ τῶν ὅπλων τῆς δικαιοσύνης τῶν δεξιῶν καὶ ἀριστερῶν, has attracted considerable attention particularly on the meaning of τῶν ὅπλων τῆς δικαιοσύνης. It has been variously understood as weapons of defence and offence in spiritual warfare,[87] weapons that the God of righteousness supplied,[88] weapons of righteousness to be wielded during times of prosperity and adversity as associated with the right and left arms respectively,[89] Paul's readiness for attack from any quarter[90] and Paul's complete equipment for the ministry of the gospel.[91] The last option is to be preferred in view of Paul's elaboration on his apostolic ministry, and this phrase may also be taken as Paul's summary statement for the list of virtues in 6.6-7.

The second and third διά phrases,[92] together with the ὡς phrases, form a series of antitheses further describing Paul's suffering. The antitheses in 6.8-10 are set out in Table 6.2 and this will assist us in evaluating the relationship between each set of descriptions.

---

86. For a helpful exposition on this, see Fee, *God's Empowering Presence*, 332–5; and Gräbe, *Power of God*, 120–31.

87. Furnish, *II Corinthians*, 346; Plummer, *Second Epistle*, 198. Contra Thrall, *II Corinthians*, I:462 and Harris, *Second Corinthians*, 478, who both rightly note that any reference to spiritual warfare is to overload the imagery.

88. Harris, *Second Corinthians*, 477–8.

89. Garland, *2 Corinthians*, 311.

90. Hughes, *Second Corinthians*, 231.

91. Barnett, *Second Epistle*, 188; Mak, 'Holistic View of Pauline Suffering', 191.

92. It is best to take these phrases to be connecting statements for the following antithesis. See Fitzgerald, *Cracks in an Earthen Vessel*, 195; Ebner, *Leidenslisten und Apostelbrief*, 260–3.

Table 6.2. *Antitheses in 2 Corinthians 6.8-10*

	Column A		Column B
1	ὡς πλάνοι	καὶ	ἀληθεῖς
	as deceivers	and yet	true
2	ὡς ἀγνοούμενοι	καὶ	ἐπιγινωσκόμενοι
	as unknown	and yet	well-known
3	ὡς ἀποθνῄσκοντες	καὶ	ἰδοὺ ζῶμεν
	as dying	and	behold we live
4	ὡς παιδευόμενοι	καὶ	μὴ θανατούμενοι
	as punished	and yet	not killed
5	ὡς λυπούμενοι	ἀεὶ δὲ	χαίροντες
	as sorrowful	but always	rejoicing
6	ὡς πτωχοὶ	πολλοὺς δὲ	πλουτίζοντες
	as poor	but	making many rich
7	ὡς μηδὲν ἔχοντες	καὶ	πάντα κατέχοντες
	as having nothing	and yet	possessing everything

Several possibilities of understanding the antitheses in Table 6.2, aptly described as 'vicissitudes of the apostolic life' by Bruce,[93] emerge:

1. Column A describes the outward appearance while column B the inner reality.[94] But items 2B, 3B, and 4B do not match this description.
2. Both Columns A and B represent two sides of assessments of Paul, with the former being the worldly standard and the latter the divine.[95] Again items 3B and 4B do not match.
3. Column A represents Paul's reputation among the Corinthians while Column B represents what they are in reality.[96] But item 1A does not match, as there is no evidence that the Corinthians consider Paul to be a deceiver.
4. Mak takes the antitheses as Paul's rebuttal of the criticisms of the opponents where Column A represents these criticisms while Column

93. Bruce, *1 & 2 Corinthians*, 212.

94. Bultmann, *Second Corinthians*, 173–4; Windisch, *Der zweite Korintherbrief*, 207. Cf. Fitzgerald, *Cracks in an Earthen Vessel*, 196, who suggests that the contrast intended here is between appearance and being.

95. Bruce, *1 & 2 Corinthians*, 212. Cf. Furnish, *II Corinthians*, 357, who suggests Column A represents the false estimate of Paul from worldly standards and Column B the true judgement from those in Christ; and Wan, *Power in Weakness*, 94, who regards Column A as a 'mistaken evaluation' of Paul and Column B as 'his vindication'. See also Barnett, *Second Epistle*, 331; Craig S. Keener, *1 & 2 Corinthians*, NCBC (Cambridge: Cambridge University Press, 2005), 188; Schiefer Ferrari, *Die Sprache des Leids*, 224–33.

96. Allo, *Seconde Épître aux Corinthiens*, 177; Watson, *Second Corinthians*, 71.

B constitutes Paul's rebuttals.[97] As I have earlier pointed out, Mak's argument stands on shaky ground as his working assumption is based on 'mirror reading' and the need for Paul to successfully defend and refute the criticisms of the opponents.

5. Both columns depict Paul as speaking for himself and not repeating what is said by others, and stating truth equally on both sides of the account.[98] The difficulty here is to admit that Paul would have thought of himself as a deceiver, as item 1A indicates.

As with the antitheses in 2 Cor. 4.8-9, it is preferable to see all the antitheses in 6.8-10 as expressing 'two concurrent and paradoxical realities' in Paul's apostolic life.[99] It cannot be discounted that some of the items in Column A illustrate ways in which Paul has been maligned and misunderstood by those who judge him (e.g., item 1A where Paul is treated as a deceiver. Cf. ESV, RSV, NRSV: 'we are treated as impostors'). As such, it is wise not to classify narrowly and neatly columns A and B into any of the categories mentioned above.

These antitheses demonstrate three important themes that are central in Paul's apostolic existence which is analogous to the Isaianic Servant of the Lord: (1) the harsh reality of apostolic suffering grounded in the story of Jesus as intrinsic to Paul's apostolic call as the Servant of the Lord; (2) the misgiving and misunderstanding of the nature of his ministry characterized by suffering; and (3) the powerful working of God's power experienced by Paul in the midst of his sufferings.[100] Seen from this perspective, Column B complements Column A in Paul's understanding of his apostolic existence. Column A portrays the actual circumstances that may have been viewed negatively as reasons for causing offence while Column B describes the deeper reality of Paul's life that can only be understood when grounded in the story of Jesus. Taken together, their cumulative effect of surprise is heightened. Paul is not a deceiver, unknown, dying, punished, sorrowful, poor or posessing nothing. This is not the whole story as there is another side to it: Paul is true, well known, lives, rejoices, makes many rich and possesses everything in Christ. Despite all the negative circumstances, God's power is at the same time working in Paul. The emphasis here is not merely on Paul's survival, but there is a wider divine purpose operative in Paul's survival ensuring that the apostolic mission is not impeded by his sufferings.

---

97. Mak, 'Holistic View of Pauline Suffering', 199–202.

98. Denney, *Second Corinthians*, 233–4.

99. Harris, *Second Corinthians*, 480; Matera, *II Corinthians*, 154.

100. Cf. Hafemann, *Suffering and the Spirit*, 78–9, who argues that Paul commends himself in two ways. Actively, Paul exhibits his apostolic experience through suffering and his great endurance as a demonstration of the qualities of the Servant of the Lord. Passively, through his sufferings, Paul displays the power of God at work in him in delivering him from death and at the same time mediating life through his suffering.

b) *The Story of Jesus in 2 Corinthians 6.4-10*. As I argued earlier, the basis of Paul's commendation is his apostolic status as a servant of God (6.4). By appealing to a detailed list of hardships, this demonstrates that underlying Paul's commendation is the recognition that his ministry embodies the tradition analogous to the Isaianic Servant of the Lord, and this is demonstrated in Paul's own citation of Isa. 49.8 in 2 Cor. 6.2. At the same time, Paul's list of sufferings also underscores his faithfulness, unswerving loyalty and dedicated commitment to the cause of the gospel of Christ which has been entrusted to him (5.19). As such, any argument that the hardships list here is to demonstrate Paul's attitude in facing all the negative experiences in his apostolic ministry or that the hardships are 'occupational hazards' completely misses the force of Paul's argument.[101]

As in Paul's earlier mention of his sufferings in 1.5-11; 2.14-16; and 4.7-12, what makes this list stand out is its Christological rationale. Paul has allowed the story of Jesus to redefine his understanding of his suffering. For Paul, suffering is what characterizes a servant of God.[102] It should not be seen as divine disfavour or some form of unfortunate circumstances that inflict him. Neither is Paul's suffering merely a consequence of his apostolic activities, for suffering is necessary and integral to his calling as a servant and apostle.[103]

i) *Treated as an Impostor*. In 2 Cor. 6.8, Paul is accused of being a deceiver or an impostor (πλάνος). In this context, πλάνος, which is derived from the verb πλανάω, carries the sense 'treated as deceiver or an imposter' (e.g., ESV, NRSV). According to early Christ-movement tradition, Jesus himself was accused of leading the people astray during his earthly ministry (πλανᾷ; Jn 7.12). After his death, he was labelled as 'that impostor' in the synoptic tradition (ὁ πλάνος; Mt. 27.63). In line with this, Scott argues: 'Just as Jesus was executed as a messianic pretender, a "deceiver" (*planos*) of the people, so also Paul – the apostle of Jesus Christ who shares in Christ's death and life … is also regarded as a *planos*.'[104] Therefore, it should not be completely discounted that Paul has the story of Jesus in mind when he reflects on the charge levelled against himself. Paul's response to this charge is to affirm his truthfulness. This is consistent with what Paul earlier declares in 2.17, 'For we are not, like so many, peddlers of God's word, but as men of sincerity, as commissioned by God, in the sight of God we speak in Christ' (ESV). Here, Paul affirms that his divine call and mission are genuine (cf. Gal. 1.1, 15-16), and his message is true (cf. 2 Cor. 4.2; 6.7).

---

101. Witherington, *Conflict & Community in Corinth*, 398–401.

102. As rightly postulated by Kruse, the true servant of God is the Suffering Servant (*Second Corinthians*, 132).

103. Cf. Manus, 'Apostolic Suffering', 46, who argues that Paul attempts to highlight his own understanding of 'the fate of a servant of Christ' in 6.4-10.

104. Scott, *2 Corinthians*, 149. Cf. Harris, *Second Corinthians*, 480, where he describes the relationship of Paul and Jesus as 'like master, like slave'.

ii) *As Dying and Behold We Live*. By asserting ὡς ἀποθνῄσκοντες καὶ ἰδοὺ ζῶ
μεν, Paul returns to the theme of death and life he earlier developed in 1.8-11;
2.14-17; and 4.7-12. The verb ἀποθνῄσκω carries the meaning 'the prospect of
death or realization of mortality'.[105] This should not surprise the Corinthians as
it is not the first time Paul foregrounds the notion of death or dying in his argument. It is a reference to Paul's continual encounters with death (e.g., 1.8-11;
4.10-12; 11.23. Cf. 1 Cor. 4.9; 15.30-1; see also Acts 9.23-5; 14.19; 21.30-2)
and the sufferings that he endured (e.g., 1.5-11; 2.14-16; 4.7-12; 11.23-33; cf.
Acts 13.50; 16.22-4; 20.23). Yet through all these, Paul can claim ζῶμεν, a
reference to ongoing physical life. It is striking that ζῶμεν is the only finite
verb in the list of antitheses and this description of Paul being alive is further
reinforced with ἰδού, which not only sets itself apart from the rest of the antitheses, but also introduces a surprising element that something new or unusual
is to follow where particular attention is required.[106] The use of ἰδού further
gives a sense that what follows will be unexpected and contrary to anticipation,
that is, Paul is expected to experience death, but the reverse is true because he
lives. The hardship list shows Paul being exposed to all kinds of afflictions to
the magnitude that even surpasses one's imagination, and yet these challenges
are put in the right perspective in the climactic paradoxical statement: as dying,
and behold we live.

This declaration of Paul, 'as dying, and behold we live', is solidly grounded
in the story of Jesus. Roetzel rightly asserts that this phrase marks Paul's most
apt 'linkage of apostolic participation in Jesus' death and resurrection in Second
Corinthians'.[107] He further argues that through this phrase, Paul 'quite explicitly ... finds his own brutal experience to parallel and to participate symbolically
in the death and resurrection of Jesus'.[108]

The crucial point that Paul is making here is not that God delivers him from
death, although this is no doubt true, but that he is the bearer of the dying of
Jesus in order that the life of Jesus, the resurrection power of God, may be made
manifest in him (cf. 2 Cor. 4.10-11).[109] The fact that Paul continues to live to
carry on his apostolic mission testifies to God's power at work within him in
this eschatological age.

As such, the story of Jesus climaxed in the death and resurrection becomes for
Paul the ultimate paradigm. Paul sees his life as belonging to the narrative of his
Lord. Neither death nor life is viewed as simply a physical reality. Seen through

---

105. BDAG, s.v.

106. BDAG, s.v. See also the use of ἰδού in 6.2 and the discussion above.

107. Calvin J. Roetzel, '"As Dying, and Behold We Live" Death and Resurrection in Paul's
Theology', *Int* 46 (1992): 5–18 (17).

108. Roetzel, 'As Dying', 17. Cf. Keener, *1 & 2 Corinthians*, 189.

109. Cf. Barnett, *Second Epistle*, 332 n. 8: 'the pattern of Paul's experiences serves to disclose
Jesus, in this case the death and the life of Jesus'. Cf. the discussion in Chapter 5.

the story of Jesus, Paul can now appreciate an alternative beginning and ending of the human story,[110] and this serves as a reinforcement of what Paul earlier articulated in 4.11-12. Paul now lives to fulfil his role as a co-worker of Jesus.

iii) *Poor yet Making Many Rich.* Ὡς πτωχοὶ πολλοὺς δὲ πλουτίζοντες is probably the most paradoxical statement in Paul's hardships list in 6.4-10 and is rightly considered as 'an oratorical climax' which serves as a fitting summary of all that has been said earlier.[111] When Paul announces ὡς πτωχοὶ πολλοὺς δὲ πλουτίζοντες, he is not applying economic sense here, that his material poverty makes others materially rich, although his material poverty is attested to elsewhere (see 1 Cor. 4.11; cf. Rom. 8.35; 2 Cor. 11.9, 27; Phil. 4.11-12). Neither does Paul have in mind that because of his material poverty the Corinthians have been spiritually enriched, although it is true that the Corinthians have been spiritually enriched in Christ in every way through Paul's ministry (1 Cor. 1.5).[112] As such, it is clear that Paul does not structure his thoughts merely according to the material poverty-material riches or material poverty-spiritual riches framework.

There is no denying that the paradigm of 'poor yet making many rich' is firmly rooted in the story of Jesus. By making this declaration, Paul is not only following after but conforming to the pattern of Jesus; as Murphy-O'Connor notes, 'it is confirmation that Paul embodies "the life of Jesus"'.[113] This is in line with my earlier argument based on 4.10-11 that Paul considers his suffering to be related to the sufferings of Christ. Grounded in the story of Jesus, Paul sees his sufferings as participating in Jesus' death and passion in fulfilling God's promises in the eschatological age.

Paul's understanding of 'poor yet making many rich' finds concrete expression elsewhere in 2 Cor. 8.9 and Phil. 2.5-11. In 2 Cor. 8.9, Paul evokes the example

110. Cf. Paul S. Minear, 'Some Pauline Thoughts on Dying: A Study of 2 Corinthians', in *From Faith to Faith: Essays in Honor of Donald G. Miller on His Seventieth Birthday*, ed. D. Y. Hadidian, PTMS 23 (Pittsburg: Pickwick, 1979), 91–106 (92–4).

111. David L. Mealand, 'As Having Nothing and Yet Possessing Everything, 2 Cor 6:10c', *ZNW* 67 (1976): 277–9 (278).

112. Cf. Keener, *1 & 2 Corinthians*, 189, who argues that it is Paul's 'sacrificial poverty that makes many rich by the gospel' and this pattern 'emulates Jesus, who became poor to make others rich'. Keener draws his argument from ancient philosophers (e.g., Plutarch *Lysander* 2.4; 30.2; Seneca *Ad Lucilium* 66.22) who despite the low status of the poor could still function as great benefactors, remaining poor to make others rich. Cf. also the dubious argument of George Wesley Buchanan, 'Jesus and the Upper Class', *NovT* 7 (1964–5): 195–209. Buchanan argues that as a wealthy businessman, Jesus took on voluntary financial self-impoverishment that produces spiritual wealth for the Corinthians. For a critique of this view, see Thrall, *II Corinthians*, II:552–3.

113. Murphy O-Connor, *Theology*, 65. Similarly, according to Morna Hooker, Paul claims that he is sharing in a very real way in the death and resurrection of Jesus, participating in his sufferings, and that these sufferings bring benefits to others (*Not Ashamed of the Gospel: New Testament Interpretations of the Death of Christ* [Grand Rapids: Eerdmans, 1994], 27–8).

of Jesus as the ground of his appeal to the Corinthians for his monetary collection for Jerusalem, 'For you know the grace of our Lord Jesus Christ, that though
he was rich (πλούσιος), yet for your sakes he became poor (ἐπτώχευσεν), so that
by his poverty (πτωχείᾳ) you might become rich (πλουτήσητε).' There have been
debates whether Paul has in mind in this context the act of Christ voluntarily
embracing human poverty, or the humiliating death of Christ by identifying with
the spiritual poverty of fallen humanity, or the event of incarnation.[114] But, as
I have argued earlier, the story of Jesus in Paul's thought would constitute the
incarnation, life, death and resurrection of Jesus in what Horrell describes as
'one seamless act'.[115] Thus, it is not necessary to limit it to a particular event
in the life of Jesus, be it the incarnation or death. That Paul has in mind the
pre-existent Christ becoming human in 8.9 is also confirmed in Phil. 2.5-11,
where Jesus is said to have 'emptied himself, taking the form of a servant, being
born in human likeness.[116] And being found in human form, he humbled himself
and became obedient to the point of death – even death on a cross' (Phil. 2.7-8;
cf. Gal. 4.4-5). Recalling the story of Jesus as the supreme exemplar[117] is to
motivate the Philippians to be humble and look out for the interests of others.

Horrell has pointed out that on both of these occasions in 2 Cor. 8.9 and
Phil. 2.5-11, Paul's retelling of the story of Jesus is to inculcate in his readers
behaviour that he wishes them to emulate.[118] In 2 Cor. 8.9, Christ is the model
for generous giving, while in Phil. 2.5-11 Christ is the model for proper attitude. But it is interesting to note that, in both these passages, Paul's appeal to
the story of Jesus becomes the ground of appeal directed towards his readers
and not himself. It is in 2 Cor. 6.10 that Paul applies the exemplar of Jesus in
becoming poor to enrich others to his apostolic ministry. While Christ's story in
relation to the redemptive significance here is inimitable, the pattern of faithful
endurance through suffering for the sake of others is clearly mirrored in Paul's
life.[119] The 'self-lowering other-regard' paradigm as suggested by Horrell is

114. See Harris, *Second Corinthians*, 578–80 and Thrall, *II Corinthians*, II:532–5, for various
options of interpretation. See also James Dunn's forceful argument for a non-incarnationalist
reading in his *Christology in the Making: A New Testament Inquiry into the Origins of the Doctrine of the Incarnation*, 2nd edn (London: SCM Press, 1989), 114–21; and *Theology of Paul*,
281–8.

115. Horrell, *Solidarity and Difference*, 212, 237. So Stegman, *Character of Jesus*, 189. See
also Harris, *Second Corinthians*, 580, where 'Christ's incarnation, life, and death-resurrection' is
to be taken 'in a single glance as "becoming poor"'. *Pace* Woods, 'St. Paul's Apostolic Weakness', 70–80, where 2 Cor. 8.9 refers narrowly to Christ's death and resurrection.

116. So Furnish, *II Corinthians*, 417; Martin, *2 Corinthians*, 263–4; Thrall, *II Corinthians*,
II:533–4.

117. For further discussion on the notion of Jesus as exemplar in Phil. 2.6-11, see Fowl, *Story
of Christ*, 49–101.

118. Horrell, *Solidarity and Difference*, 237.

119. Cf. Horrell, *Solidarity and Difference*, 210.

paradigmatically demonstrated in the central story of Jesus himself, whose self-lowering takes the movement from one extreme end to another: from the form of God (and equality with God) to the form of slave.[120] This self-giving of Jesus informs Paul's understanding of his apostolic existence and this is mirrored in Paul's proclamation to the Corinthians. This is unmistakably reflected in 4.5 where Paul declares that οὐ γὰρ ἑαυτοὺς κηρύσσομεν ἀλλὰ Ἰησοῦν Χριστὸν κύριον, ἑαυτοὺς δὲ δούλους ὑμῶν διὰ Ἰησοῦν. Here, careful attention is to be given to the parallel content of Paul's preaching: (1) Jesus Christ as Lord, *and* (as indicated by the δέ); (2) Paul as a slave of the Corinthians for Jesus' sake. This is a highly unusual statement as Paul only speaks of himself as a slave of Jesus/Christ (e.g., Rom. 1.1; Gal. 1.10; Phil. 1.1; cf. Titus 1.1) and never considers himself to be a slave of any human elsewhere, let alone making this part of his preaching. However, this is less surprising if we understand Paul's apostolic ministry as grounded in the story of Jesus and embracing the 'self-lowering other-regard' paradigm. By proclaiming himself as the slave of the Corinthians, it signifies that Paul's apostolic self-understanding modelled after Jesus is one that is orientated towards others and not for any self-benefit. This 'self-lowering other-regard' plot of the story of Christ becomes the lens through which Paul makes sense of his own experiences as he retells the story of his life to the Corinthians. Hence, it is the story of Jesus, rather than the narrative of his own life, on which Paul interprets and describes his own experience.[121]

As a slave, Paul is 'at the disposal of the Corinthians',[122] although Jesus remains his Lord as the prepositional phrase διὰ Ἰησοῦν indicates. By taking the position of a slave (cf. πᾶσιν ἐμαυτὸν ἐδούλωσα, 1 Cor. 9.19) and following the paradigm of self-humbling for the sake of others (ἐμαυτὸν ταπεινῶν, 2 Cor. 11.7), Paul's story finds its parallel in the story of Jesus narrated in Phil. 2.7-8. This pattern of conduct is so central to Paul's apostolic understanding because it represents a conformity to the self-giving of Christ for others which culminated in Christ's self-lowering and humiliation even to death.[123] It is this kind of apostolic service that later moves Paul to say that he would gladly 'spend and be spent' (2 Cor. 12.15) for the sake of the Corinthians. This is a clear demonstration that the enslavement of Paul to the Christ-community

---

120. Horrell, *Solidarity and Difference*, 210, and for a detailed treatment, see 204–45. See also the discussion by Gorman, *Cruciformity*, 242–4; Stegman, *Character of Jesus*, 188–96.

121. David G. Horrell, 'Paul's Narratives or Narrative Substructure? The Significance of "Paul's Story"', in *Narrative Dynamics in Paul: A Critical Assessment*, ed. Bruce W. Longenecker (Louisville: Westminster/John Knox, 2002), 166; and his *Solidarity and Difference*, 213 n. 35.

122. BDAG, s.v.

123. Cf. Gorman, *Cruciformity*, whose central thesis for Paul's narrative spirituality of the cross is the master story embedded in Phil. 2.5-11 where Christ the exalted one assumes lowly status, becoming like us, so that we can become exalted. This same structure is at work in 2 Cor. 6.3-10; and 8.9.

stands alongside his gospel. This fact is made even more significant in that
Paul feels he should never place any offence in the way of his ministry of
preaching the gospel (2 Cor. 6.3). This 'self-lowering other-regard' paradigm
ultimately envisages his relationship to Christ and his relationship to the
Christ-followers as one of slavery, 'as unquestioning service for the benefit
of the other, as the result of the unconditional but voluntary surrender of all
personal rights'.[124] It is this 'renunciation of one's own rights [that] makes
others rich'.[125]

In what ways has Paul made others rich? As we have seen, the logic behind
Paul's argument is clearly grounded in the story of Jesus. Working together
with Christ as his ambassador (5.20; 6.1), Paul sees his own role coloured by
the Servant figure of Isaiah in his citation of LXX Isa. 49.8 in 6.2. As such, Paul
casts himself as the voice 'saying to the prisoners, "Come out", to those who
are in darkness, "Show yourselves"' (Isa. 49.9; cf. 2 Cor. 4.6), bringing God's
people and gathering others back to God. By doing so, Paul is bringing the
riches of salvation and the eschatological blessings of God as embedded in the
Deutero-Isaiah new exodus motif to others and, as a consequence, making many
rich. The eschatological salvation and blessings of God include those presently
enjoyed by the Corinthians in Christ (1 Cor. 1.5) and those yet to come through
the final glorification. These blessings would include all those proclaimed by
Paul the minister of reconciliation as the gifts of salvation (6.2): salvation and
life (2.15-16; 4.12; cf. Rom. 6.23); new creation (5.17); reconciliation with God
(5.18-19); forgiveness of sins (5.19, 21); the righteousness of God (5.21); and
the gift of the Holy Spirit (5.5; cf. Rom. 8.23-4; Gal. 5.5). In addition, it is
very likely that Paul may also have in mind the abundant gifts of the Spirit, the
eschatological *charismata*, that are presently enjoyed by the Corinthians (8.7;
1 Cor. 1.7; 12.1-31; 14.1-25). The possession of these riches is, according to
God's promise, taking place 'now' (6.2).

It is therefore unmistakably clear that the ultimate beneficiaries of Paul's
apostolic ministry are the Corinthians themselves because they have received
both the eschatological salvation and gifts. When Paul continues his appeal
in 6.11-13 (which he earlier started in 6.1), he is once again inviting them to
see themselves as a part of this drama, either 'in solidarity with Paul ... or ...
as those being recalled from darkness to light'.[126] Seen from this perspective,
Willert is certainly right to assert that through the hardship list in 6.3-10, 'Paul
is not defending himself', but instead 'presents himself as a servant of recon-

---

124. Harris, *Second Corinthians*, 333. See 1 Cor. 9 where Paul voluntarily gives up his right to
financial support, which most likely results in him having to take up manual labour.

125. Hauck and Kasch, *TDNT* 6:329. For a similar argument, see Hafemann, *2 Corinthians*,
337–8.

126. Edith M. Humphrey, 'Ambivalent Apocalypse: Apocalyptic Rhetoric and Intertextuality
in 2 Corinthians', in *The Intertexture of Apocalyptic Discourse in the New Testament*, ed. Duane
F. Watson, SBLSymS 14 (Atlanta: Society of Biblical Literature, 2002), 113–35 (129).

ciliation in a context concerning reconciliation between God and the world'.[127] His ultimate purpose here is to persuade the Corinthians to identify themselves with the story of Jesus[128] and to see what Christ has done and, at the same time, to remind them that he has been given the ministry of reconciliation for their sake.

3. *The Function of the Catalogue of Sufferings in 2 Corinthians 6.3-10*

Based on the argument above, I may now briefly suggest three functions of Paul's catalogue of suffering in 6.3-10. This further reinforces my argument in the earlier chapters that Paul's sufferings cannot be isolated from his under-standing in relationship to his mission and the Corinthians. First, grounded in the story of Jesus, this catalogue reasserts that suffering is integral to Paul's call as a servant of God. Second, the hardships Paul experiences are all intimately connected with his missionary life and they do not constitute any cause for offence that may discredit his ministry. On the contrary, they emit a pleasing odour, both acceptable to God and salvific to the believing community (2.15-16). The life of Jesus is at work in the Corinthians because of, not despite, death being at work in Paul (4.10-12). Third, once the ground is clear that no fault may be found in his ministry, Paul launches into his appeal to the Corinthians for reconciliation (6.11-13). By doing so, Paul now turns the tables on them for it is no longer the nature of his ministry that is at stake but their faith if they choose to reject him because of his weakness and sufferings.[129]

Second Corinthians 6.1-10 clearly demonstrates that Paul places himself within God's redemptive drama. Paul's warrant for his role is found in the Scriptures and the story of Jesus. Hafemann correctly asserts that Paul's experi-ence is 'interpreted, informed, and only becomes authoritative, in light of the Scriptures and his Christology, rather than the other way around'.[130] Similarly, it is because Paul is an ambassador of Christ and a servant of God that he suffers, rather than the other way around.[131] Paul clearly sees his suffering in connection

---

127. Willert, 'Catalogues of Hardships', 236. So Fitzgerald, *Cracks in an Earthen Vessel*, 188: '6.3-10 is primarily paraenetic in function, and the apologetic aim is only secondary'. *Pace* those who see the *primary* function of this catalogue as Paul's defence, e.g., Hafemann, *Suffering and the Spirit*, 76–7; Mak, 'Holistic View of Pauline Suffering', 204; Wan, *Power in Weakness*, 92–3.

128. Cf. Sampley, *Second Corinthians*, 96.

129. Cf. Hafemann, *Suffering and the Spirit*, 79–80.

130. Hafemann, 'Paul's Argument', 282. *Pace* Lambrecht (*Second Corinthians*, 114–15): '[I]t would seem that Paul's profound Christological conviction offers him the ultimate explanation for his suffering, as well as a source of inspiration.' Lambrecht's argument is no doubt true but it misses another equally important factor at work in Paul's thought that cannot be in anyway minimized – the deep influence of Scripture.

131. *Pace* Pobee, *Persecution and Martyrdom*, 96–7.

with the story of Jesus as the fulfilment of the promises of God (1.5; 2.14-16; 4.10-11; 5.14; 6.3-10; 12.10; 13.4; cf. Col. 1.24). To be part of this narrative means that the ambassador of Christ will have to suffer just as Christ did, as rightly argued by Gignilliat, 'God's means of reconciling the world was by the suffering of the Christ. God's continued means of proclaiming the concrete fact of reconciliation is by the agency of the apostle who lives a life demonstrating the death of Jesus Christ for the other, that is, in his suffering for the benefit of the other.'[132]

If Paul's warrant for his suffering is grounded in the Scriptures and the story of Jesus, particularly the 'poor and yet making many rich' paradigm (6.10), then this is another striking fact that distinguishes Paul from the Hellenistic sages as Fitzgerald vigorously argues.[133] While it is true that moral philosophers have moral and spiritual riches despite their material poverty, the enrichment of others is not a dominant theme in their teachings. In this respect, Furnish rightly argues that 'there are no clear parallels in the descriptions of the Cynic and Stoic philosophers'.[134] The true Hellenistic sage is depicted as one 'who is sick and happy, in danger and happy, dying and happy, in exile and happy, in disgrace and happy' (Epictetus, *Diatribai* 2.19.24) and this has often been cited in support of Paul's provenance of his catalogue of suffering and in comparison with Paul's attempt to present himself in the same category as a virtuous sage. But a close examination of Paul's sufferings reveals that he is completely cast down by the hardships and is not impassive, unaffected or unmoved by the hardships.[135] Paul's great endurance should not be mistaken as a passive matter. In addition, Harrison also points out that Paul's 'poor and yet making many rich' paradigm is not rendered under compulsion and is carried out with no expectation of any return of gratitude, and this is another factor that distinguishes Paul from the Hellenistic sages.[136] Therefore, I can confidently come to a conclusion in support of Furnish that any apparent similarity between Paul and the Hellenistic sages is 'really no parallel at all'.[137]

---

132. Gignilliat, *Paul and Isaiah's Servants*, 111.

133. Fitzgerald, *Cracks in an Earthen Vessel*. The core of Fitzgerald's thesis is that Paul's catalogues of suffering have their provenance in Hellenistic thought and Paul is establishing that he is in the same category as the virtuous Hellenistic sages.

134. Furnish, *II Corinthians*, 359. Cf. Mealand, 'As Having Nothing and Yet Possessing Everything'. While Mealand notes there is similarity between Paul's use of this phrase and the Hellenistic philosophical writings, the framework from which Paul works is decidedly theological and, as such, sets him apart from them.

135. For further discussion, see Lambrecht, *Second Corinthians*, 113–14.

136. On the Hellenistic background of beneficence, see James R. Harrison, *Paul's Language of Grace in Its Graeco-Roman Context*, WUNT 2/172 (Tübingen: Mohr Siebeck, 2003), 250–68.

137. Furnish, *II Corinthians*, 357.

IV. *Concluding Summary*

In this chapter, I have argued that Paul's warrant for his apostolic suffering is grounded in the story of Jesus and Scripture. As an ambassador and co-worker of Christ in the ministry of reconciliation, Paul appeals to the Corinthians not to receive God's grace in vain. At the same time, Paul also sees his ministry as analogous to the Servant of Isaiah based on his citation of Isa. 49.8. On this basis, as a servant of God, Paul commends himself through his sufferings, thereby establishing that his suffering is not an obstacle to the progress of the gospel; neither is it merely a consequence of his apostolic activities. It is a necessary and essential part of his calling as a servant of God in carrying out the ministry of reconciliation.

Chapter 7

SECOND CORINTHIANS 11.23–12.10

I. *Introduction*

In this chapter, we turn our attention to the longest and most intense description of Paul's hardships in the Corinthian correspondence. Most commentators consider 2 Cor. 11.23-33 and 12.10 as two independent hardship lists, but I shall argue that 11.23–12.10 constitues a unified argument where 12.10 functions as the concluding statement. I shall also pay particular attention to the citation of LXX Jer. 9.22-3 in 10.17 which serves as the scriptural foundation for the theme of boasting. Finally, I shall further advance my thesis that Paul's understanding and boasting of his sufferings and weaknesses are grounded in the story of Jesus.

II. *Structure and Line of Thought*

Second Corinthians 11.23–12.10 is located within a larger literary unit (11.1–12.13) generally regarded as Paul's 'fool's speech'.[1] Together with 2 Cor. 10–13, much of this speech has been analysed primarily within the Hellenistic context using rhetorical criticism. As evident from the voluminous secondary literature, not only is this the most mined section of 2 Corinthians but also scholarly inter-

---

1.   For further discussion, see George Brown Davis, 'True and False Boasting in 2 Cor 10–13' (PhD dissertation, University of Cambridge, Cambridge, 1999); David E. Garland, 'Paul's Apostolic Authority: The Power of Christ Sustaining Weakness (2 Corinthians 10–13)', *RevExp* 86/3 (1989): 371–90; Mark Harding, 'The Classical Rhetoric of Praise and the New Testament', *RTR* 45 (1986): 73–82; Glenn S. Holland, 'Speaking like a Fool: Irony in 2 Corinthians 10–13', in *Rhetoric and the New Testament: Essays from the 1992 Heidelberg Conference*, ed. Stanley E. Porter and Thomas H. Olbricht, JSNTSup 90 (Sheffield: JSOT Press, 1993), 250–64; Jan Lambrecht, 'The Fool's Speech and Its Context: Paul's Particular Way of Arguing in 2 Cor 10–13', *Bib* 83 (2001): 305–24; Nichols, 'Strength of Weakness'; Aida Besançon Spencer, 'The Wise Fool (and the Foolish Wise): A Study of Irony in Paul', *NovT* 23 (1981): 349–60; Duane F. Watson, 'Paul's Boasting in 2 Corinthians 10–13 as Defense of His Honor: A Socio-Rhetorical Analysis', in *Rhetorical Argumentation in Biblical Texts: Essays from the Lund 2000 Conference*, ed. Anders Eriksson, Thomas H. Olbricht and Walter Überlacker (Harrisburg: Trinity, 2002), 260–75; Kasper K. H. Wong, *Boasting and Foolishness: A Study of 2 Cor 10:12-18 and 11:1a*, JDDS 5 (Hong Kong: Alliance Bible Seminary, 1998).

est is far from diminishing in view of the complex exegetical issues in these chapters.[2] These studies often assume that Paul not only is thoroughly familiar with the rhetorical school but also grounds his proclamation of the gospel and writings based on Greco-Roman conventions. The neat structure often proposed in the rhetorical analysis of these chapters according to the guidelines of the Hellenistic rhetorical handbooks may not be in reality that obvious; and even scholars differ on these structures. There is no doubt that many rhetorical devices are evident in Paul's 'fool's speech' including paradox, irony, sarcasm and play of words among others. But questions arise whether he deliberately crafts his argument according to the distinct genre employed by the professional orators when he categorically denies doing so (11.6; cf. 1 Cor. 1.17; 2.1-5).[3] As such, Hafemann is right to argue that, rather than trying to categorize the type of rhetorical speech Paul employs, 'the most fruitful approach to this passage is to trace the flow of Paul's argument'.[4]

Second Corinthians 11.23–12.10 is structured on the theme of Paul's boasting in τὰ τῆς ἀσθενείας μου (11.30; cf. 12.1, 5, 9), an act that is firmly grounded in the Scriptures as seen in the citation of LXX Jer. 9.22-3 and the explicit allusion to the story of Jesus (2 Cor. 13.4). Paul's boasting in his weaknesses is

---

2. For a sample, see Crafton, *Agency of the Apostle*; Frederick W. Danker, 'Paul's Debt to the *De Corona* of Demosthenes: A Study of Rhetorical Techniques in Second Corinthians', in *Persuasive Artistry: Studies in New Testament Rhetoric in Honor of George A. Kennedy*, ed. Duane F. Watson, JSNTSup 50 (Sheffield: Sheffield Academic Press, 1991), 262–80; Mario M. DiCicco, *Paul's Use of Ethos, Pathos, and Logos in 2 Corinthians 10–13*, MBPS 31 (Lewiston: Mellen, 1995); John T. Fitzgerald, 'Paul, the Ancient Epistolary Theorists, and 2 Corinthians 10–13', in *Greeks, Romans, and Christians: Essays in Honor of Abraham J. Malherbe*, ed. David. L. Balch, Everett Ferguson and Wayne A. Meeks (Minneapolis: Fortress Press, 1990), 190–200; Christopher Forbes, 'Comparison, Self-Praise and Irony: Paul's Boasting and the Conventions of Hellenistic Rhetoric', *NTS* 32 (1986): 1–30; Heckel, *Kraft in Schwachheit*; Long, *Ancient Rhetoric*; Johannes A. Loubser, 'A New Look at Paradox and Irony in 2 Corinthians 10–13', *Neot* 26 (1992): 507–21; Brian K. Peterson, *Eloquence and the Proclamation of the Gospel in Corinth*, SBLDS 163 (Atlanta: Scholars Press, 1998); Mark Edward Roberts, 'Weak Enough to Lead: Paul's Response to Criticisms and Rivals in 2 Corinthians 10–13, a Rhetorical Reading' (PhD dissertation, Vanderbilt University, Nashville, 2002); J. Paul Sampley, 'Paul, His Opponents in 2 Corinthians 10–13, and the Rhetorical Handbook', in *The Social World of Formative Christianity and Judaism: Essays in Tribute of Howard Clark Kee*, ed. Jacob Neusner, Peder Borgen, Ernest S. Frerichs and Richard Horsley (Philadelphia: Fortress Press, 1988), 162–77; Donald Dale Walker, *Paul's Offer of Leniency (2 Cor 10:1): Populist Ideology and Rhetoric in a Pauline Letter Fragment*, WUNT 2/152 (Tübingen: Mohr Siebeck, 2002); Charles A. Wanamaker, 'By the Power of God: Rhetoric and Ideology in 2 Corinthians 10–13', in *Fabrics of Discourse: Essays in Honor of Vernon K. Robbins*, ed. David B. Gowler, L. Gregory Bloomquist and Duane F. Watson (Harrisburg: Trinity, 2003), 194–221.

3. Cf. Lambrecht, 'Fool's Speech', 305: 'One should not probably expect too much of a rigid, balanced structure, i.e., not a rhetorical *disposition* nor another type of strict organization of the various items' (emphasis his).

4. Hafemann, *2 Corinthians*, 423.

illustrated by a series of narratives comprising: (1) an extended list of hardships (11.23-9); (2) the account of his humiliating escape from Damascus (11.30-3); (3) the account of the heavenly ascent without the anticipated revelation (12.1-6); and (4) the affliction of the 'thorn in the flesh' (12.7-9). The literary relationship between these narratives will be further explored below. A summary statement in 12.10 further reinforces the assertion that Paul's weaknesses and sufferings are experienced ὑπὲρ Χριστοῦ. This statement provides the Christological foundation for Paul's understanding of his sufferings and weakness that is further elaborated in 13.4.

As I have argued in earlier chapters, Paul develops the theme of his apostolic suffering at the crucial junctures of his argument. It is no different in 11.23–12.10. In his urgent appeal to the Corinthians, the issue of apostolic suffering not only takes centre stage but also is the most personal, intense and theologically developed section on his sufferings in 2 Corinthians.

III. *The Story of Jesus and Paul's Boasting in His Sufferings and Weaknesses*

A. *Paul's Appeal Grounded in the Story of Jesus (2 Corinthians 10.1)*

Paul begins 10.1 with a dramatic appeal: Αὐτὸς δὲ ἐγὼ Παῦλος παρακαλῶ ὑμᾶς διὰ τῆς πραΰτητος καὶ ἐπιεικείας τοῦ Χριστοῦ. This appeal is not dissimilar in tone with his earlier appeals in 5.20 and 6.1 (note the use of παρακαλέω),[5] once again signifying the urgency of the nature of the entreaty in this instance. However, compared to 5.20 and 6.1, the urgency in 10.1 is 'extraordinarily emphatic'[6] with the mention of his name and the use of intensive marker (αὐτὸς … ἐγὼ Παῦλος).

Paul's appeal is made διὰ τῆς πραΰτητος καὶ ἐπιεικείας τοῦ Χριστοῦ. Opinions are divided as to whether the attributes of πραΰτης and ἐπιείκεια allude to the kenotic revelation or to the earthly knowledge of Jesus. Leivestad argues that Paul is not referring to Jesus' 'mild and gracious attitude during his earthly life; he is alluding to the fact of the kenosis, the literal weakness and lowliness of the Lord'.[7] However, Leivestad's position has been criticized by Lambrecht who argues that Paul has 'concretely in mind the manner in which Jesus acted and behaved during his life on earth, *after birth and before death*'.[8] As I argued

---

5. See my earlier argument in Chapter 6.

6. Barnett, *Second Epistle*, 457. See also the excursus, 'The Meaning of αὐτὸς ἐγὼ Παῦλος in 2 Corinthians 10.1', in Hall, *Unity*, 106–12.

7. See Ragnar Leivestad, 'The Meekness and the Gentleness of Christ', *NTS* 12 (1966): 156–64, quotation from 163. So Barrett, *Second Corinthians*, 246; Güttgemanns, *Der leidende Apostel*, 140; Peterson, *Eloquence and the Proclamation*, 76–8.

8. Jan Lambrecht, 'Paul's Appeal and the Obedience to Christ: The Line of Thought in 2 Corinthians 10,1-6', *Bib* 77 (1996): 398–416 (413–14), (quotation from 414, emphasis mine).

earlier in Chapter 6, any dichotomy between the incarnation and the earthly life of Jesus is best avoided. That Paul has in mind the story of Jesus – the incarnation, life, death and resurrection as a seamless act – is further reinforced by his earlier allusions in 4.10-11; 5.21; 6.9-10; 8.9 (cf. Phil. 2.5-11).[9]

Why should Paul choose the attributes of πραΰτης and ἐπιείκεια as the basis for his appeal? Jennifer Larson argues that these attributes are not traits associated with masculinity and are virtues that are alien in the Hellenistic culture.[10] If this is correct, it suggests that Paul is not drawing from the cultural model that the Corinthians are familiar with but from divine standards of behaviour (cf. 10.12). Another clue that supports this argument is found in Paul's description of the criticism levelled against him – that he is ταπεινός when present with the Corinthians but θαρρῶ when he is away (10.2; cf. 10.10). Ταπεινός is a derogatory terminology carrying negative connotations of 'servile', 'abject', 'pliant' and 'inferior', qualities that would make one lose face in the Greco-Roman world.[11] This accurately describes the Corinthians' perception of Paul in 10.10 (cf. 11.7), an issue to which I shall return later. This is precisely how Paul characterizes himself when he boasts of the things that show his weaknesses (11.30), things perceived to be derogatory and humiliating in the eyes of the Corinthians. However negatively the Corinthians may have viewed him, Paul wishes to establish the fact right at the beginning of his appeal that his apostolic ministry is grounded in the story of Jesus, and this sets the tone for his subsequent argument. By recalling Jesus Christ's own character, Paul is drawing out his conformity to Christ and his willingness to surrender himself to weaknesses and sufferings through πραΰτης and ἐπιείκεια. At the same time, he is reminding the Corinthians that they are making a serious mistake if they find fault with him because he is ταπεινός.[12] Instead, what is incompatible with the πραΰτης and ἐπιείκεια of Christ is human boasting grounded in the confidence of the flesh (cf. 10.12-18; 11.17-18).

See also Bruce, *1 & 2 Corinthians*, 229; Windisch, *Der zweite Korintherbrief*, 292; Witherington, *Conflict and Community*, 437. For further discussion on πραΰτης and ἐπιείκεια see Walker, *Paul's Offer of Leniency*, 38–90, 331–40; Woods, 'St. Paul's Apostolic Weakness', 87–108.

9. Cf. Martin, *2 Corinthians*, 302; Barnett, *Second Epistle*, 460. Pace Walker, *Paul's Offer of Leniency*, 183–8, who argues that Paul is appealing not to '*the example of the earthly Jesus but ... the virtue which Christ displays in the administration of his present kingdom*. The aspect of the Christological story that most informs 2 Cor. 10.1 is not one about Christ's past or even pre-existence, but his present' (186, emphasis his).

10. Jennifer Larson, 'Paul's Masculinity', *JBL* 123 (2004): 85–97 (95–6).

11. BDAG, s.v.; Peter Marshall, 'Invective: Paul and His Enemies in Corinth', in *Perspectives on Language and Text*, ed. Edgar W. Conrad and Edward G. Newing (Winona Lake: Eisenbrauns, 1987), 359–73, argues that ταπεινός can mean 'obsequious' and has a general negative connotation in contemporary usage.

12. Cf. Leivestad, 'Meekness and the Gentleness', 164; Peterson, *Eloquence and the Proclamation*, 81; Woods, 'St. Paul's Apostolic Weakness', 106. See also my discussion in Chapter 6 on Paul's placing no obstacles in his ministry so that there would be no cause for offence.

B. *Paul's Ground for His Boasting (2 Corinthians 10.17)*

The theme of boasting not only appears frequently in 2 Cor. 10–13 but is also almost exclusively a Pauline expression. Καυχάομαι appears 37 times in the NT with the highest concentration in the Corinthian correspondence (6 times in 1 Corinthians and 20 times in 2 Corinthians)[13] particularly within 2 Cor. 10–13 (17 times). Two other boasting word groups, καύχημα and καύχησις, also have the highest concentration in 1 and 2 Corinthians.[14] On a lexical level, these statistics strongly suggest that the theme of boasting is dominant in 2 Corinthians, with its strongest expression found in chapters 10–12.

In evaluating Paul's boasting, divergent evidences emerge. On the one hand, Paul refers positively to boasting in his weaknesses (11.30; 12.1, 5, 9). On the other hand, he denies that he is boasting beyond measure (10.13-16). But on another occasion, he says he is forced to boast κατὰ σάρκα (11.16-18). Yet in the midst of his argument, Paul cites scriptural support for his boasting as 'boasting in the Lord' (10.17). Hence it is not surprising that Callan charges Paul as inconsistent in his boasting.[15] These apparent contradictory statements encourage my initial investigation on Paul's understanding of boasting. What is Paul's ground for his boasting? How does Paul evaluate boasting? Why does Paul practise boasting while apparently condemning others for doing so? In answering these questions, I shall pay close attention to Paul's citation of the boasting saying in 10.17.

1. *Paul and the Boasting of His Opponents*

What is clear is that Paul's opponents practise some kind of boasting (2 Cor. 11.12, 18, 21) concerning: (1) their Jewish heritage (11.21-3); (2) their boldness and achievements as servants of Christ (10.12-16); (3) their rhetorical eloquence (10.10); and (4) the miraculous signs and wonders they performed (12.11-12). They have also challenged the nature of Paul's apostolic authority (10.8) on several grounds: (1) his weak appearance and his less than eloquent preaching

---

13.   Apart from 1 and 2 Corinthians, καυχάομαι appears five times in Romans, twice in Galatians and once in Philippians. In Deutero-Pauline literature, καυχάομαι only appears in Ephesians. The remaining two occurrences are found in James.

14.   Καύχημα appears ten times in the NT; out of the nine times in the Pauline epistles, six appear in the Corinthian correspondence with the rest in Galatians and Philippians. The only other place where καύχημα appears outside the Pauline corpus is Hebrews. Καύχησις appears ten times in Pauline correspondence out of which seven are in the Corinthian correspondence, two in Romans and one in 1 Thessalonians. The only other place outside Pauline usage is found in James. The other rarer word group of καυχάομαι used by Paul is κατακαυχάομαι and this only appears twice both in Romans and James. For further discussion, see C. K. Barrett, 'Boasting in the Pauline Epistles', in *L'Apôtre Paul: Personnalité, style et conception du ministère*, ed. A. Vanhoye, BETL 73 (Leuven: Leuven University Press, 1986), 363–8.

15.   Terrance Callan, 'Competition and Boasting: Toward a Psychological Portrait of Paul', *ST* 40 (1986): 137–56.

(10.10; 11.6); (2) his refusal to accept financial support and his labour as an artisan to support himself (11.7-11); and (3) his lack of letters of recommendation (3.1; 12.11).[16] The interplay of these issues suggests that the opponents are boasting about their superiority against Paul (cf. 11.5; 12.11) resulting in Paul's strained relationship with the Corinthians concerning his views as to the concept and nature of apostolic ministry.

What then is the standard that the opponents use in boasting of their superiority against Paul? The clue that Paul provides is that they measure themselves by themselves and compare themselves with themselves (10.12) by employing the encomiastic topics parading physical appearance, education and achievements – a familiar Hellenistic social convention that the Corinthians readily recognize and accept.[17] By boasting about these encomiastic topics, the opponents could easily match Paul's Jewish pedigrees (11.23); however, Paul fails to match up to them and to the current acceptable standard of Hellenistic rhetorical skills, physical appearance and achievements required of any public speaker or leader (cf. 1 Cor. 1.17, 18-25, 27-31; 2.1-5, 6-7).[18]

When confronted with this widely accepted practice of boasting in one's honour, Paul has no choice but to respond to it by grounding his argument in the Scriptures as his warrant for legitimate boasting. Then he moves on to boast of the things that show his weaknesses, a practice that in the eyes of both the opponents and the Corinthians are to Paul's discredit. Finally, Paul demonstrates that his suffering and weaknesses are not dishonourable but are grounded in the story of Jesus, for Jesus himself was crucified in weakness (13.4). By doing so,

---

16. For further discussion, see Savage, *Power through Weakness*, 54–99. Cf. E. A. Judge, 'St Paul and Classical Society', *JAC* 15 (1972): 19–36 (35–6), who argues that these criticisms against Paul carry cultural overtones and reflect the social prejudices of the day.

17. Marshall, *Enmity in Corinth*, 327. Cf. Jerry L. Sumney, *'Servants of Satan'*, *'False Brothers' and Other Opponents of Paul: A Study of Those Opposed in the Letters of the Pauline Corpus*, JSNTSup 188 (Sheffield: Sheffield Academic Press, 2000), 79–133; idem, 'Studying Paul's Opponents', 14–17, 49. NLT captures this nuance well: 'they are only comparing themselves with each other, using themselves as the standard of measurement'.

18. See Forbes, 'Comparison', 2, where Paul's implies that the self-commendation of the opponents has taken the form of boasting of their authority, achievements and comparison against him, which is to his disadvantage. As Edwin A. Judge argues, 'As Paul himself complains, he was despised for *not* indulging in it ... Paul found himself a reluctant and unwelcomed competitor in the field of professional "sophistry" and ... promoted a deliberate collision with its standards of value' ('Paul's Boasting in Relation to Contemporary Professional Practice', *ABR* 16 [1968]: 37–50, quotation from 47). Cf. S. H. Travis, 'Paul's Boasting in 2 Corinthians 10–12', *SE* 6 (1973): 527–32 (528); Watson, 'Paul's Boasting in 2 Corinthians 10–13'; Bruce W. Winter, *Philo and Paul among the Sophists: Alexandrian and Corinthian Responses to a Julio-Claudian Movement*, 2nd edn (Grand Rapids: Eerdmans, 2002), 203–39. For an evaluation of honour among peers, see Savage, *Power through Weakness*, 23–4; Harry Adams Stansbury III, 'Corinthian Honor, Corinthian Conflict: A Social History of Early Roman Corinth and Its Pauline Community' (PhD dissertation, University of California, Irvine, 1990), 421–40.

Paul not only exposes the folly but also reverses the effects of the Hellenistic boasting, which he considers illegitimate. At the same time, Paul also seeks to bring about a conversion of the understanding of the Corinthians concerning his apostolic ministry.

2. *Paul's Citation of* LXX *Jeremiah 9.22-3/1 Kingdoms 2.10*

As Paul concludes the argument of 2 Cor. 10.12-18 on boasting in the divine authority given to him and expressed in his allocated sphere of ministry to the gentiles, he appeals to LXX Jer. 9.22-3: "Ὁ δὲ καυχώμενος ἐν κυρίῳ καυχάσθω".[19] Interestingly, this is the second time Paul cites this passage in addressing the Corinthians (cf. 1 Cor. 1.31). Surprisingly, not much scholarly attention has been paid to the boasting saying citation in 10.17,[20] which holds the key to unlock Paul's understanding of his boasting and the yardstick he uses to evaluate the legitimacy of boasting.

a) *Context of* LXX *Jeremiah 9.22-23/1 Kingdoms 2.10.* The messenger formula at the beginning of Jer. 9.22 (τάδε λέγει κύριος) and the ending of Jer. 9.23 (λέγει κύριος) and the phrase 'ἐγώ εἰμι κύριος' (Jer. 9.23) indicate that this is a prophetic oracle. In a series of three parallel clauses, Jeremiah warns against boasting in human wisdom, strength and riches as seen in the following structure.

> μὴ καυχάσθω ὁ σοφὸς ἐν τῇ σοφίᾳ αὐτοῦ
> καὶ
> μὴ καυχάσθω ὁ ἰσχυρὸς ἐν τῇ ἰσχύι αὐτοῦ
> καὶ
> μὴ καυχάσθω ὁ πλούσιος ἐν τῷ πλούτῳ αὐτοῦ

In contrast (as introduced by ἀλλά), Jeremiah presents the appropriate form of boasting, that is, to boast in one's understanding and knowledge of the Lord (Jer. 9.23). The fact that the theme of boasting occurs both negatively (Jer. 9.22) and positively (Jer. 9.23) suggests that the point of contrast is not in the *act* of boasting but in the *object* of one's boasting.[21] The boasting that Jeremiah speaks against involves an anthropocentric emphasis on the confidence in and reliance on one's ability in gaining wisdom, strength and wealth. This

---

19. The LXX verse numbering is being used here.

20. E.g., see Barnett, *Second Epistle*, 492; Garland, *2 Corinthians*, 457; Thrall, *II Corinthians*, II:652; Witherington, *Conflict and Community*, 440, all of which provide very brief treatment. Cf. Ulrich Heckel, 'Jer 9,22f. als Schlüssel für 2 Kor 10–13: Ein Beispiel für die methodischen Probleme in der gegenwärtigen Diskussion über den Schriftgebrauch bei Paulus', in *Schriftauslegung im antiken Judentum und im Urchristentum*, ed. Martin Hengel and Hermut Löhr (Tübingen: J. C. B. Mohr, 1994), 206–25 (206). For detailed treatment of the boasting saying, see Heckel, *Kraft in Schwachheit*, 145–72.

21. For a sample of both negative and positive boasting in the LXX, see Ps. 5.12; Prov. 25.14; 27.1; cf. Sir. 17.9; 50.20; *Ps. Sol.* 17.1. Cf. Heckel, *Kraft in Schwachheit*, 175–8.

threefold negative pronouncement is contrasted with a positive theocentric dependence on God.

The wider context of Jer. 9 provides further insights for Jeremiah's condemnation for self-centred boasting. Jeremiah begins by declaring Judah's unfaithfulness, in practising adultery, deceit and oppression by refusing to acknowledge the Lord (Jer. 9.2-6). As a result, God declares his judgement for their transgressions (Jer. 9.7-22). Following this come the pronouncement against those who place their trust in their wisdom, strength and wealth and the exhortation to boast in both understanding and knowing the Lord (Jer. 9.23-4). The chapter concludes with the pronouncement of God's impartial judgement on Judah (Jer. 9.25-6).

Jeremiah's critique on self-confidence is also reflected elsewhere. The prophet speaks against a culture of complacency brought about by the false sense of security of God's abiding presence based on the privileged status of Israel before God despite their transgressions (e.g., Jer. 6.13-15; 7.1-11; 8.8-11).[22] In addition, the prophet also provides a negative assessment of those who place their trust in their own wisdom (Jer. 8.8-9; 9.12; 10.7), strength (Jer. 17.5; 23.10) and unjustly acquired wealth (Jer. 5.26-9; 17.11). Brueggemann's comment on Jeremiah's triad criticism characterizes Israel's history:

> The prophet has constructed a new triad which intends to summarize the whole royal history which has continually reassured and deceived its key actors, but which has now brought Judah to the point of death. One could not imagine a more radical critique of the royal consciousness, for Jeremiah disposes in one stroke of all the sources of security and well-being upon which the royal establishment is built.[23]

The contrast to boasting in one's self-sufficiency is boasting in the understanding and the knowledge of God who exercises kindness, justice and righteousness on the earth. It is also interesting to note that God's attributes of love, justice and righteousness stand in sharp contrast with the attributes esteemed by Judah represented by wisdom, might and wealth. By admonishing Judah from placing their trust and glory in themselves, Jeremiah seeks to turn their attention from an *anthropocentric* boasting to *theocentric* boasting.

At the same time, Jeremiah's statement on the knowledge of God does not merely include God's attributes but also his actions in the world. As Davis has

---

22. Cf. Walter Brueggemann's argument that Jeremiah's criticism is levelled against a view described as 'royal consciousness' that is 'shaped by the conviction of Yahweh's abiding, sustaining presence on behalf of legitimated political-cultural institutions, especially the royal house and derivatively the royal temple' ('The Epistemological Crisis of Israel's Two Histories (Jer. 9:22-23)', in *Israelite Wisdom: Theological and Literary Essays in Honor of Samuel Terrien*, ed. John G. Gammie, Walter A. Brueggemann, W. Lee Humphreys and James M. Ward [Missoula: Scholars Press, 1978], 85–105 [90, 86]). For further analysis of the Jeremiah text, see Gail R. O'Day, 'Jeremiah 9:22-23 and 1 Corinthians 1:26-31: A Study in Intertextuality', *JBL* 109 (1990): 259–67 (260–2).

23. Brueggemann, 'Epistemological Crisis', 93.

noted, this emphasis raises a significant question whether boasting in the knowledge of God is *doxological* or *ethical* in nature.[24] Davis argues persuasively for a
participatory dimension where knowing God is directly related to ethical action.
Jeremiah clearly states in Jer. 9.3, 6 that the refusal of Judah to know God is
reflected in their sin and deception; and their disobedience will result in God's
judgement. As such, Davis argues that within this literary context, 'an endorsement
of a knowledge of God that is merely confessional would appear anti-climactic.
Thus the broader context of this passage suggests that one's obedient response to
God is an integral part of one's knowledge of God – the knowledge that should be
the focus of one's boast' and, as such, legitimate boasting includes 'one's active
participation in God's acts of righteousness, justice and mercy'.[25]

In the LXX version of the Song of Hannah (1 Kdgms 2.1-10), there are additional phrases similar to Jer. 9.22-3 which are missing in the MT. However, there
are also some differences. The wordings of σοφός/σοφία and ἰσχυρός/ἰσχύς in
Jeremiah are replaced with φρόνιμος/φρόνησις and δυνατός/δύναμις respectively
in 1 Kingdoms. However, the most significant difference is that the participatory dimension of Jer. 9.22-3 becomes explicit in 1 Kdgms 2.10. While Jer. 9
refers to κρίμα and δικαιοσύνη as attributes of God, in 1 Kingdoms, the content
of boasting includes understanding and knowing God and executing justice and
righteousness in the midst of the earth.[26]

In the wider context of 1 Kdgms 2.10, the Song of Hannah is a song of
praise offered up by Hannah after her prayer request for a son was granted. This
song extols God for reversing the position of the poor, weak and downtrodden
and at the same time humbling the strong, wicked and the adversaries of the
Lord (1 Kdgms 2.1-10). In this song, Hannah also speaks against self-centred
boasting (1 Kdgms 2.3) and rejoices that such boasting is ultimately overturned
by God's actions. In powerful narrative, the song describes God as the one who
'lifts up the poor from the earth, and raises the needy from the dunghill; to
seat him with the princes of the people, and causing them to inherit the throne
of glory' (1 Kdgms 2.8). Hannah's song is a testimony of her dependence on
God and a celebration of God's activity on her behalf. Therefore, in the context
of 1 Kingdoms, legitimate boasting encompasses the knowledge of God and
involvement in extending his activity in the world.

b) *Paul's Citation of LXX Jeremiah 9.22-3 in 1 Corinthians 1.31.* Since Jer.
9.22-3 is cited in 1 Cor. 1.31, a brief investigation of this passage within the
context of 1 Cor. 1 is relevant to our understanding of Paul's subsequent citation

24. Davis, 'True or False Boasting', 77–80.
25. Davis, 'True or False Boasting', 79, 80.
26. For further discussion, see Davis, 'True or False Boasting', 80–3; Emanuel Tov, 'Different
Editions of the Song of Hannah and of Its Narrative Framework', in *Tehillah le-Moshe: Biblical and Judaic Studies in Honor of Moshe Greenberg*, ed. Mordechai Cogan, Barry Eichler and
Jeffrey Tigay (Winona Lake: Eisenbrauns, 1997), 149–70 (164–8).

in 2 Cor. 10.17.[27] In 1 Cor. 1.31, the introductory formula καθὼς γέγραπται indicates not only a quotation from Scripture but also 'an explicit invitation to read Paul's text in concert with Jeremiah'.[28] Paul's quotation here and elsewhere in 2 Cor. 10.17 has generally been recognized as a condensed maxim of Jer. 9.22-3.[29] However, J. Ross Wagner has argued that the source of Paul's quotation should not be strictly limited to Jeremiah but should include 1 Kgdms 2.10 as well where the theme of the reversal of human pride in the Song of Hannah is echoed throughout 1 Cor. 1.18-31.[30]

The relationship between 1 Cor. 1.26-31 and Jer. 9.22-3/1 Kgdms 2.10 is not difficult to establish. Paul's reference to the triad of wise/powerful/noble birth (1 Cor. 1.26) can be traced to the triad of wise/strong/rich in Jer. 9.22 and 1 Kgdms 2.10.[31] In 1 Cor. 1.26-9, Paul stresses that the purpose of God choosing those who are foolish, weak, lowly and despised is to shame the wise, strong and those of noble birth so that no one might boast in the presence of God (1 Cor. 1.27-9).[32] The theme of reversal of status in the Song of Hannah is also

27. Cf. Hays, *Echoes of Scripture*, 29–32, where recurrence, one of the seven tests used in exegetical judgement of Paul's use of Scripture, concerns how often Paul cites or alludes to the same scriptural reference elsewhere. 'Where such evidence exists that Paul considered a passage of particular importance, proposed echoes from the same context should be given additional credence' (30). See Shum, *Paul's Use of Isaiah*, 8–9, for further expansion of this criteria.

28. O'Day, 'Jeremiah 9:22-23', 263.

29. O'Day, 'Jeremiah 9:22-23', 262–7, argues that Paul slightly modifies Jer. 9:23 in his quotation. Cf. Christopher D. Stanley, *Paul and the Language of Scripture: Citation Technique in the Pauline Epistles and Contemporary Literature*, SNTSMS 69 (Cambridge: Cambridge University Press, 1992), 186–8. See also Heckel, 'Jer 9,22f. als Schlüssel für 2 Kor 10–13', 208; Anthony C. Thiselton, *The First Epistle to the Corinthians*, NIGTC (Grand Rapids, Eerdmans, 2000), 196; Witherington, *Conflict and Community*, 118.

30. J. Ross Wagner, '"Not beyond the Things Which are Written": A Call to Boast Only in the Lord (1 Cor 4.6)', *NTS* 44 (1998): 279–87. See also Davis, 'True and False Boasting', 144–6; Richard B. Hays, 'The Conversion of the Imagination: Scripture and Eschatology in 1 Corinthians', *NTS* 45 (1999): 391–412 (404–6); John Paul Heil, *The Rhetorical Role of Scripture in 1 Corinthians*, SBLMS 15 (Atlanta: Society of Biblical Literature, 2005), 14, 37–9. Cf. Christopher Tuckett, 'Paul, Scripture and Ethics: Some Reflections', *NTS* 46 (2000): 403–44 (417–24).

31. O'Day, 'Jeremiah 9:22-23', 264. Contra James M. Gibbs, 'Wisdom, Power and Wellbeing', in *Studia Biblica 1978 III: Papers on Paul and Other New Testament Authors*, JSNTSup 3, ed. E. A. Livingstone (Sheffield: JSOT Press, 1980), 119–55 (120); and Willert, 'Catalogues of Hardships', 237–8, who only refer to Jer. 9.22-3 as the source of the quotation. In *1 Clem.* 13.1, Clement agrees closely with LXX Jer. 9.22-3 for the most part but it also contains a phrase that is unique to 1 Kgdms 2.10 (καὶ ποιεῖν κρίμα καὶ δικαιοσύνην). In addition, Clement appears to be heavily dependent on Paul's distinctive wording in 1 Cor. 1.31 and 2 Cor. 10.17 (ὁ καυχώμενος ἐν κυρίῳ καυχάσθω) found neither in Jer. 9.22-3 nor 1 Kgdms 2.10. At the least, this demonstrates Clement's familiarity with Jeremiah and 1 Kingdoms where he most likely conflates them with Paul's unique citation of these texts. For further discussion, see Donald A. Hagner, *The Use of the Old and New Testaments in Clement of Rome*, NovTSup 34 (Leiden: Brill, 1973), 203–4.

32. David G. Horrell, *The Social Ethos of the Corinthian Correspondence: Interests and*

prominent in 1 Cor. 1.18-31. Earlier on, Paul describes the reversal of status affected by the cross: God has made the wisdom of the world into foolishness, and he has made the foolishness of the kerygma as the means of salvation for those who believe. The Messiah crucified, a stumbling block to the Jews and foolishness to the gentiles, is now the power and wisdom of God.

Paul finds Jeremiah's critique of the source of false security of Judah compelling for the situation of the Corinthians.[33] What Paul is articulating here is a critique of the false sense of security of those who boast in the values of wisdom, strength and noble birth, and qualities of honour and status accomplished by human hands. By doing so, Paul attempts to shift from anthropocentric boasting to theocentric boasting. The redefinition of boasting results in distorted individual and societal identity grounded in the prevailing social conventions being now superseded by the true source of the community's identity that is grounded in the story of Jesus. In this context, Paul is drawing upon the Scriptures in his effort to reshape the identity of the Corinthians.[34]

As in the context of Jeremiah, the boasting element in 1 Corinthians does not merely focus on the soteriological aspects to the exclusion of the ethical dimension.[35] There are two clues that the participatory dimensions are prevalent. First, when Paul exhorts the Corinthians to boast in the Lord, he is calling them to reconfigure their identity in the light of the story of Jesus: Jesus Christ crucified (1 Cor. 2.2). Paul's exposition of the status reversal through the foolishness of the cross proves the unreliability of using these anthropocentric criteria in determining one's honour in society.[36] This is reflected in the manner in which Paul first brings the message of the gospel to Corinth; it is not grounded in eloquent rhetoric or superior wisdom but in a demonstration of the power of God (1 Cor. 1.17; 2.1-5). Paul's mode of operation is tantamount to a critique of the culture of Corinth and a rejection of the traditional means of oratory delivery expected by society.[37] The very faith of the Corinthians is most intimately linked

Ideology from 1 Corinthians to 1 Clement, SNTW (Edinburgh: T&T Clark, 1996), 134, cautions against reading 1 Cor. 1.26 simply as a piece of information concerning the sociological composition of the Christ-believers in Corinth but argues for paying attention to Paul's aim of denying all human grounds of boasting and proclaiming the only appropriate ground of boasting in the Lord.

    33. Hays, *First Corinthians*, 34; O'Day, 'Jeremiah 9:22-23', 267.

    34. For further discussion, see Hays, 'Conversion of the Imagination'. Cf. the study of Heil, *Rhetorical Role*, where his concern is to demonstrate how 'Paul's use of scripture in 1 Corinthians does not merely inform his listeners but performs a rhetorical strategy aimed at persuading and transforming them in various ways' (5). For further discussion, see William S. Campbell, *Paul and the Creation of Christian Identity*, LNTS 322 (London: T&T Clark, 2006), 159–73.

    35. See Davis, 'True and False Boasting'. 146–9.

    36. David A. DeSilva, *Honor, Patronage, Kinship and Purity: Unlocking New Testament Culture* (Downers Grove: InterVarsity, 2000), 75.

    37. For further discussion, see Winter, *Philo and Paul*, 111–239, where he compares Paul's initial proclamation of the gospel in Corinth with the *modus operandi* of well-known Sophist

to *what* Paul proclaims and not to *how* he proclaims it. As such, what Paul is attempting to do is to issue an invitation to the Corinthians to be participants in the story of Jesus. This can only become a reality if there is 'a conversion of the imagination' on their part.[38] Second, it may not be insignificant that the vocabulary of Jer. 9.22-3/1 Kdgms 2.10 reflected in the triads of fools/weak/disrepute and wise/strong/honour appears again in 1 Cor. 4.10 in the context of Paul's sufferings (1 Cor. 4.9-13).[39] Here, as in 1 Cor. 1.26-31, Paul is warning the Corinthians that their boasts are dangerously misplaced and a correction of their behaviour is urgently required (1 Cor. 4.14-15; cf. 5.2, 6). Paul points to himself as a model to imitate (1 Cor. 4.16). The Corinthians are therefore challenged to turn from judging their status and security according to the world's standard of what is wise, powerful and noble and to embrace Paul's 'way of life in Christ Jesus' (1 Cor. 4.17).

c) *Paul's Citation of LXX Jeremiah 9.22-3 in 2 Corinthians 10.17.* While Paul's critique of the wise/strong/noble birth in 1 Corinthians is obvious, it is less obvious in 2 Cor. 10. However, a close examination will reveal that the notion of boasting and the reversal of status found in Jeremiah and 1 Kingdoms remains firmly rooted in Paul's thought.

In 2 Cor. 10, Paul denounces all arguments and every lofty opinion against the knowledge of God by taking every thought captive in obedience to Christ (10.3-6). He also responds to those who place emphasis on eloquent rhetoric and personal appearance, traits that conform to contemporary acceptable standards (10.10). He also takes issue with those who measure and compare themselves with one another and calls them people 'without understanding' (10.12). Apart from his critique of the esteemed social values, Paul also describes his ministry as one that builds up and not one that destroys (10.8), echoing the language of Jeremiah. In 10.12-16, the theme of boasting comes to the fore. Paul argues

orators seeking to establish a reputation. Winter argues that the first initial contact is crucial to establish the reputation of an orator and that Paul deliberately distances himself from the conventional behaviour of visiting orators. Winter's persuasive argument explains why Paul purposely chooses a different method in his initial proclamation of the gospel. See also Winter, 'The Toppling of Favorinus and Paul by the Corinthians', in *Early Christianity and Classical Culture: Comparative Studies in Honor of Abraham J. Malherbe*, ed. John T. Fitzgerald, Thomas H. Olbright and L. Michael White, NovTSup 110 (Leiden: Brill, 2003), 291–306; E. A. Judge, 'The Conflict of Educational Aims in New Testament Thought', *JCE* 9 (1966), 32–45. See also Schnabel, *Early Christian Mission*, 2: 1325–8, 1361–2).

38. A phrase borrowed from Hays's article of the same title, 'Conversion of the Imagination', *NTS* 45 (1999): 391–412.

39. Horrell, *Social Ethos*, 136, suggests that the correspondence of these motifs is even stronger if 1 Cor. 1.27-8 is taken into account. See his diagram in 136 depicting the relationship of 1 Cor. 1.27-8 and 4.10. So Gibbs, 'Wisdom, Power and Wellbeing', 133–4; and Wagner, 'Not beyond the Things', 284–5.

that his boasting is reflected in the sphere of ministry that has been given to him by God. In a series of negative clauses, Paul describes what constitutes illegitimate boasting (10.12-15) and distances himself from the opponents who attack his credibility, and implies that they boast inappropriately. Paul concludes by repeating the quotation from Jer. 9.22-3: Ὁ δὲ καυχώμενος ἐν κυρίῳ καυχάσθω. This is then followed by a commentary in 10.18: 'For it is not those who commend themselves that are approved, but those whom the Lord commends.' In the context of 10.17, Paul associates the act of boasting with self-commendation. For Paul, self-commendation, however impressive, never constitutes the ground for boasting. Only those who boast in the Lord and the one who is commended by the Lord are legitimate servants of the Lord. The participatory dimension in 10.17-18 then becomes obvious: true boasting includes not only the privilege of knowing the Lord but also carrying out the Lord's activity on earth by being a co-worker of Jesus in a manner consistent with the story of Jesus.[40]

The significant difference in the use of the boasting sayings in 1 Cor. 1.31 and 2 Cor. 10.17 is that Paul applies the former to the Corinthians and the latter to his apostolic ministry. Both passages demonstrate that divine standards are antithetical to worldly standards. In 1 Corinthians, God has made foolish the standards of the world which include the prevailing acceptable criteria for apostleship as well as rhetorical conventions of self-praise, self-commendation, comparison and boasting. In 2 Corinthians, the possession of a letter of commendation, polished rhetoric and impressive appearance are not the appropriate foundation for boasting. The only ground for legitimate boasting is to boast in the Lord, in knowing and understanding the Lord and in carrying out his activities on earth.

d) *Paul's Evaluation of Boasting and the Function of the Citation of* LXX *Jeremiah 9.22-3 in the Light of his Ministry.* By citing the boasting saying, in 2 Cor. 10.17, Paul uses the Scriptures to establish the criteria for evaluating the legitimacy of boasting[41] based on the object of one's boast and how one's life is lived according to the object of the boasting.[42] If the object of boasting focuses on self-praise, self-commendation, comparison and accordance to the values esteemed by society, then it is rendered illegitimate, or foolish boasting.

---

40. On boasting in what one has accomplished in the Lord, see Hafemann, "Self-Commendation". This further supports my argument in Chapter 6 that Paul sees himself as a co-worker of Jesus Christ in extending the Lord's activity.

41. Contra Stanley, *Arguing with Scripture*, 98, who doubts 2 Cor. 10.17 constitutes a quotation. Even if it is, Stanley argues that it does not 'play a significant role in (Paul's) argumentation'.

42. Hafemann, *2 Corinthians*, 401. Contra Lambrecht, 'Dangerous Boasting', 338, who argues that all kinds of boasting are 'foolish and not without danger'. See also his 'Strength in Weakness: A Reply to Scott Andrews' Exegesis of 2 Cor 11.23b-33', *NTS* 43 (1997): 285–90 (289),on various degrees of legitimate or illegitimate boasting. Hafemann responds by commenting that there is no such indication in Paul's argument (*2 Corinthians*, 424 n. 4).

Such boasting is not κατὰ κύριον but κατὰ σάρκα, and does not conform to LXX Jer. 9.22-3/1 Kgdms 2.10 (cf. 2 Cor. 11.17-18).[43] In the context of both Jeremiah and 1 Kingdoms, boasting is related to understanding and knowing God, and executing actions that correspond with this knowledge. This background informs the thrust of Paul's argument. By calling his opponents 'without understanding' when they measure themselves against each other (2 Cor. 10.12), Paul is echoing the language of Jeremiah.[44] Paul charges them for preaching another Jesus, a different Spirit and a different gospel (11.5) and declares them to be false apostles (11.13) because of this. By doing so, Paul is in fact asserting that they are the enemies of the gospel.

But for Paul, the object of his boast is in the Lord (ἐν κυρίῳ). Who then is the 'Lord' (κύριος)? Is it God[45] or Christ?[46] Harris argues persuasively that there are at least four compelling reasons for taking κύριος to refer to Christ in this context.[47] First, the same citation from Jeremiah in 1 Cor. 1.30-1 refers to Christ. Second, the concept of boasting in Christ is found in Phil. 3.3 (and, in addition to Harris, we may add Rom. 15.17; 1 Cor. 15.31; Gal. 6.14; Phil. 1.26). Third, the prepositional phrase ἐν κυρίῳ regularly refers to Christ in Paul's letters. Finally, Paul regularly applies to Christ scriptural references to κύριος that clearly denote Yahweh. In addition to the reasons provided by Harris, I could add that Paul regularly attributes the title 'Lord' to Christ in his letters as well.[48] If it is correct that κύριος refers to Christ, then it is not surprising that Paul has the story of Jesus in mind when he boasts in the Lord. For Paul, Christ was crucified in weakness (13.4) and this informs his understanding of himself as an apostle. What is incompatible with the meekness and gentleness of Christ (10.1) is boasting according to the flesh. As such, Paul does not take refuge in all the signs and wonders and mighty works that he performed in Corinth (12.12), although he could. Instead, he would rather boast in those things that show his weaknesses (11.30; cf. 12.1, 5, 9) which will be further investigated below.

As I have noted, the notion of boasting is not only in understanding and knowing the Lord but also in participation in the Lord's work. This can be seen

43. In rendering boasting as foolish, Paul is not thinking of the role of the fool in Greek comedy (so L. L. Welborn, 'The Runway Paul', *HTR* 92 [1999]: 116–63 (122–61); or professional rhetoric (see the bibliography in n. 1 above), but rather of the fool portrayed in the Jewish wisdom tradition as one who refuses to acknowledge or praise God, and the boasting of the arrogant which is false boasting condemned by the prophets (so Hafemann, *2 Corinthians*, 423, and note the list of Scripture in his n. 2; Heckel, *Kraft in Schwachheit*, 194–8; idem, 'Jer 9,22f. als Schlüssel für 2 Kor 10–13', 212–13). See LXX Ps. 13.1-3.

44. Davis, 'True and False Boasting', 182.

45. So Kasper K. H. Wong, '"Lord" in 2 Corinthians 10:17', *LS* 17 (1992): 243–53.

46. So Furnish, *II Corinthians*, 474; Matera, *II Corinthians*, 235; Peterson, *Eloquence and the Proclamation*, 103.

47. See Harris, *Second Corinthians*, 725–6.

48. See, for example, Rom. 1.4, 7; 4.24; 5.1, 11; 6.23; 10.9; 14.9; 1 Cor. 1.2-3, 7-10; 8.6; 11.23; 12.3; 2 Cor. 1.2-3; 8.9; Gal. 1.3; 6.14; Phil. 1.2; 2.11; 3.20; 1 Thess. 1.3; 2.15; 3.11; 5.23.

in how Paul's citation of the boasting saying in 10.17 is closely related to his missionary work.[49] Paul's boasting is not in another's field but in his divinely apportioned missionary field. As such, Paul's boasting in the Lord should not merely be limited to the soteriological dimensions of God's activity, as suggested by Barnett,[50] but should also include the participatory dimension leading to ethical expression.[51] As such, for Paul the conduct of one's life should also reflect the character of the object of the boast.[52]

In the final analysis, for Paul, 'There is indeed only one standard by which measurement should be made – Christ ... This is the standard by which the Corinthians ought to be assessing both him and his rivals.'[53] With this position in place, I shall now investigate Paul's boasting in his weakness.

C. *Paul's Boasting of His Weaknesses (2 Corinthians 11.23–12.10)*

1. *Paul's Boast of His Weaknesses (2 Corinthians 11.23–12.9)*

As I argued earlier, Paul makes no attempt to match the boasting of the opponents according to their yardstick of measuring achievements or superiority which include boasting of boldness (2 Cor. 10.12-16), missionary success, eloquence (10.10) and miraculous signs and wonders (12.11-12). Instead, Paul boasts of his weaknesses, which are his sufferings, the very things deplored by the Corinthians, in authenticating his ministry.[54] Paul's manner of boasting in this way 'appears to be without literary precedent'.[55]

---

49. So Bruce, *1 & 2 Corinthians*, 234; Hafemann, "Self-Commendation", 82. Cf. Wong, '"Lord" in 2 Corinthians 10:17', 251–2, who rejects any notion of boasting in one's weakness.

50. Barnett, *Second Epistle*, 492.

51. Barrett, 'Boasting', 368. Cf. Callan, 'Competition and Boasting', who argues that by boasting in his missionary accomplishments, Paul is displaying his competitive character to surpass his peers. As such, to reconcile his action, Paul subsequently develops the notion of legitimate boasting in weakness by identifying himself with Jesus as a servant of the Lord. Callan's attempt to 'sketch a psychological portrait' (138) of Paul is open to objection. See Wong, *Boasting and Foolishness*, 17–21, and Barrett, 'Boasting', 363, for an evaluation of this approach. While not responding specifically to Callan, Barrett argues that 'a purely psychological account of Paul's personality ... would be inadequate and misleading'.

52. Cf. Paul's appeal in 10.1 grounded in the meekness and gentleness of Christ. For a thesis that the character of Jesus forms the linchpin of 2 Corinthians, see Stegman, *Character of Jesus*.

53. Ernest Best, *Second Corinthians*, IBC (Atlanta: John Knox, 1987), 98.

54. Barnett, *Second Epistle*, 534. The suggestion by Fitzgerald (*Cracks in an Earthen Vessel*, 25, 85–6) and Garland (*2 Corinthians*, 491) that the opponents suffered is unlikely. It is also doubtful that the letters of recommendation brought by the opponents contain lists of hardships (cf. Fiztgerald, *Cracks in an Earthen Vessel*, 25 n. 95). So Anitra Bingham Kolenkow, 'Paul and Opponents in 2 Cor 10–13 – *Theioi Andres* and Spiritual Guides', in *Religious Propaganda and Missionary Competition in the New Testament World: Essays Honoring Dieter Georgi*. NovTSup 74, ed. Lukas Bormann, Kelly Del Tredici and Angela Standhartinger (Leiden: Brill. 1994), 351–74.

55. Barnett, *Second Epistle*, 495.

In boasting of his weaknesses, Paul begins by raising four rhetorical questions related to his Jewish heritage and his status as a servant of Christ (11.22-3). This is done in response to the opponents' comparison with him. While the Jewish pedigree is to be treasured, it is Paul's weaknesses that mark him out as the authentic servant of Christ. By declaring 'I am more' (ὑπὲρ ἐγώ) as a servant of Christ in 11.23, Paul's preoccupation is not to establish who has suffered more for the sake of the gospel but to boast in the things that show his weaknesses. The phrase ὑπὲρ ἐγώ should rightly be seen as controlling the lists of weaknesses that follow in 11.24, right up to the climactic thorn in the flesh in 12.10.[56] By doing so, Paul boasts of himself as a better servant of Christ, demonstrated through sufferings, his humiliating escape from Damascus, his heavenly ascent and the incident of the thorn in the flesh, all of which magnify his weaknesses.

The word ἀσθένεια and its cognates appear frequently in 2 Cor. 11–13. The noun ἀσθένεια appears six times (in 11.30; 12.5, 9 [twice], 10; and 13.4) while the verb ἀσθενέω appears seven times (in 11.21, 29 [twice]; 12.10; 13.3, 4, and 9). The adjective ἀσθενής appears only once (in 10.10).[57] It is to be noted that ἀσθένεια does not simply refer to lack of physical strength or the persecution that one suffers.[58] As Paul's list of hardships demonstrates, this experience of suffering is not what a physically weak person would have been able to endure. It is also significant to note, as correctly argued by Forbes, that embedded in the notion of weakness are negative social connotations.[59] Weakness is not merely what is perceived by oneself, it is a result of an evaluation by others who consider it to be a humiliation (cf. 10.10; 11.21). This can be seen in the manner Paul deals with the issue of honour and shame in 1 Cor. 4.10. Here, Paul makes the connection that strong is associated with honour while weak with

---

56. So Barnett, *Second Epistle*, 538.

57. On the lexical use of the ἀσθένεια word group, see Black, *Paul, Apostle of Weakness*; and Woods, 'St. Paul's Apostolic Weakness'.

58. Bengt Holmberg, *Paul and Power: The Structure of Authority in the Primitive Church as Reflected in the Pauline Epistles*, CB 11 (Lund: C. W. K. Gleerup, 1978), 78, sees Paul's weakness as physical, while Michael L. Barré, 'Qumran and the "Weakness" of Paul', *CBQ* 42 (1980): 216–27, takes it as the persecution Paul encountered. Cf. Fitzgerald, *Cracks in an Earthen Vessel*, 138–9, who suggests that Paul's weakness is his failure to retaliate to those who abuse him.

59. Forbes, 'Comparison', particularly 18–20. See also S. Scott Bartchy, '"When I'm Weak, I'm Strong": A Pauline Paradox in Cultural Context', in *Kontexte der Schrift, Band II: Kultur, Politik, Religion, Sprache – Text; Wolfgang Stegemann zum 60 Geburtstag*, ed. Christian Strecker (Stuttgart: Kohlhammer, 2005), 49–60; Arthur J. Dewey, 'A Matter of Honor: A Social-Historical Analysis of 2 Corinthians 10', *HTR* 78 (1985): 209–17; J. Albert Harrill, 'Invective against Paul (2 Cor 10:10), the Physiognomics of the Ancient Slave Body, and the Greco-Roman Rhetoric of Manhood', in *Antiquity and Humanity: Essays on Ancient Religion and Philosophy Presented to Hans Dieter Betz on His 70th Birthday*, ed. Adela Yarbro Collins and Margaret M. Mitchell (Tübingen: Mohr Siebeck, 2001), 189–213; Larson, 'Paul's Masculinity'; Marshall, *Enmity in Corinth*, 153, 327–8; idem, 'Invective'; Pickett, *Cross in Corinth*, 85–125.

dishonour, shame, and the poor and lowly in social status. It is also significant that this negative social connotation appears within the context of his suffering (1 Cor. 4.9-13) which ends in the climactic statement emphasizing his humiliating status 'like the rubbish of the world, the dregs of all things' (1 Cor. 4.13). In the eyes of the Corinthians, Paul's apostolic ministry characterized by his sufferings is viewed negatively.

What then constitutes Paul's weaknesses in the context of 2 Corinthians? Within 11.23–12.10, Paul's weaknesses include his sufferings, his humiliating escape from Damascus, his heavenly ascent without any revelation and the mysterious thorn in the flesh. However, within the wider context, Paul's weaknesses in the eyes of the Corinthians and the opponents would have included his attitude of meekness and gentleness, personal appearance, lack of rhetorical performance, policy of self-support as an artisan and refusal of financial support (10.1, 10; 11.6, 7; cf. 5.12; 1 Cor. 1.17-25; 2.1-5).[60] But for Paul, there is another dimension to his understanding of his weakness that is grounded in the story of Jesus (2 Cor. 13.4). From the Christological perspective, Paul sees his weaknesses carrying the same sense of the rejection, suffering and humiliation of Jesus.[61] By identifying his weaknesses with the weakness of Christ (13.4) in dealing with the issues related to the cultural conventions of his day, Paul seeks to prove the unreliability of the criteria used by the Corinthians to evaluate a person's worth by appearance based on personal strengths that stand fundamentally opposed to God's values.[62] For Paul, the only sound criterion to evaluate one's worth is grounded in the Scriptures and the story of Jesus (cf. 1 Cor. 1.22-3; 2.1-5).

---

60. For further discussion, see David A. DeSilva, *The Hope of Glory: Honor Discourse and New Testament Interpretation* (Collegeville: Liturgical Press, 1999), 118–43; Gorman, *Cruciformity*, 281–93; Ronald F. Hock, 'Paul's Tentmaking and the Problems of His Social Class', *JBL* 97 (1978): 555–64; idem, *The Social Context of Paul's Ministry: Tentmaking and Apostleship* (Philadelphia: Fortress Press, 1980), 59–60; and Pickett, *Cross in Corinth*, 163–70. Marshall, *Enmity in Corinth*, 327, rightly sums up that the derogatory use of the 'encomiastic topics of physical appearance, education and achievements' forms the description of Paul as one who is weak. For further discussion on the importance of impressive physiognomy among ancient orators and how physical presence is read carefully and used either to present one's case effectively or to disparage one's opponents, see Tamsyn S. Barton, *Power and Knowledge: Astrology, Physiognomics, and Medicine under the Roman Empire* (Ann Arbor: University of Michigan Press, 1994), 95–131; Elizabeth Evans, 'Physiognomics in the Ancient World', *TAPS* 59/5 (1969): 1–101 (5–101); Dale B. Martin, *The Corinthian Body* (New Haven: Yale University Press, 1995), 34–7, 53–5; Mikeal C. Parsons, *Body and Character in Luke and Acts: The Subversion of Physiognomy in Early Christianity* (Grand Rapids: Baker, 2006), 17–65.

61. Roberts, 'Weak Enough to Lead', 233.

62. Judge rightly contends that Paul's boasting is therefore 'a systematic debunking of the Hellenic system' of placing emphasis in the competition of honour ('Conflict of Educational Aim', 39). Cf. DeSilva, *Honor*, 76.

a) *Paul's Boast as a Better Servant of Christ Demonstrated through Sufferings: 2 Corinthians 11.23-30*. Before he begins his list of hardships, Paul uses the expressions κἀγώ (four times in 2 Cor. 11.21-2) in announcing that he is equally bold in boasting compared to the opponents (11.21), followed by a series of three rhetorical questions concerning his Jewish heritage: 'Are they Hebrews?' 'Are they Israelites?' 'Are they descendants of Abraham?'; all demanding an affirmative answer. This gives the readers the impression that Paul is no less inferior to the opponents since these epithets are honourific titles describing the religious privileges of the Jews.[63] At the same time, they also heighten the expectation that, following this declaration, Paul will prove his superiority. This expectation climaxes when Paul emphatically declares ὑπὲρ ἐγώ to the next question, 'Are they better servants of Christ?' (11.23).

If Paul sets out by declaring his boldness in boasting, proceeds by establishing his equality through his Jewish heritage and pedigree, and emphatically claims superiority as a servant of Christ, then one would expect him to list impressive credentials and personal achievements to reinforce such grand claims. But in a surprising twist, Paul deflates the worldly expectations of his readers by providing the most descriptive, extensive and extended list containing 26 items of his sufferings unparalleled elsewhere in 2 Corinthians and his other canonical writings. The listing of his suffering and weaknesses (cf. 11.30; 12.1, 5, 9) in such a fashion must have proven to be undoubtedly shocking to the readers. What is even more striking is that there is no mention of the success in founding new Christ-believing communities, the number of gentiles won over to Christ, the miracles that he performed, the vast geographical coverage of his gentile mission (e.g., Rom. 15.7; 1 Cor. 15.31; 2 Cor. 1.14; 7.4; 8.24; Phil. 2.16; 4.1; 1 Thess. 2.19-20) and the Jewish pedigree/qualifications found in Phil. 3.3-6 and Gal. 1.14 (cf. Rom. 11.1). As Forbes notes: 'To be precise, [Paul] amplifies what he should minimise, and minimises what he should amplify.'[64]

Paul's catalogue of hardship (11.23-9) is rhetorically impressive,[65] and covers various aspects of his sufferings, including both Jewish and Roman

---

63. Contra Walker, *Paul's Offer of Leniency*, 305, in which he ignores the Jewish context by concluding that Paul's claims in 11.22 would sound 'ridiculous' and lack eminence compared to the pedigrees of Greco-Roman notables.

64. Forbes, 'Comparison', 19. Cf. Marshall, *Enmity in Corinth*, 351–3; and Roberts, 'Weak Enough to Lead', 225–6.

65. For extensive structural analysis of the passage, see Anton Fridrichsen, 'Zum Stil des paulinischen Peristasenkatalogs 2 Kor. 11, 23ff.', *SO* 7 (1928): 25–9; Judge, 'Paul's Boasting'; Mak, 'Holistic View of Pauline Suffering', 207–47. See also Harris's twofold analysis by construction and by content (*Second Corinthians*, 789–92).

punishments,[66] physical labours,[67] dangers in his travels,[68] experiences of death, threats from various parties, physical deprivation and the daily pressure of his concern for the believing communities and individuals. This hardship list further expands on his earlier lists in 1.3-11; 2.14-16; 4.7-12; and 6.3-10.

What then does Paul aim to achieve in enumerating his hardships? Some have pointed out that Paul's appeal to a specific statistical count of his sufferings (11.24-5) mirrors the practice of the Romans in parading their great exploits, such as those found in the *Res Gestae Divi Augusti*.[69] Obviously, the Roman practice is to highlight one's achievement, while in Paul it is to highlight his suffering and weakness; for the Romans, it is done to achieve honour, while for Paul it is dishonour. In the case of Augustus Caesar, the list highlights what he wished to be regarded as the leading glory of his reign. This is certainly not Paul's ambition in enumerating his sufferings. By comparing Paul's catalogue of sufferings with Augustus' and Pompey's accounts of their great achieve-ments, Travis concludes that 'Paul's catalogue is a carefully calculated *reductio ad absurdum* of the whole Graeco-Roman attitude to boasting'.[70]

Others suggest that Paul's boasting in difficulties serves as a standard method in gaining goodwill from an audience.[71] Peterson, a strong proponent of this reading, argues that this catalogue should not be read as Paul's boast-ing in weakness but one intended 'to match and overwhelm the claims of his opponents, to add to Paul's own *ethos* in the eyes of the Corinthians, as well as to create *pathos* in his hearers'.[72] It is difficult to see how Paul could hope to

66. On Jewish punishment, see A. E. Harvey, 'Forty Strokes Save One: Social Aspects of Judaizing and Apostasy', in *Alternative Approaches to New Testament Study*, ed. A. E. Harvey (London: SPCK, 1985), 79–96; Sven Gallas, '"Fünfmal vierzig weniger einen ...": Die an Paulus vollzogenen Synagogalstrafen nach 2 Kor 11,24', *ZNW* 81 (1990): 178–91. On Roman punish-ment, see the excursus 'Paul's Punishment and Roman Law', in Thrall, *II Corinthians*, II:739–42; Craig S. Wansink, *Chained in Christ: The Experience and Rhetoric of Paul's Imprisonment*, JSNTSup 130 (Sheffield: JSOT Press, 1996), 27–95.

67. See Hock, 'Paul's Tentmaking'; and idem, *Social Context of Paul's Ministry*.

68. Bruce W. Winter, 'Dangers and Difficulties for the Pauline Mission', in *The Gospel to the Nations: Perspectives on Paul's Mission*, ed. Peter Bolt and Mark Thompson (Downers Grove: InterVarsity, 2000), 285–95.

69. Anton Fridrichsen, 'Peristasenkatalog und Res Gestae: Nachtrag zu 2 Kor. 11, 23ff.', *SO* 8 (1929): 78–82. So Witherington, *Conflict and Community*, 438, 444, 450–2. Cf. Julius Caesar, *Civil Wars* 2.32; and Pliny, *Natural History* 7.26.97-8, for the listing of the achievements of Pompey.

70. Travis, 'Paul's Boasting', 530.

71. So Danker, *II Corinthians*, 180–1; Fitzgerald, *Cracks in an Earthen Vessel*, 24–5; Holland, 'Speaking like a Fool', 259; Peterson, *Eloquence and the Proclamation*, 115–16; Thrall, *II Cor-inthians*, II:755–8.

72. Peterson, *Eloquence and the Proclamation*, 118. See also DiCicco, *Paul's Use of Ethos*. Contra Savage, *Power through Weakness*, 63 where 11.23-9 is 'a list of personal afflictions so horrific that it would have elicited feelings of extreme contempt among his readers. By boasting of such humiliations the apostle would seem to be revelling in his disgrace.'

create *pathos* or goodwill from the Corinthians if his hardship list is nothing but what is disparaged by them.

Still others argue that this catalogue demonstrates Paul's faithful endurance in line with the tradition of the Stoic sage. As I pointed out in earlier chapters, Paul's list of hardships is not intended to reveal Paul's indifference to suffering or patient endurance corresponding to that of the Stoic virtuous sage.[73] Paul's focus here is to boast of the things that show his weaknesses and the grace and power of Christ sustaining him (11.30; 12.9-10).

Therefore, it needs to be firmly recognized that the hardship list in 11.23-9 demonstrates that it was Paul's weaknesses that set him apart from his opponents. Instead of conforming to the cultural expectation of his day in boasting of one's credentials and achievements, Paul launches a new perspective of boasting grounded in the story of Jesus. Harris is right to note that 'this technique will jolt his converts at Corinth … into recognizing the character of true apostleship, namely, the "weakness" of suffering service in imitation of the suffering ministry of Christ'.[74] This list looks forward to Paul's identification with Christ who was crucified in weakness (13.4).

While this extended and graphic list of hardships would undoubtedly have shocked the readers, what should not be overlooked is the vivid imagery that would have come to mind, such as the permanent scars on Paul's body, resulting from the beatings and floggings. The Corinthians would have been at least familiar with or seen Paul's scarred body during his extended stay at Corinth.[75] But the question is: how did the Corinthians read those scars?

Quoting Xenophon, *Agessilaus* 6.2, Fitzgerald argues that the 'scars that the good man sometimes bears on his body are visible tokens of his virtue, "so that not by hearsay but by evidence of their own eyes men can judge what manner of man he is". The endurance of hardship is thus the *proof of virtue*, the seal of integrity.'[76] By this, Fitzgerald implies that Paul's scars point to his endurance of hardships and thus tell a virtuous story. Upon close scrutiny, this argument cannot be sustained and is rightly subject to criticism. First, Scott Andrews correctly notes that Fitzgerald 'does not describe how any particular type of

---

73. So Harris, *Second Corinthians*, 798. Cf. Hodgson, 'Paul the Apostle', 61, for a thesis that 'the mythological labors of Heracles' are able to illuminate Paul's hardship list as effectively as the Stoic parallels, questioning the argument that Paul is presenting himself as a Stoic sage.

74. Harris, *Second Corinthians*, 793.

75. Jennifer A. Glancy, 'Boasting of Beatings (2 Corinthians 11:23-25)', *JBL* 123 (2004): 99–135 (103) suggests that Paul could have showed his scars and offered an interpretation of the history of its markings, reminding his audience that 'whips had similarly lacerated Jesus' flesh' and explained his stripes during chance encounters in the baths.

76. Fitzgerald, *Cracks in an Earthen Vessel*, 43 (emphasis his). Those who support Fitzgerald's position include Garland, *2 Corinthians*, 491–2; Best, *Second Corinthians*, 114; Kruse, *Second Corinthians*, 193; Lambrecht, 'Dangerous Boasting', 338.

hardship list differs in form or function'[77] from another, and so he considers Paul's bodily scars as equivalent to heroic scars sustained in battles. Second, Fitzgerald directly applies his selective quotation from Xenophon's references to battle scars to Paul's scars resulting from persecution. This practice has been rightly questioned by Glancy. By indiscriminately applying signs of virtue and courage from battle to Paul's hardship lists, Glancy charges Fitzgerald with distortion of the picture by leaving 'the impression that the endurance of any hardship, any physical ordeal, is equally exemplary'.[78] In her extensive study, Glancy persuasively argues that not all battle wounds tell the same heroic story, but in fact some testify to contemptibility and cowardice.[79] In addition, ancient audiences also make particular distinctions between the marks left by sword-slashing in battle and those left by a whip or rod. Unlike battle scars, scars that are impressed by beatings are marks of dishonour. Being subjected to the power of another man to undergo a whipping is a state that diminished any claim to manliness, and any inability to resist a whipping testified to the dishonour of the person whipped.[80] Since vulnerability to beating is a servile liability, any free person who is whipped suffers an injury to honour far in excess of whatever temporary pain or permanent mark is inflicted.[81] In addition to the Roman punishment, the Jewish punishment received by Paul also brings shame and dishonour. Josephus mentions that receiving the 'forty minus one' is so

77. Scott B. Andrews, 'Too Weak Not to Lead: The Form and Function of 2 Cor 11.23b-33', *NTS* 41 (1995): 263–76, quotation from 264. Unfortunately, Andrews goes too far to suggest that Paul became a populist or demagogue in order to claim leadership of the Corinthians (274). See the critique by Lambrecht, 'Strength in Weakness: A Reply to Scott Andrews'; and Thrall, *II Corinthians*, II:753–4.

78. Glancy, 'Boasting of Beatings', 100–1. Garland, *2 Corinthians*, 498–9, seems to fall into the same trap when he cites the account of Antipater after he was accused by Caesar of being disloyal: Antipater 'stripped off his clothes and exposed his numerous scars. His loyalty to Caesar needed ... no words from him; his body cried it aloud, were he to hold his peace' (Josephus, *Jewish War* 1.197). Garland fails to notice that these are scars of battle, not of dishonourable whipping.

79. Glancy, 'Boasting of Beatings'. Glancy points out that battle scars marking chest, throat, or face tell the story of courage in combat while scars marking a man's back tell a different story of cowardice. See her discussion and citation of ancient sources in 103–7. In addition, see Pliny, *Natural History* 7.28.10, where the account of Lucius Siccius Dentatus 'having the distinction of 45 scars in front and none at all on his back' marks him as honourable. Cf. Cicero, *De oratore* 2.28.124.

80. Glancy, 'Boasting of Beatings', 109: 'Dishonorable bodies were whippable; honorable bodies were not.'

81. Glancy, 'Boasting of Beatings', 109. Glancy refers to Philo's account of Flaccus' campaign against the Jews of Alexandria where beatings were ordered to strip the dignity of those being whipped (Flaccus, 10.75-80) and Cicero's account of the flogging of Gavius of Consa, a Roman citizen (*In Verrem* 2.62.161-3). Cf. Acts 5.40-1 where, after they were beaten, Peter and the other apostles rejoiced that they were considered worthy to suffer dishonour for the sake of Jesus' name. See also Larson, 'Paul's Masculinity', 94, where the manner of one's punishment proclaims one's social status. In the case of floggings, it is shame and humiliation.

shameful that it renders a free man at the same level as a slave.[82] Stoning (2 Cor. 11.25) is also viewed as a shameful punishment as well.[83] From these impressive pieces of evidence, I conclude that these scars on Paul's body inflicted by beatings are simply not scars of honour but scars of dishonour.

Therefore, Paul's account of his repeated beatings resulting in permanent bodily scars not only singles him out as one who is 'dishonorable, even contemptible'[84] but also proclaims to the Corinthians that 'his bodily integrity, a prerequisite of masculine dignity as well as social and political status, had been violated on numerous occasions'.[85] This is supported by clear indications that his scars, carrying the notion of shame and dishonour, have not been well received. The charge that Paul's bodily presence is weak (10.10), seen as a direct reference to his scars of dishonour, should not be discounted.[86] As such, it would be difficult to believe that Paul's offensive scars escaped the close scrutiny of both the opponents and the Corinthians.[87]

How does boasting of his beatings contribute to Paul's argument in 2 Cor. 10–13? These scars tell the story of weakness; but, more importantly, they tell the story of Jesus. This is the clearest evidence of Paul not only carrying in his body the νέκρωσις τοῦ Ἰησοῦ (4.10; cf.13.4)[88] but also the στίγματα τοῦ Ἰησοῦ (Gal. 6.17).[89] Glancy observes rightly that 'Paul perceived that in his

---

82. Josephus, *Jewish Aniquities* 4.8.21-2. Cf. Harvey, 'Forty Strokes Save One', 93–4, rightly points out that none of the other sufferings Paul undergoes 'is likely to have exceeded, in the sheer damage it caused to his physique (let alone the humiliation of his person), the five occasions on which he received from his fellow Jews the maximum judicial penalty of forty strokes save one'. So Gallas, 'Fünfmal vierzig weniger einen ...', 190.

83. See Aristophanes, *Acharnians* 285-9; Aeschines, *Against Timarchus* 163; Josephus, *Jewish Antiquities* 4.202; Philo, *On the Special Laws* 3.51; *On the Life of Moses* 2.202, 218.

84. Glancy, 'Boasting of Beatings', 111.

85. Larson, 'Paul's Masculinity', 94. See also Bartchy, 'When I'm Weak, I'm Strong'.

86. The description of Paul in the second-century *Acts of Paul and Thecla* indicates that his physical appearance may not have been that welcoming: '(A) man little of stature, thin-haired upon the head, crooked in the legs, of good state of body, with eyebrows joining, and nose somewhat hooked.' See Robert M. Grant, 'The Description of Paul in the Acts of Paul and Thecla', *VC* 36 (1982): 1–4; Abraham J. Malherbe, *Paul and the Popular Philosophers* (Minneapolis: Fortress Press, 1989), 165–70. However, my argument has shown that the charge against Paul's weak appearance is not related to any physical infirmity such as those in *Acts of Paul and Thecla* but includes reference to the scars from beatings that were considered dishonourable.

87. Commentators are chiefly concerned to establish the legal implications of the beatings by drawing Paul's Roman citizenship into the debate. See Barnett, *Second Epistle*, 543; Barrett, *Second Corinthians*, 297; Furnish, *II Corinthians*, 516; Thrall, *II Corinthians*, II:739–42. By doing so, the social implications of such beatings as perceived by the audience are overlooked.

88. Murphy-O'Connor, *Theology*, 115–16, suggests that in 11.23-5 Paul 'graphically illustrated ... "bearing in the body the dying of Jesus"'.

89. For views that the στίγματα are scars from persecutions incurred in the course of apostolic ministry, see James D. G. Dunn, *The Epistle to the Galatians*, BNTC (Peabody: Hendrickson, 1993), 347; Ronald Y. K. Fung, *The Epistle to the Galatians*, NICNT (Grand Rapids: Eerdmans,

marked body the story of Jesus' passion is legible' because the 'agonizing story of Jesus' humiliations preceding his life-giving death' is featured prominently among those humiliations.[90] What others consider shameful, Paul boasts of as legitimate expressions of his calling and commitment to his apostolic ministry as a διάκονος Χριστοῦ – one who is called by Christ and suffers for Christ, and this is possibly an echo of the Servant passage of Isa. 52.14–53.5.

Another evidence of Paul embodying the story of Jesus is reflected in his identification with those who are weak (2 Cor. 11.29). It is significant that Paul ends his hardship list with his deep concern for the believing community and also the individuals within the community (11.28-9). This can only be an expression of his love for them (cf. 1 Cor. 12.25; Phil. 2.20). By declaring τίς ἀσθενεῖ καὶ οὐκ ἀσθενῶ; τίς σκανδαλίζεται καὶ οὐκ ἐγὼ πυροῦμαι, Paul compassionately identifies himself with the weak – those who are oppressed and abused by those who exploit the Corinthians for their own benefit (cf. 2 Cor. 11.20-1; see also Rom. 14.1-23; 1 Cor. 8.9-13) – as a representative of the crucified Christ who also identified with the weak in his earthly life. Although 2 Cor. 11.29 has presented interpreters with numerous exegetical challenges,[91] it is best to take a comprehensive view in line with Harris that Paul's emphasis here is on his identification with his fellow believers in their weakness, whatever its precise nature – physical, psychological, social or spiritual.[92] Barnett suggests that Paul's use of σκανδαλίζεται may have its source in the Jesus tradition (Mt. 13.41; 16.23; 18.7; Lk. 17.1; see also Rom. 14.21; 1 Cor. 8.13) and the prophets' denunciation of those who abuse the weak (e.g., Isa. 28.7-9; Jer. 23.9-15; Ezek. 12.21–14.11).[93] If Barnett is correct, it further strengthens my argument that, like his Lord, Paul's greatest anxiety is for the Christ-believing communities that he founded.

The long list of Paul's 'achievements' as proof of being a better servant of Christ turns out to be anything but impressive; it is a catalogue of his sufferings. Through this list, Paul demonstrates that he follows the paradigm of Christ. Building on the earlier theme of suffering, Paul further advances the argument that suffering and weakness is the vehicle for the mediation and embodiment of the gospel and the character of the crucified Christ,[94] despite its negative social connotations. By doing so, Paul defines a contrary set of values

---

1988), 313; Richard N. Longenecker, *Galatians*, WBC (Dallas: Word Books, 1990), 300; J. Louis Martyn, *Galatians*, AB (New York: Doubleday, 1997), 568.

90. Glancy, 'Boasting of Beatings', 127, 133.

91. See Michael L. Barré, 'Paul as "Eschatological Person": A New Look at 2 Cor 11:29', *CBQ* 37 (1975): 500–26; Bartchy, 'When I'm Weak, I'm Strong'.

92. Harris, *Second Corinthians*, 814. So Thrall, *II Corinthians*, II:751–2; Lambrecht, *Second Corinthians*, 192.

93. Barnett, *Second Epistle*, 550 n. 48.

94. Cf. Jerry L. Sumney, 'Paul's "Weakness": An Integral Part of His Conception of Apostleship', *JSNT* 52 (1993): 71–91.

grounded in the story of Jesus and renounces those that are equated with status and power in Corinth.

b) *Paul's Boast of the Humiliating Damascus Escape: 2 Corinthians 11.30-3.* Paul's narrative of his humiliating Damascus escape is a continuation of his boasting of his weakness.[95] In 11.30, Paul spells out the necessity (δεῖ) of boasting[96] in the things that show his weakness rather that those that glory in his strength and accomplishments. This is followed by invoking the name of God in a traditional oath formula, declaring that Paul is denying any form of deceit but telling the truth in recounting these weaknesses.[97]

The vivid event of Paul being lowered down the city walls of Damascus in his escape from the Ethnarch appears not only odd but out of place, as noted by various commentators.[98] It is exceptionally humiliating even to be mentioned,

95. Barnett, *Second Epistle*, 551; Black, *Paul, Apostle of Weakness*, 144–6. Pace Harris, *Second Corinthians*, 816, who sees 11.30 as beginning a new section that stretches all the way to 12.10 where the focus is on Paul's boasting of his weaknesses. Thus Harris paraphrases 11.30: 'If I must go on boasting, then I shall change tack and boast no longer of my hardships (11:21b-29) but of my weakness' (817). This strict distinction between hardships and weakness is best avoided.

96. BDAG classifies this use of δεῖ as denoting 'of an inner necessity growing out of a given situation'. The Corinthians' fondness for boasting, as highlighted by Davis, 'True and False Boasting', 130–88; and Savage, *Power through Weakness*, 54–62, necessitates the 'given situation' for Paul's boasting. Cf. Barrett's dubious suggestion that καυχᾶσθαι δεῖ may have been one of the catchwords of the Corinthians (*Second Corinthians*, 302, 306).

97. There are disputes as to what necessitates Paul's oath. It could be: (1) the hardship list in 11.23-9 (so Bultmann, *Second Corinthians*, 218; Allan Menzies, *The Second Epistle of the Apostle Paul to the Corinthians* [London: Macmillan, 1912], 87–8; Tasker, *Second Corinthians*, 167; Windisch, *Der zweite Korintherbrief*, 362); (2) Paul's statement on his boasting of his weakness in 11.30 (so Martin, *2 Corinthians*, 384; Thrall, *II Corinthians*, II:762–3); (3) the Damascus narrative in 11.31-3 (so Bruce, *1 & 2 Corinthians*, 244; Witherington, *Conflict and Community*, 458); or (4) both the Damascus and thorn-in-the-flesh narrative in 11.30–12.10 (so Furnish, *II Corinthians*, 539–40; Harris, *Second Corinthians*, 816, 818; Hughes, *Second Corinthians*, 419–20). However, it makes better sense to apply Paul's oath to all the incidents that demonstrate his weaknesses and sufferings, beginning from 11.23 to 12.10. Cf. Plummer, *Second Epistle*, 332.

98. Eric F. F. Bishop, 'Does Aretas Belong in 2 Corinthians or Galatians?', *ExpT* 64 (1953): 188–9 (189), describes these verses as being 'out of context, out of style, quite out of connexion'. Bultmann, *Second Corinthians*, 218, sees 'no reason' for it. Cf. Windisch, *Der zweite Korintherbrief*, 363–6, who considers this an interpolation; Goudge, *Second Corinthians*, 110 and Tasker, *2 Corinthians*, 167, who see it as an afterthought; Menzies, *Second Corinthians*, 89, who considers it a postscript to the hardships list in 11.23-9. Against these proposals, see Plummer, *Second Epistle*, 332: '[T]here is no evidence that the Epistle ever existed without these verses at this place.' Apart from this, there are also persistent doubts cast on the accuracy of almost every aspect of Paul's account, including the identity and jurisdiction of the Ethnarch, the nature of Paul's escape and the danger he is in. For further discussion, see L. L. Welborn, '*Primum tirocinium Pauli* (2 Cor 11,32-33)', *BZ* 43 (1999): 49–71, who argues that there is no warrant for such scepticism. On the relationship between Paul's account and Acts 9.23-5, see Mark Harding, 'On the Historicity of Acts: Comparing Acts 9:23-5 with 2 Corinthians 11:32-3', *NTS* 39 (1993): 518–38.

let alone to boast in. If this story is so inappropriate, it is difficult to see why Paul includes it in the first instance. As such, it is best to regard this narrative as an example of Paul's humiliation and weakness.[99] To emphasize his humiliating escape, it is now commonplace for commentators to cite approvingly the novel suggestion made by Judge that Paul is engaging in a deliberate parody of the finest Roman award of *corona muralis*, the 'mural crown', awarded to the first soldier to scale a city wall in a battle attack. Far from being 'first up' Paul is 'first down' and this constitutes his boasting in weakness.[100] However, this allusion to the military award has been questioned by Harris. According to him, even if Roman Corinth were familiar with the military award, 'it is less certain that' the Corinthians 'would have recognized an allusion to this in the phrase ἐχαλάσθην διὰ τοῦ τείχους, for in the supposed reversal of imagery the crucial element of "firstness" is missing' in Paul's descent from the Damascus wall.[101]

Even if Judge's *corona muralis* theory may not be at work here, it does not discount the humiliation suffered. The facts that Paul exits through a window in the wall and down the city walls instead of the city gates; leaves in a basket, not on foot; and that the escape takes place at night, not in daylight (cf. Acts 9.23-5), sufficiently suggest that this incident is not merely 'memorable' but profoundly humiliating and certainly not worthy of one's boast.[102] It emphasizes the loss of dignity and status that Paul has to endure for the sake of his apostolic ministry. In this way, Paul maintains his legitimate boasting according to LXX Jer. 9.22-3 and in accordance with his position in Christ (2 Cor. 13.4). By boasting in his weakness, Paul is glorifying not in himself, but in the Lord who is his sufficiency in weakness (12.9).

c) *Paul's Boast of the Heavenly Ascent with Nothing to Share: 2 Corinthians 12.1-6.* Paul continues to boast of the things that show his weakness (12.1; cf. 12.5, 9) with his heavenly ascent account (12.2-6) and the thorn in the flesh experience (12.7-9). These accounts have received wide attention as demonstrated by the enormous amount of studies debating on wide-ranging issues that

---

99. Cf. Harris, *Second Corinthians*, 820. See also Barrett, *Second Corinthians*, 303; Furnish, *II Corinthians*, 541–2. *Pace* Lambrecht, *Second Corinthians*, 193.

100. Judge, 'Conflict of Educational Aims', 44–5. For a description of the *corona muralis*, see Gellius, *Attic Nights* 5.6.16; Polybius, *Histories* 6.39.5; Livy, *History* 10.46.3; 26.48.5.

101. Harris, *Second Corinthians*, 824.

102. Harris, *Second Corinthians*, 826. See also R. Splitter, 'The Limits of Ecstasy: An Exegesis of 2 Corinthians 12:1-10', in *Current Issues in Biblical and Patristic Interpretation*, ed. Gerald F. Hawthorne (Grand Rapids: Eerdmans, 1975), 259–66 (260), who describes the Damascus escape as 'both cowardly in conception ... and undignified in execution'. Paul's escape can hardly be classified as an enactment of a runaway fool drawn from the Hellenistic mime that is 'thievish, clownish, and recreant' (Welborn, 'Runaway Paul', 157). Cf. Roberts, 'Weak Enough to Lead', 236–9.

never seem to exhaust the creative imagination of commentators.[103] It is beyond my scope to evaluate these studies, as my concern is the relation of the heavenly ascent account to the mysterious thorn in the flesh that afflicts Paul (12.7-9) and to the wider narrative (11.22–12.10). Most acknowledge that Paul is responding to the opponents' boasting in visions and revelations by attempting to match their boast by recalling his rapture to heaven.[104] Others think that Paul is reluctant to boast in the visions and revelations by downplaying or denying that these are the criteria for true apostleship.[105] Still others see the connection between 11.30-3 and 12.1-10, where the former depicts Paul's humiliating descent down the walls and the latter his exhilarating ascent into the heavens,[106] while some believe that Paul is beginning a new section in 12.1.[107] There is also the suggestion that the heavenly ascent account provides Paul with a reason to be proud resulting in the infliction of the thorn to keep him humble.[108] There is yet another suggestion that 12.1-10 is a parody of rapture and healing miracles

103. See Harris, *Second Corinthians*, 868–9, for bibliography. For exegetical issues, see William Baird, 'Visions, Revelation, and Ministry: Reflections on 2 Cor 12:1-5 and Gal 1:11-17', *JBL* 104 (1985): 651–62; Nicdao, 'Power in Times of Weakness'; James D. Tabor, *Things Unutterable: Paul's Ascent to Paradise in Its Greco-Roman, Judaic, and Early Christian Contexts* (Lanham: University Press of America, 1986), 113–27; Margaret E. Thrall, 'Paul's Journey to Paradise: Some Exegetical Issues in 2 Cor 12, 2-4', in *The Corinthian Correspondence*, ed. Reimund Bieringer, BETL 125 (Leuven: Peeters, 1996), 347–63; and idem, *II Corinthians*, II:772–805; Edith M. Humphrey, *And I Turned to See the Voice: The Rhetoric of Vision in the New Testament* (Grand Rapids: Baker, 2007), 31–56.

104. Tabor is a strong proponent that the heavenly ascent is not only 'a privilege of the highest order' (21) for Paul but also an important experience to 'confirm his self-understanding of his authority as an apostle' (34). See his *Things Unutterable*, 34–45, 115–25. Tabor also argues that Paul's ascent 'has several direct connections with his message' (124). Tabor's position is questionable for several reasons. First, if the ascent is directly related to Paul's message, there is no reason why Paul is restrained from sharing it. Second, nowhere else does Paul use this experience to defend his apostleship. Paul grounds his call/conversion experience in his Damascus Christophany and not on his heavenly ascent. Cf. Black, *Paul, Apostle of Weakness*, 146–7; Janet Everts Powers, 'A Thorn in the Flesh: The Appropriation of Textual Meaning', *JPT* 18 (2001): 85–99 (91).

105. Daniel L. Akin, 'Triumphalism, Suffering, and Spiritual Maturity: An Exposition of 2 Corinthians 12:1-10 in Its Literary, Theological, and Historical Context', *CTR* 4/1 (1989): 119–44 (126, 130); Baird, 'Visions, Revelation, and Ministry', 653–4; Markus Bockmuehl, *Revelation and Mystery in Ancient Judaism and Pauline Christianity*, WUNT 2/36 (Tübingen: J. C. B. Mohr, 1990), 175; Martin, *2 Corinthians*, 390; Spittler, 'Limits'.

106. So Barnett, *Second Epistle*, 553 n. 59, 562; Harris, *Second Corinthians*, 820–1.

107. Akin, 'Triumphalism', 130; Nicdao, 'Power in Times of Weakness', 217; Thrall, *II Corinthians*, II:772.

108. So Barnett, *Second Epistle*, 555; Garland, 'Paul's Apostolic Authority', 380–1; Harris, *Second Corinthians*, 827; Powers, 'Thorn in the Flesh'; Schütz, *Paul and the Anatomy of Apostolic Authority*, 238–391; John Christopher Thomas, '"An Angel from Satan": Paul's Thorn in the Flesh (2 Corinthians 12:7-10)', *JPT* 9 (1996): 39–52 (47).

where, in the former, Paul is denied communicating what he hears while, in the latter, Paul is denied any healing.[109] Yet others believe that the heavenly ascent and the infliction of the thorn in the flesh are of the same event, with the thorn as a punishment or a ploy of Satan or his angel to prevent Paul from reaching the highest heaven.[110] Finally, another view attempts to see 11.23–12.10 as a literary unit based on Paul's theme of boasting but this appears to encounter problems in accounting for the function of the heavenly ascent in the narrative. The solution proposed is that Paul switches from boasting in his weaknesses in 11.23-33 to boasting in his strength in 12.1-6 before returning to boasting in his weaknesses in 12.7-10.[111]

From the brief survey, any satisfactory solution to account for Paul's heavenly ascent within the structure of 11.23–12.10 remains unforthcoming. Several questions remain unanswered. If the heavenly ascent episode is crucial for Paul, why does Paul break his silence only after 14 years, despite his extended stay in Corinth (cf. Acts 18.11) and several earlier visits (2 Cor. 12.14; 13.1, 2)? Why does Paul relate an incident that occurred long before his first visit to Corinth?[112] Does he not have any fresh and recent revelation? If Paul has an abundance of visions and revelations as suggested by Baird (and indicated by 12.1, 7),[113] it seems extremely strange that Paul should pick an event that is shrouded in obscurity, ambiguity and uncertainty, whether this occurs in the body or out of the body. Even worse, it has resulted in no direct revelation from God to the people. Furthermore, Paul recounts the experience in the third person, and cannot even provide details of the nature of the vision he encountered. It is even more surprising that Paul does not allude to his Damascus Christophany which remains 'the pivotal encounter with the resurrected Christ'[114] for this

109. Hans Dieter Betz, *Der Apostel Paulus und die sokratische Tradition: Eine exegetische Untersuchung zu seiner 'Apologie' 2 Korinther 10–13*, BHT 45 (Tübingen: Mohr, 1972), 72–3, 84–100.

110. R. M. Price, 'Punished in Paradise (An Exegetical Theory of II Corinthians 12:1-10)'. *JSNT* 7 (1980): 33–40.

111. Hafemann, *2 Corinthians*, 457, argues that 11.23-33 and 12.5-10 are part of Paul's boasting in his weaknesses. The heavenly ascent is Paul's boasting of his spiritual experience. So Andrew T. Lincoln, *Paradise Now and Not Yet: Studies in the Role of the Heavenly Dimension in Paul's Thoughts with Special Reference to His Eschatology*, SNTSMS 43 (Cambridge: Cambridge University Press, 1981), 75–6.

112. If 2 Corinthians were written around 57–8, then the heavenly rapture would have occurred around 42–3 prior to the beginning of Paul's active gentile mission. Cf. Barnett, *Second Epistle*, 561; Furnish, *II Corinthians*, 544; Thrall, *II Corinthians*, II:784.

113. Baird, 'Visions, Revelation, and Ministry', 653. Cf. Acts 9.3-9; 16.9-10; 18.9-10; 22.17-21; 23.11; 26.19; 27.23-4; Gal. 1.12; 2.1. See Harris, *Second Corinthians*. 836–7 for a chart of Paul's visions known from his letters and Acts.

114. Scott, *2 Corinthians*, 223. Cf. Seyoon Kim, *The Origin of Paul's Gospel*, 2nd edn, WUNT 2/4 (Tübingen: J.C.B. Mohr, 1984). Taylor, 'Apostolic Identity', argues that Paul's apostolic identity lies in his claim for his Damascus road call/conversion experience from which he derives

could have been a more credible and forceful argument against the opponents if Paul wanted to establish his apostolic credentials. If the account in Acts 18.9-10 is historically accurate, Paul's extended stay in Corinth is also a result of divine revelation, then why not allude to this account in his response to the challenges of the opponents of his right of ministry in Corinth, as this would have constituted a more persuasive counter-argument? More importantly, why does Paul relate this particular account in relation to his boasting in his weaknesses?

If Tabor is right that Paul's heavenly ascent is crucial for his understanding of his apostleship and is 'closely tied in with his gospel message', it is even more astonishing that Paul makes no mention of the content of the revelation.[115] If this experience is so important, why does Paul choose to disclose it now within the context of boasting in weaknesses? Surely an event 14 years ago is unlikely to place Paul in a favourable position compared to his opponents' recent or more up-to-date claims. If Paul sees himself in the tradition of the prophet, any revelation he receives is to be proclaimed for the benefit of the people and not to be kept in silence for such a long time.

The above argument highlights that any tendency to read 12.1-6 apart from Paul's earlier recitals of his sufferings and weaknesses and the subseqeunt thorn-in-the-flesh account not only misses the force of his argument but also distorts the entire argument. But if 11.23–12.10 is taken as a literary unit, as I have argued earlier,[116] where the theme of boasting in weaknesses is the thread that binds the entire argument, and if we take this as the starting point, a different picture emerges in our understanding of the heavenly ascent account.

In this respect, Paula Gooder argues that Paul's journey to paradise is not what is commonly accepted as a successful ascent but constitutes a failed journey.[117] To substantiate her argument, Gooder sets out to compare the connection of 12.1-6 with the heavenly ascent texts from *1 Enoch*, *Testament of Levi*, Slavonic Enoch, *3 Baruch*, Revelation, *Ascension of Isaiah*, Coptic *Apocalypse*

---

that authority which he defends as apostleship. If Taylor is right, all the more one would expect the Christophany to be included in 2 Corinthians, and it is surprising and significant that this is absent.

115. Tabor, *Things Unutterable*, 21, 34–45. Cf. Gal. 1.11-16, where the Damascus revelation Paul received becomes the foundation of his kerygma.

116. Although both Akin, 'Triumphalism', 123, and Spittler, 'Limits', 262–5, suggest that 11.23–12.10 should be seen as a literary unit, none sees the heavenly ascent as Paul's boasting in his weaknesses. The farthest they go is to suggest that the theme that binds 11.23–12.10 is boasting, but not boasting *in weaknesses*. Similarly, Nicdao, 'Power in Times of Weakness', 215–17, argues that 11.21b–12.10 is a unit with two sub-units of 11.21b-33 and 12.1-10 in which 12.1 signifies the movement to another topic. Cf. Baird, 'Visions, Revelation, and Ministry', 651; Johannes A. Loubser, 'Paul and the Politics of Apocalyptic Mysticism: An Exploration of 2 Cor 11:30–12:10', *Neot* 34 (2000): 191–206 (192).

117. Paula R. Gooder, *Only the Third Heaven? 2 Corinthians 12.1-10 and Heavenly Ascent*, LNTS 313 (London: T&T Clark, 2006).

of Paul, Sepher Hekhalot, Hekhalot Rabbati 4QShirShabb and 4QBerakhot.[118] Focusing on the parallels between these texts and Paul's account, Gooder concludes that the similarity of Paul's account to the other heavenly texts is only superficial, with the differences ignored by almost all commentators.[119] In particular, Gooder notes that in 12.1-6 all the major characteristics of the heavenly ascent texts are absent in that there is no mention of the setting for Paul's account, the throne vision, description of what Paul sees in the ascent, and the goal of the heavenly ascent, which is reaching the throne of God. At the same time, Paul's mention of a precise dating, his doubt about the nature of the ascent, a condensed version of only a few verses, and the use of the third person in his narrative all point to characteristics that are alien to the heavenly texts. Based on these premises, Gooder concludes that Paul's narrative is not a classic heavenly ascent text, and suggests that it is a narrative of a failed ascent.[120] Based on a seven-heaven cosmology, Gooder argues. 'An ascent to the third heaven with no subsequent ascent into higher levels of heaven certainly suggests some element of failure. In a genre where the goal of ascent is so regularly the throne of God the lack of mention of it here must be important'.[121]

If Gooder is correct, it further reinforces Paul's boasting in his weaknesses. As such, Paul is certainly not describing the 'grandeur of the experience',[122] or including the account merely to counter his opponents' boasts of similar experiences. Neither does Paul simply switch from boasting in his weaknesses to strength and then back to his weaknesses again. In this failed ascent there is no revelation, and it results in nothing being communicated (12.4). Paul could easily have boasted of his other visions and revelations which had direct implications on his gentile mission (e.g., Acts 9.3-9; 16.9-10; 18.9-10; 22.17-21; 23.11; 26.19; 27.23-4; Gal. 1.12; 2.1) but he refrained and chose this failed ascent to boast of his weaknesses.

---

118. Gooder, *Only the Third Heaven?*, 23–161. Note the table in 157 summarizing the major characteristics of the heavenly ascent texts.

119. Gooder, *Only the Third Heaven?*, 165–89.

120. Gooder, *Only the Third Heaven?*, 190–211.

121. Gooder, *Only the Third Heaven?*, 191. For treatment on seven heavens in Jewish apocalyptic literature, see Adela Yarbro Collins, *Cosmology and Eschatology in Jewish and Christian Apocalypticism*, JSJSup 50 (Leiden: Brill, 1996), 21–54; Helmut Traub, 'οὐρανός οὐράνιος κτλ.', *TDNT* 5: 511. However, Harris, *Second Corinthians*, 840, strongly objects to the seven heaven schema. 'It is unlikely that Paul was operating with a cosmological scheme of seven heavens, for if he could claim to have ascended only to the third of seven heavens, his opponents could easily depreciate the significance of his ascent, especially if they were able to claim ascent to a higher heaven.' This is precisely my argument that Paul is relating a failed ascent. Harris's premise that Paul is relating a successful ascent hinders him from seeing the force of Paul's argument. Cf. Plummer, *Second Epistle*, 344, who notes that, if Paul has seven heavens in mind, 'the third is of a very inferior origin, with somewhat earthly characteristics'.

122. Barnett, *Second Epistle*, 562.

d) *Paul's Boast of the Thorn in the Flesh: 2 Corinthians 12.7-9.* Paul continues the theme of boasting in his weaknesses by recounting the thorn in the flesh afflicting him (12.7-9) without providing any precise identification of the thorn, resulting in numerous suggestions being proposed. I shall not enter into detailed evaluation of these proposals, as this has been done elsewhere.[123] Paul's silence on the identity of the thorn is intentional, and any further attempt to identify it remains speculative and will further distract us from appreciating Paul's primary purpose in giving another example of his boasting in his weaknesses (12.5; cf. 11.30; 12.1, 9).

There is no doubt that the humiliating thorn in Paul's flesh is visible to the Corinthians, who perceive Paul to be weak because of it. This is confirmed in 12.6 where Paul explicitly states that he repudiates the option of self-promotion and boasting in his status and achievements (as indicated by φείδομαι δέ) so that the Corinthians are able to form an accurate assessment of him and his ministry based on their own observation of what they *see* in him and *hear* from him in his teaching (ὃ βλέπει με ἢ ἀκούει τι ἐξ ἐμοῦ). Paul again is careful in hammering home his point that it is his weaknesses that the Corinthians see, and the preaching of Jesus the Messiah and the Messiah crucified in weakness that they hear (1.19; 4.5; 5.11; 11.3-4; 13.4; cf. 1 Cor. 1.17, 23-5; 2.1-5).[124] He makes it clear that his embodiment of the story of Jesus is not restricted to his preaching only but to the very manner of his apostolic existence that is visible to the Corinthians. Therefore, it is no coincidence that Paul places the pair of 'hearing' and 'seeing' in the framework of his narrative of the thorn in the flesh.

What the Corinthians hear about, the weakness and power of Christ (13.4), is also replicated visibly in Paul's experience of the thorn. When Paul's request for the removal of the thorn is denied,[125] he receives the assurance that the supply of Christ's grace is never lacking and the promise that Christ's power is made perfect in his weakness (ἡ γὰρ δύναμις ἐν ἀσθενείᾳ τελεῖται) is 'permanently

---

123. See Harris, *Second Corinthians*, 858–9, 868–9 for a summary and bibliography of the proposals for Paul's thorn. For extensive surveys of the interpretations, see Nicdao, 'Power in Times of Weakness', 524–94; Furnish, *II Corinthians*, 547–50; Ulrich Heckel, 'Der Dorn im Fleisch: Die Krankheit des Paulus in 2 Kor 12,7 and Gal 4,13f.', *ZNW* 84 (1993): 65–92; Thrall, *II Corinthians*, II:809–18.

124. Barnett, *Second Epistle*, 565, notes that what the Corinthians 'see' (i.e. Paul's weaknesses) and 'hear' (i.e. Paul's preaching of Christ) are closely connected, as the pair 'see' and 'hear' is also used elsewhere in an idiomatic sense (e.g., Isa. 6.9; 29.18; Jer. 5.21; Ezek. 12.2; Rom. 11.8; 15.21; 1 Cor. 2.9; Phil. 4.9). Cf. Harris, *Second Corinthians*, 850, where seeing and hearing encompass the two primary ways an evaluation of a person can be undertaken – by observing conduct and by listening to what is said.

125. Both Barnett, *Second Epistle*, 572; and Tasker, *Second Corinthians*, 178, suggest that Paul's threefold request mirrors Christ's threefold petition in Gethsemane. See also Jerry W. McCant, 'Paul's Thorn of Rejected Apostleship', *NTS* 34 (1988): 550–72 (571), and his *2 Corinthians*, 152–3, for an outline of eight possible parallels between Jesus and Paul.

valid',[126] particularly in the bearing of the sufferings and the consequences of the thorn in the flesh. The notion of grace recalls the story of Jesus in 8.9, where Jesus' impoverishment of himself is for the enrichment of salvation to his people, and the notion of power and weakness looks forward to the story of Jesus' death and resurrection in 13.4. As such, Barnett correctly maintains that the response Paul receives is given 'in terms of the very gospel of the death and resurrection of Christ that the apostles proclaimed'.[127]

Following Christ's direct affirmation in 12.9a, Paul continues to recount this truth in 12.9b: ἥδιστα οὖν μᾶλλον καυχήσομαι ἐν ταῖς ἀσθενείαις μου, ἵνα ἐπισκηνώσῃ ἐπ' ἐμὲ ἡ δύναμις τοῦ Χριστοῦ. This statement clearly sets out the ground for Paul's boasting in the Lord, and further expands on his citation of Jer. 9.22-3/1 Kgdms 2.10. Paul does not hesitate to boast in his weaknesses (note the move from the singular ἀσθενείᾳ in 12.9a to the plural ἀσθενείαις in 12.9b) as Christ's power 'finds its consummation or reaches perfection in [the presence of] weakness'[128] in him. The choice of words in describing Christ's power dwelling in him (ἐπισκηνώσῃ) is also significant. Barnett suggests that this is the vocabulary of the tabernacle in the Scriptures as applied to God pitching his tent with his people in Exod. 40.34 (cf. Exod. 25.6; Ezek. 37.27; 2 Cor. 6.16).[129] If Barnett is right, this imagery suggests that Christ 'pitches his tent' with Paul in his weaknesses, signifying the guarantee of Christ's presence.

That Christ's power is made perfect in Paul's weakness should not be limited to Paul's experience of the thorn in his flesh. Paul's subsequent statement (as indicated by the conjunction οὖν) that he will boast all the more gladly of his weaknesses (as indicated by the plural ἀσθενείαις), so that the power of Christ may dwell in him, without doubt includes his list of sufferings (11.23-9), the humiliating Damascus escape (11.30-3) and his failed ascent to the heavens (12.1-5). In addition, it is not impossible for Paul to have in mind his earlier references to his sufferings as expressed in 1.5-11; 2.14-16; 4.7-12; and 6.3-10.

The δύναμις τοῦ Χριστοῦ that Paul experiences is not power as defined by the opponents or according to the Corinthians' perception but power that is radically redefined by the event of the cross. It is power not demonstrated in authoritative lineage and charismatic signs but power 'manifested in apostolic weakness, demonstrated in afflictions suffered for the sake of the gospel, and legitimated by the crucifixion of Jesus as God's powerful invasion of the old

---

126. Harris, *Second Corinthians*, 862, as indicated by the present τελεῖται.

127. Barnett, *Second Epistle*, 573. See also Alexandra R. Brown, 'The Gospel Takes Place: Paul's Theology of Power-in-Weakness in 2 Corinthians', *Int* 52/3 (1998): 271–85 (279).

128. BDAG, s.v. Cf. Thrall, *II Corinthians*, II:828, that the visibility of Christ's power is also intended here.

129. Barnett, *Second Epistle*, 575. In the NT, this imagery is used to describe the incarnate life of the Word of God in Jn 1.14 and God's future dwelling with his people in Rev. 7.14; 12.12; 13.6; 21.3. See also BDAG, s.v., 'to use a place for lodging, take up quarters, take up one's abode'.

world's enslaving convictions – including convictions about the use of power by human beings to divide and dominate the world'.[130] As such for Paul, the story of Jesus must always be the yardstick for his life and ministry, and not the standards imposed on him by the Corinthians and the opponents that are based on the cultural conventions of the day. It is his διακονία (6.4-10; cf. 1.3-11; 2.14-16; 4.7-12; 11.23-30) characterized by sufferings integral to his apostolic ministry that constitutes the participatory dimension forming appropriate boasting in the Lord.

2. *Summary Statement: Sufferings on the Account of Christ (2 Corinthians 12.10)*

Paul summarizes his boasting of his weaknesses in a most climactic way: διὸ εὐδοκῶ ἐν ἀσθενείαις, ἐν ὕβρεσιν, ἐν ἀνάγκαις, ἐν διωγμοῖς καὶ στενοχωρίαις, ὑπὲρ Χριστοῦ· ὅταν γὰρ ἀσθενῶ, τότε δυνατός εἰμι (12.10). Paul not only boasts of his weaknesses, but he is able to be content (εὐδοκῶ) in them, not in the sense that he finds pleasure in his weaknesses or is resigned to the fate of his sufferings, but he 'joyfully use[s] them as occasions to know and prove the resurrection power of Christ'.[131]

The phrase ἐν ἀσθενείαις is to be taken as a general summary statement for the hardship list in 12.10 which carries the force 'in weaknesses such as ...'[132] This is followed by four instances of weaknesses, ἐν ὕβρεσιν, ἐν ἀνάγκαις, ἐν διωγμοῖς καὶ στενοχωρίαις, describing in general terms the sufferings Paul endures in his ministry. Paul's earlier narratives provided concrete examples of boasting in weaknesses. Instead of listing his successful track record of impressive achievement and success, he lists his hardships and sufferings. Instead of being a brave soldier aiming at winning the *corona muralis* for scaling the walls, he has to flee in a humiliating manner. Instead of receiving sensational messages, he has no revelation to announce in his ascent; and finally, instead of being rid of the thorn, he receives the message that he has to bear it. All these point to Paul being a better servant of Christ, not because he suffers more but because he embodies the story of Jesus and through him the life of Jesus is revealed. At the same time, the summary statement in 12.10 also refers back to Paul's earlier catalogues of his sufferings in 1.5-11; 2.12-16; 4.7-12; and 6.3-10.

The emphatic position of ὑπὲρ Χριστοῦ towards the end of the clause suggests that it should be connected to the list of weaknesses[133] signifying that it

---

130. Brown, 'Gospel Takes Place', 279.

131. Harris, *Second Corinthians*, 866–7. According to Goudge, *Second Corinthians*, 122, 'I take pleasure' is a 'misleading translation'. See KJV, NKJV and NLT.

132. So Harris, *Second Corinthians*, 867; Thrall, *II Corinthians*, II:829. Cf. 6.6 and 11.26 where the first item in both the catalogues is taken to be a general rubric.

133. So Harris, *Second Corinthians*, 867; Barnett, *Second Epistle*, 575–6. However, Furnish,

is to be taken as representational, where Paul's weaknesses in ministry are also sufferings on Christ's behalf. The phrase ὑπὲρ Χριστοῦ recalls Paul's earlier appeal to the Corinthians to be reconciled to God in 5.20. As an ambassador of Christ entrusted with the ministry of reconciliation, Paul suffers for the Corinthians, as his catalogues of sufferings make clear.

Paul wraps up his argument by reiterating this paradoxical principle that is the central reality in his life and ministry: 'For whenever I am weak, then I am strong' (12.10b). This statement raises another issue: whether weakness is a precondition of power. Harris argues that weakness 'is both a prerequisite and a concomitant of Christ's power'.[134] However, O'Collins argues that grammatically Paul's statement is not a conditional statement. As such, weakness is a ground for Christ's power, not a condition.[135] It is also the ground for Paul's boasting in the Lord. Through Paul's weaknesses, the Corinthians are able to see not only the weaknesses, afflictions, persecutions, difficulties and sufferings that characterized Paul's ministry but also the embodiment of the story of Jesus and the living out of the very message of the gospel that Paul preaches: Christ crucified.[136] This is what authenticates Paul's ministry, and this reveals his 'modus operandi'[137] as one whom the Corinthians can see and hear (12.6) and one in whom weaknesses are occasions for God's grace and power to be made manifest. As such, Hafemann is right to argue that '*(t)hus, the revelation of Christ's power in Paul's weakness (v. 9b) and Paul's consequent contentment (v. 10a) form the high point of his argument in this passage and, in doing so, provide a summary of the theological substructure of 2 Corinthians as a whole*'.[138]

II Corinthians, 531; and Thrall, *II Corinthians*, II:830, suggest that ὑπὲρ Χριστοῦ is to be taken together with εὐδοκέω. This would make better sense if ὑπὲρ Χριστοῦ is positioned at the beginning of the clause or immediately after εὐδοκέω rather than remotely towards the end of the clause.

134. Harris, *Second Corinthians*, 864. So Black, *Paul, Apostle of Weakness*, 147; Leivestad, 'Meekness and the Gentleness', 162.

135. Gerald G. O'Collins, 'Power Made Perfect in Weakness: 2 Cor 12:9-10', *CBQ* 33 (1971): 528–37. If weakness is a precondition, O'Collins sees this as a 'psychological trend in interpretation that can distract us from the Christological setting in which Paul sees his ministry' (536).

136. Cf. Harris, *Second Corinthians*, 868: 'Behind δυνατός εἰμι we should see an allusion, not to Paul's own ability to cope with adversity by harnessing all his personal resources, but to his experience of Christ's power ... always in equipping him for effective service.' Note also Martyn, *Galatians*, 569, on Gal. 6:17: 'Paul's physical body is thus a place in which one finds a sign of the present activity of the redeemer in the world ... The glad tidings of Jesus' redemptive death is preached by the one who inevitably participates in that death, and whose apostolic sufferings are paradoxically the locus of God's gift of life, being the present form of Jesus' own death-life pattern.'

137. Gorman, *Cruciformity*, 281.

138. Hafemann, *2 Corinthians*, 465 (emphasis his).

D. *Paul's Weaknesses Grounded in the Story of Jesus (2 Corinthians 13.3-4)*

So far, Paul has been responding to the challenge to satisfy the demand for some visible proof (cf. δοκιμὴν ζητεῖτε) that he is Christ's genuine apostle (13.3a). His challengers most likely expect some convincing evidence, including miraculous signs (12.12), polished rhetoric (10.10), letters of recommendation (3.1), that would at least match the stature of the opponents and correspond to the prevailing cultural expectations that Christ's power is at work in Paul. By issuing this challenge, the Corinthians are questioning not only the validity of Paul's nature of apostleship and his ministry of reconciliation but also the nature of the gospel that Paul proclaims. As such, Paul once again employs the weakness–power antithesis grounded in the story of Jesus in his response (13.3-4) as depicted in the following structure.[139]

ὃς εἰς ὑμᾶς οὐκ ἀσθενεῖ	ἀλλὰ	δυνατεῖ ἐν ὑμῖν.
καὶ γὰρ ἐσταυρώθη ἐξ ἀσθενείας,	ἀλλὰ	ζῇ ἐκ δυνάμεως θεοῦ.
καὶ γὰρ ἡμεῖς ἀσθενοῦμεν ἐν αὐτῷ,	ἀλλὰ	ζήσομεν σὺν αὐτῷ ἐκ δυνάμεως θεοῦ εἰς ὑμᾶς.

The common element in the above three sentences is the motif of ἀσθένεια and δύναμις. What is striking is that Paul is drawing a parallel between his weakness and the crucifixion of Christ, and his present life sustained by the power of the resurrection.

How is the phrase ἐσταυρώθη ἐξ ἀσθενείας to be understood? What is the function of the preposition ἐξ? What constitutes the weakness of Christ? In this context ἐξ could mean 'by reasons of, as a result of, because of'.[140] The weakness of Christ has been suggested to refer to: (1) his human, bodily existence, which he willingly took on in order to humble himself by becoming a servant to God's people and by dying on a cross for their sins;[141] (2) the helplessness or defencelessness of Christ before unjust accusation;[142]or, (3) his weakness inherent in mortal human existence.[143] However, as we have earlier argued, the weakness of Christ in 13.4 should not be limited to the event surrounding the passion. Rather it should be seen in a wider perspective to include the kenotic revelation where

---

139. For the grammatical and structural construction of 13.3b-4, see Harris, *Second Corinthians*, 913–17; Jan Lambrecht, 'Philological and Exegetical Notes on 2 Cor 13,4', *Bijdragen* 46 (1985): 261–9.

140. BDAG, s.v.

141. Hafemann, *2 Corinthians*, 491; Barnett, *Second Epistle*, 603 n. 57. Note Hafemann's critique on the history of interpretation on this verse in *2 Corinthians*, 491 n. 10.

142. Garland, *2 Corinthians*, 544. So Belleville, 'Gospel and Kerygma', 156.

143. Thrall, *II Corinthians*, II:884; Black, *Paul, Apostle of Weakness*, 162.

Christ emptied himself of his glory by fully accepting the conditions of human life leading to his crucifixion (cf. Phil. 2.8),[144] an act carrying negative social connotations of degradation and dishonour and one that is 'a stumbling block to Jews and foolishness to Gentiles' (1 Cor. 1.23). As such, ἐσταυρώθη ἐξ ἀσθενείας is to be understood as meaning that Jesus was crucified as a result of weakness, which is '*the culmination of a life lived for the sake of others*, a life characterized by humility and suffering in giving oneself for the service of others'.[145]

Why is Paul so insistent on the story of Jesus, especially in responding to the challenge of the Corinthians for proof that he is the mouthpiece of Christ? Why is there a parallel in the experience of Christ and Paul as indicated by ἐν αὐτῷ ... σὺν αὐτῷ structure in 13.4? Barnett suggests the possibility that the importance of the life of the earthly Jesus, and in particular his death, has been overlooked by the Corinthians who are more interested in the triumphal nature of the gospel.[146] This argument remains unconvincing, as Paul has explicitly made clear the centrality of the cross and the crucified Messiah in his proclamation of the gospel to the Corinthians (1 Cor. 1.17–2.5). The issue at the heart of the conflict with the Corinthians is primarily Paul's relationship with them and the way he exercises his apostolic ministry that does not correspond with accepted social conventions. This can be seen in the issues of dispute related to Paul's weaknesses, as highlighted earlier. As I have already argued, weakness was often scorned in the Hellenistic culture of Paul's day, and this same basis was being used in evaluating Paul's ministry. As such, Pickett suggests that Paul's weakness is not only humiliation in the eyes of the Corinthians: his deliberate adoption of the posture of a socially and economically disadvantaged person also embarrasses the Corinthians because they expect Paul to assume the role of a leader in the socially accepted sense.[147] The parallels between Christ and Paul go beyond the idea of service for others but point further to the standard by which Paul's apostleship should be judged. Paul also endures the same kind of suffering and social humiliation associated with crucifixion.[148] It is this social stigma (cf. 1 Cor. 1.18-25) that is powerfully accentuated in 2 Cor. 10–13. Therefore, by insisting on the story of Jesus as the canon by which all apostolic proclamation and ministry must be judged, Paul reminds the Corinthians that Christ too was weak for their sakes (13.3) and calls into question all the ways in which the Corinthians join Hellenistic society in idealizing the value of power, eloquence and beauty, and in impugning any form of weakness.[149] To

144. Goudge, *Second Corinthians*, 129; Matera, *II Corinthians*, 307.

145. Stegman, *Character of Jesus*, 208. Cf. Barrett, *Second Corinthians*, 335–6.

146. Barnett, *Second Epistle*, 604.

147. Pickett, *Cross in Corinth*, 169.

148. On the social stigma attached to crucifixion, see Hengel, *Crucifixion*, 69–83.

149. Peterson, *Eloquence and the Proclamation*, 154. Cf. Martin, *2 Corinthians*, 479: 'Paul is not a minister who was intended to pass any sort of qualifying examination which would turn him into a candidate approved by the Corinthians.'

Paul, this faulty understanding of weakness among the Corinthians, pressed to an extreme, led them to a faulty and dangerous misunderstanding of the more important truth behind the story of Jesus. In failing to understand *Paul's* weakness, the Corinthians fail to understand who *Jesus* was, whose character Paul embodies.

By grounding his argument in the crucifixion of Christ, the story of Jesus becomes the supreme instance of the weakness and foolishness of God that stands against the world's wisdom. This act of weakness contradicts the idea that victory/success is gained through the display of what the prevalent culture in Corinth goes after, that is, polished rhetoric, personal appearance, status and achievements. For Paul, the powerful salvation of God is not brought to completion in eloquent rhetoric, impressive appearance and visions and revelations, but had been wrought in the weakness of the crucified One and demonstrated through his story (cf. 1 Cor. 2.1-5). This same framework is operative in Paul as he connects his gentile ministry to the story of Jesus.[150] Paul never divorces the experiences of God's power from the experience of the cross as the centre of the divine power; as Gorman notes: 'The life-giving power of God is most fully experienced by Paul in the cross of Christ and in the life of cruciform power that shares in that cross.'[151] It is in his weaknesses, sufferings and humiliation that Paul demonstrates his likeness to, fellowship with and participation in Christ who was crucified in weakness (cf. Phil. 3.10). Paul's experience of 'carrying the dying of Jesus' in daily, bodily existence, of 'being given up to death', so that the life of Jesus may be paradoxically present in that dying (4.10-12), is precisely the embodiment of the story of Jesus, for the life of Jesus is being manifested in his death. As such, for Paul, weakness is not a hindrance to his apostolic ministry, but is in fact the necessary mark of an apostle in embodying what he proclaims, and that is, above all the cross of Jesus. For Paul, 'We ... preach Jesus Christ *as Lord*' (4.5) is not a contradiction of 'We preach Christ *crucified*' (1 Cor. 1.23). Paul is adamant in refusing to alter his apostolic lifestyle or his self-presentation to win the defecting Corinthians back from other more accommodating apostles.[152] His attempt to win them back involves his appeal grounded in the story of Jesus.

E. *The Story of Jesus and the Corinthians (2 Corinthians 13.5)*

After responding to the challenge by the Corinthians for evidence (δοκιμή) that he is Christ's agent, Paul now issues his challenge to the Corinthians in 13.5: Ἑαυτοὺς πειράζετε εἰ ἐστὲ ἐν τῇ πίστει, ἑαυτοὺς δοκιμάζετε. By employing two

---

150. Harris, *Second Corinthians*, 917: 'Paul is asserting that Christ's career is the pattern for his own ministry.' Cf. Peterson, *Eloquence and the Proclamation*, 137; Black, *Paul, Apostle of Weakness*, 163.

151. Gorman, *Cruciformity*, 280. Cf. Lambrecht, 'Philological and Exegetical Notes', 267–8.

152. Cf. Horrell, *Social Ethos*, 228–9.

imperatives, πειράζετε and δοκιμάζετε, both modified by the repeated reflexive pronoun ἑαυτούς in emphatic position, Paul states that the Corinthians are the ones who ought to examine their own status and conduct to see whether they are true believers of Christ.[153] This is followed by a rhetorical question to which Paul expects an affirmative answer: ἢ οὐκ ἐπιγινώσκετε ἑαυτοὺς ὅτι Ἰησοῦς Χριστὸς ἐν ὑμῖν, and an ironical statement: εἰ μήτι ἀδόκιμοί ἐστε.[154] Paul's play on the δοκιμάζω word group (once in 13.3 and twice in 13.5) related to Christ and faith in Christ is significant. The Corinthians first seek for evidence (δοκιμή) that Paul is Christ's agent, and now Paul challenges them to examine themselves (δοκιμάζετε) so that they do not fail to meet the test (ἀδόκιμος). This stern challenge by Paul strongly suggests that the Corinthians fail to allow the story of Jesus to lead them into transformation through effecting the conversion of the imagination. Paul now turns the tables on the Corinthians: they are the ones who must be examined, not according to the canon established by the cultural conventions of the day but according to the story of Jesus.

From Paul's perspective, the situation in Corinth must be serious enough to warrant his tone of urgency and the strong language used. In 10.1, Paul begins his appeal grounded in the meekness and gentleness of Christ. This is followed by the warfare imagery to destroy arguments and every proud obstacle raised up against the knowledge of God, and to take every thought captive to obey Christ (10.3-6). Paul's subsequent allusion to the marriage metaphor (11.2) recalls the representation of Israel as betrothed to God (e.g., Isa. 49.18; 50.1-2; 54.1-8; 62.5; Jer. 3.1; Ezek. 16.23-33; Hos. 2.19-20), signifying that Paul does not want the history of Israel's spiritual adultery to be repeated by the Corinthians (cf. 1 Cor. 10.13; 2 Cor. 3.7-18). Together with subsequent references to the fall (2 Cor. 11.3) and the disapproving behaviour (12.20-1), these indications not only point to the refusal of the Corinthians to embody the story of Jesus in their lives as a community of Christ-followers but also reveal how serious the danger facing the Corinthians really is. As such, Hafemann correctly remarks, 'Paul is fighting for the faithfulness of the Corinthians.'[155]

This can be seen further in Paul's deep awareness of his constructive aim in building up the community. Paul's language of building up the community (10.6, 8; 12.19; 13.5-6, 9, 10; cf. 1.6; 2.4; 2.12-13; 4.12, 15; 7.3; 11.11; 1 Cor. 3.9; 4.15; 14.3),[156] the jealousy he feels towards them (11.2) and his commercial metaphor of parents being spent for their children (12.14-15) reinforce that what is at stake is nothing less than the salvation of the community for which

153. As indicated by ἐν τῇ πίστει. So Harris, *Second Corinthians*, 919.

154. So Barnett, *Second Epistle*, 608; Harris, *Second Corinthians*, 921; Martin, *2 Corinthians*, 479.

155. Hafemann, *2 Corinthians*, 426.

156. The language echoes the vocabulary of Jeremiah concerning Yahweh's relationship with Israel (e.g., Jer. 24.6; 38.27-8; 51.54). See also Pickett, *Cross in Corinth*, 183–92.

Christ died and for which Paul has laboured. Failure to do what is necessary to bring the community back to conformity to Paul's gospel grounded in the story of Jesus is tantamount to a betrayal of his divine commission as an apostle of Jesus Christ. As such, Paul goes to great lengths to ensure that the Corinthians do not misunderstand his apostleship characterized by suffering. If the Corinthians misunderstand his apostleship, they also misunderstand the very essence of the gospel. Paul's primary task is 'to convince his people to abandon a view of faith, the church, and ministry that is supported by the standards and values of the society around them, and to accept a model that will mean the end of such values and quests for them: a cruciform model'.[157] This explains why Paul interprets his own weaknesses in terms of the weakness of the crucifixion, 'with a view to implementing in the Corinthian community the values symbolized in this event and embodied in his own apostleship'.[158] The Corinthians must not forget that the same Christ who lives in them is the Christ who suffered and died. Similarly, they must not forget that the apostle who brings this message of Christ crucified to them is also carrying the dying of Jesus so that they may experience life (4.10-12).

Seen from this perspective, 2 Cor. 10–13, and in fact the entire 2 Corinthians, is primarily hortatory in function.[159] Second Corinthians 10–13 begins (10.1-2, 11, 17) and ends (13.5, 11-12) with entreaty and admonition with the aim of inviting the Corinthians to participate in the story of Jesus.

IV. *Concluding Summary*

In the longest description of his hardships, Paul adopts the strategy of boasting in his weaknesses in responding to those who challenge the nature of his apostolic ministry. Paul's boasting of his weakness is governed by his scriptural understanding of boasting in the Lord, as Jer. 9.22-3/1 Kgdms 2.10 had affirmed, and a theological interpretation of weakness that is grounded in the story of Jesus, the Messiah crucified in weakness but now reigning by the power of God (2 Cor. 13.4). This same paradigm is replicated in Paul's own weaknesses, as demonstrated through his sufferings, his humiliating escape from Damascus, his failed heavenly ascent, and the thorn in the flesh that afflicts him. In the same way, Paul's ministry is empowered by the same divine power at work in the resurrection of Christ to the benefit of the Corinthians, with the

---

157. Peterson, *Eloquence and the Proclamation*, 167.

158. Pickett, *Cross in Corinth*, 211. Cf. Martin, *2 Corinthians*, lx–lxi: 'The cross ... is not a station on the road to glory or a temporary diversion quickly to be passed over in the retelling of the story of Christ ... Rather the cross is of the *esse* of Christian existence.'

159. Furnish, *II Corinthians*, 8; Talbert, *Reading Corinthians*, 129. Cf. Schütz, *Paul and the Anatomy of Apostolic Authority*, 203, where he argues that Paul's suffering is 'really designed not as *apostolic defense* but as *apostolic warning*' (emphasis mine).

final challenge and invitation to the believing community to be participants in the story of Jesus. For Paul, the story of Jesus and Paul's self-presentation are congruent with each other, with the latter being a specific embodiment of the former. Paul presents this to the Corinthians in order to shape them in their embodiment of the story of Jesus, both through his theological reflections and his own life.

Chapter 8

CONCLUSION

At the beginning of this study, I noted that Paul develops the theme of suffering at critical points in his argument in 2 Corinthians and raised the question why the theme of suffering is central to Paul's argument. My analysis of previous studies on Paul's suffering, in Chapter 1, reveals that there is no satisfactory answer to this question, prompting the direction of the study. I proposed that the narrative approach could profitably be used in this study, drawing on the story of Jesus to analyse Paul's suffering in 2 Corinthians.

In Chapter 2, after suggesting that Paul's voice in addressing the Corinthians must, above all, be heard, and not the reconstructed voice of the opponents, I investigated the function of the epistolary thanksgiving in 2 Cor. 1.3-11 in relation to the overall argument of the letter. I identified five key motifs related to the theme of suffering in this section that are subsequently developed in 2 Corinthians. I also suggested that the story of Jesus in Paul's suffering is the unifying theme of the letter.

From Chapters 3 to 7, I began the exposition of my thesis that Paul's understanding of his suffering is grounded in the story of Jesus. Exegesis of the passages that speak of Paul's suffering, namely, 1.3-11; 2.14-16; 4.7-12; 6.1-10; and 11.23–12.10, are carried out in these five chapters respectively. The summaries of my exegesis are provided in the concluding summary sections in these chapters.

In this chapter, I bring together my investigation and highlight several significant findings of this study that explain the reason why the theme of suffering is dominant in 2 Corinthians.

1. Paul's understanding of his suffering is not to be divorced from his apostolic mission. Whenever Paul mentions his suffering in 2 Corinthians, it is directly related to his apostolic mission. His suffering is a proclamation of the gospel of the crucified Messiah (2.14-15; 4.10) in which the power of God is revealed (4.7; 12.9-10; 13.4). While Paul lives, his existence is cruciform, for in this mode Paul makes known the crucified and risen Christ. As such, Paul views his suffering as necessary and integral to his gentile mission, and it does not impede the progress of the gospel (6.3).

2. Paul claims that his suffering has positive missiological benefits for
    the Corinthians. Paul clearly states that it is through his suffering that
    the Corinthians receive comfort and salvation (1.6) and life (2.15-16;
    4.10-12; 13.4). His sufferings result in life being awakened in those
    who believe in the gospel and in giving birth to a Christ-believing
    community in Corinth.

3. For Paul, the story of Jesus does not end at the cross; it is to be lived
    out not only in his life but also in the life of the community he founded.
    The gospel of Jesus Christ is not simply an objective fact to believe
    in but it is also a story to be lived in. Paul's telling and retelling of
    the story is not to invite the Corinthians to continue to dwell in their
    own world supported by the values of the society around them, but to
    invite them to participate in this story. Since Paul's understanding of
    the story of Jesus defines the character of his mission, the Corinthians
    should also see that the same story of Jesus should define, shape and
    transform their way of life as well. There is a clear correspondence
    between the story of Jesus, the suffering of Paul as an apostle and the
    life of the Pauline Christ-believing community.

4. Paul's understanding of his suffering is also inspired by the Scriptures.
    I highlighted the surprising neglect of Paul's allusion to and citation of
    Scripture in relation to his suffering in 2 Corinthians. Paul's references
    to Scripture demonstrate not only that he lives in the world of the
    Scriptures but also the deep influence the Scriptures have in shaping
    his understanding of his suffering and mission to the gentiles. I argued
    that in 2.14-16 Paul draws on the image of God as Divine Warrior
    leading the triumphal procession through Christ the Messiah. This
    evokes the tradition of the Isaianic new exodus and establishes Paul as
    God's servant in manifesting the fragrance of the knowledge of Christ
    through his suffering. By citing Isa. 49.8 in 2 Cor. 6.2, Paul sees his
    apostolic mission in bringing the gentiles back to God as analogous
    to the tradition of the Servant of the Lord and in fulfilment of God's
    promises. His boasting of his weaknesses and sufferings (11.23–12.10)
    is also governed by his scriptural understanding of boasting in the Lord
    as LXX Jer. 9.22-3/1 Kdgms 2.10 affirmed.

5. Paul's interpretation of his suffering in this letter is not simply his
    personal defence of his *call* to apostleship but his specific exposition
    of the *nature* of his apostleship and his ministerial lifestyle that is
    transformed by and embedded in the story of Jesus; it is a restatement
    of the story of Jesus. It is this story that Paul wants his life and ministry
    to tell; it is this story that Paul appeals to the Corinthians to embrace.
    If the Corinthians cannot understand and appreciate his cruciformed
    life and ministry as demonstrated by weakness and suffering grounded
    in the story of Jesus, how can they understand the cross and the weak-

ness and suffering of Christ and apply it to their own lives?[1] Thus, by paying close attention to Paul's deep concern for the Corinthians expressed in this letter, I suggest reading 2 Corinthians as primarily parenaetic in nature.

In Chapter 1, I indicated that while the narrative approach has gained significant acceptance in Pauline studies it has largely been concentrated on studies in Romans and Galatians. It is hoped that this study has, in some ways, successfully pushed the developments of the narrative approach beyond the boundaries of Romans and Galatians to 2 Corinthians.

---

1. Paul's understanding of his suffering as necessary and integral to his proclamation of the gospel may be difficult for some to accept and may even sound irrelevant in the contemporary world. Therefore, the question whether there is any contemporary significance to the present study may be raised. I have offered some reflections from the perspective of a Christian minority living in the multi-religious, multi-ethnic and multi-cultural context of Malaysia where Islam is the dominant religion. See my 'Is There a Place for Suffering in Mission? Perspectives from Paul's Sufferings in 2 Corinthians', in *The Soul of Mission: Perspectives on Christian Leadership, Spirituality and Mission in East Asia*: Essays in Appreciation of Dr David Gunaratnam, ed. Kang San Tan (Petaling Jaya: Pustaka Sufes, 2007), 64–78.

BIBLIOGRAPHY

Adams, Edward, 'Paul's Story of God and Creation: The Story of How God Fulfils His Purposes in Creation', in *Narrative Dynamics in Paul: A Critical Assessment*, ed. Bruce W.
Longenecker (Louisville: Westminster/John Knox, 2002), 19–43.

Adams, Edward, and David G. Horrell, eds, *Christianity at Corinth: The Quest for the Pauline
Church* (Louisville: Westminster/John Knox, 2004).

Ådna, Jostein, and Hans Kvalbein, eds, *The Mission of the Early Church to Jews and Gentiles*, WUNT 127 (Tübingen: Mohr, 2000).

Ahern, Barnabas Mary, 'The Fellowship of His Sufferings (Phil. 3.10): A Study of St. Paul's
Doctrine on Christian Suffering', *CBQ* 22 (1960): 1–32.

Akin, Daniel L., 'Triumphalism, Suffering, and Spiritual Maturity: An Exposition of 2 Corinthians 12:1-10 in Its Literary, Theological, and Historical Context', *CTR* 4 (1989):
119–44.

Alary, Laura Dawn, 'Good Grief: Paul as Sufferer and Consoler in 2 Corinthians 1:3-7: A
Comparative Investigation' (PhD dissertation, University of St. Michael's College,
Toronto, 2003).

Allison, Dale C., *The End of the Ages Has Come: An Early Interpretation of the Passion and
Resurrection of Jesus*, SNTW (Edinburgh: T&T Clark, 1985).

Allo, E. B., *Saint Paul: Seconde Épître aux Corinthiens*, 2nd edn, EB (Paris: J. Gabala,
1956).

Amador, J. D. H., 'Revisiting 2 Corinthians: Rhetoric and the Case for Unity', *NTS* 46 (2000):
92–111.

—, 'The Unity of 2 Corinthians: A Test Case for a Rediscovered and Re-invented Rhetoric',
Neot 33 (1999): 411–32.

Andrews, Scott B., 'Too Weak Not to Lead: The Form and Function of 2 Cor 11.23b-33', *NTS*
41 (1995): 263–76.

Artz, Peter, 'The "Epistolary Introductory Thanksgiving" in the Papyri and in Paul', *NovT*
36 (1994): 29–46.

Attridge, Harold W., 'Making Scents of Paul: The Background and Sense of 2 Cor 2:14-17',
in *Early Christianity and Classical Culture: Comparative Studies in Honor of Abraham
J. Malherbe*, NovTSup 110, ed. John T. Fitzgerald, Thomas H. Olbright and L. Michael
White (Leiden: Brill, 2003), 71–88.

Aus, Roger D., *Imagery of Triumph and Rebellion in 2 Corinthians 2:14-17 and Elsewhere in
the Epistle: An Example of the Combination of Greco-Roman and Judaic Traditions in
the Apostle Paul*, SJ (Lanham: University Press of America, 2005).

—, 'Paul's Travel Plans to Spain and the "Full Number of the Gentiles" of Rom 11.25', *NovT*
21 (1979): 232–62.

Baird, William, 'Visions, Revelation, and Ministry: Reflections on 2 Cor 12:1-5 and Gal 1:11-
17', *JBL* 104 (1985): 651–62.

Baker, David W., ed., *Looking into the Future: Evangelical Studies in Eschatology* (Grand
Rapids: Baker, 2001).

Balch, David L., Everett Ferguson and Wayne A. Meeks, eds, *Greeks, Romans, and Christians: Essays in Honor of Abraham J. Malherbe* (Minneapolis: Fortress Press, 1990).

Balz, H., and G. Schneider, eds, *Exegetical Dictionary of the New Testament*, 3 vols (Grand Rapids: Eerdmans, 1990–1993).

Barclay, John M. G., 'Jesus and Paul', *DPL*, 492–503.

—, 'Mirror-Reading a Polemical Letter: Galatians as a Test Case', *JSNT* 31 (1987): 73–93.

—, 'Paul's Story: Theology as Testimony', in *Narrative Dynamics in Paul: A Critical Assessment*, ed. Bruce W. Longenecker (Louisville: Westminster/John Knox, 2002), 133–56.

—, 'Thessalonica and Corinth: Social Contrasts in Pauline Christianity', *JSNT* 47 (1992): 49–74.

Barnett, Paul W., *The Second Epistle to the Corinthians*, NICNT (Grand Rapids: Eerdmans, 1997).

Barré, Michael L., 'Paul as "Eschatological Person": A New Look at 2 Cor 11:29', *CBQ* 37 (1975): 500–26.

—, 'Qumran and the "Weakness" of Paul', *CBQ* 42 (1980): 216–27.

Barrett, C. K., 'Paul's Opponents in 2 Corinthians', *NTS* 17 (1971): 233–54.

—, *The Second Epistle to the Corinthians*, BNTC (London: A. & C. Black, 1973).

—, 'Boasting in the Pauline Epistles', in *L'Apôtre Paul: Personnalité, style et conception du ministère*, ed. A. Vanhoye, BETL 73 (Leuven: Leuven University Press, 1986), 363–8.

—, *The First Epistle to the Corinthians*, BNTC, 2nd edn (London: A. & C. Black, 1992).

Bartchy, S. Scott, '"When I'm Weak, I'm Strong": A Pauline Paradox in Cultural Context', in *Kontexte der Schrift, Band II: Kultur, Politik, Religion, Sprache – Text; Wolfgang Stegemann zum 60 Geburtstag*, ed. Christian Strecker (Stuttgart: Kohlhammer, 2005), 49–60.

Bartlett, David L., Review of *The Paradox of the Cross in the Thought of St Paul* by A. T. Hanson, *Int* 42 (1988): 434–6.

Bartling, Victor, 'God's Triumphant Captive, Christ's Aroma for God', *CTM* 22 (1951): 883–94.

Barton, Tamsyn S., *Power and Knowledge: Astrology, Physiognomics, and Medicine under the Roman Empire* (Ann Arbor: University of Michigan Press, 1994).

Bauckham, Richard, 'Colossians 1:24 Again: The Apocalyptic Motif', *EvQ* 47 (1975): 168–70.

—, 'Weakness – Paul's and Ours', *Themelios* 7/3 (1982): 4–6.

Baumert, Norbert, *Täglich sterben und auferstehen: Der Literalsinn von 2 Kor 4,12–5,10*, SANT 34 (München: Kösel-Verlag, 1973).

Beale, Gregory K., 'The Old Testament Background of Reconciliation in 2 Corinthians 5–7 and Its Bearing on the Literary Problem of 2 Corinthians 6:14–7:1', *NTS* 35 (1989): 550–81.

Beard, Mary, *The Roman Triumph* (Cambridge: Belknap Press of Harvard University Press, 2007).

Becker, Jürgen, *Paul: Apostle to the Gentiles* (Louisville: Westminster/John Knox, 1993).

Beker, Johan Christiaan, *Paul the Apostle: The Triumph of God in Life and Thought* (Philadelphia: Fortress Press, 1980).

Belleville, Linda L., 'Gospel and Kerygma in 2 Corinthians', in *Gospel in Paul: Studies on Corinthians, Galatians and Romans for Richard N. Longenecker*, JSNTSup 108, ed. L. Ann Jervis and Peter Richardson (Sheffield: Sheffield Academic Press, 1994), 134–64.

—, 'A Letter of Apologetic Self-Commendation: 2 Cor 1:8–7:16', *NovT* 31 (1989): 142–63.

—, *2 Corinthians*, IVPNTC (Downers Grove: InterVarsity, 1996).

Bellinger, William H., Jr., and William R. Farmer, eds, *Jesus and the Suffering Servant: Isaiah 53 and Christian Origins* (Harrisburg: Trinity, 1998).

Best, Ernest, *A Critical and Exegetical Commentary on Ephesians*, ICC (Edinburgh: T&T Clark, 1998).

—, *Second Corinthians*, IBC (Atlanta: John Knox, 1987).

Betz, Hans Dieter, *Der Apostel Paulus und die sokratische Tradition: Eine exegetische Unter-suchung zu seiner 'Apologie' 2 Korinther 10–13*, BHT 45 (Tübingen: Mohr, 1972).

—, *2 Corinthians 8 and 9*, Hermeneia (Philadelphia: Fortress Press, 1985).

Bieringer, Reimund, ed., *The Corinthian Correspondence*, BETL 125 (Leuven: Peeters, 1996).

—, 'Teilungshypothesen zum 2 Korintherbrief: Ein Forschungsüberblick', in *Studies on 2 Corinthians*, BETL 112, ed. Reimund Bieringer and Jan Lambrecht (Leuven: Leuven University Press, 1994), 67–105.

Bieringer, Reimund, Veronica Koperski and B. Lataire, eds, *Resurrection in the New Testa-ment: Festschrift J. Lambrecht*, BETL 165 (Leuven: Leuven University Press, 2002).

Bieringer, Reimund, and Jan Lambrecht, *Studies on 2 Corinthians*, BETL 112 (Leuven: Leuven University Press, 1994).

Bishop, Eric F. F., 'Does Aretas Belong in 2 Corinthians or Galatians?', *ExpT* 64 (1953): 188–9.

Black, David A., *Paul, Apostle of Weakness: Astheneia and Its Cognates in the Pauline Lit-erature* (New York: Lang, 1984).

Blenkinsopp, Joseph, *Isaiah 40–55: A New Translation with Introduction and Commentary*, AB (New York: Doubleday, 2000).

—, *Isaiah 56–66: A New Translation with Introduction and Commentary*, AB (New York: Doubleday, 2003).

Blomberg, Craig, 'Messiah in the New Testament', in *Israel's Messiah in the Bible and the Dead Sea Scrolls*, ed. Richard S. Hess and M. Daniel Carroll R. (Grand Rapids: Baker, 2003), 111–41.

Bockmuehl, Markus, *Revelation and Mystery in Ancient Judaism and Pauline Christianity*, WUNT 2/36 (Tübingen: J. C. B. Mohr, 1990).

Boers, Hendrikus, '2 Corinthians 5:14–6:2: A Fragment of Pauline Christology', *CBQ* 64 (2002): 527–47.

Bolt, Peter, and Mark Thompson, eds, *The Gospel to the Nations: Perspectives on Paul's Mission* (Downers Grove: InterVarsity, 2000).

Bookidis, Nancy, 'Religion in Corinth: 146 B.C.E. to 100 C.E.', in *Urban Religion in Roman Corinth: Interdisciplinary Approaches*, ed. Daniel N. Schowalter and Steven J. Friesen, HTS 53 (Cambridge: Harvard University Press, 2005), 141–64.

Borgen, Peder, and Soren Giversen, eds, *The New Testament and Hellenistic Judaism* (Aarhus: Aarhus University Press, 1995).

Bormann, Lukas, Kelly Del Tredici and Angela Standhartinger, eds, *Religious Propaganda and Missionary Competition in the New Testament World: Essays Honoring Dieter Georgi*, NovTSup 74 (Leiden: Brill, 1994).

Bosch, David, *Transforming Mission: Paradigm Shifts in Theology of Mission* (Maryknoll: Orbis, 1991).

Bouttier, Michel, 'La souffrance de l'apôtre: 2 Cor 4:7-18', in *The Diakonia of the Spirit (2 Co 4:7–7:4)*, ed. Lorenzo De Lorenzi, Benedictina 10 (Rome: Benedictina, 1989), 29–74.

Bowers, Paul, ' Mission', *DPL*, 617–18.

—, 'Studies in Paul's Understanding of His Mission' (PhD dissertation, University of Cam-bridge, Cambridge, 1977).

Bowker, J. W., '"Merkabah" Visions and the Visions of Paul', *JSS* 16 (1971): 157–73.

Brettler, Marc, 'Images of YHWH the Warrior in Psalms', *Semeia* 61 (1993): 135–65.

Breytenbach, Cilliers, 'Paul's Proclamation and God's "Thriambos" (Notes on 2 Corinthians 2.14-16b)', *Neot* 24 (1990): 255–71.

—, *Versöhnung: Eine Studie zur paulinischen Soteriologie*, WMANT 60 (Neukirchen-Vluyn: Neukirchener Verlag, 1989).

Brondos, David A., *Paul on the Cross: Reconstructing the Apostle's Story of Redemption* (Minneapolis: Fortress Press, 2006).

Brown, Alexandra R., 'The Gospel Takes Place: Paul's Theology of Power-in-Weakness in 2 Corinthians', *Int* 52/3 (1998): 271–85.

Brown, Colin, ed., *New International Dictionary of New Testament Theology*, 4 vols (Grand Rapids: Zondervan, 1975–1985).

Bruce, F. F., *1 & 2 Corinthians*, NCB (London: Oliphants, 1971).

Brueggemann, Walter A., 'The Epistemological Crisis of Israel's Two Histories (Jer 9:22-23)', in *Israelite Wisdom: Theological and Literary Essays in Honor of Samuel Terrien*, ed. John G. Gammie, Walter A. Brueggemann, W. Lee Humphreys and James M. Ward (Missoula: Scholars Press, 1978), 85–105.

—, *Isaiah 40–66*, WestBC (Louisville: Westminster/John Knox, 1998).

Buchanan, George Wesley, 'Jesus and the Upper Class', *NovT* 7 (1964–65): 195–209.

Bultmann, Rudolf, *The Second Letter to the Corinthians* (Minneapolis: Augsburg, 1957).

—, *Der Stil der paulinischen Predigt und die kynisch-stoische Diatribe*, FRLANT 13 (Göttingen: Vandenhoeck & Ruprecht, 1910).

Burke, Trevor J., and J. K. Elliott, eds, *Paul and the Corinthians: Studies on a Community in Conflict, Essays in Honour of Margaret Thrall*, NovTSup 109 (Leiden: Brill, 2003).

Byrnes, Michael, *Conformation to the Death of Christ and the Hope of Resurrection: An Exegetico-Theological Study of 2 Corinthians 4,7-15 and Philippians 3,7-11*, TGST 99 (Rome: Editrice Pontificia Universita Gregoriana, 2003).

Byron, John, *Slavery Metaphors in Early Judaism and Pauline Christianity: A Traditio-Historical and Exegetical Examination*, WUNT 2/162 (Tübingen: Mohr Siebeck, 2003).

Cahill, Michael, 'The Neglected Parallelism in Col 1:24-25', *ETL* 68 (1992): 142–7.

Callan, Terrance, 'Competition and Boasting: Toward a Psychological Portrait of Paul', *ST* 40 (1986): 137–56.

Calvin, John, *Commentary on the Epistles of Paul the Apostle to the Corinthians*, 2 vols, trans. John Pringle (Edinburgh: Calvin Translation Society, 1848).

Campbell, Douglas A., *The Quest for Paul's Gospel*, JSNTSup 274 (New York: T&T Clark, 2005).

Campbell, William S., 'Israel', *DPL*, 441–6.

—, *Paul and the Creation of Christian Identity*, LNTS 322 (London: T&T Clark, 2006).

Carroll, John T., and Joel B. Green, eds, *The Death of Jesus in Early Christianity* (Peabody: Hendrickson, 1995).

Carson, D. A., and H. G. M. Williamson, eds, *It Is Written: Scripture Citing Scripture. Essays in Honour of Barnabas Lindars* (Cambridge: Cambridge University Press, 1988).

Cartledge, Mark J., 'A Model of Hermeneutical Method: An Exegetical Missiological Reflection upon Suffering in 2 Corinthians 4:7-15', *ERT* 17 (1993): 472–83.

Chang, Steven S. H., 'The Integrity of 2 Corinthians: 1980–2000', *TTJ* 5 (2002): 167–202.

Childs, Brevard S., *Isaiah*, OTL (Louisville: Westminster/John Knox, 2001).

Chilton, Bruce D., and Caig A. Evans, eds, *The Missions of James, Peter and Paul: Tensions in Early Christianity*, NovTSup 115 (Leiden: Brill, 2005).

Cogan, Mordechai, Barry Eichler and Jeffrey Tigay, eds, *Tehillah le-Moshe: Biblical and Judaic Studies in Honor of Moshe Greenberg* (Winona Lake: Eisenbrauns, 1997).

Collange, Jean-François, *Enigmes de la deuxième épître de Paul aux Corinthiens: Étude exégétique de 2 Cor. 2:14–7:4*, SNTSMS 18 (Cambridge: Cambridge University Press, 1972).

Collins, Adela Yarbro, *Cosmology and Eschatology in Jewish and Christian Apocalypticism*, JSJSup 50 (Leiden: Brill, 1996).

Collins, Adela Yarbro, and Margaret M. Mitchell, eds, *Antiquity and Humanity: Essays on Ancient Religion and Philosophy Presented to Hans Dieter Betz on His 70th Birthday* (Tübingen: Mohr Siebeck, 2001).

Collins, John N., 'The Mediatorial Aspect of Paul's Role as *Diakonos*', *ABR* 40 (1992): 34–44.

Collins, Raymond F., *First Corinthians*, SP (Collegeville: Liturgical, 1999).

Conrad, Edgar W., and Edward G. Newing, eds, *Perspectives on Language and Text* (Winona Lake: Eisenbrauns, 1987).

Cousar, Charles B., 'Paul and the Death of Jesus', *Int* 52/1 (1998): 32–52.

—, *A Theology of the Cross: The Death of Jesus in the Pauline Letters* (Minneapolis: Fortress Press, 1990).

Crafton, Jeffrey A., *The Agency of the Apostle: A Dramatistic Analysis of Paul's Responses to Conflict in 2 Corinthians*, JSNTSup 59 (Sheffield: JSOT Press, 1991).

Cranfield, C. E. B., 'Changes of Person and Number in Paul's Epistles', in *Paul and Paulinism*, ed. Morna D. Hooker and S. G. Wilson (London: SPCK, 1982), 280–9.

Cross, Frank Moore, *Canaanite Myth and Hebrew Epic: Essays in the History of the Religion in Israel* (Cambridge: Harvard University Press, 1973).

Cullmann, Oscar, 'Le caractère eschatologique du devoir missionaire et de la conscience apostolique de S. Paul: Étude sur le κατέχον (-ων) de 2. Thess. 2:6-7', *RHPR* 16 (1936): 210–45.

—, 'Der eschatologische Charakter des Missionsauftrags und des apostolischen Selbstbewusstseins bei Paulus', in *Oscar Cullmann: Vorträge und Aufsätze, 1925–1962*, ed. Karlfried Fröhlich (Tübingen: Mohr, 1966), 305–36.

Dahl, Nils Alstrup, *The Crucified Messiah, and Other Essays* (Minneapolis: Augsburg, 1974).

—, ed. 'The Messiahship of Jesus in Paul', in *The Crucified Messiah and Other Essays*, ed. Nils Alstrup Dahl (Minneapolis: Augsburg, 1974), 37–47.

Dahl, Nils Alstrup, and Paul Donahue, *Studies in Paul: Theology for the Early Christian Mission* (Minneapolis: Augsburg, 1977).

Danker, Frederick W., 'Paul's Debt to the *De Corona* of Demosthenes: A Study of Rhetorical Techniques in Second Corinthians', in *Persuasive Artistry: Studies in New Testament Rhetoric in Honor of George A. Kennedy*, ed. Duane F. Watson, JSNTSup 50 (Sheffield: Sheffield Academic Press, 1991), 262–80.

—, *II Corinthians*, ACNT (Minneapolis: Augsburg, 1989).

Davids, Peter H., 'Why Do We Suffer? Suffering in James and Paul', in *The Missions of James, Peter and Paul: Tensions in Early Christianity*, NovTSup 115, ed. Bruce D. Chilton and Craig A. Evans (Leiden: Brill, 2005), 435–66.

Davies, W. D., 'Paul and the New Exodus', in *The Quest for Context and Meaning: Studies in Biblical Intertextuality in Honor of James A. Sanders*, ed. Craig A. Evans and Shemaryahu Talmon (Leiden: Brill, 1997), 443–63.

Davis, George Brown, 'True and False Boasting in 2 Cor 10–13' (PhD dissertation, University of Cambridge, Cambridge, 1999).

De Boer, Willis P., *The Imitation of Paul: An Exegetical Study* (Kampen: Kok, 1962).

De Lorenzi, Lorenzo, ed., *The Diakonia of the Spirit (2 Co 4:7–7:4)*, Benedictina 10 (Rome: Benedictina, 1989).

Denney, James, *The Second Epistle to the Corinthians* (London: Hodder & Stoughton, 1894).

DeSilva, David A., *An Introduction to the New Testament: Contexts, Methods & Ministry Formation* (Downers Grove: InterVarsity, 2004).

—, *Honor, Patronage, Kinship and Purity: Unlocking New Testament Culture* (Downers Grove: InterVarsity, 2000).

—, *The Hope of Glory: Honor Discourse and New Testament Interpretation* (Collegeville: Liturgical Press, 1999).

—, 'Measuring Penultimate against Ultimate Reality: An Investigation of the Integrity and Argumentation of 2 Corinthians', *JSNT* 52 (1993): 41–70.

Dewey, Arthur J., 'A Matter of Honor: A Social-Historical Analysis of 2 Corinthians 10', *HTR* 78 (1985): 209–17.

DiCicco, Mario M., *Paul's Use of Ethos, Pathos, and Logos in 2 Corinthians 10–13*, MBPS 31 (Lewiston: Mellen, 1995).

Dickson, John P., *Mission-Commitment in Ancient Judaism and in the Pauline Communities: The Shape, Extent and Background of Early Christian Mission*, WUNT 2/159 (Tübingen: Mohr Siebeck, 2003).

Dillon, Richard J., 'The "Priesthood" of St Paul, Romans 15:15-16', *Worship* 74 (2000): 156–68.

Dinter, Paul E., 'Paul and the Prophet Isaiah', *BTB* 13 (1983): 48–52.

Dippenaar, M. C., 'Prayer and Epistolarity: The Function of Prayer in the Pauline Letter Structure', *TJT* 16 (1994): 147–88.

—, 'Reading Paul's Letters: Epistolarity and the Epistolary Situation', *TJT* 15 (1993): 141–57.

Dubis, Mark, 'First Peter and the "Sufferings of the Messiah"', in *Looking into the Future: Evangelical Studies in Eschatology*, ed. David W. Baker (Grand Rapids: Baker, 2001), 85–96.

—, *Messianic Woes in First Peter: Suffering and Eschatology in 1 Peter 4:12-19*, SBL 33 (New York: Peter Lang, 2002).

Duff, Paul Brooks, 'Apostolic Suffering and the Language of Processions in 2 Corinthians 4.7-10', *BTB* 21 (1991): 158–65.

—, 'Glory in the Ministry of Death: Gentile Condemnation and Letters of Recommendation in 2 Cor. 3:6-18', *NovT* 46 (2004): 313–37.

—, 'The March of the Divine Warrior and the Advent of the Greco-Roman King: Mark's Account of Jesus' Entry into Jerusalem', *JBL* 111 (1992): 55–71.

—, 'Metaphor, Motif, and Meaning: The Rhetorical Strategy behind the Image "Led in Triumph" in 2 Corinthians 2:14', *CBQ* 53/1 (1991): 79–92.

Dunn, James D. G., ed., *Cambridge Companion to St Paul* (Cambridge: Cambridge University Press, 2003).

—, *Christology in the Making: A New Testament Inquiry into the Origins of the Doctrine of the Incarnation*, 2nd edn (London: SCM Press, 1989).

—, *The Epistle to the Galatians*, BNTC (Peabody: Hendrickson, 1993).

—, *The Theology of Paul the Apostle* (Grand Rapids: Eerdmans, 1998).

—, 'The Narrative Approach to Paul: Whose Story?', in *Narrative Dynamics in Paul: A Critical Assessment*, ed. Bruce W. Longenecker (Louisville: Westminster/John Knox, 2002), 217–30.

—, 'Paul's Theology', in *The Face of New Testament Studies: A Survey of Recent Research*, ed. Scot McKnight and Grant R. Osborne (Grand Rapids: Baker, 2004), 326–48.

Ebner, Martin, *Leidenslisten und Apostelbrief: Untersuchungen zu Form, Motivik und Funktion der Peristasenkataloge bei Paulus*, FB 66 (Wurzburg: Echter Verlag, 1991).

Edelman, Diana, 'The Meaning of *Qiṭṭēr*', *VT* 35 (1985): 395–404.

Egan, R. B., 'Lexical Evidence on Two Pauline Passages', *NovT* 19 (1977): 34–62.

Ehrensperger, Kathy, '"Be Imitators of Me as I am of Christ": A Hidden Discourse of Power and Domination in Paul?', *LTQ* 38 (2003): 241–61.

—, Review of *Narrative Dynamics in Paul: A Critical Assessment*, ed. Bruce W. Longenecker, *JBV* 24 (2003): 377–80.

Ekblad, Eugene Robert, Jr., *Isaiah's Servant Poems according to the Septuagint: An Exegetical and Theological Study*, CBET 23 (Leuven: Peeters, 1999).

Ellis, E. Earle, 'Paul and His Co-Workers', *NTS* 17 (1971): 437–52.

—, 'Paul and His Opponents: Trends in Research', in *Christianity, Judaism and Other Greco-Roman Cults: Studies for Morton Smith at Sixty, Part One: New Testament*, SJLA 12, ed. Jacob Neusner (Leiden: Brill, 1975), 264–98.

Engels, Donald, *Roman Corinth: An Alternative Model for the Classical City* (Chicago: University of Chicago Press, 1990).

Eriksson, Anders, Thomas H. Olbricht and Walter Überlacker, eds, *Rhetorical Argumentation in Biblical Texts: Essays from the Lund 2000 Conference* (Harrisburg: Trinity, 2002).

Evans, Craig A., and Peter W. Flint, eds, *Eschatology, Messianism, and the Dead Sea Scrolls*, SDSSRL (Grand Rapids: Eerdmans, 1997).

Evans, Craig A., and James A. Sanders, eds, *Paul and Scriptures of Israel*, JSNTSup 83 (Sheffield: JSOT Press, 1993).

Evans, Craig A., and Shemaryahu Talmon, eds, *The Quest for Context and Meaning: Studies in Biblical Intertextuality in Honor of James A. Sanders* (Leiden: Brill, 1997).

Evans, Elizabeth, 'Physiognomics in the Ancient World', *TAPS* 59/5 (1969): 1–101.

Fee, Gordon D., *The First Epistle to the Corinthians*, NICNT (Grand Rapids: Eerdmans, 1987).

—, *God's Empowering Presence: The Holy Spirit in the Letters of Paul* (Peabody: Hendrickson, 1994).

Ferrari, Markus Schiefer, *Die Sprache des Leids in den paulinischen Peristasenkatalogen* (Stuttgart: Verlag Katholisches Bibelwerk, 1991).

Field, Frederick, *Notes on the Translation of the New Testament* (Cambridge: Cambridge University Press, 1899).

Finlan, Stephen, *The Background and Contents of Paul's Cultic Atonement Metaphors*, AcBib 19 (Leiden: Brill, 2004).

Finney, Mark T., 'Christ Crucified and the Inversion of Roman Imperial Ideology in 1 Corinthians', *BTB* 35 (2005): 20–33.

Fitzgerald, John T., *Cracks in an Earthen Vessel: An Examination of the Catalogue of Hardships in the Corinthian Correspondence*, SBLDS 99 (Atlanta: Scholars Press, 1988).

—, 'Paul, the Ancient Epistolary Theorists, and 2 Corinthians 10–13', in *Greeks, Romans, and Christians: Essays in Honor of Abraham J. Malherbe*, ed. David L. Balch, Everett Ferguson and Wayne A. Meeks (Minneapolis: Fortress Press, 1990), 190–200.

Fitzgerald, John T., Thomas H. Olbright and L. Michael White, eds, *Early Christianity and Classical Culture: Comparative Studies in Honor of Abraham J. Malherbe*, NovTSup 110 (Leiden: Brill, 2003).

Fitzmyer, Joseph, *The One Who Is to Come* (Grand Rapids: Eerdmans, 2007).

Flemington, W. F., 'On the Interpretation of Colossians 1:24', in *Suffering and Martyrdom in the New Testament: Studies Presented to G. M. Styler*, ed. William Horbury and Brian McNeil (Cambridge: Cambridge University Press, 1981), 84–90.

Forbes, Christopher, 'Comparison, Self-Praise and Irony: Paul's Boasting and the Conventions of Hellenistic Rhetoric', *NTS* 32 (1986): 1–30.

Fortna, Robert T., and Beverly Roberts Gaventa, eds, *The Conversation Continues: Studies in Paul and John in Honor of J. Louis Martyn* (Nashville: Abingdon, 1990).

Fowl, Stephen E., *The Story of Christ in the Ethics of Paul: An Analysis of the Function of the Hymnic Material in the Pauline Corpus*, JSNTSup 36 (Sheffield: JSOT Press, 1990).

Frankemölle, Hubert, and Karl Kartelge, eds, *Vöm Urchristentum zu Jesus: Für Joachim Gnilka* (Freiberg: Herder, 1989).

Fredrickson, David E., 'Paul's Sentence of Death (2 Corinthians 1:9)', in *God, Evil and Suffering: Essays in Honor of Paul R. Sponheim*, ed. T. Fretheim and C. Thompson, WWSup 4 (St Paul: Word & World, 2000), 99–107.

Fredrikson, H., *Jahwe als Krieger* (Lund: C. E. K. Gleerup, 1945).

Freedman, David Noel, ed., *The Anchor Bible Dictionary*, 6 vols (New York: Doubleday, 1992).

—, ed., *Eerdmans Dictionary of the Bible* (Grand Rapids: Eerdmans, 2000).

Fretheim, T., and C. Thompson, eds, *God, Evil and Suffering: Essays in Honor of Paul R. Sponheim*, WWSup 4 (St Paul: Word & World, 2000).

Fridrichsen, Anton, 'Peristasenkatalog und Res Gestae: Nachtrag zu 2 Kor. 11, 23ff', *SO* 8 (1929): 78–82.

—, 'Zum Stil des paulinischen Peristasenkatalogs 2 Kor. 11, 23ff', *SO* 7 (1928): 25–9.

Fröhlich, Karlfried, ed., *Oscar Cullmann: Vorträge und Aufsätze, 1925–1962* (Tübingen: Mohr, 1966).

Fung, Ronald Y. K., *The Epistle to the Galatians*, NICNT (Grand Rapids: Eerdmans, 1988).

Furnish, Victor Paul, '"He Gave Himself (Was Given) Up …": Paul's Use of a Christological Assertion', in *The Future of Christology: Essays in Honor of Leander E. Keck*, ed. Abraham J. Malherbe and Wayne A. Meeks (Minneapolis: Fortress Press, 1993), 109–21.

—, 'Paul and the Corinthians: The Letters, the Challenges of Ministry, the Gospel', *Int* 52 (1998): 229–45.

—, *II Corinthians*, AB (Garden City: Doubleday, 1984).

Gallas, Sven, '"Fünfmal vierzig weniger einen …": Die an Paulus vollzogenen Synagogalstrafen nach 2 Kor 11,24', *ZNW* 81 (1990): 178–91.

Gammie, John G., Walter A. Brueggemann, W. Lee Humphreys and James M. Ward, eds, *Israelite Wisdom: Theological and Literary Essays in Honor of Samuel Terrien* (Missoula: Scholars Press, 1978).

Garland, David E., 'Paul's Apostolic Authority: The Power of Christ Sustaining Weakness (2 Corinthians 10–13)', *RevExp* 86/3 (1989): 371–90.

—, *2 Corinthians*, NAC (Nashville: Broadman & Holman, 1999).

Garrett, Susan R., 'The God of This World and the Affliction of Paul: 2 Cor 4:1–12', in *Greeks, Romans, and Christians: Essays in Honor of Abraham J. Malherbe*, ed. David L. Balch, Everett Ferguson and Wayne A. Meeks (Minneapolis: Fortress Press, 1990), 99–117.

—, 'Paul's Thorn and Cultural Models of Affliction', in *The Social World and the First Christians: Essays in Honor of Wayne A. Meeks*, ed. L. Michael White and O. Larry Yarbrough (Minneapolis: Fortress Press, 1995), 82–99.

Gempf, Conrad, 'The Imagery of Birth Pangs in the New Testament', *TynBul* 45 (1994): 119–35.

Georgi, Dieter, *The Opponents of Paul in Second Corinthians* (Philadelphia: Fortress Press, 1986).

Gibbs, James M., 'Wisdom, Power and Wellbeing', in *Studia Biblica 1978 III: Papers on Paul and Other New Testament Authors*, ed. E. A. Livingstone, JSNTSup 3 (Sheffield: JSOT Press, 1980), 119–55.

Gignilliat, Mark Salem, *Paul and Isaiah's Servants: Paul's Theological Reading of Isaiah 40–66 in 2 Corinthians 5.14–6.10*, LNTS 330 (London: T&T Clark, 2007).

—, '2 Corinthians 6:2: Paul's Eschatological "Now" and Hermeneutical Invitation', *WTJ* 67 (2005): 147–61.

—, 'A Servant Follower of the Servant: Paul's Eschatological Reading of Isaiah 40–66 in 2 Corinthians 5:14–6:10', *HBT* 26 (2004): 98–124.

—, 'Who Is Isaiah's Servant? Narrative Identity and Theological Potentiality', *SJT* 61 (2008): 125–36.

Glancy, Jennifer A., 'Boasting of Beatings (2 Corinthians 11:23-25)', *JBL* 123 (2004): 99–135.

Gloer, W. Hulitt, *An Exegetical and Theological Study of Paul's Understanding of New Creation and Reconciliation in 2 Cor 5:14-21*, MBPS 42 (Lampeter: Edwin Mellen, 1996).

Gombis, Timothy, 'Ephesians 2 as a Narrative of Divine Warfare', *JSNT* 26 (2004): 403–18.

—, 'The Triumph of God in Christ: Divine Warfare in the Argument of Ephesians' (PhD dissertation, University of St Andrews, St Andrews, 2005).

Gooder, Paula R., *Only the Third Heaven? 2 Corinthians 12.1-10 and Heavenly Ascent*, LNTS 313 (London: T&T Clark, 2006).

Gorman, Michael J., *Apostle of the Crucified Lord: A Theological Introduction to Paul and His Letters* (Grand Rapids: Eerdmans, 2003).

—, *Cruciformity: Paul's Narrative Spirituality of the Cross* (Grand Rapids: Eerdmans, 2001).

Goudge, H. L., *The Second Epistle to the Corinthians*, WC (London: Methuen, 1927).

Goulder, Michael D., *Paul and the Competing Mission in Corinth* (Peabody: Hendrickson, 2001).

—, 'Visions and Revelations of the Lord (2 Corinthians 12:1-10)', in *Paul and the Corinthians: Studies on a Community in Conflict, Essays in Honour of Margaret Thrall*, ed. Trevor J. Burke and J. K. Elliott, NovTSup 109 (Leiden: Brill, 2003), 302–12.

Gowler, David B., L. Gregory Bloomquist and Duane F. Watson, eds, *Fabrics of Discourse: Essays in Honor of Vernon K. Robbins* (Harrisburg: Trinity International Press, 2003).

Gräbe, Petrus J., 'The All-Surpassing Power of God through the Holy Spirit in the Midst of Our Broken Earthly Existence: Perspectives on Paul's Use of *Dýnamis* in 2 Corinthians', *Neot* 28/1 (1994): 147–56.

—, '*Dýnamis* (Power) in Paul's Ministry as Portrayed in His Main Letters', *NGTT* 32/2 (1991): 201–13.

—, *The Power of God in Paul's Letters*, WUNT 2/123 (Tübingen: Mohr Siebeck, 2000).

Grams, Rollin G., 'Gospel and Mission in Paul's Ethics' (PhD dissertation, Duke University, Durham, 1989).

Grant, Robert M., 'The Description of Paul in the Acts of Paul and Thecla', *VC* 36 (1982): 1–4.

Grayston, Kenneth, *Dying, We Live: A New Inquiry into the Death of Christ in the New Testament* (New York: Oxford University Press, 1990).

Green, Joel B., 'The Death of Jesus and the Ways of God: Jesus and the Gospels on Messianic Status and Shameful Suffering', *Int* 52/1 (1998): 24–37.

—, 'Paul's Theology of the Cross', in *The Death of Jesus in Early Christianity*, ed. John T. Carroll and Joel B. Green (Peabody: Hendrickson, 1995), 113–32.

Greene, Michael D., Review of *Persecution and Martyrdom in the Theology of Paul*, by John S. Pobee, *PRS* 16 (1989): 169–72.

Grieb, A. Katherine, *The Story of Romans: A Narrative Defense of God's Righteousness* (Louisville: Westminster/John Knox, 2002).

Gundry-Volf, Judith M., *Paul and Perseverance: Staying in and Falling away*, WUNT 2/37 (Tübingen: J. C. B. Mohr, 1990).

Gunther, John J., *St. Paul's Opponents and Their Background: A Study of Apocalyptic and Jewish Sectarian Teachings*, NovTSup 35 (Leiden: Brill, 1973).

Gustafson, Henry A., 'Afflictions of Christ: What Is Lacking?', *BR* 8 (1963): 28–42.

Guting, Eberhard W., and David L. Mealand, *Asyndeton in Paul: A Text-Critical and Statistical Enquiry into Pauline Style*, SBEC 39 (Lewiston: Queenston, 1998).

Güttgemanns, Erhardt, *Der leidende Apostel und sein Herr: Studien zur paulinischen Christologie*, FRLANT 90 (Göttingen: Vandenhoeck & Ruprecht, 1966).

Hadidian D. Y., ed., *From Faith to Faith: Essays in Honor of Donald G. Miller on His Seventieth Birthday*, PTMS 23 (Pittsburg: Pickwick, 1979).

Hafemann, Scott J., '"Because of Weakness" (Galatians 4:13): The Role of Suffering in the Mission of Paul', in *The Gospel to the Nations: Perspectives on Paul's Mission*, ed. Peter Bolt and Mark Thompson (Downers Grove: InterVarsity, 2000), 131–46.

—, 'The Comfort and Power of the Gospel: The Argument of 2 Corinthians 1–3', *RevExp* 86/3 (1989): 325–45.

—, *Paul, Moses and the History of Israel: The Letter/Spirit Contrast and the Argument from Scripture in 2 Corinthians 3*. Peabody: Hendrickson, 1996.

—, 'Paul's Argument from the Old Testament and Christology in 2 Cor 1–9', in *The Corinthian Correspondence*, ed. R. Bieringer, BETL 125 (Leuven: Leuven University Press, 1996), 277–303.

—, 'Paul's Use of the Old Testament in 2 Corinthians', *Int* 52/3 (1998): 246–57.

—, 'The Role of Suffering in the Mission of Paul', in *The Mission of the Early Church to Jews and Gentiles*, ed. Jostein Ådna and Hans Kvalbein (Tübingen: Mohr, 2000), 165–84.

—, *2 Corinthians*, NIVAC (Grand Rapids: Zondervan, 2000).

—, '"Self-Commendation" and Apostolic Legitimacy in 2 Corinthians: A Pauline Dialectic?', *NTS* 36 (1990): 66–88.

—, *Suffering and Ministry in the Spirit: Paul's Defense of His Ministry in II Corinthians 2:14–3:3* (Grand Rapids: Eerdmans, 1990).

—, *Suffering and the Spirit: An Exegetical Study of II Cor. 2:14–3:3 within the Context of the Corinthian Correspondence*, WUNT 2/19 (Tübingen: J. C. B. Mohr, 1986).

Hagner, A. Donald, *The Use of the Old and New Testaments in Clement of Rome*, NovTSup 34 (Leiden: Brill, 1973).

Hall, David R., *The Unity of the Corinthian Correspondence*, JSNTSup 251 (New York: T&T Clark, 2003).

Hanson, Anthony Tyrrell, *Jesus Christ in the Old Testament* (London: SPCK, 1965).

—, *The Paradox of the Cross in the Thought of St Paul*, JSNTSup 17 (Sheffield: JSOT Press, 1987).

Hanson, Paul D., *The Dawn of Apocalyptic: The Historical and Sociological Roots of Jewish Apocalyptic Eschatology*, rev. edn (Philadelphia: Fortress Press, 1979).

—, *Isaiah 40–66*, IBC (Louisville: Westminster/John Knox, 1995).

Haran, Menahem, 'Uses of Incense in the Ancient Israelite Ritual', *VT* 10 (1960): 113–29.

Harding, Mark, 'The Classical Rhetoric of Praise and the New Testament', *RTR* 45 (1986): 73–82.

—, 'On the Historicity of Acts: Comparing Acts 9:23-5 with 2 Corinthians 11:32-3', *NTS* 39 (1993): 518–38.

Harrill, J. Albert, 'Invective against Paul (2 Cor 10:10), the Physiognomics of the Ancient Slave Body, and the Greco-Roman Rhetoric of Manhood', in *Antiquity and Humanity: Essays on Ancient Religion and Philosophy Presented to Hans Dieter Betz on His 70th Birthday*, ed. Adela Yarbro Collins and Margaret M. Mitchell (Tübingen: Mohr Siebeck, 2001), 189–213.

—, *Slaves in the New Testament: Literary, Social, and Moral Dimensions* (Philadelphia: Fortress Press, 2005).

Harris, Murray J., 'Preparations and Theology in the Greek New Testament', *NIDNTT*, 3: 1192–3.

—, *The Second Epistle to the Corinthians*, NIGTC (Grand Rapids: Eerdmans, 2005).

Harrison, James R., *Paul's Language of Grace in Its Graeco-Roman Context*, WUNT 2/172 (Tübingen: Mohr Siebeck, 2003).

Harrisville, Roy A., *Fracture: The Cross as Irreconcilable in the Language and Thought of the Biblical Writers* (Grand Rapids: Eerdmans, 2006).

Harvey, A. E., ed. *Alternative Approaches to New Testament Study* (London: SPCK, 1985).

—, 'Forty Strokes Save One: Social Aspects of Judaizing and Apostasy', in *Alternative Approaches to New Testament Study*, ed. A. E. Harvey (London: SPCK, 1985), 79–96.

—, *Renewal through Suffering: A Study of 2 Corinthians*, SNTW (Edinburgh: T&T Clark, 1996).

Hawthorne, Gerald F., ed., *Current Issues in Biblical and Patristic Interpretation* (Grand Rapids: Eerdmans, 1975).

Hawthorne, Gerald F., and Otto Betz, eds, *Tradition and Interpretation in the New Testament: Essays in Honor of E. Earle Ellis for His 60th Birthday* (Grand Rapids: Eerdmans, 1987).

Hawthorne, Gerald F., Ralph Martin and Daniel G. Reid, eds, *Dictionary of Paul and His Letters* (Downers Grove: InterVarsity, 1993).

Hay, David M., ed., *Pauline Theology*, Vol. II (Minneapolis: Fortress Press, 1993).

Hayes, John W., 'Roman Pottery from the South Stoa at Corinth', *Hesperia* 42 (1973): 416–70.

Hays, J. Daniel, *From Every People and Nation: A Biblical Theology of Race*, NSBT 14 (Downers Grove: InterVarsity, 2003).

Hays, Richard B., *The Conversion of the Imagination: Paul as Interpreter of Israel's Scripture* (Grand Rapids: Eerdmans, 2005).

—, 'The Conversion of the Imagination: Scripture and Eschatology in 1 Corinthians', *NTS* 45 (1999): 391–412.

—, *Echoes of Scripture in the Letters of Paul* (New Haven: Yale, 1989).

—, *The Faith of Jesus Christ: The Narrative Substructure of Galatians 3:1–4:11*, 2nd edn (Grand Rapids: Eerdmans, 2001).

—, *First Corinthians*, IBC (Louisville: John Knox Press, 1997).

—, 'Is Paul's Gospel Narratable?', *JSNT* 27 (2004): 217–39.

—, '"Who Has Believed Our Message?": Paul's Reading of Isaiah', *SBLSP* 37/1 (1998): 205–25.

Heckel, Ulrich, 'Der Dorn im Fleisch: Die Krankheit des Paulus in 2 Kor 12,7 and Gal 4,13f', *ZNW* 84 (1993): 65–92.

—, 'Jer 9,22f. als Schlüssel für 2 Kor 10–13: Ein Beispiel für die methodischen Probleme in der gegenwärtigen Diskussion über den Schriftgebrauch bei Paulus', in *Schriftauslegung im antiken Judentum und im Urchristentum*, ed. Martin Hengel and Hermut Löhr (Tübingen: J. C. B. Mohr, 1994), 206–25.

—, *Kraft in Schwachheit: Untersuchungen zu 2. Kor 10–13*, WUNT 2/56 (Tübingen: Mohr Siebeck, 1993).

Heil, John Paul, *The Rhetorical Role of Scripture in 1 Corinthians*, SBLMS 15 (Atlanta: Society of Biblical Literature, 2005).

Hemer, Colin J., 'A Note on 2 Corinthians 1:9', *TynBul* 23 (1972): 103–7.

Hengel, Martin, *Between Jesus and Paul: Studies in the Earliest History of Christianity*, trans. John Bowden (London: SCM Press, 1983).

—, *Crucifixion in the Ancient World and the Folly of the Message of the Cross* (London: SCM Press, 1977).

—, *Studies in Early Christology* (Edinburgh: T&T Clark, 1995).

Hengel, Martin, and Hermut Löhr, eds, *Schriftauslegung im antiken Judentum und im Urchristentum* (Tübingen: J. C. B. Mohr, 1994).

Hensell, Eugene, Review of *The Paradox of the Cross in the Thought of St Paul*, by A. T. Hanson, *CBQ* 51 (1989): 559–60.

Héring, Jean, *The Second Epistle of Saint Paul to the Corinthians* (London: Epworth, 1967).

Hess, Richard S., and M. Daniel Carroll R., eds, *Israel's Messiah in the Bible and the Dead Sea Scrolls* (Grand Rapids: Baker, 2003).

Hickling, C. J. A., 'Is the Second Epistle to the Corinthians a Source for Early Church History?', *ZNW* 66 (1975): 284–7.

—, 'Paul's Reading of Isaiah', in *Studia Biblica 1978 III: Papers on Paul and Other New Testament Authors* ed. E. A. Livingstone, JSNTSup 3 (Sheffield: JSOT Press, 1980), 215–23.

Hiebert, Theodore, 'Warrior, Divine', *ABD* 6:76–9.

Hock, Ronald F., 'Paul's Tentmaking and the Problems of His Social Class', *JBL* 97 (1978): 555–64.

—, *The Social Context of Paul's Ministry: Tentmaking and Apostleship* (Philadelphia: Fortress Press, 1980).

Hodge, Charles, *An Exposition of the Second Epistle to the Corinthians*, 6th edn (London: James Nisbert, 1883).

Hodgson, Robert, 'Paul the Apostle and First Century Tribulation Lists', *ZNW* 74 (1983): 59–80.

Hogeterp, Albert L. A., *Paul and God's Temple: A Historical Interpretation of Cultic Imagery in the Corinthian Correspondence*, BTS 2 (Leuven: Peeters, 2006).

Holland, Glenn S., 'Speaking like a Fool: Irony in 2 Corinthians 10–13', in *Rhetoric and the New Testament: Essays from the 1992 Heidelberg Conference*, ed. Stanley E. Porter and Thomas H. Olbricht, JSNTSup 90 (Sheffield: JSOT Press, 1993), 250–64.

Holland, Tom, *Contours of Pauline Theology: A Radical New Survey of the Influences on Paul's Biblical Theology* (Fearn, Ross-shire: Christian Focus, 2004).

—, Review of *Paul's Seven Explanations of the Suffering of the Righteous*, by Barry D. Smith, *Themelios* 29 (2003): 89–91.

Holmberg, Bengt, *Paul and Power: The Structure of Authority in the Primitive Church as Reflected in the Pauline Epistles*, CB 11 (Lund: CWK Gleerup, 1978).

Hooker, Morna, 'Did the Use of Isaiah 53 to Interpret His Mission Begin with Jesus?', in *Jesus and the Suffering Servant: Isaiah 53 and Christian Origins*, ed. William H. Bellinger, Jr. and William R. Farmer (Harrisburg: Trinity, 1998), 88–103.

—, *From Adam to Christ: Essays on Paul* (Cambridge: Cambridge University Press, 1990).

—, 'Interchange and Suffering', in *Suffering and Martyrdom in the New Testament: Studies Presented to G. M. Styler*, ed. William Horbury and Brian McNeil (Cambridge: Cambridge University Press, 1981), 71–83.

—, 'Interchange in Christ', *JTS* 22/2 (1971): 349–61.

—, 'Interchange in Christ and Ethics', *JSNT* 25 (1985): 3–17.

—, *Jesus and the Servant: The Influence of the Servant Concept of Deutero-Isaiah in the New Testament* (London: SPCK, 1959).

—, *Not Ashamed of the Gospel: New Testament Interpretations of the Death of Christ* (Grand Rapids: Eerdmans, 1994).

Hooker, Morna, and S. G. Wilson, eds, *Paul and Paulinism* (London: SPCK, 1982).

Horbury, William, and Brian McNeil, eds, *Suffering and Martyrdom in the New Testament: Studies Presented to G. M. Styler* (Cambridge: Cambridge University Press, 1981).

Horrell, David G., 'Paul's Narratives or Narrative Substructure? The Significance of "Paul's Story"', in *Narrative Dynamics in Paul: A Critical Assessment*, ed. Bruce W. Longenecker (Louisville: Westminster/John Knox, 2002), 157–71.

—, *The Social Ethos of the Corinthian Correspondence: Interests and Ideology from 1 Corinthians to 1 Clement*, SNTW (Edinburgh: T&T Clark, 1996).

—, *Solidarity and Difference: A Contemporary Reading of Paul's Ethics* (London: T&T Clark, 2005).

Hübner, Hans, *Vetus Testamentum in Novo Band 2: Corpus Paulinum* (Göttingen: Vanderhoeck & Ruprecht, 1997).

Hugenberger, Gordon P., 'The Servant of the Lord in the "Servant Songs" of Isaiah: A Second Moses Figure', in *The Lord's Anointed: Interpretation of Old Testament Messianic Texts*, ed. Philip E. Satterthwaite, Richard S. Hess and Gordon J. Wenham (Grand Rapids: Baker, 1995), 105–40.

Hughes, Philip E., *Paul's Second Epistle to the Corinthians*, NICNT (Grand Rapids: Eerdmans, 1962).

Hultgren, Artland J., *Paul's Gospel and Mission* (Philadephia: Fortress Press, 1985).

Humphrey, Edith M., 'Ambivalent Apocalypse: Apocalyptic Rhetoric and Intertextuality in 2 Corinthians', in *The Intertexture of Apocalyptic Discourse in the New Testament*, ed. Duane F. Watson, SBLSymS 14 (Atlanta: Society of Biblical Literature, 2002), 113–35.

—, *And I Turned to See the Voice: The Rhetoric of Vision in the New Testament* (Grand Rapids: Baker, 2007).

Hunter, W. Bingham, 'Prayer', *DPL*, 725–34.

Hurtado, Larry W., *Lord Jesus Christ: Devotion to Jesus in Earliest Christianity* (Grand Rapids: Eerdmans, 2003).

Innasimuthu, Arulsamy, 'Comfort in Affliction: An Exegetical Study of 2 Corinthians 1:3-11' (PhD dissertation, Catholic University of Leuven, Leuven, 1995).

Janowski, Bernd, and Peter Stuhlmacher, eds, *The Suffering Servant: Isaiah 53 in Jewish and Christian Sources* (Grand Rapids: Eerdmans, 2004).

Jervis, L. Ann, and Peter Richardson, eds, *Gospel in Paul: Studies on Corinthians, Galatians and Romans for Richard N. Longenecker*, JSNTSup 108 (Sheffield: Sheffield Academic Press, 1994).

Judge, E. A., 'The Conflict of Educational Aims in New Testament Thought', *JCE* 9 (1966): 32–45.

—, 'Paul's Boasting in Relation to Contemporary Professional Practice', *ABR* 16 (1968): 37–50.

—, 'St Paul and Classical Society', *JAC* 15 (1972): 19–36.

Kaiser, Walter C., *Messiah in the Old Testament* (Grand Rapids: Zondervan, 1995).

Kaithakottil, Joyce. '"Death in Us, Life in You" Ministry and Suffering: A Study of 2 Cor 4,7-15', *BiBh* 28 (2002): 433–60.

Kang, Sa-Moon, *Divine War in the Old Testament and in the Ancient Near East*, BZAW 117 (Berlin: Walter de Gruyter, 1989).

Keener, Craig S., *1 & 2 Corinthians*, NCBC (Cambridge: Cambridge University Press, 2005).

Kerrigan, Alexander, 'Echoes of Themes from the Servant Songs in Pauline Theology', in *Studiorum Paulinorum Congressus Internaionalis Catholicus 1961*, Vol. 2, AnBib 17–18 (Rome: Pontificio Instituto Biblico, 1963), 217–28.

Kim, Chan-Hie, *Form and Structure of the Familiar Letter of Recommendation*, SBLDS 4 (Missoula: Society of Biblical Literature, 1972).

Kim, Seyoon, *The Origin of Paul's Gospel*, 2nd edn, WUNT 2/4 (Tübingen: J. C. B. Mohr. 1984).

Kittel, G., and G. Friedrich, eds, *Theological Dictionary of the New Testament*, 10 vols, trans. G. W. Bromiley (Grand Rapids: Eerdmans, 1964–76).

Klein, William W., '*Christos*: Jewish Title or Hellenistic Name? A Response to Craig L. Blomberg', in *Israel's Messiah in the Bible and the Dead Sea Scrolls*, ed. Richard S. Hess and M. Daniel Carroll R. (Grand Rapids: Baker, 2003), 143–50.

Kleinknecht, Karl Theoder, *Der leidende Gerechtfertigte: Die alttestamentlich-jüdische Tradition vom 'leidenden Gerechten' und ihre Rezeption bei Paulus*, WUNT 2/13 (Tübingen: Mohr, 1984).

Klingbeil, Martin, *Yahweh Fighting from Heaven: God as Warrior and as God of Heaven in the Hebrew Psalter and Ancient Near Eastern Iconography*, OBO 169 (Göttingen: Vandenhoeck & Ruprecht, 1999).

Koenig, John, 'The Knowing of Glory and Its Consequences (2 Corinthians 3–5)', in *The Conversation Continues: Studies in Paul and John in Honor of J. Louis Martyn*, ed. Robert T. Fortna and Beverly R. Gaventa (Nashville: Abingdon, 1990), 158–69.

Koester, Helmut, 'Suffering Servant and Royal Messiah: From Second Isaiah to Paul, Mark and Matthew', *TD* 51 (2004): 103–24.

Kolenkow, Anitra Bingham, 'Paul and Opponents in 2 Cor 10–13 – *Theioi Andres* and Spiritual Guides', in *Religious Propaganda and Missionary Competition in the New Testament World: Essays Honoring Dieter Georgi*, ed. Lukas Bormann, Kelly Del Tredici and Angela Standhartinger, NovTSup 74 (Leiden: Brill, 1994), 351–74.

Kraftchick, Steven J., 'Death in Us, Life in You: The Apostolic Medium', in *Pauline Theology*, Vol. 2, ed. David M. Hay (Minneapolis: Fortress Press, 1993), 156–81.

Kramer, Werner, *Christ, Lord, Son of God*, SBT 50 (London: SCM Press, 1966).

Kremer, J., 'βλῖγις, εως, ἡ; βλίβω', *EDNT* 2: 152–3.

Kruse, Colin G., 'The Relationship between the Opposition to Paul Reflected in 2 Corinthians 1–7 and 10–13', *EvQ* 61 (1989): 195–202.

—, *The Second Epistle of Paul to the Corinthians: An Introduction and Commentary*, TNTC (Leicester: InterVarsity, 1987).

Ladd, George E., *A Theology of the New Testament*, Rev. Donald A. Hagner (Grand Rapids: Eerdmans, 1993).

Lambrecht, Jan, 'Brief Anthropological Reflections on 2 Corinthians 4:6–5:10', in *Paul and the Corinthians: Studies on a Community in Conflict, Essays in Honour of Margaret Thrall*, ed. Trevor J. Burke and J. K. Elliott, NovTSup 109 (Leiden: Brill, 2003), 259–66.

—, 'Dangerous Boasting: Paul's Self-Commendation in 2 Corinthians 10–13', in *The Corinthian Correspondence*, ed. R. Bieringer, BETL 125 (Leuven: Peeters, 1996), 325–46.

—, 'The Defeated Paul, Aroma of Christ: An Exegetical Study of 2 Corinthians 2:14-16b', *LS* 20 (1995): 170–86.

—, 'The Eschatological Outlook in 2 Cor 4:7-15', in *To Tell the Mystery: Essays on New Testament Eschatology in Honor of Robert H. Gundry*, ed. Thomas E. Schmidt and Moisés Silva, JSNTSup 100 (Sheffield: JSOT Press, 1994), 122–39.

—, 'The Favourable Time: A Study of 2 Cor 6,2a in Its Context', in *Vöm Urchristentum zu Jesus: Für Joachim Gnilka*, ed. Hubert Frankemölle and Karl Kartelge (Freiberg: Herder, 1989), 377–91.

—, 'The Fool's Speech and Its Context: Paul's Particular Way of Arguing in 2 Cor 10–13', *Bib* 83 (2001): 305–24.

—, 'The *Nekrōsis* of Jesus: Ministry and Suffering in 2 Cor 4:7-15', in *L'Apôtre Paul: Personnalité, style et conception du ministère*, ed. A. Vanhoye, BETL 73 (Leuven: Leuven University Press, 1986), 120–43.

—, 'Paul and Suffering', in *God and Human Suffering*, ed. Jan Lambrecht and Raymond Collins (Louvain: Peeters, 1990), 47–67.

—, 'Paul's Appeal and the Obedience to Christ: The Line of Thought in 2 Corinthians 10,1-6', *Bib* 77 (1996): 398–416.

—, 'Paul's Boasting about the Corinthians: A Study of 2 Cor. 8:24–9:5', *NovT* 40/4 (1998): 352–68.

—, 'Philological and Exegetical Notes on 2 Cor 13,4', *Bijdragen* 46 (1985): 261–9.

—, '"Reconcile Yourselves …": A Reading of 2 Cor 5,11-21', in *The Diakonia of the Spirit (2 Co 4:7–7:4)*, ed. Lorenzo De Lorenzi, Benedictina 10 (Rome: Benedictina, 1989), 161–209.

—, *Second Corinthians*, SP (Collegeville: Liturgical, 1999).

—, 'Strength in Weakness: A Reply to Scott Andrews' Exegesis of 2 Cor 11.23b-33', *NTS* 43 (1997): 285–90.

—, 'Structure and Line of Thought in 2 Cor 2,14–4,6', *Bib* 64 (1983): 344–80.

Lambrecht, Jan, and Raymond Collins, eds, *God and Human Suffering* (Louvain: Peeters, 1990).

Lanci, John R., *A New Temple for Corinth: Rhetorical and Archaeological Approaches to Pauline Imagery*, SBL 1 (New York: Peter Lang, 1997).

Lane, William, 'Covenant: The Key to Paul's Conflict at Corinth', *TynBul* 33 (1982): 3–29.

Larson, Jennifer, 'Paul's Masculinity', *JBL* 123 (2004): 85–97.

Leivestad, Ragnar, 'The Meekness and the Gentleness of Christ', *NTS* 12 (1966): 156–64.

Lim, Kar Yong, 'Is there a Place for Suffering in Mission? Perspectives from Paul's Sufferings in 2 Corinthians', in *The Soul of Mission: Perspectives on Christian Leadership, Spirituality and Mission in East Asia: Essays in Appreciation of Dr David Gunaratnam*, ed. Kang San Tan (Petaling Jaya: Pustaka Sufes, 2007), 64–78.

—, Review of *Cruciformity: Paul's Narrative Spirituality of the Cross*, by Michael J. Gorman. *JBV* 25 (2004): 114–16.

Lincoln, Andrew T., *Paradise Now and Not Yet: Studies in the Role of the Heavenly Dimension in Paul's Thoughts with Special Reference to His Eschatology*, SNTSMS 43 (Cambridge: Cambridge University Press, 1981).

Lind, Millard C., *Yahweh Is a Warrior: The Theology of Warfare in Ancient Israel* (Scottdale: Herald, 1980).

Lindgård, Fredrik, *Paul's Line of Thought in 2 Corinthians 4:16–5:10*, WUNT 2/189 (Tübingen: Mohr Siebeck, 2005).

Litwak, Kenneth D., 'Echoes of Scripture? A Critical Survey of Recent Works on Paul's Use of the Old Testament', *CR:BS* 6 (1998): 260–88.

Livingstone, E. A., *Studia Biblica 1978 III: Papers on Paul and Other New Testament Authors*, JSNTSup 3 (Sheffield: JSOT Press, 1980).

Long, Fredrick J., *Ancient Rhetoric and Paul's Apology: The Compositional Unity of 2 Corinthians*, SNTSMS 131 (Cambridge: Cambridge University Press, 2004).

Longenecker, Bruce W., 'The Narrative Approach to Paul: An Early Retrospective', *CBR* 1 (2002): 88–111.

—, ed., *Narrative Dynamics in Paul: A Critical Assessment* (Louisville: Westminster/John Knox, 2002).

—, 'Narrative Interest in the Study of Paul: Retrospective and Prospective', in *Narrative Dynamics in Paul: A Critical Assessment*, ed. Bruce W. Longenecker (Louisville: Westminster/John Knox, 2002), 3–16.

—, 'Sharing in Their Spiritual Blessings? The Stories of Israel in Galatians and Romans', in *Narrative Dynamics in Paul: A Critical Assessment*, ed. Bruce W. Longenecker (Louisville: Westminster/John Knox, 2002), 58–84.

Longenecker, Richard N., *Galatians*, WBC (Dallas: Word Books, 1990).

Longman, Tremper, III, 'The Divine Warrior: The New Testament Use of an Old Testament Motif', *WTJ* 44 (1982): 290–307.

—, 'Psalm 98: A Divine Warrior Victory Song', *JETS* 27 (1984): 267–74.

Longman, Tremper, III, and Daniel G. Reid, *God Is a Warrior* (Grand Rapids: Zondervan, 1995).

Loubser, Johannes A., 'A New Look at Paradox and Irony in 2 Corinthians 10–13', *Neot* 26 (1992): 507–21.

—, 'Paul and the Politics of Apocalyptic Mysticism: An Exploration of 2 Cor 11:30–12:10', *Neot* 34 (2000): 191–206.

Luz, Ulrich, and Hans Weder, eds, *Die Mitte des Neuen Testaments: Einheit und Vielfalt neutestamentlicher Theologie: Festschrift für Eduard Schweizer zum siebzigsten Geburtstag* (Göttingen: Vandenhoeck & Ruprecht, 1983).

Lyons, George, *Pauline Autobiography: Toward a New Understanding*, SBLDS 73 (Atlanta: Scholars Press, 1985).

McCant, Jerry W., 'Paul's Thorn of Rejected Apostleship', *NTS* 34 (1988): 550–72.

—, *2 Corinthians*, Readings (Sheffield: Sheffield Academic Press, 1999).

McClelland, Scott E., '"Super-Apostles, Servants of Christ, Servants of Satan": A Response', *JSNT* 14 (1982): 82–7.

McDonald, James I. H., 'Paul and the Preaching Ministry: A Reconsideration of 2 Cor 2:14-17 in Its Context', *JSNT* 17 (1983): 35–50.

McKnight, Scot, and Grant R. Osborne, eds, *The Face of New Testament Studies: A Survey of Recent Research* (Grand Rapids: Baker, 2004).

Mak, Alexander, '2 Corinthians 4:7-12: Life Manifesting in Death', *CMSJ* 3 (2003): 109–35.

—, 'Towards a Holistic View of Pauline Suffering: A Contextual Study of 2 Corinthians' (ThD dissertation, Bible College of Victoria, Melbourne, 1996).

Malherbe, Abraham J., *Paul and the Popular Philosophers* (Minneapolis: Fortress Press, 1989).

Malherbe, Abraham J., and Wayne A. Meeks, eds, *The Future of Christology: Essays in Honor of Leander E. Keck* (Minneapolis: Fortress Press, 1993).

Malherbe, Abraham J., Frederick W. Norris and James W. Thompson, eds, *The Early Church in Its Context: Essays in Honor of Everett Ferguson* (Leiden: Brill, 1998).

Manson, T. W., '2 Cor 2:14-17: Suggestions towards an Exegesis', in *Studia Paulina*, ed. J. Sevenster and W. C. van Unnik (Haarlem: Erven F. Bohn, 1953), 155–62.

Manus, Chris Ukachuku, 'Apostolic Suffering (2 Corinthians 6.4-10): The Sign of Christian Existence and Identity', *AJT* 1 (1987): 41–54.

Marshall, Peter, *Enmity in Corinth: Social Conventions in Paul's Relationship with the Corinthians*, WUNT 2/23 (Tübingen: J. C. B. Mohr, 1987).

—, 'Invective: Paul and His Enemies in Corinth', in *Perspectives on Language and Text*, ed. Edgar W. Conrad and Edward G. Newing (Winona Lake: Eisenbrauns, 1987), 359–73.

—, 'A Metaphor of Social Shame: ΘΡΙΑΜΒΕΥΕΙΝ in 2 Cor 2:14', *NovT* 25/4 (1983): 302–17.

Martin, Dale B., *The Corinthian Body* (New Haven: Yale University Press, 1995).

Martin, Ralph P., 'The Opponents of Paul in 2 Corinthians: An Old Issue Revisited', in *Tradition and Interpretation in the New Testament: Essays in Honor of E. Earle Ellis for His 60th Birthday*, ed. Gerald F. Hawthorne and Otto Betz (Grand Rapids: Eerdmans, 1987), 279–89.

—, *Reconciliation: A Study of Paul's Theology* (London: Marshall, Morgan & Scott, 1981).

—, *2 Corinthians*, WBC (Waco: Word Books Publishers, 1986).

Martyn, J. Louis, *Galatians*, AB (New York: Doubleday, 1997).

Matera, Frank J., 'Apostolic Suffering and Resurrection Faith Distinguishing Between Appearance and Reality (2 Cor 4,7–5,10)', in *Resurrection in the New Testament: Festschrift J. Lambrecht*, ed. Reimund Bieringer, Veronica Koperski and B. Lataire, BETL 165 (Leuven: Leuven University Press, 2002), 387–405.

—, *Galatians*, SP (Collegeville: Liturgical Press, 1992).

—, *II Corinthians: A Commentary* (NTL. Louisville: Westminster/John Knox, 2003).

Matlock, R. Barry, 'The Arrow and the Web: Critical Reflections on a Narrative Approach to Paul', in *Narrative Dynamics in Paul: A Critical Assessment*, ed. Bruce W. Longenecker (Louisville: Westminster/John Knox, 2002), 44–57.

Mealand, David L., 'As Having Nothing and Yet Possessing Everything, 2 Cor 6:10c', *ZNW* 67 (1976): 277–9.

Meeks, Wayne A., *The First Urban Christians: The Social World of the Apostle Paul*, rev. edn (New Haven: Yale University Press, 2003).

Menzies, Allan, *The Second Epistle of the Apostle Paul to the Corinthians* (London: Macmillan, 1912).

Metzger, Bruce M., *A Textual Commentary on the Greek New Testament*, 2nd edn (Stuttgart: United Bible Society, 1994).

Meyer, H. A. W., *Critical and Exegetical Hand-Book to the Epistles to the Corinthians* (New York: Funk and Wagnalls, 1884).

Michaelis, W., 'πάσχω, παθητός, κτλ', *TDNT* 5:904–39.

Middleton, Paul, *Radical Martyrdom and Cosmic Conflict in Early Christianity*, LNTS 307 (London: T&T Clark, 2006).

Miller, Patrick D., Jr., *The Divine Warrior in Early Israel* (Cambridge: Harvard University Press, 1973).

Minear, Paul S., 'Some Pauline Thoughts on Dying: A Study of 2 Corinthians', in *From Faith to Faith: Essays in Honor of Donald G. Miller on His Seventieth Birthday*, ed. D. Y. Hadidian (PTMS 23. Pittsburg: Pickwick, 1979), 91–106.

Mitchell, Margaret M., 'New Testament Envoys in the Context of Greco-Roman Diplomatic and Epistolary Conventions: The Example of Timothy and Titus', *JBL* 111 (1992): 641–62.

Motyer, J. Alec, *The Prophecy of Isaiah: An Introduction & Commentary* (Downers Grove: InterVarsity, 1993).

Moyise, Steve, and Maarten J. J. Menken, eds, *Isaiah in the New Testament: The New Testament and the Scriptures of Israel* (New York: T&T Clark, 2005).

Mullins, Terrance Y., 'Paul's Thorn in the Flesh', *JBL* 76 (1957): 299–303.

Munck, Johannes, *Paul and the Salvation of Mankind*, trans. Frank Clarke (London: SCM Press, 1959).

Murphy-O'Connor, Jerome, '"Another Jesus" (2 Cor 11:4)', *RB* 97 (1990): 238–51.

—, 'Faith and Resurrection in 2 Cor 4:13-14', *RB* 95 (1988): 543–50.

—, 'Pneumatikoi and Judaizers in 2 Cor 2:14–4:6', *ABR* 34 (1986): 42–58.

—, *St. Paul's Corinth: Texts and Archaeology*, 3rd edn (Collegeville: Liturgical Press, 2002).

—, *The Theology of the Second Letter to the Corinthians* (Cambridge: Cambridge University Press, 1991).

Neufeld, Tom Yoder, *Put on the Armour of God: The Divine Warrior from Isaiah to Ephesians*, JSNTSup 140 (Sheffield: Sheffield Academic Press, 1997).

Neusner Jacob, ed., *Christianity, Judaism and Other Greco-Roman Cults: Studies for Morton Smith at Sixty, Part One: New Testament*, SJLA 12 (Leiden: Brill, 1975).

Neusner, Jacob, Peder Borgen, Ernest S. Frerichs and Richard Horsley, eds, *The Social World of Formative Christianity and Judaism: Essays in Tribute of Howard Clark Kee* (Philadelphia: Fortress Press, 1988).

Neyrey, Jerome H., *Paul in Other Words: A Cultural Reading of His Letters* (Louisville: Westminster/John Knox, 1990).

Nicdao, Victor S., 'Power in Times of Weakness according to 2 Corinthians 12,1-10: An Exegetical Investigation of the Relationship between Dynamism and Asthéneia' (PhD dissertation, Catholic University of Leuven, Leuven, 1997).

Nichols, David R., 'The Strength of Weakness, the Wisdom of Foolishness: A Theological Study of Paul's Theologia Crucis' (PhD dissertation, Marquette University, Milwaukee, 1992).

North, Christopher R., 'The "Former Things" and the "New Things" in Deutero-Isaiah', in *Studies in Old Testament Prophecy*, ed. H. H. Rowley (New York: Charles Scribner's Sons, 1950), 111–26.

O'Brien, Peter Thomas, *Gospel and Mission in the Writings of Paul: An Exegetical and Theological Analysis* (Grand Rapids: Baker, 1995).

—, *Introductory Thanksgivings in the Letters of Paul*, NovTSup 49 (Leiden: Brill, 1977).

O'Collins, Gerald G., 'Power Made Perfect in Weakness: 2 Cor 12:9-10', *CBQ* 33 (1971): 528–37.

O'Day, Gail R., 'Jeremiah 9:22-23 and 1 Corinthians 1:26–31: A Study in Intertextuality', *JBL* 109 (1990): 259–67.

Odendaal, D. H., 'The "Former" and the "New Things" in Isaiah 40–48', *OTWSA* 10 (1967): 64–75.

Omanson, Roger L., and John Ellington, *A Handbook on Paul's Second Letter to the Corinthians* (New York: United Bible Societies, 1993).

Oropeza, B. J., 'Echoes of Isaiah in the Rhetoric of Paul: New Exodus, Wisdom, and the

Humility of the Cross in Utopian-Apocalyptic Expectations', in *The Intertexture of Apocalyptic Discourse in the New Testament*, ed. Duane F. Watson, SBLSymS 14 (Atlanta: Society of Biblical Literature, 2002), 87–112.

Oss, Douglas A., 'A Note on Paul's Use of Isaiah', *BBR* 2 (1992): 105–12.

Oswalt, John N., *The Book of Isaiah: Chapters 40–66*, NICOT (Grand Rapids: Eerdmans, 1998).

Pao, David W., *Acts and the Isaianic New Exodus*, WUNT 2/130 (Tübingen: Mohr Siebeck, 2000).

—, *Thanksgiving: An Investigation of a Pauline Theme*, NSBT 13 (Downers Grove: Inter-Varsity, 2002).

Papahatzis, Nicos, *Ancient Corinth: The Museums of Corinth, Isthmia and Sicyon* (Athens: Ekdotike Athenon, 1977).

Park, David M., 'Interpretative Value of Paul's Metaphors', *SEAJT* 18 (1977): 37–40.

—, 'Paul's ΣΚΟΛΟΨ ΤΗ ΣΑΡΚΙ: Thorn or Stake? (2 Cor 12 7)', *NovT* 22/2 (1980): 179–83.

—, 'The Value of Biblical Metaphor: 2 Cor 2:14-17', in *Metaphor and Religion (Theolinguistics 2)*, ed. Jean-Pierre Van Noppen (Brussels: Vrije Universiteit, 1983), 253–68.

Parsons, Mikeal C., *Body and Character in Luke and Acts: The Subversion of Physiognomy in Early Christianity* (Grand Rapids: Baker, 2006).

Pate, C. Marvin, *Adam Christology as the Exegetical and Theological Substructure of 2 Corinthians 4:7–5:21* (Lanham: University Press of America, 1991).

—, *The Glory of Adam and the Afflictions of the Righteous: Pauline Sufferings in Context* (Lewiston: Edwin Mellen, 1993).

Pate, C. Marvin, J. Scott Duvall, J. Daniel Hays, E. Randolph Richards, W. Dennis Tucker, Jr. and Preben Vang, *The Story of Israel: A Biblical Theology* (Downers Grove: Inter-Varsity, 2004).

Pathrapankal, J. M., '"When I Am Weak, then I Am Strong" (2 Cor 12:10): Pauline Understanding of Apostolic Sufferings', *Jeevadhara* 18 (1988): 140–51.

Peerbolte, Bert Jan Lietaert, 'Romans 15:14-29 and Paul's Missionary Agenda', in *Persuasion and Dissuasion in Early Christianity, Ancient Judaism, and Hellenism*, ed. Pieter W. van der Horst, Maarten J. J. Menken, Joop F. M. Smit and Geert Van Oyen, CBET 33 (Leuven: Peeters, 2003), 143–59.

Perriman, Andrew, 'Between Troas and Macedonia: 2 Cor 2:13-14', *ExpT* 101 (1989–90): 39–41.

—, 'The Pattern of Christ's Sufferings: Colossians 1:24 and Philippians 3:10-11', *TynBul* 42/1 (1991): 62–79.

Peterson, Brian K., *Eloquence and the Proclamation of the Gospel in Corinth*, SBLDS 163 (Atlanta: Scholars Press, 1998).

Pickett, Raymond, *The Cross in Corinth: The Social Significance of the Death of Jesus*, JSNTSup 143 (Sheffield: Sheffield Academic Press, 1997).

Plummer, A., *A Critical and Exegetical Commentary on the Second Epistle of St. Paul to the Corinthians*, ICC (Edinburgh: T&T Clark, 1915).

Plummer, Robert L., 'Imitation of Paul and the Church's Missionary Role in 1 Corinthians', *JETS* 44 (2001): 219–35.

—, *Paul's Understanding of the Church's Mission: Did the Apostle Paul Expect the Early Christian Communities to Evangelize?*, PBM (Milton Keynes: Paternoster, 2006).

Plunkett-Dowling, Regina, 'Reading and Restoration: Paul's Use of Scripture in 2 Corinthians 1–9' (PhD dissertation, Yale University, New Haven, 2001).

Pobee, John S., *Persecution and Martyrdom in the Theology of Paul*, JSNTSup 6 (Sheffield: JSOT Press, 1985).

Polhill, John B., 'Reconciliation at Corinth: 2 Corinthians 4–7', *RevExp* 86 (1989): 345–57.

Porter, Stanley E., ed. *Paul and His Opponents*, Pauline Studies 2 (Leiden: Brill, 2005).

—, ed., *The Pauline Canon*, Pauline Studies 1 (Leiden: Brill, 2004).

Porter, Stanley E., and Thomas H. Olbricht, eds, *Rhetoric and the New Testament: Essays from the 1992 Heidelberg Conference*, JSNTSup 90 (Sheffield: JSOT Press, 1993).

Powers, Janet Everts, 'A Thorn in the Flesh: The Appropriation of Textual Meaning', *JPT* 18 (2001): 85–99.

Price, R. M., 'Punished in Paradise (An Exegetical Theory of II Corinthians 12:1-10)', *JSNT* 7 (1980): 33–40.

Price, Simon R. F., *Rituals and Power: The Roman Imperial Cult in Asia Minor* (Cambridge: Cambridge University Press, 1984).

Proudfoot, C. Merrill, 'The Apostle Paul's Understanding of Christian Suffering' (PhD dissertation, Yale University, New Haven, 1956).

—, 'Imitation or Realistic Participation: A Study of Paul's Concept of "Suffering with Christ"', *Int* 17 (1963): 140–60.

Pryor, John W. 'Paul's Use of Iēsous: A Clue for the Translation of Romans 3:26?', *Colloquium* 16 (1983): 31–45.

Reed, Jeffrey T., 'Are Paul's Thanksgivings "Epistolary"?', *JSNT* 61 (1996): 87–99.

Renwick, David A., *Paul, the Temple and the Presence of God*, BJS 224 (Atlanta: Scholars Press, 1991).

Richardson, Peter, and John C. Hurd, eds, *From Jesus to Paul: Studies in Honour of Francis Wright Beare* (Waterloo: Wilfrid Laurier University Press, 1984).

Roberts, Mark Edward, 'Weak Enough to Lead: Paul's Response to Criticisms and Rivals in 2 Corinthians 10–13, A Rhetorical Reading' (PhD dissertation, Vanderbilt University, Nashville, 2002).

Roetzel, Calvin J., '"As Dying, and Behold We Live", Death and Resurrection in Paul's Theology', *Int* 46 (1992): 5–18.

Rowley, H. H., ed., *Studies in Old Testament Prophecy* (New York: Charles Scribner's Sons, 1950).

Sampley, J. Paul, 'Paul, His Opponents in 2 Corinthians 10–13, and the Rhetorical Handbooks', in *The Social World of Formative Christianity and Judaism: Essays in Tribute of Howard Clark Kee*, ed. Jacob Neusner, Peder Borgen, Ernest S. Frerichs and Richard Horsley (Philadelphia: Fortress Press, 1988), 162–77.

—, *The Second Letter to the Corinthians*, NIB 11 (Nashville: Abingdon Press, 2000).

—, *Walking between the Times: Paul's Moral Reasoning* (Minneapolis. Fortress Press, 1991).

Sanders, Boykin, 'Imitating Paul: 1 Cor 4:16', *HTR* 74 (1981): 353–63.

Sanders, E. P., *Jesus and Judaism* (London: SCM Press, 1985).

Sanders, Jack T., 'The Transition from Opening Epistolary Thanksgiving to Body in the Letters of the Pauline Corpus', *JBL* 81 (1962): 348–62.

Sandnes, Karl Olav, *Paul – One of the Prophets? A Contribution to the Apostle's Self-Understanding*, WUNT 2/43. Tübingen: Mohr Siebeck, 1991).

Satterthwaite, Philip E., Richard S. Hess and Gordon J. Wenham, eds, *The Lord's Annointed: Interpretation of Old Testament Messianic Texts* (Grand Rapids: Baker, 1995).

Savage, Timothy B., *Power through Weakness: Paul's Understanding of the Christian Ministry in 2 Corinthians*, SNTSMS 86 (Cambridge: Cambridge University Press, 1996).

Schiefer Ferrari, Markus, *Die Sprache des Leids in den paulinischen Peristasenkatalogen* (Stuttgart: Verlag Katholisches Bibelwerk, 1991).

Schlier, Heinrich, 'θλίβω, θλῖψις'. *TDNT* 3: 139–48.

Schmidt, Thomas E., and Moisés Silva, eds, *To Tell the Mystery: Essays on New Testament Eschatology in Honor of Robert H. Gundry*, JSNTSup 100 (Sheffield: JSOT Press, 1994).

Schmidt, T. E., 'Mark 15.16-32: The Crucifixion Narrative and the Roman Triumphal Procession', *NTS* 41 (1995): 1–18.

Schnabel, Eckhard, *Early Christian Mission: Paul and the Early Church*, Vol. 2 (Downers Grove: InterVarsity, 2004).

Schowalter, Daniel N., and Steven J. Friesen, eds, *Urban Religion in Roman Corinth. Interdisciplinary Approaches*, HTS 53 (Cambridge: Harvard University Press, 2005).

Schrage, Wolfgang, 'Leid, Kreuz und Eschaton: Die Peristasenkatologe als Merkmale paulinischer theologia crucis und Eschatologie', *EvT* 34 (1974): 141–75.

Schreiner, Thomas R., *Paul, Apostle of God's Glory in Christ: A Pauline Theology* (Downers Grove: InterVarsity, 2001).

Schubert, Paul, *Form and Function of the Pauline Thanksgivings*, BZNW 20 (Berlin: Töpelmann, 1939).

Schütz, John Howard, *Paul and the Anatomy of Apostolic Authority*, SNTSMS 26 (Cambridge: Cambridge University Press, 1975).

Schweitzer, Albert, *The Mysticism of Paul the Apostle*, trans. William Montgomery (New York: H. Holt & Co, 1931).

Scott, James M., *Adoption as Sons of God: An Exegetical Investigation into the Background of YIOTHESIA in the Pauline Corpus*, WUNT 2/48 (Tübingen: Mohr Siebeck, 1992).

—, 'Paul's Use of Deuteronomic Tradition', *JBL* 112 (1993): 645–65.

—, *2 Corinthians*, NIBC (Peabody: Hendrickson, 1998).

—, 'Throne-Chariot Mysticism in Qumran and in Paul', in *Eschatology, Messianism, and the Dead Sea Scrolls*, ed. Craig A. Evans and Peter W. Flint, SDSSRL (Grand Rapids: Eerdmans, 1997), 101–19.

—, 'The Triumph of God in 2 Cor 2.14: Additional Evidence of Merkabah Mysticism in Paul', *NTS* 42 (1996): 260–81.

—, 'The Use of Scripture in 2 Corinthians 6.16c-18 and Paul's Restoration Theology', *JSNT* 56 (1994): 73–99.

Senior, Donald, and Carroll Stuhlmueller, *The Biblical Foundations for Mission* (Maryknoll: Orbis, 1983).

Sevenster, J., and W. C. van Unnik, eds, *Studia Paulina* (Haarlem: Erven F. Bohn, 1953).

Shum, Shiu-Lun, *Paul's Use of Isaiah in Romans: A Comparative Study of Paul's Letter to the Romans and the Sibylline and Qumran Sectarian Texts*, WUNT 2/156 (Tübingen: Mohr Siebeck, 2002).

Slane, Kathleen W., 'Corinth's Roman Pottery: Quantification and Meaning', in *Corinth: The Centenary, 1896–1996*, ed. Charles K. Williams II and Nancy Bookidis, Corinth 20 (Princeton: American School of Classical Studies at Athens, 2003), 321–36.

—, *The Sanctuary of Demeter and Kore: The Roman Pottery and Lamps*, Corinth 18.2 (Princeton: American School of Classical Studies at Athens, 1990).

Smith, Barry D., *Paul's Seven Explanations of the Suffering of the Righteous*, SBL 47 (New York: Peter Lang, 2002).

Smith, D. Moody, 'The Pauline Literature', in *It Is Written: Scripture Citing Scripture*: *Essays in Honour of Barnabas Lindars*, ed. D. A. Carson and H. G. M. Williamson (Cambridge: Cambridge University Press, 1988), 265–91.

Smith, Neil Gregor, 'The Thorn That Stayed: An Exposition of II Corinthians 12:7-9', *Int* 13/4 (1959): 409–16.

Spencer, Aida Besançon, *Paul's Literary Style: A Stylistic and Historical Comparison of II Corinthians 11:16–12:13, Romans 8:9-39 and Philippians 3:2–4:13* (Lanham: University of America Press, 1998).

—, 'The Wise Fool (and the Foolish Wise): A Study of Irony in Paul', *NovT* 23 (1981): 349–60.

Spicq, C., 'L'image sportive de II Corinthians', *ETL* 14 (1937): 209–29.

—, ed. *Theological Lexicon of the New Testament*, 3 vols, trans. and ed. James D. Ernest (Peabody: Henrickson, 1994).

Splitter, R., 'The Limits of Ecstasy: An Exegesis of 2 Corinthians 12:1-10', in *Current Issues in Biblical and Patristic Interpretation*, ed. Gerald F. Hawthorne (Grand Rapids: Eerdmans, 1975), 259–66.

Stanley, Christopher D., *Arguing with Scripture: The Rhetoric of Quotations in the Letters of Paul* (New York: T&T Clark, 2004).

—, *Paul and the Language of Scripture: Citation Technique in the Pauline Epistles and Contemporary Literature*, SNTSMS 69 (Cambridge: Cambridge University Press, 1992).

Stanley, David M., 'The Theme of the Servant of Yahweh in Primitive Christian Soteriology, and Its Transposition by St. Paul', *CBQ* 16 (1954): 385–425.

—, 'Imitations in Paul's Letters: Its Significance for His Relationship to Jesus and to His Own Christian Foundations', in *From Jesus to Paul: Studies in Honour of Francis Wright Beare*, ed. Peter Richardson and John C. Hurd (Waterloo: Wilfrid Laurier University Press, 1984), 127–41.

Stansbury, Harry Adams, III, 'Corinthian Honor, Corinthian Conflict: A Social History of Early Roman Corinth and Its Pauline Community' (PhD dissertation, University of California, Irvine, 1990).

Stanton, Graham N., '"I Think, When I Read That Sweet Story of Old": A Response to Douglas Campbell', in *Narrative Dynamics in Paul: A Critical Assessment*, ed. Bruce W. Longenecker (Louisville: Westminster/John Knox, 2002, 125–32).

Stegman, Thomas Dennis, 'The Character of Jesus: The Linchpin to Paul's Argument in 2 Corinthians' (PhD dissertation, Emory University, Atlanta, 2003).

—, *The Character of Jesus: The Linchpin to Paul's Argument in 2 Corinthians*, AnBib 158 (Rome: Editrice Pontifico Istituto Biblico, 2005).

Stettler, Hanna, 'An Interpretation of Colossians 1:24 in the Framework of Paul's Mission Theology', in *The Mission of the Early Church to Jews and Gentiles*, WUNT 127, ed. Jostein Ådna and Hans Kvalbein (Tübingen: Mohr, 2000), 185–208.

Stevens, Bruce A., 'Jesus as the Divine Warrior', *ExpT* 94 (1983): 326–9.

—, '"Why 'Must' the Son of Man Suffer?" The Divine Warrior in the Gospel of Mark', *BZ* 31 (1987): 101–10.

Still, Todd, ed., *Jesus and Paul Reconnected: Fresh Pathways into an Old Debate* (Grand Rapids: Eerdmans, 2007).

Stirewalt, M. Luther, Jr., *Paul, the Letter Writer* (Grand Rapids: Eerdmans, 2003).

Stowers, Stanley K., *Letter Writing in Greco-Roman Antiquity*, LEC 5 (Philadelphia: Westminster, 1986).

Strachan, R. H., *The Second Epistle of Paul to the Corinthians*, MNTC (London: Hodder & Stoughton, 1935).

Strange, E., 'Diktierpausen in den Paulusbriefen', *ZNW* 18 (1917): 109–17.

Strauss, Steve, 'Missions Theology in Romans 15:14-33', *BibSac* (2003): 457–74.

Strecker, Christian, ed., *Kontexte der Schrift, Band II: Kultur, Politik, Religion, Sprache – Text; Wolfgang Stegemann zum 60 Geburtstag* (Stuttgart: Kohlhammer, 2005).

Sumney, Jerry L., *Identifying Paul's Opponents: The Question of Method in 2 Corinthians*, JSNTSup 40 (Sheffield: JSOT Press, 1990).

—, 'Paul's "Weakness": An Integral Part of His Conception of Apostleship', *JSNT* 52 (1993): 71–91.

—, *'Servants of Satan', 'False Brothers' and Other Opponents of Paul: A Study of Those Opposed in the Letters of the Pauline Corpus*, JSNTSup 188 (Sheffield: Sheffield Academic Press, 2000).

—, 'Studying Paul's Opponents: Advances and Challenges', in *Paul and His Opponents*, Pauline Studies 2, ed. Stanley E. Porter (Leiden: Brill, 2005), 7–58.

Tabor, James D., *Things Unutterable: Paul's Ascent to Paradise in Its Greco-Roman, Judaic, and Early Christian Contexts* (Lanham: University Press of America, 1986).

Talbert, Charles H., *Reading Corinthians: A Literary and Theological Commentary*, rev. edn (Macon: Smyth and Helwys, 2002).

Tan, Che-Bin, 'The Idea of "Suffering with Christ" in the Pauline Epistles: An Exegetical and Historical Study' (PhD dissertation, University of Manchester, Manchester, 1978).

Tannehill, Robert C., *Dying and Rising with Christ: A Study in Pauline Theology* (Berlin: Verlag Alfred Topelmann, 1967).

Tasker, R. V. G., *The Second Epistle of Paul to the Corinthians: An Introduction and Commentary*, TNTC (London: Tyndale Press, 1958).

Taylor, Justin, 'The Ethnarch of King Aretas at Damascus: A Note on 2 Cor 11:32-33', *RB* 99 (1992): 719–28.

Taylor, Nicholas H., 'Apostolic Identity and the Conflicts in Corinth and Galatia', in *Paul and His Opponents*, Pauline Studies 2, ed. Stanley E. Porter (Leiden: Brill, 2005), 99–127.

Theissen, Gerd, *The Social Setting of Pauline Christianity* (Edinburgh: T&T Clark, 1982).

Thiselton, Anthony C., *The First Epistle to the Corinthians*, NIGTC (Grand Rapids: Eerdmans, 2000).

Thomas, John Christopher, '"An Angel from Satan": Paul's Thorn in the Flesh (2 Corinthians 12:7-10)', *JPT* 9 (1996): 39–52.

Thorsteinsson, Runar M., *Paul's Interlocutor in Romans 2: Function and Identity in the Context of Ancient Epistolography*, CBNTS 40 (Stockholm: Almqvist & Wiksell, 2003).

Thrall, Margaret E., *A Critical and Exegetical Commentary on the Second Epistle to the Corinthians*, Vol. 1, ICC (Edinburgh: T&T Clark, 1994).

—, *A Critical and Exegetical Commentary on the Second Epistle to the Corinthians*, Vol. 2, ICC (Edinburgh: T&T Clark. 2000).

—, 'Paul's Journey to Paradise: Some Exegetical Issues in 2 Cor 12, 2-4', in *The Corinthian Correspondence*, ed. Reimund Bieringer, BETL 125 (Leuven: Peeters, 1996), 347–63.

—, 'A Second Thanksgiving Period in II Corinthians', *JSNT* 16 (1982): 101–24.

Thurston, Bonnie Bowman, '2 Corinthians 2:14-16a: Christ's Incense', *ResQ* 29/2 (1987): 65–9.

Tinsley, E. J., *The Imitation of God in Christ: An Essay on the Biblical Basis of Christian Spirituality* (Philadelphia: Westminster, 1960).

Tov, Emanuel, 'Different Editions of the Song of Hannah and of Its Narrative Framework', in *Tehillah le-Moshe: Biblical and Judaic Studies in Honor of Moshe Greenberg*, ed. Mordechai Cogan, Barry Eichler and Jeffrey Tigay (Winona Lake: Eisenbrauns, 1997), 149–70.

Travis, S. H., 'Paul's Boasting in 2 Corinthians 10–12', *SE* 6 (1973): 527–32.

Trudinger, L. Paul, 'Further Brief Note on Colossians 1:24', *EvQ* 45 (1973): 36–8.

Tuckett, Christopher. 'Paul, Scripture and Ethics: Some Reflections', *NTS* 46 (2000): 403–24.

Turner, David L., 'Paul and the Ministry of Reconciliation in 2 Cor 5:11–6:2', *CTR* 4 (1989): 77–95.

Van der Horst, Pieter W., Maarten J. J. Menken, Joop F. M. Smit and Geert Van Oyen, eds, *Persuasion and Dissuasion in Early Christianity, Ancient Judaism, and Hellenism*, CBET 33 (Leuven: Peeters, 2003).

Van Noppen, Jean-Pierre, ed., *Metaphor and Religion (Theolinguistics 2)* (Brussels: Vrije Universitiet, 1983).

Vanhoye, A., ed., *L'Apôtre Paul: Personnalité, style et conception du ministère*, BETL 73 (Leuven: Leuven University Press, 1986).

Versnel, H. S., *Triumphus: An Inquiry into the Origin, Development and Meaning of Roman Triumph* (Leiden: Brill, 1970).

Wagner, J. Ross, 'The Heralds of Isaiah and the Mission of Paul', in *Jesus and the Suffering*

Servant: Isaiah 53 and Christian Origins, ed. William H. Bellinger, Jr. and William R. Farmer (Harrisburg: Trinity, 1998), 193–222.

—, *Heralds of the Good News: Isaiah and Paul 'in Concert' in the Letter of Romans*, NovTSup 101 (Leiden: Brill, 2002).

—, '"Not beyond the Things Which are Written": A Call to Boast Only in the Lord (1 Cor 4.6)', *NTS* 44 (1998): 279–87.

Wallace, Daniel B., *Greek Grammar beyond the Basics: An Exegetical Syntax of the New Testament* (Grand Rapids: Zondervan, 1996).

Walker, Donald Dale, *Paul's Offer of Leniency (2 Cor 10:1): Populist Ideology and Rhetoric in a Pauline Letter Fragment*, WUNT 2/152 (Tübingen: Mohr Siebeck, 2002).

Wan, Sze-Kar, *Power in Weakness: The Second Letter of Paul to the Corinthians*, NTC (Harrisburg: Trinity, 2000).

Wanamaker, Charles A., 'By the Power of God: Rhetoric and Ideology in 2 Corinthians 10–13', in *Fabrics of Discourse: Essays in Honor of Vernon K. Robbins*, ed. David B. Gowler, L. Gregory Bloomquist and Duane F. Watson (Harrisburg: Trinity, 2003), 194–221.

Wansink, Craig S., *Chained in Christ: The Experience and Rhetoric of Paul's Imprisonment*, JSNTSup 130 (Sheffield: JSOT Press, 1996).

Ware, James Patrick, *The Mission of the Church in Paul's Letter to the Philippians in the Context of Ancient Judaism*, NovTSup 120 (Leiden: Brill, 2005).

Watson, Duane F., 'Amplification Techniques in 1 John: The Interaction of Rhetorical Style and Invention', *JSNT* 51 (1993): 99–123.

ed. *The Intertexture of Apocalyptic Discourse in the New Testament*, SBLSymS 14 (Atlanta: Society of Biblical Literature, 2002).

—, 'Paul's Boasting in 2 Corinthians 10–13 as Defense of His Honor: A Socio-Rhetorical Analysis', in *Rhetorical Argumentation in Biblical Texts: Essays from the Lund 2000 Conference*, ed. Anders Eriksson, Thomas H. Olbricht and Walter Überlacker (Harrisburg: Trinity, 2002), 260–75.

—, ed., *Persuasive Artistry: Studies in New Testament Rhetoric in Honor of George A. Kennedy*, JSNTSup 50 (Sheffield: Sheffield Academic Press, 1991).

Watson, Nigel M., '"The Philosopher Should Bathe and Brush His Teeth": Congruence between Word and Deed in Graeco-Roman Philosophy and Paul's Letters to the Corinthians', *ABR* 42 (1994): 1–16.

—, *The Second Epistle to the Corinthians*, EC (London: Epworth, 1993).

—, '"To Make Us Rely not on Ourselves but on God Who Raises the Dead": 2 Corinthians 1.9b as the Heart of Paul's Theology', in *Die Mitte des Neuen Testaments: Einheit und Vielfalt neutestamentlicher Theologie: Festschrift für Eduard Schweizer zum siebzigsten Geburtstag*, ed. Ulrich Luz and Hans Weder (Göttingen: Vandenhoeck & Ruprecht, 1983), 384–98.

Watts, John D. W., *Isaiah 34–66*, WBC (Waco: Word Books, 1987).

Watts, Rikki E., 'Consolation or Confrontation? Isaiah 40–55 and the Delay of the New Exodus', *TynBul* 41 (1990): 31–59.

—, *Isaiah's New Exodus and Mark*, WUNT 2/88 (Tübingen: Mohr Siebeck, 1997).

Webb, Robert L., *John the Baptizer and Prophet: A Socio-Historical Study*, JSNTSup 62 (Sheffield: JSOT Press, 1991).

Webb, William J., *Returning Home: New Covenant and Second Exodus as the Context for 2 Corinthians 6:14–7:1*, JSNTSup 85 (Sheffield: JSOT, 1993).

Wedderburn, A. J. M., ed. *Paul and Jesus: Collected Essays*, JSNTSup 37 (Sheffield: JSOT Press, 1989).

—, 'Paul and the Story of Jesus', in *Paul and Jesus: Collected Essays*, JSNTSup 37, ed. A. J. M. Wedderburn (Sheffield: JSOT Press, 1989), 161–89.

Welborn, L. L., '*Primum tirocinium Pauli* (2 Cor 11,32-33)', *BZ* 43 (1999): 49–71.

—, 'The Runaway Paul', *HTR* 92 (1999): 115–63.

Wenham, David, *Paul: Follower of Jesus or Founder of Christianity?* (Grand Rapids: Eerdmans, 1995).

White, John L., 'Introductory Formulae in the Body of the Pauline Letter', *JBL* 90 (1971): 91–7.

White, L. Michael, and O. Larry Yarbrough, eds, *The Social World and the First Christians: Essays in Honor of Wayne A. Meeks* (Minneapolis: Fortress Press, 1995).

Wiles, Gordon P., *Paul's Intercessory Prayers: The Significance of the Intercessory Prayer Passages in the Letters of St Paul*, SNTSMS 24 (Cambridge: Cambridge University Press, 1974).

Wilk, Florian, 'Isaiah in 1 and 2 Corinthians', in *Isaiah in the New Testament: The New Testament and the Scriptures of Israel*, ed. Steve Moyise and Maarten J. J. Menken (New York: T&T Clark, 2005), 133–58.

Willert, Niels, 'The Catalogues of Hardships in the Pauline Correspondence: Background and Function', in *The New Testament and Hellenistic Judaism*, ed. Peder Borgen and Soren Giversen (Aarhus: Aarhus University Press, 1995), 217–43.

Williams, Charles K., II, and Nancy Bookidis, eds, *Corinth: The Centenary, 1896–1996*, Corinth 20 (Princeton: American School of Classical Studies at Athens, 2003).

Williams, David J., *Paul's Metaphors: Their Context and Character* (Peabody: Hendrickson, 1999).

Williamson, Lamar, Jr., 'Led in Triumph: Paul's Use of *Thriambeuo*', *Int* 22/3 (1968): 317–32.

Windisch, Hans, *Der zweite Korintherbrief*, 9th edn, KEK (Göttingen: Vandenhoeck & Ruprecht, 1924).

Winter, Bruce W., *After Paul Left Corinth: The Influence of Secular Ethics and Social Change* (Grand Rapids: Eerdmans, 2001).

—, 'Dangers and Difficulties for the Pauline Mission', in *The Gospel to the Nations: Perspectives on Paul's Mission*, ed. Peter Bolt and Mark Thompson (Downers Grove: InterVarsity, 2000), 285–95.

—, *Philo and Paul among the Sophists: Alexandrian and Corinthian Responses to a Julio-Claudian Movement*, 2nd edn (Grand Rapids: Eerdmans, 2002).

—, 'The Toppling of Favorinus and Paul by the Corinthians', in *Early Christianity and Classical Culture: Comparative Studies in Honor of Abraham J. Malherbe*, ed. John T. Fitzgerald, Thomas H. Olbright and L. Michael White, NovTSup 110 (Leiden: Brill, 2003), 291–306.

Wire, Antoinette Clark, 'Reconciled to Glory in Corinth? 2 Cor 2:14–7:4', in *Antiquity and Humanity: Essays on Ancient Religion and Philosophy Presented to Hans Dieter Betz on His 70th Birthday*, ed. Adela Yarbro Collins and Margaret M. Mitchell (Tübingen: Mohr Siebeck, 2001), 263–75.

Witherington, Ben, III, *Paul's Narrative Thought World: The Tapestry and Tragedy of Triumph* (Louisville: Westminster/John Knox, 1994).

—, *Jesus the Sage: The Pilgrimage of Wisdom* (Minneapolis: Augsburg, 1994).

—, *Conflict and Community in Corinth: A Socio-Rhetorical Commentary on 1 and 2 Corinthians* (Grand Rapids: Eerdmans, 1995).

Wong, Kasper K. H., *Boasting and Foolishness: A Study of 2 Cor 10:12-18 and 11:1a*, JDDS 5 (Hong Kong: Alliance Bible Seminary, 1998).

—, '"Lord" in 2 Corinthians 10:17', *LS* 17 (1992): 243–53.

Wood, John E., 'Death at Work in Paul', *EvQ* 54 (1983): 151–5.

Woods, L. E., 'Opposition to a Man and His Message: Paul's "Thorn in the Flesh" (2 Cor 12:7)', *ABR* 39 (1991): 44–53.

—, 'St. Paul's Apostolic Weakness' (PhD dissertation, University of Manchester, Manchester, 1986).

Wright, N. T., *The Climax of the Covenant: Christ and the Law in Pauline Theology*. Minneapolis: Fortress Press, 1993.

—, *Jesus and the Victory of God*, COQG 2 (London: SPCK, 1996).

—, *The New Testament and the People of God*, COQG 1 (Minneapolis: Fortress Press, 1992).

—, *Paul: Fresh Perspectives* (Minneapolis: Fortress Press, 2005).

—, *The Resurrection of the Son of God*, COQG 3 (Minneapolis: Fortress Press, 2003).

Yates, Roy, 'Note on Colossians 1:24', *EvQ* 42 (1970): 88–92.

—, 'Paul's Affliction in Asia: 2 Corinthians 1:8', *EvQ* 53 (1981): 241–5.

Young, Frances M., and David F. Ford, *Meaning and Truth in 2 Corinthians* (Grand Rapids: Eerdmans, 1988).

Zanker, Paul, *The Power of Images in the Age of Augustus*, trans. Alan Shapiro (Ann Arbor: University of Michigan Press, 1988).

INDEX OF ANCIENT SOURCES

OLD TESTAMENT

Genesis		2.3	166	29.18	187
1–3	9	2.8	166	30.14	101
2–3	9			34.3	71
		2 Samuel		35.10	89
Exodus		22	79	37.26	85
3.11	103			40.1	33
5.21	71	*Psalms*		40.1-10	81
13.21-2	82	5.12	164	40.3-4	133
14.19	82	18	89	40.10	82
15	79, 82	21	89	40.10-11	82
19.9-11	82	24	89	40.28-31	33
25.6	188	30.13	101	40–55	81, 82,
40.34	188	31.12	101		135
		34.18	104	40–66	81, 85
Leviticus		46	89	41.8-9	132
6.21	101	68	89	41.17-20	33
15.12	101	76	89	41.21	89
25.8-10	133	96-8	89	41.22-7	85
26.31	71	114	89	41.25	102
		124-5	89	42.1-9	132, 135
Deuteronomy		136	89	42.1-12	132
30.12-20	95			42.5-9	33
33	79	*Proverbs*		42.6	82
		25.14	164	42.7	132
Judges		27.1	164	42.9	85, 136
5	79			42.9	136
6.15	103	*Isaiah*		42.10-13	133
		2.2-4	82	42.13	79, 82
1 Samuel		6.9	187	43.5-6	82
18.23	103	9.1	85	43.6	133
		11.1-2	83	43.9-19	85
1 Kingdoms		22.11	85	43.10	132
2.1-10	166, 188	25.1	85	43.15	88
2.10	14, 164,	25.6-10	82	43.18-19	85, 136
	166, 167,	26.16–27.6	79	43.19	136
	171, 195,	28.7-9	180	44.1-2	132
	198,	29.6	102	44.6-8	85

OTHER ANCIENT SOURCES

INDEX OF AUTHORS